W9-CID-396

Stereotyping and Prejudice

This volume presents a contemporary and comprehensive overview of the great diversity of theoretical interests, new ideas, and practical applications that characterize social psychological approaches to stereotyping and prejudice.

All the contributions are written by renowned scholars in the field, with some chapters focusing on fundamental principles, including research questions about the brain structures that help us categorize and judge others, the role of evolution in prejudice, and how prejudice relates to language, communication, and social norms. Several chapters review a new dimension that has frequently been understudied—the role of the social context in creating stereotypes and prejudice. Another set of chapters focuses on applications, particularly how stereotypes and prejudice really matter in everyday life. These chapters include studies of their impact on academic performance, their role in small group processes, and their influence on everyday social interactions.

The volume provides an essential resource for students, instructors, and researchers in social and personality psychology, and is also an invaluable reference for academics and professionals in related fields who have an interest in the origins and effects of stereotyping and prejudice.

Charles Stangor is Professor of Psychology at the University of Maryland. His research interests pertain to the development of stereotypes and prejudice and their influences upon individuals who are potential victims of discrimination. He is also researching the psychology of learning and achievement, particularly among college students.

Christian S. Crandall is Professor of Psychology at the University of Kansas. His research concerns issues related to how the expression of prejudice is different from the underlying "genuine" prejudice and the justification of prejudice, particularly through ideology, values, stereotypes, the kinds of explanations people make for bad outcomes, and the underlying psychological nature of political ideology.

FRONTIERS OF SOCIAL PSYCHOLOGY

Series Editors:
Arie W. Kruglanski, *University of Maryland at College Park*
Joseph P. Forgas, *University of New South Wales*

Frontiers of Social Psychology is a series of domain-specific handbooks. Each volume provides readers with an overview of the most recent theoretical, methodological, and practical developments in a substantive area of social psychology, in greater depth than is possible in general social psychology handbooks. The editors and contributors are all internationally renowned scholars whose work is at the cutting edge of research.

Scholarly, yet accessible, the volumes in the *Frontiers* series are an essential resource for senior undergraduates, postgraduates, researchers, and practitioners and are suitable as texts in advanced courses in specific subareas of social psychology.

Published Titles

Negotiation Theory and Research, Thompson
Close Relationships, Noller & Feeney
Evolution and Social Psychology, Schaller, Simpson, & Kenrick
Social Psychology and the Unconscious, Bargh
Affect in Social Thinking and Behavior, Forgas
The Science of Social Influence, Pratkanis
Social Communication, Fiedler
The Self, Sedikides & Spencer
Personality and Social Behavior, Rhodewalt
Attitudes and Attitude Change, Crano & Prislin
Social Cognition, Strack & Förster
Social Psychology of Consumer Behavior, Wänke
Social Metacognition, Briñol & DeMarree
Social Motivation, Dunning
Intergroup Conflicts and their Resolution, Bar-Tal
Goal-directed Behavior, Aarts & Elliot
Social Metacognition, Briñol & DeMarree
Social Judgment and Decision Making, Krueger
Group Processes, Levine
Stereotyping and Prejudice, Stangor & Crandall

Forthcoming Titles

Explorations in Political Psychology, Krosnick & Chiang
Behavioral Economics, Zeelenberg

For continually updated information about published and forthcoming titles in the Frontiers of Social Psychology series, please visit:
www.psypress.com/frontiers

Stereotyping and Prejudice

Edited by
Charles Stangor
and
Christian S. Crandall

Ψ Psychology Press
Taylor & Francis Group

NEW YORK AND LONDON

First published 2013
by Psychology Press
711 Third Avenue, New York, NY 10017

Simultaneously published in the UK
by Psychology Press
27 Church Road, Hove, East Sussex BN3 2FA

Psychology Press is an imprint of the Taylor & Francis Group, an informa business

© 2013 Taylor & Francis

The right of the editors to be identified as the authors of the editorial material, and of the authors for their individual chapters, has been asserted in accordance with sections 77 and 78 of the Copyright, Designs and Patents Act 1988.

All rights reserved. No part of this book may be reprinted or reproduced or utilised in any form or by any electronic, mechanical, or other means, now known or hereafter invented, including photocopying and recording, or in any information storage or retrieval system, without permission in writing from the publishers.

Trademark notice: Product or corporate names may be trademarks or registered trademarks, and are used only for identification and explanation without intent to infringe.

Library of Congress Cataloging in Publication Data
Stereotyping and prejudice / edited by Charles Stangor and Chris Crandall.—1st Edition.
pages cm.—(Frontiers of social psychology series; 22)
1. Stereotypes (Social psychology) 2. Prejudices. I. Stangor, Charles. II. Crandall, Chris.
BF323.S63S747 2013
303.3′85—dc23
2012037464

ISBN: 978-1-84169-455-9 (hbk)
ISBN: 978-1-84872-644-4 (pbk)
ISBN: 978-0-203-56770-8 (ebk)

Typeset in Caledonia and Korinna
by Book Now Ltd, London

SCIENCE
BF
323
.S63
S747
2013

Contents

List of Illustrations

FIGURES

TABLES

Contributors

David M. Amodio, New York University

Joshua Aronson, New York University

Angela J. Bahns, Wellesley College

Catherine A. Cottrell, New College of Florida

Christian S. Crandall, University of Kansas

Mark A. Ferguson, University of Wisconsin, Stevens Point

Mikki Hebl, Rice University

Kristin E. Henkel, Western Connecticut State University

Cheryl R. Kaiser, University of Washington

Yoshihisa Kashima, University of Melbourne

Eden King, George Mason University

I-Ching Lee, National Chengchi University

Mary C. Murphy, Indiana University

Carlos David Navarrete, Michigan State University

Julia D. O'Brien, University of Maryland

Justin H. Park, University of Bristol

Felicia Pratto, University of Connecticut

Jenessa R. Shapiro, University of California, Los Angeles

Kerry E. Spalding, University of Washington

Charles Stangor, University of Maryland

Joshua M. Tybur, University of New Mexico

Gregory M. Walton, Stanford University

Preface
Introductory Remarks

Over the past years, the study of stereotyping and prejudice, rather than reaching a zenith and fading in popularity as many research topics do, has continued its overpowering presence within social psychological theory and research. This is perhaps in part because the topic is so central to person perception, social cognition, interpersonal attraction, aggression, and other social psychological topics. But is almost certainly the case that the topic remains vital because it matters so much.

Over time the research has been transformed, in part by becoming more fine-grained in its approaches but also by broadening into many different content areas. The study of stereotyping and prejudice remains vibrant, seems likely to continue that way, and thus is an outstanding topic for a volume in the *Frontiers* series.

The chapters represented in this volume were chosen to represent the diversity of theoretical interests, new ideas, and practical applications that currently characterize social psychological approaches to stereotyping and prejudice. Some represent a focus on fundamental principles, including research questions about the brain structures that help us categorize and judge others, the role of evolution in prejudice, and how prejudice relates to language, communication, and social norms. Several chapters focus on a new dimension that has frequently been understudied—the role of the social context in creating them. Others focus more on applications, particularly how stereotypes and prejudice really matter in everyday life. These chapters include studies of their impact on academic performance, their role in small-group processes, and their influence on everyday social interactions.

Taken together, it is our pleasure to present you with these informative and exciting contributions, and hope both that you will enjoy them and that they will inform your own thinking and research.

Charles Stangor
Christian S. Crandall

1

The Social Neuroscience of Prejudice

Then, Now, and What's to Come

DAVID M. AMODIO

New York University

*P*rejudice researchers are typically interested in two things, neither of which directly concerns the brain: the situational causes and conse-quences of prejudice for individuals in society and the psychological mechanisms that drive biased perceptions and discriminatory behavior. Perhaps surprisingly, the field of intergroup relations is the domain in which social neuroscience research has been arguably the most active. This is partly due to a coincidence—many of first social psychologists with neuroscience training happened to be interested in intergroup questions (Amodio, Harmon-Jones, & Devine, 2003; Bartholow, Pearson, Gratton, & Fabiani, 2003; Ito & Urland, 2003; Phelps et al., 2000; Vanman, Paul, Ito, & Miller, 1997). A more substantive reason, however, is that the field of intergroup relations provides one of the most fertile, multi-faceted areas of research for studying the inter-play of multiple psychological processes at multiple levels of analysis. And, at its core, the social neuroscience approach is interested in connections across levels of analysis. By studying intergroup processes, social neuroscientists can exam-ine the rich interplay of neural function with cognition, emotion, and behavior as they operate within the individual, dyads, groups, and societies. Prejudice researchers who take this approach hope to probe the psychological mechan-isms of intergroup bias while also elucidating brain function.

Social neuroscientists have studied intergroup bias from many different angles (see reviews by Amodio, 2008; Ito & Bartholow, 2009; Quadflieg & Macrae, 2011; Van Bavel & Cunningham, 2011). This chapter focuses on how neuroscience has helped to advance the psychological understanding of inter-group processes, primarily in the context of race. My review begins by describing early physiological approaches to the study of prejudice that date back over half a century. I then describe contemporary research that has applied theories and methods of neuroscience to address critical questions about psychological mechanisms underlying prejudice and intergroup behavior.

THEN: THE SOCIAL PSYCHOPHYSIOLOGY OF PREJUDICE

Long before the term "social neuroscience" was conceived, social psychologists used physiological assessments to gauge the racial attitudes of White American research participants (Rankin & Campbell, 1955; see Guglielmi, 1999, for a review). This early research took place during the emergence of the American Civil Rights Movement—a time when White Americans became increasingly concerned with concealing their prejudices. To psychologists interested in prejudiced attitudes, physiological methods provided a way to assess responses to race while circumventing participants' concerns about self-presentation. These methods were also sensitive to responses to race that were inaccessible to conscious awareness (i.e., *implicit*; see Amodio & Mendoza, 2010). Thus, psychophysiological methods offered new and arguably more direct ways to assess participants' responses to race and to examine the relation between these responses and participants' self-reported attitudes and beliefs. Although these methods were not used to probe the socio-cognitive mechanisms of intergroup bias, they provided useful indicators that could nonetheless inform theories about mechanism.

Mid-Century Modern Prejudice

Psychophysiological approaches to prejudice were first conducted in the mid-1900s. In what may be the first of such studies, Rankin and Campbell (1955) examined White participants' reactions to racial ingroup and outgroup members using a measure of the skin conductance response (SCR; alternatively called the *galvanic skin response*). The SCR assesses changes in sweat gland activity, usually from one's fingertips or palm. This reflects activation of the autonomic nervous system, which may be interpreted as representing an anxiety response that is largely uncontrollable and often implicit. In Rankin and Campbell's study, participants completed a bogus experimental task during which two different experimenters—one White and one Black—entered the participant chamber at different times, ostensibly to check the electrode connections on each participant's hand. This provided a pretense for the experimenters to interact with and even touch the wrist of the participants while the SCRs were recorded. At the end of the study, participants reported their liking of each of the experimenters on a questionnaire. As expected, the authors observed larger SCRs during interactions with the Black experimenter than the White experimenter. However, participants reported liking the Black and

White experimenters to the same degree, in apparent contradiction of the SCR results. Rankin and Campbell (1955) found these results to be somewhat puzzling and, in their discussion of the results, questioned the validity of their measures. However, this dissociation pattern is now very familiar to prejudice researchers (e.g., Devine, 1989) and, in retrospect, Rankin and Campbell's finding was likely the first demonstration of implicit prejudice.

In experiments conducted around the same time, Cooper and his colleagues measured skin conductance responses of White subjects while these subjects heard favorable or derogatory statements about different racial groups that, in an earlier testing session, had been rated as highly liked or disliked by the participant (Cooper & Siegel, 1956; Cooper & Singer, 1956). As expected, when subjects heard statements that contradicted their previously assessed attitude toward a particular group, they exhibited larger SCRs. This was especially true when highly disliked groups were described in a positive light, as compared with negative statements about liked groups. The authors argued, on the basis of these results, that prejudiced attitudes were "emotionally fortified"—that is, deeply ingrained in affective processes—and that conflicting thoughts about these groups created an unsettling emotional conflict. Vidulich and Krevanick (1966) extended this work by showing that participants with stronger anti-Black bias evidenced larger SCRs to pictures of Black people's faces and of Black–White social interactions than did low-prejudice participants. In doing so, this work demonstrated the role of individual differences in physiological responses to race.

Together, these early psychophysiological studies of prejudice established the critical role of emotion in prejudiced responses, and their findings presaged the idea of modern prejudice (Guglielmi, 1999). But, just as these groundbreaking findings emerged in the literature, the theoretical zeitgeist of psychology shifted sharply toward cognitive explanations of social phenomena. Interest in emotional processes waned, and thus the innovations made by these early psychophysiological studies of prejudice had relatively little impact.

The Re-emergence of Social Psychophysiology

After a period of virtual dormancy, interest in emotion and affective processes resurged in the 1990s, driven in part by advances in neuroscience research on fear and anxiety (e.g., Davidson, 1992; LeDoux, 1996). With this resurgence came a renewed interest in physiological approaches to prejudice, particularly in the handful of laboratories that specialized in physiological approaches to social psychological questions. In addition, new theories to explain the dissociation between explicit beliefs and implicit responses to social outgroups had been developed (Devine, 1989; Greenwald & Banaji, 1995), and so researchers were in a better position to interpret observed differences between self-reported and physiological responses to race.

Vanman et al. (1997) used facial electromyography (EMG) to measure facial expressions of White participants' responses to pictures of White and Black people. They found that more highly prejudiced participants exhibited increased corrugator activity (i.e., brow furrowing) and decreased zygomaticus activity (i.e., smiling) when viewing outgroup faces compared with ingroup faces, despite their self-reported preference for the Black faces. Low-prejudice participants did not show different EMG patterns to ingroup and outgroup faces. These effects presumably occurred without subjects' conscious awareness, and thus this research provided further evidence that prejudice may be expressed in implicit emotional responses. Other research provided updated and elaborated replications of peripheral responses to intergroup interactions (Vrana & Rollock, 1998). Research by Blascovich, Mendes, and their colleagues examined patterns of cardiovascular activity as a way to assess participants' appraisals of intergroup situations in terms of challenge or threat (e.g., Mendes, Blascovich, Lickel, & Hunter, 2002).

As methodological technologies advanced, researchers began to use direct measures of brain activity to examine individuals' responses to race. Ito and Urland (2003) used an event-related potential (ERP) measure of brain activity to examine differences in attention to outgroup and ingroup faces. By using ERP measures, which track changes in brain activity on the order of milliseconds, these researchers could probe the timing of evaluative and cognitive responses to race. Ito and Urland's study suggested that the brain registered a Black target person's race in as little as 121 milliseconds (ms). Bartholow and his colleagues used ERPs to assess the activation of stereotypes concerning both gender (Bartholow, Fabiani, Gratton, & Bettencourt, 2001) and race (Bartholow et al., 2003). By examining an ERP component that is sensitive to semantic expectancy violation when viewing the words of a sentence one at a time, they observed that violations of stereotype-based expectations were registered in the brain in as little as 450 ms. The major finding in both programs of research was that race-based evaluation and stereotype activation occurs very quickly, prior to conscious awareness and the availability of intentional control. This finding corroborated prior behavioral research regarding the automatic and implicit nature of racial bias, but with a measure that could track these effects as they unfolded online.

This body of social psychophysiological research on intergroup bias is characterized by two major features. First, most of this research focused on the critical role of affect in intergroup responses, whereas much of the behavioral research concentrated on cognitive aspects of intergroup bias. Second, these studies used the physiological approach primarily for its measurement features. That is, they did not yet apply ideas from the neuroscience literature about brain function, in part because the field's understanding of the neural mechanisms behind these physiological responses was still developing. Thus, the approach was not typically used to interrogate specific neural or psychological mechanisms.

NOW: SOCIAL COGNITIVE NEUROSCIENCE APPROACHES

The contemporary social neuroscience approach to prejudice is characterized by the emphasis on neuroimaging measures and the greater focus on mechanism. Whereas social psychophysiology approaches provide useful indicators of psychological responses, the cognitive neuroscience approach offers new theoretical models of complex neural function, which can be used to generate new and increasingly refined models of socio-cognitive processes relevant to intergroup bias. Because of the major influence of cognitive neuroscience in this approach, it is often referred to as *social cognitive neuroscience* (but, in this chapter, *social neuroscience* is used to describe the overarching field).

To date, most social neuroscience studies on intergroup bias have focused on identifying neural correlates of intergroup responses. These studies ask, "Which brain regions are activated during responses to race?" Brain mapping studies, such as these, are important for delineating the basic layout of brain function, but they do not typically address theoretical issues relevant to social psychology (see Amodio, 2010a). However, some research has sought to advance psychological theories of intergroup bias by applying well-established models of neurocognitive function to probe socio-cognitive mechanisms. In this section, I describe some of the ways in which this approach has already begun to shed light on enduring questions about the psychology of intergroup bias.

Seeing Race

Intergroup interactions often begin with the perception of a face. Humans are expert face perceivers, and a large body of neuroscience research has identified specific regions of the brain that appear to be dedicated to face processing, such as the fusiform gyrus (Figure 1.1; Kanwisher, McDermot, & Chun, 1997; cf. Haxby, Hoffman, & Gobbini, 2000). Face perception occurs very rapidly, too. Faces are also known to elicit a characteristic ERP component that peaks just 170 ms after the presentation of a face (Bentin, Allison, Puce, Perez, & McCarthy, 1996; Carmel & Bentin, 2002). Known as the "N170" for its timing and its negative electrical polarity at occipito-temporal scalp sites, this ERP component is believed to reflect the structural encoding process—that is, the point at which the brain recognizes that an object is a conspecific's face.

Prejudice researchers have applied neuroscience models of face perception to ask questions about the role of perceptual processes in intergroup bias. For example, are faces of ingroup members processed differently than those of outgroup members? And at what stage of face processing does a person's group membership influence perception? Social psychologists have begun to address these questions in order to understand the mechanisms through which intergroup bias affects social behavior.

In an early study on this topic, Golby, Eberhardt, Chiao, and Gabrieli (2001) observed greater activity in the fusiform gyrus in response to ingroup as compared to outgroup faces (Figure 1.2A), and this difference predicted later recognition of the faces. These results suggest that ingroup members are given priority in face processing because of their social relevance. More recently, Ratner and Amodio (2013) used a minimal group procedure to assign participants to novel groups, and then had participants view faces of people purported

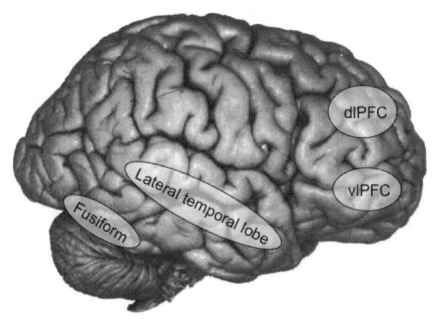

Figure 1.1 Lateral aspect of the right hemisphere of the brain illustrating the dorsolateral prefrontal cortex (dlPFC), ventrolateral prefrontal cortex (vlPFC), lateral temporal lobe, and fusiform regions.

to belong to their arbitrary ingroup or outgroup (holding race constant). The authors observed larger N170 responses to ingroup members as compared to outgroup members, suggesting that ingroup faces are favored at the stage of face encoding (Figure 1.2B). This finding extended that of Golby et al., and it was consistent with the idea that, in minimal group situations, intergroup bias primarily concerns preference for the ingroup (Brewer, 1999).

Studies have also investigated differences in the N170 response to members of existing groups. Most of these have examined White American participants' responses to pictures of Black and White people (i.e., of African and European heritage, respectively). However, the findings have been mixed, with some studies observing no differences (Caldara, Rossion, Bovet, & Hauert, 2004; Caldara et al., 2003; Wiese, Stahl, & Schweinberger, 2009), some finding larger N170 effects for ingroup faces (Ito & Urland, 2005) and some finding larger N170 effects for outgroup faces (Walker, Silvert, Hewstone, & Nobre, 2008). These inconsistent findings are likely due to differences in the tasks and stimulus features (e.g., stimuli that did not control for luminance and contrast differences between White and Black face images).

Ofan, Rubin, and Amodio (2011) investigated the N170 response to Black and White faces that were equated for luminance and contrast (i.e., using

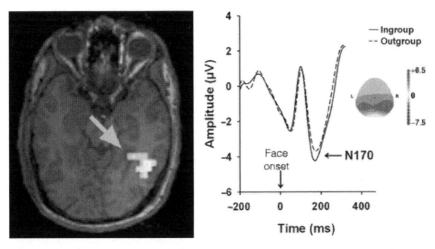

Figure 1.2   In passive viewing paradigms, visual processing of ingroup faces is enhanced relative to outgroup faces, as indicated by (A) activity in the fusiform gyrus (Golby et al., 2001) and (B) greater activity in the face-specific N170 event-related potential, which occurs just 170 ms following face presentation (Ratner & Amodio, 2013).

"two-toned" face stimuli that were composed of equal proportions of black and white pixels). Ofan et al. found that participants with stronger automatic pro-White bias, as indicated by responses on a behavioral evaluative race priming task, exhibited significantly larger N170 responses to Black than to White faces. This finding is consistent with the idea that, in the context of existing groups with known conflict, outgroup members are seen as threatening. So, whereas ingroup faces elicited larger N170s in a minimal group paradigm (Ratner & Amodio, 2013), outgroup faces elicited larger N170s in a race paradigm involving White vs. Black American faces (Ofan et al., 2011). So far, however, many inconsistencies remain in the race perception literature, and the resolution of these inconsistencies will require new theorizing and research. Nevertheless, the extant findings from this literature suggest that implicit racial attitudes can tune the perception of a face, such that attitudes modulate the initial physiognomic encoding of a face within 170 ms of its presentation.

Implicit Bias and the Brain

The perception of an outgroup member often triggers automatic racial attitudes and stereotypes (Devine, 1989). Although the effects of automatic and implicit forms of bias have been studied extensively in behavioral research (for reviews, see Amodio & Mendoza, 2010; Fazio & Olson, 2003), the mechanisms that drive these effects have been difficult to identify. Some of the first social neuroscience studies sought to use neuroscience techniques to shed light on the processes driving automatic and implicit forms of racial bias.

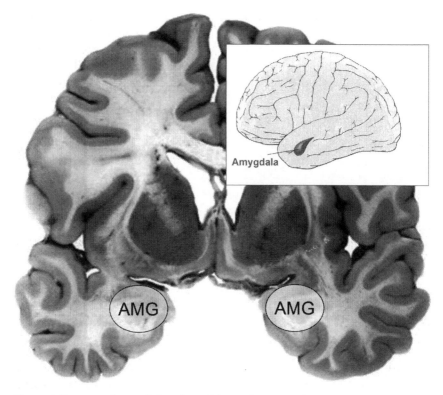

Figure 1.3   View of coronal slice through brain illustrating the amygdala (AMG).

While interest in implicit forms of racial bias surged in the field of social psychology, new findings were emerging from the animal neuroscience literature regarding the neural structures underlying fear and classical conditioning. This neuroscience work focused on the amygdala as a key neural substrate for the learning and expression of threat cues (Figure 1.3; Davis, 1992; Fendt & Fanselow, 1999; LeDoux, Iwata, Cicchetti, & Reis, 1988). Given other research suggesting that fear-related affect might underlie observations of implicit racial bias (Fazio, Jackson, Dunton, & Williams, 1995; Greenwald, McGhee, & Schwartz, 1998), the amygdala seemed like a strong candidate for a neural substrate of implicit prejudice.

A pair of early studies, by Hart et al. (2000) and Phelps et al. (2000), used functional magnetic resonance imaging (fMRI) to measure participants' brain activity while they viewed faces of ingroup and outgroup members. The goal was to see whether the amygdala might be a neural correlate of implicit prejudice. Both studies used blocked designs, such that White American participants would view a series of all White faces in one block and a series of all Black faces in a different block. Faces were viewed for several seconds, and measures of brain activity were averaged across the entire blocks, as a function of race. Thus, these studies focused on identifying the location of brain activity while viewing Black compared with White faces, but were unable to discern the timing of these responses.

Interestingly, neither study found a significant difference in amygdala activity between the viewing of Black and White faces. The effects were more complex. Hart et al. (2000) observed that, although passive viewing of both ingroup and outgroup faces elicited a similar degree of amygdala activity, amygdala responses to ingroup faces habituated more quickly than responses to outgroup faces. In Phelps et al. (2000), subjects viewed faces in the context of a memory task, indicating whether each face was the same as or different from the one presented on a previous trial. Although the authors did not observe a difference in amygdala activity for Black compared with White faces, individual differences in amygdala response to Black vs. White faces from the fMRI measure were correlated with subjects' scores on a behavioral measure of implicit racial bias, the Implicit Association Test (IAT), and also with scores on a startle-eyeblink measure of amygdala activity. None of these measures were associated with explicit self-report measures of prejudiced beliefs.

These neuroimaging findings suggested that amygdala activity might be correlated with implicit responses to race. This made sense, given that the amygdala was already known to respond quickly to threat. But did these findings have something new to say about implicit bias? From a social psychological perspective, perhaps not. Yet, by identifying a neural substrate of implicit racial bias, one could draw on knowledge about this brain structure from the neuroscience literature to shed new light on psychological models of implicit bias, such as how implicit associations are learned, activated, expressed in behavior, and potentially extinguished (Amodio, 2008; Amodio & Ratner, 2011). For example, the amygdala is known to respond very rapidly to learned threats and to engage physiological responses associated with inhibition (i.e., freezing) and active avoidance. This would correspond to inhibited and awkward social behavior in human interactions. The amygdala-based fear response also operates without conscious deliberation and, once a fear association is acquired through amygdalar circuitry, is extremely difficult to extinguish. This suggests that strategies to override implicit biases, rather than directly to undo them, might be more effective for reducing prejudice. Furthermore, whereas the amygdala response is associated with emotion, motivation, and behavior, it is not directly associated with language and high-level cognition. This suggests that knowledge about amygdala function might inform intergroup emotion and motivation, but probably not stereotypes.

Amodio et al. (2003) sought to move beyond a brain-mapping analysis by considering the theoretical implications of the amygdala as a neural substrate of implicit racial bias. Instead of fMRI, Amodio et al. used the startle-eyeblink method to assess amygdala activity in response to faces of White and Black people. The eyeblink is part of the whole-body startle reflex, and this reflex is reliably amplified when a startling event (e.g., a sudden loud noise) occurs when one is already in a threatened state (Lang, Bradley, & Cuthbert, 1990). By contrast, the reflex is reduced, or inhibited, when one is already in an appetitive state. Therefore, the relative size of one's blink reflex indicates one's emotional state just prior to the onset of the startle probe. Importantly, this "affective modulation" of the startle-eyeblink response is driven by the amygdala. The advantage of the startle-eyeblink measure is that it is able to index changes in amygdala activity within milliseconds of a stimulus being presented. Furthermore, the startle-eyeblink measure is sensitive to activity in the central nucleus of the amygdala—the specific region of the amygdala associated with fear conditioning and responses to threat. Both of these measurement attributes were critical for establishing the implicit nature of participants' response to race. By comparison, fMRI's slow temporal resolution, on the order of seconds, allows for both awareness and control. Moreover, although the spatial resolution of fMRI is better than that of electroencephalography (EEG), it is still too coarse to discern the different nuclei of the amygdala such as the central nucleus, which is associated with threat processing, from other nuclei such as the basal nucleus, which is associated with appetitive processing.

Amodio et al. (2003) found that, on average across participants, startle-eyeblink amplitudes were larger to Black than to White faces, evidencing differential amygdala activity in response to race for the first time. By associating implicit racial bias with activity in the amygdala's central nucleus, this finding linked implicit bias to a uniquely affective response that is associated with a classical fear-conditioning learning mechanism. Through this link, we can draw on the fear-conditioning literature to develop a model of how implicit affective associations may be learned, expressed, and potentially unlearned. As noted above, fear-conditioned responses are learned rapidly, often after a single exposure to the stimulus in a threatening context, and they are expressed primarily in autonomic responses and nonverbal behaviors (such as freezing and avoidance). Furthermore, such associations are very difficult and perhaps impossible to extinguish (Bouton, 1994; but see Schiller, Freeman, Mitchell, Uleman, & Phelps, 2009). Instead of being unlearned, fear-conditioned responses can be overridden by newer learned responses. Interestingly, most theories of implicit social cognition suggest that implicit associations are learned slowly, only after repeated exposure, and that they can be unlearned through the same mechanism (e.g., Smith & DeCoster, 2000)—a model that is inconsistent with the fear-conditioning mechanism. In addition, behavioral studies have shown that measures of implicit evaluative bias predict nonverbals associated with freezing and avoidance (Amodio & Devine, 2006; Dovidio, Kawakami, Johnson, Johnson, & Howard, 1997; Fazio et al., 1995), consistent with the models of amygdala-based learning.

A second goal of Amodio et al. (2003) was to examine individual differences in amygdala responses to Black vs. White faces as a function of internal and external motivations to respond without prejudice. Previous research showed that among self-avowed egalitarians (i.e., who reported low-prejudice attitudes), are more prone to expressions of implicit prejudice than others (Devine, Plant,

Amodio, Harmon-Jones, & Vance, 2002). Devine et al. showed that, among participants who reported strong internal motivation to respond without prejudice, those who also reported being highly concerned about social pressures to respond without prejudice exhibited more prejudice on implicit measures than participants who were not worried about such pressures. Amodio et al. (2003) tested whether differences in amygdala response to race might help to explain the difference in these two behavioral profiles. To this end, the authors found that participants who were motivated only for internal reasons showed a similar degree of startle response to both Black and White faces—a pattern suggesting no difference in amygdala response and, hence, the absence of racial bias. However, participants who were internally motivated to respond without prejudice but also worried about social pressures (i.e., high external motivation) showed a much larger startle response to Black than to White faces, suggesting greater amygdala activity to Black faces. This effect was similar in magnitude to the difference observed among highly prejudiced participants (i.e., those reporting low internal motivation; Figure 1.4A). This finding suggested that high internal/high external subjects, who typically report egalitarian attitudes but show evidence of implicit prejudice (Devine et al., 2002), expressed implicit bias because of deeply rooted fear-conditioned associations with Black people. It is notable that Amodio et al. (2003) initially assumed the startle-eyeblink responses measured 4,000 ms after the presentation of a face could reflect a controlled emotional response (whereas eyeblink responses occurring only 400 ms following face presentation could not). However, their results showed no evidence of control at 4,000 ms; rather, control was expressed only in behavior,

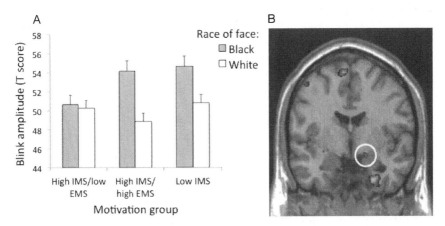

Figure 1.4   Affective forms of implicit bias toward Black faces, compared with White faces, may be reflected in amygdala activity, as indicated by (A) the startle-eyeblink response occurring at 4,000 ms for individuals varying in internal and external motivations to respond without prejudice (IMS/EMS; Amodio et al., 2003) and (B) amygdala activity measured using fMRI (Cunningham et al., 2004).

in the form of self-reported emotional responses to Black faces compared to White faces (Study 2, Amodio et al., 2003). This pattern comports with other work suggesting that the amygdala response underlying the startle effect is not subject to direct control (described below).

Since these initial studies, several event-related fMRI studies have observed that amygdala activity is greater to outgroup than to ingroup faces under some conditions but not others, and that these effects are typically subtle (Figure 1.4B; Cunningham et al., 2004; Lieberman, Hariri, Jarcho, Eisenberger, & Bookheimer, 2005; Wheeler & Fiske, 2005; Ronquillo et al., 2007; Van Bavel, Packer, & Cunningham, 2008). These studies reveal that differences in amygdala activity to Black vs. White faces tend to emerge most strongly in the context of a minimally demanding task, such as during the passive viewing of faces. As tasks become more demanding, such as when searching for a "dot" on the image, when imagining whether the target likes a particular vegetable, or when attempting to match the face to written group labels, amygdala activations tend to diminish. Other research suggests that amygdala effects are lessened when the outgroup face is not looking directly at the subject (i.e., has averted gaze; Richeson, Todd, Trawalter, & Baird, 2008). These studies collectively help to demarcate the boundaries conditions for the amygdala's role in implicit bias.

An important implication of this broader program of work is that, although implicit attitudes are conceived in terms of positive vs. negative valence in social psychological models, the mechanisms underlying implicit prejudice do not conform to a simple valence-based organization. That is, no brain region corresponds to "good" or "bad" (cf. Cunningham, Raye, & Johnson, 2004). Rather, neural and biological processes are organized around behavioral processes, such as approach, inhibition, and avoidance (Harmon-Jones, 2003; Harmon-Jones, Harmon-Jones, Amodio, & Gable, 2011), as well as perceptual processes, and the amygdala in particular reflects this organization (Amodio, 2008; Lang et al., 1990). As such, behavior-based measures of implicit prejudice should be related more directly to goals, motivations, and behaviors than to abstract (i.e., cognitive) appraisals of whether an outgroup member is "good" or "bad" (e.g., Amodio & Devine, 2006; Dovidio et al., 1997; Fazio et al., 1995).

Stereotyping   Whereas much research has examined the neural correlates of race-related affect and evaluation, very little has investigated social stereotypes. Stereotypes are cognitive structures stored in memory that represent attributes associated with a social group (Stangor & Lange, 1994). Amodio and Devine (2006; see also Amodio, 2008; Amodio & Mendoza, 2010) proposed that stereotypes are rooted in mechanisms of semantic memory and selection, which are associated with neural activity in the temporal lobe (Figure 1.1) and lateral posterior prefrontal cortex (PFC; e.g., Brodmann areas 45 and 47). Behavioral and neuroscience research on semantic learning systems has uncovered the dynamics of how such associations are learned and expressed in behavior. Neuroscience research on the connectivity of these brain regions provides further clues about other psychological processes that are influenced most directly by these semantic associations (Gabrieli, 1998). By linking stereotypes to this literature, researchers can apply findings from the memory literature to understand stereotyping processes (Amodio, 2008; Amodio & Ratner, 2011). For example, whereas affective associations are learned quickly and are relatively indelible, semantic associations may be learned and unlearned through a process of repeated exposure to pairings and non-pairings. As suggested by studies of neural connectivity, semantic associations are more likely to be expressed in trait impressions, goal representations, and instrumental behaviors in comparison to affective associations, and they are also more likely to emerge in verbal responses (Amodio & Devine, 2006).

Some fMRI studies have examined neural activity associated with the completion of stereotyping tasks (Knutson, Mah, Manly, & Grafman, 2007; Mitchell, Ames, Jenkins, & Banaji, 2009; Quadflieg et al., 2009), but this work has not yet addressed the mechanisms of stereotypes per se. Rather, these studies have focused on brain activity associated with more general aspects of task completion, such as response conflict and inhibition or face perception. In a related brain lesion study, patients with damage to their medial prefrontal cortex (mPFC; Figure 1.5) did not show bias on a male vs. female IAT (Milne & Grafman, 2001). However, it is likely that this finding reflects the important role of the mPFC in the cognitive control processes that give rise to the IAT

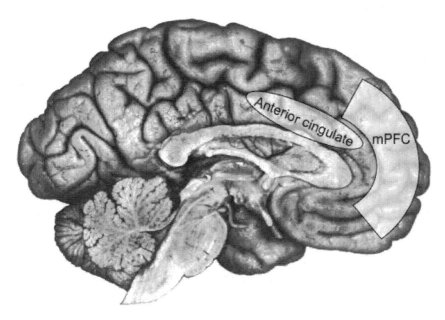

Figure 1.5   Medial aspect of the left hemisphere of the brain showing the anterior cingulate and medial frontal regions (mPFC = medial prefrontal cortex).

effect, rather than suggesting that the mPFC contains a representation of stereotype knowledge (a function typically ascribed to lateral regions of the PFC and the temporal lobes). Thus, the neural mechanisms of stereotyping remain largely untested, although researchers have already applied findings from the broader cognitive neuroscience literature on semantic selection and representation to help understand the functions of stereotypes (Amodio, 2008).

Control and the Regulation of Intergroup Bias

Today, most Americans espouse egalitarian values and oppose discrimination on the basis of race. But at the same time, by virtue of being exposed to prejudices and stereotypes in their environment, they have acquired implicit race-biased associations. In order to respond in accordance with one's beliefs, one must find a way to override the influence of implicit associations on behavior (Crandall & Eshleman, 2003; Devine, 1989). Neuroscience research has already had a substantial influence on social psychologists' understanding of how expressions of intergroup bias are regulated (Amodio, Devine, & Harmon-Jones, 2007; Amodio & Devine, 2010; Bartholow, Dickter, & Sestir, 2006). In this section, I describe the most significant influences of neuroscience research on theories regarding the control of prejudiced responses.

Detecting the Need for Control   Recent neuroscience models posit that control involves two major components: conflict monitoring and regulative control (Botvinick, Braver, Barch, Carter, & Cohen, 2001). *Conflict monitoring* is the process for detecting the need for control, and it refers specifically to conflict between higher-level response goals and lower-level motor responses. *Regulative control* refers to the process of implementing an intended response after the need for control has been detected. Amodio et al. (2004) proposed that this model of control could explain a puzzling phenomenon: Despite holding non-prejudiced beliefs, many self-avowed egalitarians still often express stereotypes and racial bias in their behavior. Amodio et al. wondered whether such "slips" might reflect a failure to detect the need for control by the conflict-monitoring system or, rather, a failure to implement control once its need has been detected. To test these competing hypotheses, the authors examined participants' attempts to control stereotype-biased responses while measuring patterns of brain activity associated with conflict monitoring in the anterior cingulate cortex (ACC; Figure 1.5). The behavioral task in this study was Payne's (2001) weapons identification task. This sequential priming task requires enhanced control to override an automatic stereotype on some trials but not others. Therefore, it provided the necessary conditions to examine responses when control was needed compared with when it was not needed.

Amodio et al. (2004) focused on two event-related potential (ERP) indices of ACC activity—the *error-related negativity* (ERN) component and the *N2* component (associated with successful control; also called the *correct-related negativity*)—and found that both were more strongly activated on trials where control over stereotypes was needed (Figure 1.6A; see also Bartholow, Dickter, & Sestir, 2006; Correll, Urland, & Ito, 2006). Importantly, heightened ACC activity was observed both when control succeeded and when it failed. This finding suggested that participants were generally good at detecting the need for control, and, when unintentional expressions of bias occurred, they failed to implement the intended response. This new perspective on control helped to explain why racial biases sometimes slip through into behavior despite a person's egalitarian intentions.

In a follow-up study, Amodio, Devine, and Harmon-Jones (2008) used this neuroscience model of control to address why some low-prejudice people—those who have strong internal motivation to respond without prejudice but are also very concerned about external social pressures—are especially prone to unintended expressions of bias. The authors proposed that these individuals might have trouble controlling their expressions of bias because their neural systems are less sensitive to conflicts between activated stereotypes and

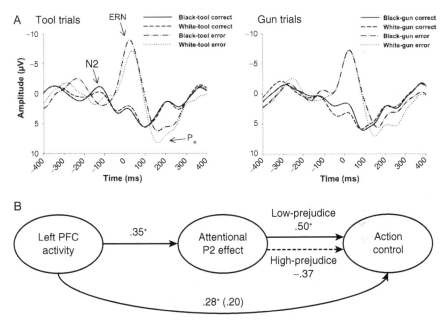

Figure 1.6   The successful regulation of a race-biased response involves two major processes: (A) Detection of conflict between a stereotype-biased tendency and one's task goal, associated with the rapid activation of the anterior cingulate cortex and indexed by the error-related negativity (ERN) and the N2 (or correct-related negativity) components of the event-related potential (Amodio et al., 2004); and (B) the engagement of regulative control, associated with increased prefrontal cortical (PFC) activity, which in turn predicts greater rapid attentional processing of racial cues, indexed by the P2 event-related potential, and greater action control, as indicated by task performance (Amodio, 2010b).

egalitarian response goals. Consistent with this hypothesis, these high-internal/ high-external motivation subjects showed low levels of ACC activity on trials that required control over automatic stereotypes—a pattern matching that of participants with high-prejudice beliefs. By contrast, participants who were highly internally motivated and unconcerned about external pressures showed strong ACC responses when stereotype control was needed, and they were better at exerting control in their behavior. Other research suggests that mechanisms for engaging control in response to external cues (e.g., cues from other people) involve activity in more anterior regions of the ACC and in the mPFC (Amodio, Kubota, Harmon-Jones, & Devine, 2006)—regions shown in other work to be important for inferring the perspective of another person and coordinating behavior with that person (Amodio & Frith, 2006).

Together, these social neuroscience studies have revealed an important component of control that was missing in prior social psychological models, whereby conflict between an automatic tendency and one's intended response is detected and the need for control is registered. This work has also distinguished the processes of detecting conflict involving one's own goals from conflict involving the goals of other people (e.g., peers or authority figures). By invoking neuroscience models, and by using physiological methods, researchers have begun to answer longstanding questions about why some people have more trouble regulating their intergroup behavior than others.

Implementing Control   Many theories in social and cognitive psychology posit that, once the need for control is detected, other mechanisms are engaged to implement a controlled response (Devine, 1989; Shiffrin & Schneider, 1977). Neuroscience research has implicated the PFC in this function (Figure 1.1; Botvinick et al., 2001; Kerns et al., 2004; Badre & Wagner, 2007). However, the specific target of control is not always clear—it could be the emotional response to an outgroup member, the stereotype itself, the behavior tendency, one's perception of the outgroup member, or some other process. Although social psychological theories typically consider each of these targets of control to be equally plausible, an analysis of the neural circuitry of the PFC suggests that some of these processes are more likely to be modulated by control mechanisms than others. In particular, this circuitry suggests that the PFC modulates goal-directed action processes as well as sensory input and perceptual processing (Miller & Cohen, 2001). By contrast, the PFC has few connections to subcortical regions associated with emotion, such as the amygdala. Given that the amygdala is often identified as a neural correlate of implicit bias, this analysis suggests that the notion of direct down-regulation of implicit bias is unlikely.

Several studies have observed patterns of PFC activity in response to race, such as when White participants view pictures of White and Black people. However, the role of these PFC activations in controlled processing is not always clear. In the earliest example, Richeson et al. (2003) had White American subjects view Black and White faces while measuring brain activity using fMRI. Later, these participants had an interaction with a Black experimenter, after which they completed a behavioral measure of cognitive control. The authors found that participants who showed stronger PFC activity to Black than to White faces in the first session performed more poorly on the cognitive control task following an interracial interaction. The authors reasoned that subjects who showed greater PFC activity when viewing faces had engaged in spontaneous control and were thus also more likely to engage control during the interracial interaction, which in turn produced a more "depleted" pattern of performance on the Stroop task. Although provocative, it was very difficult to know whether the PFC activity observed during the fMRI session had anything to do with "control," as it was unclear what participants were controlling while they simply viewed pictures of faces.

A study by Cunningham, Johnson, et al. (2004) also measured brain activity in response to viewing faces of Black and White people using fMRI. Participants simply indicated whether each face appeared on the right or left side of the visual field. Like Richeson et al. (2003), Cunningham, Johnson, et al. (2004) assumed that people spontaneously engage some form of control when simply viewing faces passively, but the basis for this assumption is unclear. Similarly, a study by Lieberman et al. (2005) found an increase in some PFC regions (e.g., the right ventrolateral PFC; Figure 1.1) when participants viewed Black vs. White faces and were instructed to match the faces to written labels. But what exactly was being controlled in these studies? Because they did not measure brain activity in a context in which the control of racial responses was relevant, and because they did not include behavioral indices of control, it is difficult to know.

Using experimental tasks designed to elicit the control of racially biased tendencies, my own research has shown that PFC activity is associated with specific intentions to respond without prejudice (Amodio et al., 2007) and with the control of attention to racial cues and the behavioral control of racial bias (Amodio, 2010b; Figure 1.6B), but not with the direct regulation of amygdala activity in response to racial outgroups (Amodio et al., 2003). These findings comport with Monteith's (1993) self-regulation model, which posits that, once the goal to control intergroup responses is formed, an individual becomes vigilant to cues that control is needed and that these cues facilitate behavioral forms of regulation (see also Richeson & Trawalter, 2008). But these neuroscience findings do not support the idea that prejudice can be controlled by directly down-regulating one's emotional response to an outgroup member or by intentionally inhibiting stereotypic thoughts. The specificity of neuroscience models with regard to the targets of control represents another unique contribution of neuroscience to the psychological study of intergroup bias.

Intergroup Anxiety   Actual intergroup situations often elicit social anxiety. Based on earlier work suggesting that anxiety can interfere with performance and controlled processing (e.g., Easterbrook, 1959; Baumeister & Showers, 1986), prejudice researchers have proposed that intergroup anxiety might undermine the regulation of intergroup responses, leading to greater expressions of prejudice (Lambert et al., 2003; Richeson & Trawalter, 2005).

However, the mechanism through which anxiety might interfere with control has been unclear, particularly because self-report assessments of anxiety are typically uncorrelated with changes in behavioral control. Neuroscience models linking neural substrates of anxiety with those of control have begun to shed light on this mechanism. For example, Amodio (2009) proposed that intergroup anxiety would cause a person to become hyper-sensitive to conflict between automatic race-biased tendencies and one's egalitarian intentions, and that this hyper-sensitivity would interfere with the effective control of behavior. In other words, the extreme sensitivity to conflict makes it harder to focus on one's main task goals. This hypothesis was based on a neuroscience model addressing the interaction between the ACC and the neurotransmitter *norepinephrine* (Aston-Jones & Cohen, 2005) and tested by Amodio (2009) in a behavioral experiment using salivary measures of the hormone cortisol as a downstream proxy for norepinephrine levels. This study revealed that, indeed, heightened arousal during an interracial interaction, as indicated by cortisol, was associated with worse control on a stereotype inhibition task. This research suggests a specific mechanism through which intergroup anxiety might enhance some aspects of control (e.g., vigilance) but impair other aspects (e.g., response implementation) during an intergroup interaction.

Mentalizing/Dehumanization

A particularly active area in the social neuroscience field examines brain activity involved in "social cognition"—that is, the process of inferring another person's thoughts, perspective, and motives (also referred to as *mentalizing*; Amodio & Frith, 2006; Mitchell, 2009). In the intergroup domain, researchers have asked whether perceivers engage in a lesser degree of mentalizing toward outgroup members than toward ingroup members, and whether this process underlies aspects of racial discrimination. Although few studies in the social neuroscience literature have addressed these questions about intergroup bias directly, they are consistent with research on related topics. For example, Harris and Fiske (2006) proposed that mPFC activity is associated with the process of humanization—viewing another individual as possessing agentic and uniquely human properties (Haslam, 2006). Prior theorizing by Fiske, Cuddy, Glick, and Xu (2002) related humanization to two major factors of person perception—warmth and competence—and suggested that individuals who are perceived as low on both dimensions are seen as less than human, or *dehumanized*. Analyses of participants' warmth and competence ratings of a host of different social groups showed that, among these, African Americans were perceived as lower on both dimensions than White Americans. That is, compared with Whites, Blacks were seen as less human.

In an effort to link humanization to social neuroscience studies of mentalizing, Harris and Fiske (2006) had participants view pictures of people from groups classified as humanized (e.g. middle-class Americans) and dehumanized (e.g., homeless people), on the basis of Fiske et al.'s (2002) model. As expected, a comparison of brain activity for humanized vs. dehumanized targets yielded significant activation in the same regions of mPFC linked previously to mentalizing. That is, humanization was related to greater mPFC activity and, by association, to the process of mentalizing. This interpretation was corroborated by the authors' finding that, for dehumanized targets, lower mPFC activity was associated with ratings of lower feelings of warmth (Harris & Fiske, 2009). An implication of these findings is that the regulation of intergroup responses may involve a process of "rehumanization," whereby formerly dehumanized individuals come to be viewed as worthy of social engagement. According to this analysis, regulation involves not the suppression of unwanted thoughts and feelings but, rather, the process of seeing a person in a new light and adopting a motivation to engage socially (Amodio, 2008). Although this hypothesis has not yet been tested, the broader literature on mentalizing, dehumanization, and the mPFC suggests new ways of thinking about the regulation of prejudice.

Summary

Contemporary social neuroscience research has already illuminated several important psychological processes involved in prejudice and intergroup bias. Because the brain is inherently a mechanism, neuroscience approaches have been most useful for examining the socio-cognitive mechanisms underlying intergroup phenomena, such as implicit bias, the self-regulation of intergroup responses, and humanization/dehumanization.

WHAT'S TO COME

The social neuroscience approach has already yielded some important contributions to social psychological theories of intergroup bias and self-regulation. But this is just the tip of the iceberg. The neurosciences represent one of the fastest growing areas within the biomedical and psychological fields, and these scientific advances will continue to make their way to the study of intergroup processes. Although the possibilities are boundless, I describe, here, just a few currently breaking trends.

Hyperscanning of Intergroup Interactions

Intergroup processes concern interactions between (at least) two people, yet most existing research has examined individuals only in private, non-social laboratory contexts. To address this issue, researchers are increasingly using a technique known as "hyperscanning," in which two or more participants interact remotely (e.g., over an Internet connection) while their brain activity is recorded in separate scanners. Hyperscanning refers to the simultaneous recording of fMRI, EEG, or other brain imaging techniques. To date, hyperscanning has been used primarily to study brain activity associated with economic negotiations or in studies of social exclusion (King-Casas et al., 2005; or, for simulated hyperscanning, Eisenberger, Lieberman, & Williams, 2003), but it has clear applications to intergroup interactions.

Modeling of Neural Networks and Micro-Systems

Currently, most social neuroscience studies focus on the role of a particular brain region associated with a socio-cognitive process. However, the socio-cognitive processes of interest to prejudice researchers are very complex, and it is unlikely that any high-level process reflects the activity of a single brain structure. Psychologists are increasingly recognizing the need to examine *networks* of brain structures, and the degree of functional connectivity among them, in order to understand complex psychological processes such as social perception and social cognition. At the same time, social neuroscientists are increasingly appreciative of the complexity within neural structures. For example, the amygdala is thought to comprise up to 13 different nuclei, each with different functions, connected within an inhibitory network. Thus, the amygdala cannot be interpreted as supporting just one function. Furthermore, popular neuroimaging techniques, such as fMRI, are limited in their ability to discern important structures that are smaller than the spatial resolution of these measures. Because fMRI is a measure of blood flow, its resolution is limited by the spacing of cerebral capillaries. For reasons such as these, social and cognitive neuroscientists alike are constantly looking for better neuroimaging technologies. Most importantly, a better understanding of socio-cognitive mechanisms will require researchers to study the functions of multiple structures within broader networks of brain activity.

Molecular Genetics

Major advances in molecular genetics have been made in recent years, and the study of genetic and epigenetic processes will soon begin to contribute to the study of intergroup relations. Genes—the components of DNA that provide the blueprint for our biological (and, hence, psychological) development—are increasingly appreciated for their complexity and their propensity for adaptation. Measures of genes and gene variation (i.e., *polymorphisms*) provide a powerful assessment of dispositional factors. Research connecting gene polymorphisms to personality traits, attitudes, beliefs, and behavioral tendencies will help to refine psychological models of dispositional factors in intergroup relations. By using the genetics approach, researchers can refine psychological models of traits and dispositions to match better the biological contours that underlie them. The emerging field of epigenetics is especially relevant to social processes. Epigenetics concerns the study of gene expression, and research in this field has shown that the expression of genes is continuously being modulated by environmental and situational factors, including social factors (Champagne & Mashoodh, 2009).

As the field of genetics advances, researchers are more and more interested in including gene measures in their research on social cognition. However, an obvious challenge in this endeavor is that, to connect these two areas of inquiry, one must traverse many levels of analysis, both physiologically and psychologically. It is very possible that the conceptual distance between genetic mechanisms and intergroup processes is just too great to produce theoretically useful information. That is, researchers will most certainly find correlations between gene polymorphisms and some aspects of intergroup processes (and, of course, they will speculate on the meaning of these correlations), but whether this approach can render a substantive advance in psychological theories of prejudice remains to be seen.

Endocrine Systems

Although most social neuroscience studies of intergroup processes have focused on measures of brain activity, other physiological processes are increasingly seen as relevant. In particular, hormones operate in both the brain and the periphery, functioning to orchestrate complex psychobiological processes. Steroidal hormones, such as testosterone and cortisol, are known to be responsive to social factors such as social evaluation, competition, and attachment (Dickerson & Kemeny, 2004; Mehta & Josephs, 2006; Baumgartner, Heinrichs, Vonlanthen, Fischbacher, & Fehr, 2008; Eisenegger, Naef, Snozzi, Heinrichs, & Fehr, 2010). Although most intergroup studies have included hormones as physiological outcome measures of social stress (e.g., Mendes, Gray, Mendoza-Denton, Major, & Epel, 2007; Page-Gould, Mendes, & Major, 2010) or indicators of neural mechanisms involved in the control of stereotyping (e.g., Amodio, 2009), research has yet to study the role of hormones in guiding complex intergroup responses.

Psychoneuroimmunology and Health Disparities

Another important area of intergroup bias research concerns the effect of prejudice on its victims. Several researchers have examined the effect of social stigma on health (Halim, Yoshikawa, & Amodio, 2013; Major & O'Brien, 2005), and those taking a social neuroscience approach are beginning to look at the effects of stigma on biological health factors, such as stress-related hormones and immune variables. Ratner, Halim, and Amodio (2013) found that greater perceived stigmatization among Black and Latina community members was associated with higher baseline interleukin-6 (IL-6)—a proinflammatory cytokine associated with infection—whereas more positive ingroup attitudes were associated with higher baseline levels of Dehydroepiandrosterone (DHEA)—a steroid with many complex biological functions that, in the health literature, is generally associated with resilience. These effects on IL-6 and DHEA remained after statistically adjusting for variability in general perceived stress and several socio-economic factors. This finding suggests that the psychological experience of prejudice is directly associated with a poorer biological health profile, but that positive ingroup attitudes may promote biological resilience. This psychoneuroimmunological approach to intergroup bias promises to provide a powerful method for understanding the impact of prejudice on its victims and the implications of this effect for health disparities.

CONCLUSIONS

Although the social neuroscience approach to intergroup bias is still relatively new, it has already made significant contributions to the psychological literature on prejudice, stereotyping, and discrimination. Early social psychophysiological approaches provided researchers with invaluable methods for assessing prejudiced responses that were otherwise concealed in overt behaviors and self-reports. More recently, social neuroscientists have begun to invoke models of brain structure and function to understand the socio-cognitive and emotional mechanisms that underlie implicit racial bias and the regulation of these biases. In doing so, this research has already begun to provide important theoretical advances that would not have been anticipated by traditional behavioral approaches to the study of intergroup bias.

Given the rapid expansion of social neuroscience across scientific disciplines, and the growing acceptance and incorporation of neuroscience ideas by psychologists who study intergroup bias, the influence of this approach on the intergroup literature is sure to grow. My hope is that behavioral psychologists will recognize and embrace the contributions of social neuroscience to the understanding of the social mind, and that intergroup researchers will integrate this approach in their efforts to understand and address the critical problems of prejudice, discrimination, and social justice.

REFERENCES

Amodio, D. M. (2008). The social neuroscience of intergroup relations. *European Review of Social Psychology, 19*, 1–54.

Amodio, D. M. (2009). Intergroup anxiety effects on the control of racial stereotypes: A psychoneuroendocrine analysis. *Journal of Experimental Social Psychology, 45*, 60–67.

Amodio, D. M. (2010a). Can neuroscience advance social psychological theory? Social neuroscience for the behavioral social psychologist. *Social Cognition, 28*, 695–716.

Amodio, D. M. (2010b). Coordinated roles of motivation and perception in the regulation of intergroup responses: Frontal cortical asymmetry effects on the P2 event-related potential and behavior. *Journal of Cognitive Neuroscience, 22*, 2609–2617.

Amodio, D. M., & Devine, P. G. (2006). Stereotyping and evaluation in implicit race bias: Evidence for independent constructs and unique effects on behavior. *Journal of Personality and Social Psychology, 91*, 652–661.

Amodio, D. M., & Devine, P. G. (2010). Regulating behavior in the social world: Control in the context of intergroup bias. In R. R. Hassin, K. N. Ochsner, and Y. Trope (Eds.), *Self control in society, mind and brain* (pp. 49–75). New York: Oxford University Press.

Amodio, D. M., Devine, P. G., & Harmon-Jones, E. (2007). A dynamic model of guilt: Implications for motivation and self-regulation in the context of prejudice. *Psychological Science, 18*, 524–530.

Amodio, D. M., Devine, P. G., & Harmon-Jones, E. (2008). Individual differences in the regulation of intergroup bias: The role of conflict monitoring and neural signals for control. *Journal of Personality and Social Psychology, 94,* 60–74.

Amodio, D. M., & Frith, C. D. (2006). Meeting of minds: The medial frontal cortex and social cognition. *Nature Reviews Neuroscience, 7,* 268–277.

Amodio, D. M., Harmon-Jones, E., & Devine, P. G. (2003). Individual differences in the activation and control of affective race bias as assessed by startle eyeblink responses and self-report. *Journal of Personality and Social Psychology, 84,* 738–753.

Amodio, D. M., Harmon-Jones, E., Devine, P. G., Curtin, J. J., Hartley, S. L., & Covert, A. E. (2004). Neural signals for the detection of unintentional race bias. *Psychological Science, 15,* 88–93.

Amodio, D. M., Kubota, J. T., Harmon-Jones, E., & Devine, P. G. (2006). Alternative mechanisms for regulating racial responses according to internal vs. external cues. *Social Cognitive and Affective Neuroscience, 1,* 26–36.

Amodio, D. M., & Mendoza, S. A. (2010). Implicit intergroup bias: Cognitive, affective, and motivational underpinnings. In B. Gawronski and B. K. Payne (Eds.), *Handbook of implicit social cognition* (pp. 353–374). New York: Guilford Press.

Amodio, D. M., & Ratner, K. G. (2011). A memory systems model of implicit social cognition. *Current Directions in Psychological Science, 20,* 143–148.

Aston-Jones, G., & Cohen, J. D. (2005). An integrative theory of locus coeruleus-norepinephrine function: Adaptive gain and optimal performance. *Annual Review of Neuroscience, 28,* 403–450.

Badre D., and Wagner, A. D. (2007). Left ventrolateral prefrontal cortex and the control of memory. *Neuropsychologia, 45,* 2883–2901.

Bartholow, B. D., Dickter, C. L., & Sestir, M. A. (2006). Stereotype activation and control of race bias: Cognitive control of inhibition and its impairment by alcohol. *Journal of Personality and Social Psychology, 90,* 272–287.

Bartholow, B. D., Fabiani, M., Gratton, G., & Bettencourt, B. A. (2001). A psychophysiological analysis of cognitive processing of and affective responses to social expectancy violations. *Psychological Science, 12,* 197–204.

Bartholow, B. D., Pearson, M. A., Gratton, G., & Fabiani, M. (2003). Effects of alcohol on person perception: A social cognitive neuroscience approach. *Journal of Personality and Social Psychology, 85,* 627–638.

Baumeister, R. F., & Showers, C. J. (1986). A review of paradoxical performance effects: Choking under pressure in sports and mental tests. *European Journal of Social Psychology, 16,* 361–383.

Baumgartner, T., Heinrichs, M., Vonlanthen, A., Fischbacher, U., & Fehr, E. (2008). Oxytocin shapes the neural circuitry of trust and trust adaptation in humans. *Neuron, 58,* 639–650.

Bentin, S., Allison, T., Puce, A., Perez, E., & McCarthy, G. (1996). Electrophysiological studies of face perception in humans. *Journal of Cognitive Neuroscience, 8,* 551–565.

Botvinick, M. M., Braver, T. S., Barch, D. M., Carter, C. S., & Cohen, J. D. (2001). Conflict monitoring and cognitive control. *Psychological Review, 108,* 624–652.

Bouton, M. E. (1994). Conditioning, remembering, and forgetting. *Journal of Experimental Psychology: Animal Behavior Processes, 20,* 219–231.

Brewer, M. B. (1999). The psychology of prejudice: Ingroup love or outgroup hate? *Journal of Social Issues, 55,* 429–444.

Caldara, R., Rossion, B., Bovet, P., & Hauert, C. (2004). Event-related potentials and time course of the "other-race" face classification advantage. *Neuroreport, 15,* 905.

Caldara, R., Thut, G., Servoir, P., Michel, C., Bovet, P., & Renault, B. (2003). Face versus non-face object perception and the "other-race" effect: A spatio-temporal event-related potential study. *Clinical Neurophysiology, 114*, 515–528.

Carmel, D., & Bentin, S. (2002). Domain specificity versus expertise: Factors influencing distinct processing of faces. *Cognition, 83*, 1–29.

Champagne, F. A., & Mashoodh, R. (2009). Genes in context: Gene–environment interplay and the origins of individual differences in behavior. *Current Directions in Psychological Science, 18*, 127–131.

Cooper, J. B., & Siegel, H. E. (1956). The galvanic skin response as a measure of emotion in prejudice. *Journal of Psychology, 42*, 149–155.

Cooper, J. B., & Singer, D. N. (1956). The role of emotion in prejudice. *Journal of Social Psychology, 44*, 241–247.

Correll, J., Urland, G. R., & Ito, T. A. (2006). Event-related potentials and the decision to shoot: The role of threat perception and cognitive control. *Journal of Experimental Social Psychology, 42*, 120–128.

Crandall, C. S., & Eshleman, A. (2003). A justification-suppression model of the expression and experience of prejudice. *Psychological Bulletin, 129*, 414–446.

Cunningham, W. A., Johnson, M. K., Raye, C. L., Gatenby, J. C., Gore, J. C., & Banaji, M. R. (2004). Separable neural components in the processing of Black and White faces. *Psychological Science, 15*, 806–813.

Cunningham, W. A., Raye, C. L., & Johnson, M. K. (2004). Implicit and explicit evaluation: fMRI correlates of valence, emotional intensity, and control in the processing of attitudes. *Journal of Cognitive Neuroscience, 16*, 1717–1729.

Davidson, R. J. (1992). Emotion and affective style: Hemispheric substrates. *Psychological Science, 3*, 39–43.

Davis, M. (1992). The role of the amygdala in fear and anxiety. *Annual Review of Neuroscience, 15*, 353–375.

Davis, M. (2006). Neural systems involved in fear and anxiety measured with fear-potentiated startle. *American Psychologist, 61*, 741–756.

Devine, P. G. (1989). Stereotypes and prejudice: Their automatic and controlled components. *Journal of Personality and Social Psychology, 56*, 5–18.

Devine, P. G., Plant, E. A., Amodio, D. M., Harmon-Jones, E., & Vance, S. L. (2002). The regulation of explicit and implicit race bias: The role of motivations to respond without prejudice. *Journal of Personality and Social Psychology, 82*, 835–848.

Dickerson, S. S., & Kemeny, M. E. (2004). Acute stressors and cortisol responses: A theoretical integration and synthesis of laboratory research. *Psychological Bulletin, 130*, 355–391.

Dovidio, J. F., Kawakami, K., Johnson, C., Johnson, B., & Howard, A. (1997). On the nature of prejudice: Automatic and controlled processes. *Journal of Experimental Social Psychology, 33*, 510–540.

Easterbrook, J. A. (1959). The effect of emotion on cue utilization and the organization of behavior. *Psychological Review, 66*, 183–201.

Eisenberger, N. I., Lieberman, M. D., & Williams, K. D. (2003). Does rejection hurt? An fMRI study of social exclusion. *Science, 302*, 290–292.

Eisenegger, C., Naef, M., Snozzi, R., Heinrichs, M., & Fehr, E. (2010). Prejudice and the truth about the effect of testosterone on human bargaining behavior. *Nature, 463*, 356–361.

Fazio, R. H., Jackson, J. R., Dunton, B. C., & Williams, C. J. (1995). Variability in automatic activation as an unobtrusive measure of racial attitudes: A bona fide pipeline? *Journal of Personality and Social Psychology, 69*, 1013–1027.

Fazio, R. H., & Olson, M. A. (2003). Implicit measures in social cognition: Their meaning and use. *Annual Review of Psychology, 54*, 297–327.

Fendt, M., & Fanselow, M. S. (1999). The neuroanatomical and neurochemical basis of conditioned fear. *Neuroscience & Biobehavioral Reviews, 23*, 743–760.

Fiske, S. T., Cuddy, A. J. C., Glick, P., & Xu, J. (2002). A model of (often mixed) stereotype content: Competence and warmth respectively follow from perceived status and competition. *Journal of Personality and Social Psychology, 82*, 878–902.

Gabrieli, J. D. (1998). Cognitive neuroscience of human memory. *Annual Review of Psychology, 49*, 87–115.

Golby, A. J., Eberhardt, J. L., Chiao, J. Y., & Gabrieli, J. D. E. (2001). Fusiform response to same and other race faces. *Nature Neuroscience, 4*, 845–850.

Greenwald, A. G., & Banaji, M. R. (1995). Implicit social cognition: Attitudes, self-esteem, and stereotypes. *Psychological Review, 102*, 4–27.

Greenwald, A. G., McGhee, D. E., & Schwartz, J. K. L. (1998). Measuring individual differences in implicit cognition: The Implicit Association Test. *Journal of Personality and Social Psychology, 74*, 1464–1480.

Guglielmi, R. S. (1999). Psychophysiological assessment of prejudice: Past research, current status, and future directions. *Personality and Social Psychology Review, 3*, 123–157.

Halim, M. L., Yoshikawa, H., & Amodio, D. M. (2013). Cross-generational effects of discrimination in immigrant mothers: Perceptions of bias predict child's healthcare visits for illness. *Health Psychology, 32*, 203–211.

Harmon-Jones, E. (2003). Clarifying the emotive functions of asymmetrical frontal cortical activity. *Psychophysiology, 40*, 838–848.

Harmon-Jones, E., Harmon-Jones, C., Amodio, D. M., & Gable, P. A. (2011). Attitudes toward emotions: Conceptualization and measurement of evaluations of specific emotions. *Journal of Personality and Social Psychology, 101*, 1332–1350.

Harris, L. T., & Fiske, S. T. (2006). Dehumanizing the lowest of the low: Neuro-imaging responses to extreme outgroups. *Psychological Science, 17*, 847–853.

Harris, L. T., & Fiske, S. T. (2009). Social neuroscience evidence for dehumanised perception. *European Review of Social Psychology, 20*, 192–231.

Hart, A. J., Whalen, P. J., Shin, L. M., McInerney, S. C., Fischer, H., & Rauch, S. L. (2000). Differential response in the human amygdala to racial outgroup vs. ingroup face stimuli. *NeuroReport, 11*, 2351–2355.

Haslam, N. (2006). Dehumanization: An integrative review. *Personality and Social Psychology Review, 10*, 252–264.

Haxby, J., Hoffman, E., & Gobbini, M. (2000). The distributed human neural system for face perception. *Trends in Cognitive Sciences, 4*, 223–232.

Ito, T. A., & Bartholow, B. D. (2009). The neural correlates of race. *Trends in Cognitive Sciences, 13*, 524–531.

Ito, T. A., & Urland, G. R. (2003). Race and gender on the brain: Electrocortical measures of attention to race and gender of multiply categorizable individuals. *Journal of Personality and Social Psychology, 85*, 616–626.

Ito, T., & Urland, G. (2005). The influence of processing objectives on the perception of faces: An ERP study of race and gender perception. *Cognitive, Affective, & Behavioral Neuroscience, 5*, 21–36.

Kanwisher, N. G., McDermott, J., & Chun, M. M. (1997). The fusiform face area: A module in human extrastriate cortex specialized for face perception. *Journal of Neuroscience, 17*, 4302–4311.

Kerns, J. G., Cohen, J. D., MacDonald, A. W., Cho, R. Y., Stenger, V. A., & Carter, C. S. (2004). Anterior cingulate conflict monitoring and adjustments in control. *Science, 303*, 1023–1026.

King-Casas, B., Tomlin, D., Anen, C., Camerer, C. F., Quartz, S. R., Montague, P. R. (2005). Getting to know you: Reputation and trust in a two-person economic exchange. *Science, 308*, 78–83.

Knutson, K. M., Mah, L., Manly, C. F., and Grafman, J. (2007). Neural correlates of automatic beliefs about gender and race. *Human Brain Mapping, 28*, 915–930.

Lambert, A. J., Payne, B. K., Jacoby, L. L., Shaffer, L. M., Chasteen, A. L., & Khan, S. R. (2003). Stereotypes as dominant responses: On the "social facilitation" of prejudice in anticipated public contexts. *Journal of Personality and Social Psychology, 84*, 277–295.

Lang, P. J., Bradley, M. M., & Cuthbert, B. N. (1990). Emotion, attention, and the startle reflex. *Psychological Review, 97*, 377–395.

LeDoux, J. E. (1996). *The emotional brain*. New York: Simon & Schuster.

LeDoux, J. E., Iwata, J., Cicchetti, P., & Reis, D. J. (1988). Different projections of the central amygdaloid nucleus mediate autonomic and behavioral correlates of conditioned fear. *Journal of Neuroscience, 8*, 2517–2529.

Lieberman, M. D., Hariri, A., Jarcho, J. M., Eisenberger, N. I., & Bookheimer, S. Y. (2005). An fMRI investigation of race-related amygdala activity in African-American and Caucasian-American individuals. *Nature Neuroscience, 8*, 720–722.

Major, B., & O'Brien, L. T. (2005). The social psychology of stigma. *Annual Review of Psychology, 56*, 393–421.

Mehta, P. H., & Josephs, R. A. (2006). Testosterone change after losing predicts the decision to compete again. *Hormones and Behavior, 50*, 684–692.

Mendes, W. B., Blascovich, J., Lickel, B., & Hunter, S. (2002). Challenge and threat during social interactions with White and Black men. *Personality and Social Psychology Bulletin, 28*, 939–952.

Mendes, W. B., Gray, H. M., Mendoza-Denton, R., Major, B., & Epel, E. (2007). Why egalitarianism might be good for your health: Physiological thriving during stressful intergroup encounters. *Psychological Science, 18*, 991–998.

Miller, E. K., & Cohen, J. D. (2001). An integrative theory of prefrontal cortex function. *Annual Review of Neuroscience, 24*, 167–202.

Milne, E., & Grafman, J. (2001). Ventromedial prefrontal cortex lesions in humans eliminate implicit gender stereotyping. *Journal of Neuroscience, 21*, 1–6.

Mitchell, J. P. (2009). Social psychology as a natural kind. *Trends in Cognitive Sciences, 13*, 246–251.

Mitchell, J. P., Ames, D. L., Jenkins, A. C., & Banaji, M. R. (2009). Neural correlates of stereotype application. *Journal of Cognitive Neuroscience, 21*, 594–604.

Monteith, M. J. (1993). Self-regulation of prejudiced responses: Implications for progress in prejudice-reduction efforts. *Journal of Personality and Social Psychology, 65*, 469–485.

Ofan, R. H., Rubin, N., & Amodio, D. M. (2011). Seeing race: N170 responses to race and their relation to automatic racial attitudes and controlled processing. *Journal of Cognitive Neuroscience, 23*, 3152–3161.

Page-Gould, E., Mendes, W. B., & Major, B. (2010). Intergroup contact facilitates physiological recovery following stressful intergroup interactions. *Journal of Experimental Social Psychology, 46*, 854–858.

Payne, B. K. (2001). Prejudice and perception: The role of automatic and controlled processes in misperceiving a weapon. *Journal of Personality and Social Psychology, 81*, 181–192.

Phelps, E. A., O'Connor, K. J., Cunningham, W. A., Funayama, E. S., Gatenby, J. C., Gore, J. C., & Banaji, M. R. (2000). Performance on indirect measures of race evaluation predicts amygdala activation. *Journal of Cognitive Neuroscience, 12*, 729–738.

Quadflieg, S., & Macrae, C. N. (2011). Stereotypes and stereotyping: What's the brain got to do with it? *European Review of Social Psychology, 22*, 215–273.

Quadflieg, S., Turk, D. J., Waiter, G. D., Mitchell, J. P., Jenkins, A. C., & Macrae, C. N. (2009). Exploring the neural correlates of social stereotyping. *Journal of Cognitive Neuroscience, 21*, 1560–1570.

Rankin, R. E., & Campbell, D. T. (1955). Galvanic skin response to Negro and White experimenters. *Journal of Abnormal and Social Psychology, 51*, 30–33.

Ratner, K. G., & Amodio, D. M. (2013). Seeing "us vs. them": Minimal group effects on the rapid neural processing of faces. *Journal of Experimental Social Psychology, 49*, 298–301.

Ratner, K. G., Halim, M. L., & Amodio, D. M. (2013). Perceived stigmatization, ingroup pride, and immune and endocrine activity: Evidence from a Black and Latina community sample. *Social Psychological and Personality Science, 4*, 81–91.

Richeson, J. A., Baird, A. A., Gordon, H. L., Heatherton, T. F., Wyland, C. L., Trawalter, S., & Shelton, J. N. (2003). An fMRI investigation of the impact of interracial contact on executive function. *Nature Neuroscience, 6*, 1323–1328.

Richeson, J. A., Todd, A. R., Trawalter, S., & Baird, A. A. (2008). Eye-gaze direction modulates race-related amygdala activity. *Group Processes and Intergroup Relations, 11*, 233–246.

Richeson, J. A., & Trawalter, S. (2005). Why do interracial interactions impair executive function? A resource depletion account. *Journal of Personality and Social Psychology, 88*, 934–947.

Richeson, J. A., & Trawalter, S. (2008). The threat of appearing prejudiced and race-based attentional biases. *Psychological Science, 19*, 98–102.

Ronquillo, J., Denson, T. F., Lickel, B., Lu, Z., Nandy, A., & Maddox, K. B. (2007). The effects of skin tone on race-related amygdala activity: An fMRI investigation. *Social Cognitive and Affective Neuroscience, 2*, 39–44.

Schiller, D., Freeman, J. D., Mitchell, J. P., Uleman, J. S., & Phelps, E. A. (2009). A neural mechanism of first impressions. *Nature Neuroscience, 12*, 508–514.

Shiffrin, R., & Schneider, W. (1977). Controlled and automatic human information processing, II: Perceptual learning, automatic attending, and a general theory. *Psychological Review, 84*, 127–190.

Smith, E. R., & DeCoster, J. (2000). Dual process models in social and cognitive psychology: Conceptual integration and links to underlying memory systems. *Personality and Social Psychology Review, 4*, 108–131.

Stangor, C., & Lange, J. (1994). Mental representations of social groups: Advances in understanding stereotypes and stereotyping. *Advances in Experimental Social Psychology, 26*, 357–416.

Van Bavel, J. J., & Cunningham, W. A. (2011). A social neuroscience approach to self and social categorisation: A new look at an old issue. *European Review of Social Psychology, 21*, 237–284.

Van Bavel, J. J., Packer, D. J., & Cunningham, W. A. (2008). The neural substrates of in-group bias: A functional magnetic resonance imaging investigation. *Psychological Science, 19*, 1131–1139.

Vanman, E. J., Paul, B. Y., Ito, T. A., & Miller, N. (1997). The modern face of prejudice and structural features that moderate the effect of cooperation on affect. *Journal of Personality and Social Psychology, 73*, 941–959.

Vidulich, R. N., & Krevanick, F. W. (1966). Racial attitudes and emotional response to visual representations of the Negro. *Journal of Social Psychology, 68*, 85–93.

Vrana, S. R., & Rollock, D. (1998). Physiological response to a minimal social encounter: Effects of gender, ethnicity, and social context. *Psychophysiology, 35*, 462–469.

Walker, P., Silvert, L., Hewstone, M., & Nobre, A. (2008). Social contact and other-race face processing in the human brain. *Social Cognitive and Affective Neuroscience, 3*, 16–25.

Wheeler, M. E., & Fiske, S. T. (2005). Controlling racial prejudice: Social cognitive goals affect amygdala and stereotype activation. *Psychological Science, 16*, 56–63.

Wiese, H., Stahl, J., & Schweinberger, S. R. (2009). Configural processing of other-race faces is delayed but not decreased. *Biological Psychology, 81*, 103–109.

2

Evolutionary Perspectives on Prejudice

CATHERINE A. COTTRELL

New College of Florida

JUSTIN H. PARK

University of Bristol

The purpose of this chapter is to examine insights offered by an evolutionary approach for the study of prejudice, to summarize recent empirical findings that were generated from an evolutionary framework, and to highlight important research questions for future research. As we reflected on the news of the past several years, four diverse stories jumped out as examples of the psychological processes we seek to describe here.

First, in January of 2009, nine Muslim Americans were removed from a flight departing from Washington, DC, after fellow passengers overheard what they characterized as a "suspicious remark" from one of the Muslim passengers. In particular, these other travelers were concerned that this remark reflected a desire to cause harm to the airplane, its passengers, and people on the ground. Second, in the summer and fall of 2009, people around the world were taking extra care to avoid contracting the H1N1 influenza (i.e., "swine flu"), which originated in Veracruz, Mexico. As this pandemic reached its pinnacle, airplanes originating from Mexico faced increased scrutiny when they attempted to land in international destinations. At least once, healthy Mexican travelers were held in forced isolation at an international airport out of concern that they were carrying the highly contagious flu. Third, in November of 2008, California voters approved Proposition 8, which amended the state constitution to restrict marriage to opposite-sex couples only, thereby overturning an earlier legal ruling that same-sex couples have a constitutional right to marry. Its supporters argued that this proposition protects the institution of marriage from corruption by gay and lesbian couples. Last, in April of 2010, the governor of Arizona signed into effect a state law that required law-enforcement officials to inquire about the immigration status of anyone who is suspected of being in the United States illegally. According to its proponents, this law allows for improved identification, prosecution, and deportation of illegal immigrants, who place a substantial burden on state social programs (because illegal immigrants are thought to benefit from these programs without contributing taxes).

These four news stories have received a substantial amount of coverage in the last couple of years. Beyond this common tie, however, they also share another important quality—each offers valuable insight into human prejudices. In each case, a group of people was believed to threaten another group in a specific way: The Muslim American travelers were perceived as wanting to cause bodily harm to others; the Mexican travelers were thought to carry a contagious illness; gay/lesbian couples were seen as holding inferior values and morals; and illegal immigrants were perceived as taking state resources without contributing to them. These perceived threats then ostensibly motivated specific actions (i.e., removal from an airplane, quarantine, constitutional amendment, and state law) intended to neutralize the perceived threat.

This idea that specific discriminatory reactions are functionally relevant responses to specific perceived threats sits at the heart of an evolutionary approach to prejudice. We elaborate on this perspective below. We begin by describing evolutionary approaches to human social behavior in general terms, then present an illustrative set of specific threats that might underlie prejudices, describe the nature of the resultant prejudice and discrimination responses, and summarize personality and situational influences on these responses. We close by discussing the contributions of an evolutionary approach for understanding prejudice, as well as the future of research on prejudice from this perspective.

AN OVERVIEW OF EVOLUTIONARY APPROACHES TO HUMAN BEHAVIOR

Evolution-informed perspectives have recently been applied to the study of a broad range of human social phenomena (e.g., social cognition, familial relationships, prosocial behavior; for a recent overview, see Neuberg, Kenrick, & Schaller, 2010). According to evolutionary psychology, human psychological processes reflect adaptations "designed" by natural selection to solve recurrent problems faced by ancestral humans (Cosmides, Tooby, & Barkow, 1992; Kenrick, Schaller, & Simpson, 2006; Neuberg et al., 2010). Simply put, an evolutionary approach suggests that our contemporary affect, cognition, and behavior reflect what tended to increase the reproductive fitness of our ancestors. Although evidence indicates that evolutionarily recent cultural and ecological changes (occurring within the past 10,000 years) may have driven substantial genetic evolution (Hawks, Wang, Cochran, Harpending, & Moyzis, 2007), many of the principal psychological mechanisms are expected to be adapted to recurrent problems that human (and prehuman) populations faced for a much longer duration (Tooby & Cosmides, 2005). Moreover, it is important to note that psychological adaptations do not operate in a cultural vacuum; rather, the capacity for culture is a core human adaptation (Richerson & Boyd, 2005), and this has important implications for understanding the development of and flexibility in behavioral tendencies, as well as variation across cultures and historical periods.

Several aspects of contemporary evolutionary psychological approaches deserve further elaboration. First, central to this assertion is a focus on domain-specific psychological processes. That is, psychological mechanisms are assumed to solve specific recurrent problems that threatened the reproductive fitness of ancestral humans (e.g., keeping oneself safe, maintaining one's health, managing relations with others). It is important to note that solutions to different problems are expected to take different forms (e.g., what it takes to stay safe is different from what it takes to stay healthy). Second, these psychological mechanisms are those that *tended* to enhance our ancestors' reproductive fitness across situations. They may not *always* do so—a point clearly made by error management theory (Haselton & Buss, 2000; Haselton & Nettle, 2006). Third, these psychological mechanisms are those that benefited our ancestors in their environment, and they may not actually produce notable advantage in a contemporary social environment. Fourth, evolution-inspired analyses do not imply that human social behavior is genetically fixed. Such analyses, rather, speak volumes about the environmental variables that may moderate the occurrence of a particular behavior (e.g., Neuberg et al., 2010; Schaller, Park, & Kenrick, 2007), a point that we consider further below. Last, these theories do not imply that what "is" represents what "should be" (i.e., the naturalistic fallacy). The light shed by an evolution-based analysis is intended to expose features of human social behavior that tended to enhance reproductive success; it is not intended to present these features as morally or ethically appropriate.

ASSUMPTIONS OF AN EVOLUTIONARY APPROACH TO PREJUDICE

In social psychology, prejudice has traditionally been treated as a psychologically unitary phenomenon, being defined simply as negative attitudes toward members of specific social categories. Reflecting this tradition, most theoretical approaches (e.g., social identity, self-affirmation, terror management) have conceptualized different instances of prejudice (e.g., prejudice against racial/ethnic outgroups, gay people, elderly people) as products of a common underlying psychological process, such as self-esteem maintenance (e.g., Fein & Spencer, 1997; Greenberg et al., 1990; Tajfel & Turner, 1979). While it is clear that such general psychological processes do contribute to prejudice, and while these theoretical approaches fruitfully predict variation in prejudice, we believe that evolutionary perspectives may usefully complement such general-process accounts.

From an evolutionary perspective, we should expect discernible patterns in the kinds of social categories that frequently inspire prejudice and in the kinds of psychological responses that are typically associated with those prejudices. For instance, throughout history, and around the world, certain groups of individuals (e.g., ethnic outgroups) have more often inspired aggression compared to other groups of individuals (e.g., elderly people). Likewise, some groups of individuals (e.g., those with visually conspicuous symptoms of disease) have more often inspired avoidance. With its focus on specific psychological processes, an evolutionary analysis of prejudice may be especially well equipped to explain and predict these different responses toward different social categories.

From an evolutionary perspective, people may hold stereotypes, express prejudices, and act in discriminatory ways because these cognitive, affective, and behavioral responses enhanced the reproductive fitness of ancestral humans. Why would it have been adaptive to respond to others with such negative reactions? To understand this, we need to appreciate the role of sociality in human life. Like many animals, humans evolved as social creatures, living in groups containing no more than around 150 individuals (Dunbar, 1998). The tendency to live in groups (rather than solitarily) likely evolved because it decreased predation risk and allowed the individual to accomplish more than one could alone. Individuals working together could forage for more berries, hunt larger game, and build better shelters than could an individual working alone. People living in groups could also share knowledge with one another, learn from one another, and exchange favors with one another. Such benefits likely offered group-living ancestral humans substantial fitness advantages over solitary-living humans (Brewer, 1999).

However, living in groups introduced new problems that ancestral humans needed to manage. To illustrate, people living in small groups can steal from one another, physically harm (or even kill) one another, and spread contagious diseases to one another. Furthermore, groups themselves may compete with other groups for resources, introducing the problem of hostile outgroup members—individuals who may be inclined to cause others harm, simply because they belong to a different group. In all, people gain access to many (potential) fitness-enhancing benefits from sociality while also facing many (potential) fitness-reducing costs. How could ancestral humans avoid (or perhaps just minimize) these harmful costs? From an evolutionary perspective, natural selection may have "engineered" psychological mechanisms that monitored humans' social environment for potential threats to their group's well-being, and thus to their own individual well-being (for related ideas, see Stangor & Crandall, 2000). Ancestral humans who detected these threats and responded to them appropriately would have gained more fitness-enhancing benefits from sociality than those who did not detect and respond to such threats. Once a potential threat is detected, people must also respond with appropriate affective (e.g., fear, disgust), cognitive (e.g., ascription of stereotypes), and behavioral (e.g., aggression, avoidance) reactions that are focused on eliminating (or at least reducing) the perceived threat. It is important to note that these reactions must be appropriate to the specific perceived threat. Just as different medical maladies require different treatments, different specific perceived threats to one's group also require different affective, cognitive, and behavioral responses to the ostensible source of that threat.

Apart from the notion of specific psychological mechanisms attuned to specific threats, two additional key ideas in evolutionary psychology have informed research on prejudice: *error management theory* and *functional flexibility*. To respond adaptively to threat, it must first be detected. But the presence of threat is often uncertain and must be inferred from imperfect cues, which means that any particular inference strategy entails inference errors (this is an example of a signal-detection problem; see also Amodio, chapter 1 in this volume). An evolutionary approach to these errors suggests that inferential mechanisms may evolve to be biased toward minimizing the more costly form of error, even though this inevitably leads to an increase in the less costly form of error (this idea is known as *error management theory*; Haselton & Buss, 2000; Haselton & Nettle, 2006). The implications of this theory for threat perception are illustrated in greater detail below.

Moreover, even though the tendencies to overperceive threats and to respond with specific aversive cognitions and emotions may have evolved for adaptive reasons, they are not unconditionally adaptive. Excessive overperception of threat and excessive aversive responses can impose net costs on reproductive fitness. Over human evolutionary history, it is likely that individuals encountered fluctuating levels of vulnerability to threat, and psychological mechanisms may have evolved to be *functionally flexible*, varying their responses as a function of threat-connoting factors (Schaller et al., 2007). Defensive and aversive responses may be amplified when one's (perceived) vulnerability to threat is greater—when their benefits are more likely to outweigh their costs. Information suggesting vulnerability to threat may be present within the individual (e.g., chronically heightened fear) or in the environment (e.g., outbreak of war). Conveniently, this allows psychologists to predict (and test) specific person, situation, and person-by-situation effects on different kinds of prejudice.

Specific Threats and Their Functional Psychological and Behavioral Responses

What specific threats would be relevant to reproductive fitness in ancestral times? Evolutionary psychologists have grappled with this question and have proposed a number of threats to which humans are likely attuned (see also Stangor & Crandall, 2000). Below we describe four kinds of threats that have been identified by evolutionary psychologists, and we discuss psychological and behavioral responses that may have evolved to manage those threats. More importantly, we summarize research testing hypotheses derived from an evolutionary analysis, which have yielded data relevant to our understanding of prejudice.

Threats to Physical Safety   To thrive in their environment, ancestral humans needed to survive to reproductive age and then stay alive long enough to raise their offspring. It therefore seems likely that physical safety was a primary concern for ancestral humans (Kenrick, Griskevicius, Neuberg, & Schaller, 2010; Kenrick, Li, & Butner, 2003). For our current purposes, this means that people should be attuned to others who ostensibly seek to inflict bodily harm (e.g., the Muslim American travelers in our opening example). Cues to these safety threats may include signs of others' harmful intentions (e.g., an angry facial expression, possession of a weapon, a history of harm in the past); threat may also be indicated simply by coalitional group membership. Ancestral humans who effectively detected and responded to such safety threats would have been able to stay alive longer to reproduce and raise their offspring in comparison with those who failed to detect such threats.

Humans evolved in tribal contexts characterized by high prevalence of intergroup violence. Although it is tempting to think that deaths from war have been more common in recent history, the percentage of deaths caused by warfare was likely far higher in prehistoric hunter-gatherer societies, often exceeding 25% (Keeley, 1996; Pinker, 2011). Correspondingly, many present-day hunter-gatherer groups are highly territorial and violent (e.g., Chagnon, 1988; Eibl-Eibesfeldt, 1974; Kelly, 1995). Given the recurrent problem posed by potentially harmful outgroup members, there likely evolved psychological mechanisms that facilitate avoidance of such harmful encounters (Kurzban & Leary, 2001; Sidanius & Pratto, 1999). In fact, intergroup violence and the resultant intergroup vigilance appear to predate humans: group categorization and vigilance toward outgroup members have been experimentally demonstrated in nonhuman primates as well (Mahajan et al., 2011). Humans are highly attentive to cues suggesting coalitional alliance and quickly discriminate ingroup members from outgroup members; moreover, the perception of potentially harmful outgroup members activates cognitive and emotional responses (e.g., fear, anxiety, danger-relevant thoughts) that facilitate adaptive behavior (e.g., avoidance, caution; Kurzban & Neuberg, 2005; Schaller & Neuberg, 2008). White Americans' general reactions to African Americans illustrate this pattern—Whites associate Blacks with a threat to safety, report fear toward them, and indicate a willingness to engage in escape-related actions to avoid them (e.g., Cottrell & Neuberg, 2004, 2005).

When we consider the fact that humans may possess psychological mechanisms specialized for dealing with coalitional alliances—not only for forming coalitions but also for besting rival coalitions—it becomes clear that not all social categorizations are equal. In fact, although social psychologists tend to use the term "group" to refer to just about any social category, only a subset of these may be psychologically meaningful "groups" (Park, 2012). More specifically, humans are likely to have evolved coalition-detection mechanisms that are responsive to various indicators of tribal alliances (Kurzban, Tooby, & Cosmides, 2001). In contemporary contexts, cues such as skin color, speech patterns, and linguistic labels—regardless of whether they reliably signal tribal alliances—may be perceived as indicators of coalitional alliances (Kurzban et al., 2001; Schaller, Park, & Faulkner, 2003). Perhaps equally important, many other salient cues—gender, age, eye color—may be far less likely to engage the coalitional psychology.

When people's coalitional alliances are not perfectly obvious, there may be classification errors. One could perceive a harmless ingroup member as a harmful outgroup member (false positive); or one could perceive a harmful outgroup member as a harmless ingroup member (false negative). The costs associated with these two errors are asymmetrical, and error management theory implies that people may be biased toward erroneously perceiving ambiguous others as hostile outgroup members. Moreover, the logic of functional flexibility suggests that this bias may be further exaggerated when perceivers feel vulnerable to harm, either because of the perceiver's characteristics or because of the situation. Miller, Maner, and Becker (2010) found that White individuals were more likely to categorize racially ambiguous targets as Black when perceptions of threat were heightened (e.g., when the target moved toward the perceiver or when the perceiver felt fearful). Even when the targets were racially unambiguous, the level of threat had a noticeable effect: When perceivers were under time pressure, White male faces holding angry (threatening) expressions were more likely to be categorized as Black than vice versa.

One cue that suggests threat to physical safety is ambient darkness. A series of studies examined the effects of ambient darkness on functionally specific psychological responses. In one study, Schaller, Park, and Faulkner (2003) asked Canadian students to rate the ingroup (Canadians) and an outgroup (Iraqis) on four trait dimensions, two of which were danger relevant (hostile, trustworthy) and two of which were not (ignorant, open-minded). The ratings were made in either a dark room or a well-lit room and, based on these ratings, ingroup favoritism scores were created. The results showed that, for the traits unrelated to danger, ingroup favoritism was identical across the dark and light conditions; however, for traits connoting danger, ingroup favoritism was higher in the dark. A subsequent study (reported by Schaller, Park, & Faulkner, 2003) showed that the effect of darkness on ingroup favoritism for danger-relevant traits is limited to people who tend to believe that the world is a dangerous place, as measured via a questionnaire (see Figure 2.1). While it is clear that there is a general ingroup-favoritism effect, it is also clear that perceptions of danger-relevant traits in ingroup and outgroup members are closely tied to perceived threat to physical safety. Implicit measures have revealed conceptually similar effects. Using reaction-time methodology, Schaller, Park, and Mueller (2003) found that students sitting in a dark room were more likely to implicitly associate members of an outgroup (Africans) with danger-relevant negative words (but not with danger-irrelevant negative words), and these effects were specific to participants with chronically heightened beliefs about danger. We see these latter interaction effects as especially notable because they illustrate nicely a functional person-by-situation effect that is predicted from the concept of functional flexibility.

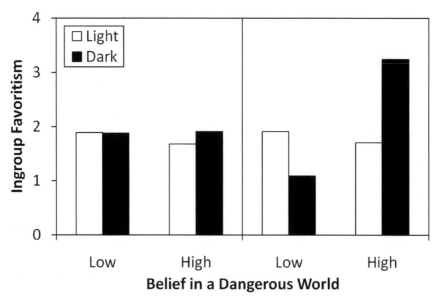

Figure 2.1 Interactive effects of ambient darkness (manipulated between subjects) and belief in a dangerous world (median split) on ingroup favoritism for danger-irrelevant (left panel) and danger-relevant (right panel) traits. Participants (69 students from the University of British Columbia, Canada) were asked to rate "men from Canada" (ingroup) and "men from Iraq" (outgroup). Higher values indicate more positive ratings of ingroup relative to outgroup members. (Figure based on results reported in Schaller, Park, & Faulkner, 2003).

In addition to attributing danger-relevant stereotypes to potentially danger-ous outgroup members, another sort of functional response is to (mis)perceive aggressive intention in such people (again, inferring nonexistent aggressive intent is less costly than failing to perceive existent aggressive intent). Maner et al. (2005) termed this tendency *functional projection*, and they proposed that people may tend to perceive anger in the faces of outgroup members (espe-cially males) even if those people are holding neutral expressions. They found that an experimentally heightened self-protective motive (which involved show-ing participants scenes from the movie *Silence of the Lambs*) increased the ten-dency among White American participants to perceive anger in the faces of Black men and Arab men (but not in the faces of White men or women).

In all, it seems that humans possess psychological mechanisms designed to motivate avoidance of potentially harmful others, and we have suggested that this threat alarm system may tend to be activated over-inclusively. In addition, we have noted the functional flexibility of this system. That is, the safety-related responses are especially pronounced among those who believe the world is an especially dangerous place or who are currently in especially dangerous contexts.

Threats to Health and Well-Being   To thrive in their environment, ancestral humans needed not just to stay alive but also to remain healthy enough to reproduce and to devote energy to raising their offspring. As such, it seems likely that humans developed psychological mechanisms to monitor their social environment for threats to their physical health, such as contagious disease (Schaller & Park, 2011). In particular, health concerns might be especially relevant for women of reproductive age, as they need to bear children and nurse their young. This means that people should be attuned to others who ostensibly spread contagious disease (e.g., the Mexican travelers in our opening example). Among possible cues to these contagion threats are outward signs of disease (e.g., sores on the skin, sunken cheeks, cough) and anomalous behaviors, including foreign practices of exotic cultures (see below). Ancestral humans who effectively detected and responded to such threats would have been able to remain healthier than those who failed to do so. It is instructive to note here that many physical features typically considered attractive (e.g., clear skin, lustrous hair, body symmetry) may signal good health, suggesting that natural selection also created psychological mechanisms that draw people toward healthy others (Fink & Penton-Voak, 2002; Rhodes, 2006). Adaptive responses to the perception of disease-connoting cues may involve specific emotional responses such as disgust (e.g., Curtis, Aunger, & Rabie, 2004) and the activation of disease-relevant cognitions such as appraisals of contagion and contamination (e.g., Rozin, Millman, & Nemeroff, 1986; Woody & Teachman, 2000). Indeed, the desire to avoid diseased others is correlated with the perceived contagiousness of the disease (Bishop, 1991; Crandall & Moriarty, 1995). As an example of these processes, gay men are often viewed as threats to others' health (ostensibly via a stereotypic association with contagious illnesses, such as AIDS), which predicts disgust felt toward them and behavioral inclinations focused on preventing contamination to others (e.g., Cottrell & Neuberg, 2004, 2005).

Error management theory suggests that psychological disease-detection mechanisms may respond over-inclusively (Haselton & Nettle, 2006; Kurzban & Leary, 2001; Nesse, 2005). This is because, in the domain of disease detection, false-negative errors (inferring that a diseased person is healthy) impose substantially greater fitness costs than false-positive errors (inferring that a healthy person is diseased). Thus, any gross deviation from what is considered "normal" appearance or behavior in a given society (even in the absence of contagious disease) may be interpreted as evidence of infection, automatically triggering an aversive response (Kurzban & Leary, 2001; Schaller & Duncan, 2007; Schaller & Park, 2011). Moreover, people's automatic aversive responses are likely to be functionally flexible—being especially strong when the benefits of avoiding disease are high (and are likely to exceed the costs). Information concerning the benefits of avoidance behavior may be present in the environment (e.g., outbreak of disease in the local area) or within individuals (e.g., suppressed immune system). Simply put, the motivation to avoid individuals bearing disease-connoting cues is expected to be particularly powerful among people with heightened (perceived) susceptibility to pathogens (Schaller & Duncan, 2007).

These implications have led to several lines of inquiry and interesting discoveries. One set of studies investigated the degree to which physical disabilities (regardless of whether they have infectious causes) may be perceived as a heuristic cue for pathogens (Park, Faulkner, & Schaller, 2003). In one study conducted in Canada, Park et al. (2003) found that students with chronically heightened concerns about disease are less likely to have friends with physical disabilities. In another study, employing a computer-based reaction-time task, Park et al. (2003) found that the perception of physically disabled people automatically activates disease-relevant cognitions, even though perceivers were fully aware that the physical disabilities had noninfectious causes. Moreover, this effect was stronger among people with chronically or experimentally heightened concerns about disease (at least among European Canadian participants; among Asian Canadians, disgust sensitivity was a better predictor of the tendency to implicitly associate disability with disease-relevant cognitions). Other studies have found that the perception of a facial birthmark automatically activates disease cognitions, even when perceivers are aware that no contagious disease is present (Schaller & Duncan, 2007).

A wide range of physical cues seems to trigger the disease-avoidance process. In cultures in which thin body types are considered the norm, gross obesity may be perceived as a disease cue, leading to aversive responses. In one recent study (Klaczynski, 2008), seven- and ten-year-old American and Chinese children were asked to sample drinks "created" by obese and average-weight children (the weight status of the drink maker was manipulated via photos on the package label). After sampling the drinks, children gave lower taste ratings to the drinks made by obese children; more telling, they believed that the drinks made by obese children were more likely to cause illness, especially among those who, prior to sampling the drinks, had read a story about an ill child who had infected other children by coughing (in the control condition, the ill child coughed but the other children did not become ill).

In a study with university students, Park, Schaller, and Crandall (2007) found that those with chronically heightened concerns about disease harbor more strongly negative attitudes toward fat people (see also Lieberman, Tybur, & Latner, in press). This relationship emerged especially strongly among people who had viewed images of obese people immediately prior to expressing their anti-fat attitudes, consistent with the idea that it is the visual perception of physical deviation that activates the behavioral immune system. In another study, employing a computer-based reaction-time task, Park et al. (2007) found that the perception of obese people automatically activates disease-relevant cognitions, especially following experimentally induced pathogen salience. In both of these studies, additional methods and analyses ruled out the possibility that the effects are due simply to nonspecific (disease-irrelevant) negativity toward obesity.

Disease-connoting cues come in the form not only of morphological deviation but also of cultural outgroupness. This follows from the fact that humans have historically lived in small groups, and contact with members of other groups often introduced diseases to which individuals had no immunity (Diamond, 1999). For people within any given culture, some outgroups may appear especially foreign with respect to food preparation and hygiene practices. Because each culture has developed (via cultural evolution) its own set of practices for preventing infection, cultures with different practices—especially in the domains of food preparation and hygiene—may be perceived as posing disease threats. Thus, the perception of outgroups, particularly those that are subjectively foreign, may activate disease-avoidance responses.

Evidence for this hypothesis came from a series of studies conducted by Faulkner, Schaller, Park, and Duncan (2004). They found that Canadian participants with chronically heightened concerns about disease tend to harbor more strongly negative attitudes toward cultural outgroup members, but only those outgroup members perceived to be subjectively foreign in the disease-relevant domains (e.g., Africans, Sri Lankans); such effects were not found for outgroup members perceived to be subjectively familiar (e.g., East Asians, Europeans). Faulkner et al. (2004) also found analogous effects in studies in which concerns about disease were experimentally manipulated.

Other studies, employing somewhat different methodologies, have replicated and extended these findings. One study found that chronically heightened concerns about disease are associated with both outgroup negativity and ingroup positivity, even after controlling for concerns about death (Navarrete & Fessler, 2006). Another study found that individual differences in disgust sensitivity are associated with both negativity toward outgroups and positivity toward the ingroup (Navarrete & Fessler, 2006). Yet another study examined reactions of pregnant women. In the first trimester of pregnancy, both the fetus and the mother are more susceptible to infection (due to suppressed immune responses), implying the hypothesis that women in this period may exhibit stronger psychological disease-avoidance responses. In a cross-sectional study of pregnant women, Navarrete, Fessler, and Eng (2007) found that women in the first trimester exhibit stronger ingroup positivity and outgroup negativity.

In sum, findings from several lines of research suggest that humans possess psychological mechanisms designed to motivate avoidance of potentially diseased others. Owing to the design features of these mechanisms, aversive responses are activated automatically and over-inclusively, sometimes even in the face of conflicting rational assessments of contagiousness. In most of the studies described above, the people or groups that activated the disease-avoidance response posed no real threat of infection.

It is also important to note that these automatic responses are flexible, in a manner consistent with functional cost–benefit considerations. Most of the studies described above revealed that the aversive responses are especially pronounced among people with heightened sensitivity to disease because of either internal or external events. By adopting an evolutionary perspective, not only have these research lines provided clues toward understanding the ultimate function of emotional–motivational responses associated with disease avoidance (e.g., disgust, desire for physical distance), they have also produced a more detailed picture of the contextual and individual variables that are involved in phenomena generally classified as "stigmatization."

So far, we have offered in-depth discussions of adaptive responses to perceived threats to safety and health. These two threat systems have been the focus of much of the evolution-inspired research to date. Next, we consider other threat attunement systems and their associated "prejudice syndromes." Although the following discussions are more speculative than those presented above, they are based on the same principles, including error management processes and functional flexibility.

Threats to Values and Morals   Groups of ancestral humans likely developed their own sets of customs, values, and morals. Why would common group values benefit individuals within a group? They create a common identity, establish rules for everyday interactions, and provide a means of common socialization of future generations. They also create a clear dividing line to distinguish members of the ingroup from members of outgroups. Indeed, common values may be a universal feature of human social groups (Brown, 1991).

Given these benefits, we might expect that people are attuned to others who ostensibly possess or advocate values divergent from their own (e.g., the gay and lesbian couples in our opening example). Ancestral humans who effectively detected and responded to such values threats would have been able to identify others with "corrupt" values and reject them before they could contaminate the group's values systems. More generally, to the extent that values systems are a reliable indicator of outgroup status, an attunement to divergent values would also help identify outgroup members, who might be somewhat more likely to threaten an ingroup in other ways as well.

The moral contamination response system may operate similarly to the pathogen contamination response system just described. Many theorists have hypothesized that evolutionary processes may have expanded the original physical disgust system—designed to cope with contaminants and pathogens—to include adaptive responses to moral violations (Chapman, Kim, Susskind, & Anderson, 2009; Rozin, Haidt, & Fincher, 2009; Rozin, Haidt, & McCauley, 2008). We may expect instances of moral contamination to evoke disgust toward the apparent contaminant, as well as adaptive cognitions and actions focused on preventing the offending others from "infecting" others with their corrupt values, morals, and ideas.

This could explain how both fundamentalist Christians and feminists tend to be viewed as posing values threats, evoking disgust and action tendencies focused on reducing the threat (e.g., opposing the teaching of the outgroup's values in the community, preventing children from being exposed to members of the outgroup; Cottrell & Neuberg, 2004, 2005). Gay men may be seen both as disease contaminants (via a heuristic association with HIV/AIDS) and as moral contaminants (due to the perception that they threaten traditional American values related to marriage and family), evoking substantial amounts of disgust (Cottrell & Neuberg, 2005). Recent research suggests that this perceived threat to American values predicts opposition to social policies grant-ing gay rights, a relationship that is partially mediated by the disgust felt toward gays and lesbians (Cottrell, Richards, & Nichols, 2010).

Along these lines, an interesting area of research has demonstrated close links between disgust and morality. Studies have found that people's responses to immorality mirror responses to disease contaminants—seen, for instance, in their increased desire to cleanse themselves physically when their moral purity is threatened (Zhong & Liljenquist, 2006). Disgust has also been found to mor-alize activities relevant to "purity" (Horberg, Oveis, Keltner, & Cohen, 2009). Does this imply that people do not distinguish morality threats from disease threats? Not necessarily. An evolutionary analysis points to important distinc-tions between these threats, and it has been empirically demonstrated that morality-relevant disgust is distinct from disease-relevant disgust (Schaich Borg, Lieberman, & Kiehl, 2008; Tybur, Lieberman, & Griskevicius, 2009). Additional research is thus required to enable a better understanding of the psychological mechanisms underlying responses to morality threats, especially with respect to elucidating the morality-relevant disgust and associated func-tional cognitions and behaviors.

As with the other threat systems, we expect the moral contamination system to exhibit functional flexibility according to environmental inputs. For instance, values threat attunement may be enhanced in contexts involving children, who are particularly impressionable and vulnerable to novel ideas, or those involving heightened influence over others. We might expect that individuals thought to threaten values are viewed as especially dangerous in elementary schools, politi-cal arenas, or religious organizations (more so than in other settings). One study found that simply being reminded of one's role as a parent increases the ten-dency to oppose offensive acts (Eibach, Libby, & Ehrlinger, 2009). As another example, we might expect increased perception of values threat in environments cuing physical danger because different values systems may help identify out-group members who are more likely to represent safety threats, as described above. There are certainly many untested hypotheses related to perceived values threats, and we encourage researchers to examine them closely in future work.

Threats to Reciprocal Relations   Groups of ancestral humans likely estab-lished reciprocity-based relationships both within and between their groups. Such relationships would allow people to trade fitness-enhancing favors and information—I help you now, you help me in the future. Indeed, cooperative relationships and reciprocal exchange may be considered central components within human social groups (Brewer, 1999; Gouldner, 1960). It would be adap-tive for people to be attuned to others who ostensibly violate the terms of these reciprocity-based relationships (e.g., the illegal immigrants in our opening example). Ancestral humans who effectively detected and responded to such reciprocity threats would have been able to protect their sizable investments in social relationships better than those who failed to detect such threats. Along these lines, people respond negatively to those who violate reciprocity in interpersonal relationships (Cotterell, Eisenberger, & Speicher, 1992). We might expect a similar process to extend to intergroup relationships (Kurzban & Neuberg, 2005). Perceived threats to reciprocity should evoke anger toward the offending group, which then motivates actions focused on terminating the imbalanced relationship and (potentially) reclaiming the owed resources (Cottrell & Neuberg, 2005; Neuberg & Cottrell, 2002).

Several pieces of data illustrate these ideas. White American students reported that Mexican Americans take more than they contribute to society (i.e., a reciprocity threat); these participants also indicated that they felt increased anger toward Mexican Americans (Cottrell & Neuberg, 2005). In addition, consistent with the idea that White Americans view Black Americans as "free-loading" (Devine, 1989), Cottrell et al. (2010) found that the reciprocity threat White Americans associate with African Americans was related to decreased support for programs to aid Hurricane Katrina victims (many of whom are African Americans); this effect was partially mediated by anger felt toward African Americans. Although currently untested, we might expect that the intensity of the prejudice syndrome resulting from a perceived reciprocity threat will vary as a function of an individual's belief in the Protestant work ethic, as well as any economic stress in one's current environment (Neuberg & Cottrell, 2006).

Summary of Threats

In all, we have just outlined four illustrative social threats to which people may be attuned. For each threat, we presented research that linked a specific group to a specific threat. For example, African Americans were viewed as safety threats, disabled people were viewed as health threats, feminists were viewed as values threats, and Mexican Americans were viewed as reciprocity threats. How can researchers best map perceived threats onto social groups to understand and predict responses within a given intergroup context? In some situations, it may be relatively straightforward to connect specific threats to specific social groups. The best example here involves perceived health threats: Individuals with obvious cues to disease (e.g., skin lesions, coughs) or morphological abnormalities (e.g., missing limbs, asymmetrical features) will likely be thought to threaten others' health. However, more often, this mapping between group and threat is a function of the historical and contemporary relationships between the involved groups. Have the groups been in competition for jobs or other material resources? Has one group held more power or status than the other? We should expect that different intergroup interdependencies will create different configurations of perceived threats, though this is clearly an area where further research is required.

In addition, we do not intend to suggest that any given group or individual may pose only one threat. Indeed, an individual might perceive multiple threats from a given social category. For instance, some people believe gay men both possess morally inferior values and spread contagious diseases (e.g., HIV/AIDS; Cottrell & Neuberg, 2005). These multiple threats may not be perceived to equivalent degrees; it seems likely that, for a given group, the prominence of a specific perceived threat (and its associated psychological responses) will vary across contexts and perceivers. That is, for perceptions of gay men, a values threat may be especially pronounced in contexts that sensitize people to values and for perceivers who are dispositionally attuned to values, whereas a health threat may be especially pronounced in contexts that sensitize people to health and for perceivers who are dispositionally attuned to health. We encourage researchers to test this idea in future studies.

Furthermore, as we have emphasized, perceivers are not necessarily accurate in their assessment of threats. Because the presence of many threats is inferred on the basis of imperfect cues, there is always room for error, and an evolutionary analysis of such situations suggests that perceivers may have evolved to overperceive (rather than underperceive) threats (Haselton & Nettle, 2006). Regardless of whether people's reactions are calibrated to the actual level of threat, when the alarm is sounded to indicate a specific perceived threat, individuals appear to respond with functionally appropriate affective, cognitive, and behavioral responses, and they do so largely automatically (Park & Buunk, 2011).

CONTRIBUTIONS OF AN EVOLUTIONARY APPROACH TO PREJUDICE

It is important to consider what an evolutionary approach contributes to the extant social psychological literature. We see several valuable contributions of a threat-based evolutionary approach to prejudice.

First, an evolutionary approach focuses explicitly on the contents of prejudice-related processes. Many theories of prejudice are not equipped to make statements about specific cognitive, affective, and behavioral responses. In contrast, an evolutionary perspective focuses squarely on specific content related to different threats—threats to safety, health, values, reciprocity, etc.—and their associated functionally appropriate responses. This consideration of content is particularly valuable because it tends to yield hypotheses that are more nuanced than those arising from alternative theoretical approaches (Neuberg et al., 2010).

An evolutionary approach highlights the notion that prejudice syndromes might be best understood in terms of *specific* threat perceptions, emotional reactions, and behavioral reactions to others (rather than in terms of general cognitive, affective, and behavioral responses). We should note that this idea has also emerged from other theoretical approaches, including intergroup emotions theory (e.g., Mackie, Devos, & Smith, 2000), the stereotype content model (e.g., Fiske, Cuddy, Glick, & Xu, 2002), and image theory (e.g., Alexander, Brewer, & Herrmann, 1999). However, an evolutionary perspective puts functionally specific responses at its very core. This focus is important because it gives scholars a far broader and richer spectrum with which to understand, predict, and improve intergroup emotion and action. Focusing on positive versus negative reactions offers limited insight on intergroup interactions.

As we have stressed, all negative emotions and actions are not the same. Fear, anger, and disgust are each negatively valenced, but they tend to motivate quite different behavioral inclinations (escape, attack, and rejection, respectively). With an understanding of these specific cognitive, affective, and behavioral responses, we can better understand intergroup interactions.

An evolutionary approach suggests novel prejudice-reduction strategies (Park, 2012). Although demonstrated to be moderately effective (Pettigrew & Tropp, 2006), intergroup contact theory, which hypothesizes that particular forms of contact reduce prejudice, is a general strategy; it does not offer different guidelines for different prejudices. By contrast, an examination of specific forms of prejudice affords more focused interventions. An intervention that effectively reduces a perceived safety threat (and its resultant fear-related reactions) will look different from one that effectively reduces a perceived reciprocity threat (and its resultant anger-related reactions). Scholars who focus on prejudice reduction will benefit greatly from carefully evaluating the nature of the specific perceived threats in a particular intergroup context before constructing an intervention program.

As one last note, an evolutionary approach suggests motivational and situational variables that are not easily generated from alternative approaches. We have already shown that belief in a dangerous world, perceived vulnerability to disease, and stage in pregnancy are important moderating variables of prejudice reactions, and the approach has not yet been exhausted.

THE FUTURE OF THREAT-BASED RESEARCH

In addition to the suggested future research noted above, we see several fruitful avenues for the future of prejudice research from an evolutionary perspective. We must continue to map out the relevant psychological processes in greater detail. For instance, while researchers have identified links between fear-inducing stimuli (e.g., darkness, movie clips) and functional psychological responses (e.g., danger-relevant stereotyping, functional projection), we are far from having a complete catalog of the most important environmental triggers and of the key psychological responses. We should expect systematic connections among threat-relevant environmental stimuli, threat-relevant individual differences, threat-relevant psychological responses, and groups thought to pose specific threats. For example, health-relevant environmental stimuli (but not other stimuli, such as safety-relevant ones) should increase disgust-relevant responses (but not other negative responses, such as fear-relevant ones) toward groups thought stereotypically to pose health threats (but not toward other groups, such as those posing safety threats); and these effects should be strongest for perceivers who are chronically attuned to health threats (but not other concerns, such as physical safety). Although the work described above tackles some of these connections, it is clear that much more research is needed to delineate these relationships fully. In addition, some of this work will be usefully complemented by research on the neurophysiology underlying the psychological processes. As specific emotions are associated with specific neural structures and responses, research charting the links between social perception and brain activity will help guide future theories of prejudice (e.g., Harris & Fiske, 2006).

Researchers have tended to focus on the majority ethnic group's perceptions of minority ethnic groups rather than on each minority group's perceptions of the majority group (and other minority groups). For example, we know a great deal about White Americans' affective, cognitive, and behavioral reactions to Black Americans, Asian Americans, Hispanic Americans, and so on, but we know much less about how these other groups perceive White Americans and one another. Our social world is a heterogeneous one involving many complex interdependent networks, and a more thorough consideration of how different groups view one another may offer valuable means to improve often strained relationships within those social networks (Cottrell & Neuberg, 2012).

Research on prejudice is not merely academic but is intended to find possible solutions to societal problems. Given that an evolutionary approach implies specific kinds of interventions, future research will need to rigorously test the effectiveness of those interventions. For example, we should expect that an intervention targeting perceived safety threats (perhaps by making the perceivers feel more physically secure) will effectively reduce prejudice toward groups that stereotypically threaten safety but not toward groups that stereotypically threaten health. Moreover, it will be important to determine the extent to which domain-specific interventions yield benefits above and beyond those yielded by domain-general ones (given that, all else being equal, domain-general interventions are more likely to be cost-effective).

Another potentially fruitful avenue involves integrating the social/ evolutionary perspectives with developmental perspectives. Although prejudice is typically studied among adults, it is not a phenomenon that suddenly appears in adulthood; it has developmental antecedents, being influenced by inborn tendencies and by events that occur during childhood and adolescence. Although no social psychologist would deny the role of development, there has been lack of integration with developmental psychologists who have generated rich theories of the operation of psychological processes in early childhood. Children are not passive recipients of ambient norms but are endowed with psychological mechanisms that bias them toward certain ways of perceiving their social world and toward learning certain things. Understanding what children are innately equipped with, what they learn, and how that learning translates into prejudice is a task that will require increased cooperation among social, developmental, and evolutionary psychologists (Kinzler, Shutts, & Correll, 2010).

Finally, tendencies toward prejudice differ not only across individuals and situations but across societies as well. Some societies are more tolerant of "deviant" individuals and outgroups than are others. Some of this variation might be understood by applying the principle of functional flexibility described above. For instance, some societies may be located in parts of the world in which certain threats are more common, resulting in stronger norms and practices that neutralize that threat. One kind of threat that varies widely across world regions is contagious disease, and researchers have found that societies located in more disease-prevalent regions are more likely to have norms and practices that are geared toward excluding deviant individuals and outgroup members (e.g., Fincher, Thornhill, Murray, & Schaller, 2008; Murray, Trudeau, & Schaller, 2011; Van Leeuwen, Park, Koenig, & Graham, in press). We encourage researchers to examine cross-cultural variability in other threat sensitivities.

CONCLUDING THOUGHTS

We opened our discussion with four different instances of prejudice responses from recent news events. On the surface, they may seem unrelated to one another. However, an evolutionary perspective highlights a common thread: Each represents a functionally specific response to a perceived threat thought to originate with the target of the prejudice. It is important to note that each response was specific to its situation (and thus to the particular perceived threat). The nine Muslim American travelers were removed from an airplane—not prohibited from marrying—whereas gay and lesbian citizens of California were prohibited from marrying—not kept off a plane. This nicely illustrates the specificity of the prejudice processes that emerge from an evolutionary analysis (Neuberg & Cottrell, 2006).

The opening example also demonstrates the tendency for the threat alarm to sound over-inclusively. The Mexican travelers—quarantined over concern that they carried the swine flu—did not *actually* represent a contagion threat. However, the decision to isolate these individuals reflects the tendency to manage costly errors (Haselton & Buss, 2000; Haselton & Nettle, 2006). That is, inferring that they were healthy (and thus permitted to enter an international destination) if they were actually ill would impose significant fitness costs (as compared to inferring that they were ill if they were actually healthy).

We have also stressed that these threat systems are flexible in response to person and situation factors (Schaller et al., 2007). Again, our opening example is illustrative here. We noted above that people might be more sensitive to threats to reciprocity during times of economic stress. We think it is no coincidence that the Arizona law—proposed to protect state resources from illegal immigrants who ostensibly do not contribute taxes to state funds—was developed and enacted during a period of economic downturn.

We have presented these examples from recent news, as well as those from the research described above, to highlight the insights offered by an evolutionary approach to prejudice. In particular, an evolution-inspired analysis suggests that natural selection has created threat-attunement mechanisms to protect individuals from fitness-decreasing threats to themselves and their fellow group members. Once detected, these specific threat perceptions evoke specific affective, cognitive, and behavioral responses focused on reducing the perceived threat. Building on this research and its underlying theoretical rationale, we believe prejudice researchers will gain valuable traction for understanding, predicting, and reducing different forms of prejudice.

REFERENCES

Alexander, M. G., Brewer, M. B., & Herrmann, R. K. (1999). Images and affect: A functional analysis of out-group stereotypes. *Journal of Personality and Social Psychology, 77*, 78–93.

Bishop, G. D. (1991). Lay disease representations and responses to victims of disease. *Basic and Applied Social Psychology, 12*, 115–132.

Brewer, M. B. (1999). The psychology of prejudice: Ingroup love or outgroup hate? *Journal of Social Issues, 55*, 429–444.

Brown, D. E. (1991). *Human universals.* New York: McGraw-Hill.

Chagnon, N. A. (1988). Life histories, blood revenge, and warfare in a tribal population. *Science, 239*, 985–992.

Chapman, H., Kim, D., Susskind, J., & Anderson, A. (2009). In bad taste: Evidence for the oral origins of moral disgust. *Science, 323*, 1222–1226.

Cosmides, L., Tooby, J., & Barkow, J. (1992). Evolutionary psychology and conceptual integration. In J. Barkow, L. Cosmides, & J. Tooby (Eds.), *The adapted mind: Evolutionary psychology and the generation of culture.* New York: Oxford University Press.

Cotterell, N., Eisenberger, R., & Speicher, H. (1992). Inhibiting effects of reciprocation wariness on interpersonal relationships. *Journal of Personality and Social Psychology, 62*, 658–668.

Cottrell, C. A., & Neuberg, S. L. (2004, January). *From threat to emotion to action: A sociofunctional analysis of intergroup interactions.* Paper presented at the annual meeting of the Society for Personality and Social Psychology, Austin, Texas.

Cottrell, C. A., & Neuberg, S. L. (2005). Different emotional reactions to different groups: A sociofunctional threat-based approach to "prejudice." *Journal of Personality and Social Psychology, 88*, 770–789.

Cottrell, C. A., & Neuberg, S. L. (2012). *Do different ethnic groups view one another differently? Textured intergroup beliefs and emotions in college and national samples.* Unpublished manuscript, University of Florida.

Cottrell, C. A., Richards, D. A. R., & Nichols, A. L. (2010). Predicting policy attitudes from general prejudice versus specific intergroup emotions. *Journal of Experimental Social Psychology, 46*, 247–254.

Crandall, C. S., & Moriarty, D. (1995). Physical illness stigma and social rejection. *British Journal of Social Psychology, 34*, 67–83.

Curtis, V., Aunger, R., & Rabie, T. (2004). Evidence that disgust evolved to protect from risk of disease. *Proceedings of the Royal Society of London, Series B, 271*, S131–S133.

Devine, P. (1989). Stereotypes and prejudice: Their automatic and controlled components. *Journal of Personality and Social Psychology, 56*, 5–18.

Diamond, J. (1999). *Guns, germs, and steel: The fates of human societies.* New York: W. W. Norton.

Dunbar, R. I. M. (1998). The social brain hypothesis. *Evolutionary Anthropology: Issues, News, and Reviews, 6*, 178–190.

Eibach, R. P., Libby, L. K., & Ehrlinger, J. (2009). Priming family values: How being a parent affects moral evaluations of harmless but offensive acts. *Journal of Experimental Social Psychology, 45*, 1160–1163.

Eibl-Eibesfeldt, I. (1974). The myth of the aggression-free hunter and gatherer society. In R. L. Holloway (Ed.), *Primate aggression, territoriality, and xenophobia* (pp. 435–457). New York: Academic Press.

Faulkner, J., Schaller, M., Park, J. H., & Duncan, L. A. (2004). Evolved disease-avoidance mechanisms and contemporary xenophobic attitudes. *Group Processes and Intergroup Behavior, 7,* 333–353.

Fein, S., & Spencer, S. J. (1997). Prejudice as self-image maintenance: Affirming the self through derogating others. *Journal of Personality and Social Psychology, 73,* 31–44.

Fincher, C. L., Thornhill, R., Murray, D. R., & Schaller, M. (2008). Pathogen prevalence predicts human cross-cultural variability in individualism/collectivism. *Proceedings of the Royal Society B: Biological Sciences, 275,* 1279–1285.

Fink, B., & Penton-Voak, I. (2002). Evolutionary psychology of facial attractiveness. *Current Directions in Psychological Science, 11,* 154–158.

Fiske, S. T., Cuddy, A. J., Glick, P., & Xu, J. (2002). A model of (often mixed) stereotype content: Competence and warmth respectively follow from perceived status and competition. *Journal of Personality and Social Psychology, 82,* 878–902.

Gouldner, A. W. (1960). The norm of reciprocity: A preliminary statement. *American Sociological Review, 25,* 161–178.

Greenberg, J., Pyszczynski, T., Solomon, S., Rosenblatt, A., Veeder, M., Kirkland, S., & Lyon, D. (1990). Evidence for terror management theory II: The effects of mortality salience reactions to those who threaten or bolster the cultural worldview. *Journal of Personality and Social Psychology, 58,* 308–318.

Harris, L. T., & Fiske, S. T. (2006). Dehumanizing the lowest of the low: Neuro-imaging responses to extreme outgroups. *Psychological Science, 17,* 847–853.

Haselton, M. G., & Buss, D. M. (2000). Error management theory: A new perspective on biases in cross-sex mind reading. *Journal of Personality and Social Psychology, 78,* 81–91.

Haselton, M. G., & Nettle, D. (2006). The paranoid optimist: An integrative evolutionary model of cognitive biases. *Personality and Social Psychology Review, 10,* 47–66.

Hawks, J., Wang, E. T., Cochran, G. M., Harpending, H. C., & Moyzis, R. K. (2007). Recent acceleration of human adaptive evolution. *Proceedings of the National Academy of Sciences, 104,* 20753–20758.

Horberg, E. J., Oveis, C., Keltner, D., & Cohen, A. B. (2009). Disgust and the moralization of purity. *Journal of Personality and Social Psychology, 97,* 963–976.

Keeley, L. (1996). *War before civilization.* New York: Oxford University Press.

Kelly, R. L. (1995). *The foraging spectrum: Diversity in hunter-gatherer lifeways.* Washington, DC: Smithsonian Institution Press.

Kenrick, D. T., Griskevicius, V., Neuberg, S. L., & Schaller, M. (2010). Renovating the pyramid of needs: Contemporary extensions built upon ancient foundations. *Perspectives on Psychological Science, 5,* 292–314.

Kenrick, D. T., Li, N. P., & Butner, J. (2003). Dynamical evolutionary psychology: Individual decision-rules and emergent social norms. *Psychological Review, 110,* 3–28.

Kenrick, D. T., Schaller, M., & Simpson, J. A. (2006). Evolution is the new cognition. In M. Schaller, J. A. Simpson, & D. T. Kenrick (Eds.), *Evolution and social psychology* (pp. 1–13). New York: Psychology Press.

Kinzler, K. D., Shutts, K., & Correll, J. (2010). Priorities in social categories. *European Journal of Social Psychology, 40,* 581–592.

Klaczynski, P. A. (2008). There's something about obesity: Culture, contagion, rationality, and children's responses to drinks "created" by obese children. *Journal of Experimental Child Psychology, 99,* 58–74.

Kurzban, R., & Leary, M. R. (2001). Evolutionary origins of stigmatization: The functions of social exclusion. *Psychological Bulletin, 127*, 187–208.

Kurzban, R., & Neuberg, S. L. (2005). Managing ingroup and outgroup relationships. In D. M. Buss (Ed.), *Handbook of evolutionary psychology* (pp. 653–675). New York: John Wiley & Sons.

Kurzban, R., Tooby, J., and Cosmides, L. (2001). Can race be erased? Coalitional computation and social categorization. *Proceedings of the National Academy of Sciences, 98*, 15387–15392.

Lieberman, D. L., Tybur, J. M., & Latner, J. D. (in press). Disgust sensitivity, obesity stigma, and gender: Contamination psychology predicts weight bias for women, not men. *Obesity*.

Mackie, D. M., Devos, T., & Smith, E. R. (2000). Intergroup emotions: Explaining offensive action tendencies in an intergroup context. *Journal of Personality and Social Psychology, 79*, 602–616.

Mahajan, N., Martinez, M. A., Gutierrez, N. L., Diesendruck, G., Banaji, M. R., & Santos, L. R. (2011). The evolution of intergroup bias: Perception and attitudes in rhesus macaques. *Journal of Personality and Social Psychology, 100*, 387–405.

Maner, J. K., Kenrick, D. T., Becker, D. V., Robertson, T. E., Hofer, B., Neuberg, S. L., Delton, A. W., Butner, J., & Schaller, M. (2005). Functional projection: How fundamental social motives can bias interpersonal perception. *Journal of Personality and Social Psychology, 88*, 63–78.

Miller, S. L., Maner, J. K., & Becker, D. V. (2010). Self-protective biases in group categorization: What shapes the psychological boundary between "Us" and "Them"? *Journal of Personality and Social Psychology, 99*, 62–77.

Murray, D. R., Trudeau, R., & Schaller, M. (2011). On the origins of cultural differences in conformity: Four tests of the pathogen prevalence hypothesis. *Personality and Social Psychology Bulletin, 37*, 318–329.

Navarrete, C. D., & Fessler, D. M. T. (2006). Disease avoidance and ethnocentrism: The effects of disease vulnerability and disgust sensitivity on intergroup attitudes. *Evolution and Human Behavior, 27*, 270–282.

Navarrete, C. D., Fessler, D. M. T., & Eng, S. J. (2007). Elevated ethnocentrism in the first trimester of pregnancy. *Evolution and Human Behavior, 28*, 60–65.

Nesse, R. M. (2005). Natural selection and the regulation of defenses: A signal detection analysis of the smoke detector principle. *Evolution and Human Behavior, 26*, 88–105.

Neuberg, S. L., & Cottrell, C. A. (2002). Intergroup emotions: A biocultural approach. In D. M. Mackie & E. R. Smith (Eds.), *From prejudice to intergroup emotions: Differentiated reactions to social groups* (pp. 265–283). New York: Psychology Press.

Neuberg, S. L., & Cottrell, C. A. (2006). Evolutionary bases of prejudices. In M. Schaller, J. A. Simpson, & D. T. Kenrick (Eds.), *Evolution and social psychology* (pp. 163–187). New York: Psychology Press.

Neuberg, S. L., Kenrick, D. T., & Schaller, M. (2010). Evolutionary social psychology. In S. T. Fiske, D. T. Gilbert, & G. Lindzey (Eds.), *Handbook of social psychology* (5th ed., Vol. 2, pp. 761–796). New York: John Wiley & Sons.

Park, J. H. (2012). Evolutionary perspectives on intergroup prejudice: Implications for promoting tolerance. In S. C. Roberts (Ed.), *Applied evolutionary psychology* (pp. 186–200). Oxford, UK: Oxford University Press.

Park, J. H., & Buunk, A. P. (2011). Interpersonal threats and automatic motives. In D. Dunning (Ed.), *Social motivation* (pp. 11–35). New York: Psychology Press.

Park, J. H., Faulkner, J., & Schaller, M. (2003). Evolved disease-avoidance processes and contemporary anti-social behavior: Prejudicial attitudes and avoidance of people with physical disabilities. *Journal of Nonverbal Behavior, 27*, 65–87.

Park, J. H., Schaller, M., & Crandall, C. S. (2007). Pathogen-avoidance mechanisms and the stigmatization of obese people. *Evolution and Human Behavior, 28*, 410–414.

Pettigrew, T. F., & Tropp, L. R. (2006). A meta-analytic test of intergroup contact theory. *Journal of Personality and Social Psychology, 90*, 751–783.

Pinker, S. (2011). *The better angels of our nature: Why violence has declined.* New York: Viking.

Rhodes, G. (2006). The evolutionary psychology of facial beauty. *Annual Review of Psychology, 57*, 199–226.

Richerson, P. J., & Boyd, R. (2005). *Not by genes alone: How culture transformed human evolution.* Chicago: University of Chicago Press.

Rozin, P., Haidt, J., & Fincher, K. (2009). From oral to moral. *Science, 323*, 1179–1180.

Rozin, P., Haidt, J., & McCauley, C. R. (2008). Disgust. In M. Lewis, J. M. Haviland-Jones, & L. F. Barrett (Eds.), *Handbook of emotions* (3rd ed., pp. 757–776). New York: Guilford Press.

Rozin, P., Millman, L., & Nemeroff, C. (1986). Operation of the laws of sympathetic magic in disgust and other domains. *Journal of Personality and Social Psychology, 50*, 703–712.

Schaich Borg, J., Lieberman, D., & Kiehl, K. A. (2008). Infection, incest, and iniquity: Investigating the neural correlates of disgust and morality. *Journal of Cognitive Neuroscience, 20*, 1529–1546.

Schaller, M., & Duncan, L. A. (2007). The behavioral immune system: Its evolution and social psychological implications. In J. P. Forgas, M. G. Haselton, & W. von Hippel (Eds.), *Evolution and the social mind: Evolutionary psychology and social cognition* (pp. 293–307). New York: Psychology Press.

Schaller, M., & Neuberg, S. L. (2008). Intergroup prejudices and intergroup conflicts. In C. Crawford & D. L. Krebs (Eds.), *Foundations of evolutionary psychology* (pp. 399–412). Mahwah, NJ: Lawrence Erlbaum Associates.

Schaller, M., & Park, J. H. (2011). The behavioral immune system (and why it matters). *Current Directions in Psychological Science, 20*, 99–103.

Schaller, M., Park, J. H., & Faulkner, J. (2003). Prehistoric dangers and contemporary prejudices. *European Review of Social Psychology, 14*, 105–137.

Schaller, M., Park, J. H., & Kenrick, D. T. (2007). Human evolution and social cognition. In R. I. M. Dunbar & L. Barrett (Eds.), *The Oxford handbook of evolutionary psychology* (pp. 491–504). Oxford, UK: Oxford University Press.

Schaller, M., Park, J. H., & Mueller, A. (2003). Fear of the dark: Interactive effects of beliefs about danger and ambient darkness on ethnic stereotypes. *Personality and Social Psychology Bulletin, 29*, 637–649.

Sidanius, J., & Pratto, F. (1999). *Social dominance: An intergroup theory of social hierarchy and oppression.* New York: Cambridge University Press.

Stangor, C., & Crandall, C. S. (2000). Threat and the social construction of stigma. In T. F. Heatherton, R. E. Kleck, M. R. Hebl, and J. G. Hull (Eds.), *The social psychology of stigma* (pp. 62–87). New York: Guilford Press.

Tajfel, H., & Turner, J. C. (1979). An integrative theory of intergroup conflict. In W. G. Austin & S. Worchel (Eds.), *The social psychology of intergroup relations* (pp. 33–47). Monterey, CA: Brooks/Cole.

Tooby, J., & Cosmides, L. (2005). Conceptual foundations of evolutionary psychology. In D. M. Buss (Ed.), *The handbook of evolutionary psychology* (pp. 5–67). Hoboken, NJ: John Wiley & Sons.

Tybur, J. M., Lieberman, D., & Griskevicius, V. (2009). Microbes, mating, and morality: Individual differences in three functional domains of disgust. *Journal of Personality and Social Psychology, 97*, 103–122.

Van Leeuwen, F., Park, J. H., Koenig, B. L., & Graham, J. (in press). Regional variation in pathogen prevalence predicts endorsement of group-focused moral concerns. *Evolution and Human Behavior.*

Woody, S., & Teachman, B. (2000). Intersection of disgust and fear: Normative and pathological views. *Clinical Psychology: Science and Practice, 7*, 291–311.

Zhong, C. B., & Liljenquist, K. (2006). Washing away your sins: Threatened morality and physical cleansing. *Science, 313*, 1451–1452.

3

When We See Prejudice

The Normative Window and Social Change

CHRISTIAN S. CRANDALL

University of Kansas

MARK A. FERGUSON

University of Wisconsin, Stevens Point

ANGELA J. BAHNS

Wellesley College

> All social inequalities which have ceased to be considered expedient, assume the character not of simple inexpediency, but of injustice, and appear so tyrannical, that people are apt to wonder how they ever could have been tolerated; forgetful that they themselves perhaps tolerate other inequalities under an equally mistaken notion of expediency, the correction of which would make that which they approve seem quite as monstrous as what they have at last learnt to condemn.
>
> (John Stuart Mill, *Utilitarianism, Liberty & Representative Government*)

Social psychologists use everyday experience to shape their thinking about the world. Despite sophisticated theories about the social processes, the very definitions of basic social psychological phenomena tend to be founded in popular discourse. Prejudice is no different; Allport's (1954) foundational book defines prejudice as "antipathy based upon a faulty and inflexible generalization" (p. 9) or "thinking ill of others without sufficient warrant" (p. 6), and "whenever a negative attitude is sustained by a spurious overgeneralization, we encounter the syndrome of prejudice" (p. 12). These definitions are thoughtful, provocative, and useful to social scientists. But they come primarily from Allport's thoughtfulness rather than from extensive scientific experience with the phenomenon.

WHAT IS THE PHENOMENON?

Phaedrus: And what is the other principle, Socrates?
Socrates: That of dividing things again by classes, where the natural joints are, and not trying to break any part, after the manner of a bad carver.

(Plato, Phaedrus, 265d–266a)

The kinds of definitions that Allport (1954) gives us confuse psychological processes with both factual and value judgments. He argues that prejudices must be inaccurate, that they must not have a substantial basis in fact. But absolute social truth is never discernible, as even Allport (1954) argues (in his chapter 6, "The Scientific Study of Group Differences") it is difficult if not impossible to demonstrate reliably the factual basis behind a prejudice. "The study of groups, so far as it has gone, does not permit us to say that hostility toward a group is to any appreciable extent based on 'well-deserved reputation'" (Allport, 1954, p. 125).

But, even more importantly, the "truth" is functionally irrelevant to individual endorsement of feelings and belief. People believe in their beliefs—they endorse their own understandings of the world. It is the rare person who peruses the pages of *American Sociological Review* to compare their own attitudes toward adolescent drug users with the best available data or the pages of the *Journal of the American Geriatrics Society* to test their stereotypes of the elderly. Attitudes are experienced as real—scientists may call such attitudes beliefs, but *people experience them as knowledge.* Definitions that include inaccuracy as a component fail to cut the psychological process where the natural joints are; they are poor carvery.

We define prejudice as "a negative evaluation of a social group or a negative evaluation of an individual that is significantly based on the individual's group membership" (Crandall & Eshleman, 2003, p. 414). In contrast to Allport (1954), we do not argue that a prejudice need be "unfounded" or "lack basis in fact" (p. 7), and we do not rely on the ineffable quality of "objective reality" to sort out what counts as shrewd judgment and what is prejudice. Instead, we follow Lewin (1951) in suggesting that the definition of any psychological concept should be psychological—based on the phenomenological reality of the perceiver and not on the reality of any observer, lay or professional.

The theoretical and empirical consequences of defining prejudice as a psychological process, without including value judgments or "social truth" standards, are profound—it brings into the study of prejudice *any* kind of group-based animosity as prejudiced and distinguishes judgments about the social acceptability of prejudice as a distinct area of study. It also allows for the study of change in the normative appropriateness of prejudice, which brings

to our attention attitudes that were once socially acceptable as now being prejudiced and worthy of remediation. By removing "values" and "truth" from the
definition of prejudice, social scientists can examine the broader processes of
"prejudice," rather than narrowly focusing on particular "prejudices."

WHAT WE STUDY AND WHAT WE DON'T

Prejudice against groups runs the entire gamut of social acceptability, from
completely unquestioning acceptance to complete and utter unacceptability
(Crandall, Eshleman, & O'Brien, 2002). But we find that social psychologists
prefer to study prejudice toward a comparatively narrow range of groups; the
majority of prejudice research focuses on groups based on race, ethnicity, gender, and religion, with some strong development in sexual orientation or physical disability, age, and weight. It should be no surprise that psychologists are
studying those very groups that are being protected by legislation (e.g., the
Civil Rights Act of 1964, the Americans with Disabilities Act of 1990); these
laws both reflect and create the social change that researchers study.

This is in no way the universe of possible prejudice targets. But these groups
grab our attention because attitudes toward them are both varied and changing.
Prejudice as a psychological phenomenon has not "gone underground"
(Dovidio, 2001) or slowly diminished over time (Arkes & Tetlock, 2004), but
rather *some* prejudices have done so. And the prejudices that have reduced in
the recent past are the ones that receive the most empirical attention.

Since the publication of Gordon Allport's (1954) *The Nature of Prejudice*,
theory and research on prejudice has been grounded largely in a definition of
prejudice as "antipathy based upon a faulty and inflexible generalization" (p. 9).
Thus, prejudice is considered to be *irrational* (i.e., based on ignorance, narrow-
mindedness, or intolerance), with the implication that individuals should be
evaluated on their individual characteristics rather than on their social group
membership. This definition effectively excludes many targets of prejudice
from scientific scrutiny. This oversight is problematic for several reasons, including
the creation and use of a prejudice definition based on non-psychological
dimensions, a questionable standard of demonstrating a certain prejudice to be
irrational, and the preclusion of present animosities as prejudiced (e.g., Allport
was silent on sexual orientation). Much of the problem is really based on a naïve
definition of what prejudice is—it's something that's "bad."

While this standard meaning might seem like common sense, it glosses over
two distinct meanings of prejudice (see Williams, 1993). There is first a *descriptive meaning*, which defines prejudice as a psychological process. When prejudice is defined as an affective process, it reflects the descriptive meaning.
Second, there is an *evaluative meaning* of prejudice, which conceptualizes prejudice as irrational and unjust (see Biernat, 2003; Shadish, Cook, & Campbell,
2002). This meaning does not reflect prejudice as a psychological process;
rather, it reflects *how researchers feel* about the prejudices they study. When
the standard meaning of prejudice focuses on the necessity of examining and

alleviating prejudices toward particular social groups because they are "irrational" and "unjust" (e.g., socially disadvantaged groups), it reflects the evaluative meaning. These two distinct meanings coexist in the modern usage of prejudice as a concept in theory and research throughout psychology (e.g., American Psychological Association, 2006).

These two meanings of prejudice are not synonymous, but rather reflect a much deeper value conflict in the field of prejudice. That is, should researchers call affect that is consistent with scientific values, but inconsistent with political values, an instance of prejudice? If an individual has negative affect toward rapists, but having such affect appears consistent with rational and just thinking, should this be considered prejudiced? Considering current practice, the answer to these questions appears to be an emphatic (and slightly defensive) "No!" In this way, social scientists are studying prejudice as "the moral evaluation placed by a culture on some of its own practices" (Allport, 1954, p. 11).

Prejudice researchers appear to resolve this value conflict by prioritizing the evaluative meaning of prejudice above its descriptive meaning. Rather than focusing on the complete range available for study, researchers tend to focus on a more select range of prejudices implied by the evaluative meaning. Groups who appear to receive unfair outcomes are examined as targets of prejudice, while groups who appear to receive rational, fair, or deserved outcomes are overlooked. This essentially denounces particular prejudices while seemingly supporting others that are consistent with existing social norms about what is (or is not) rational and just. Although this resolution might further particular political ideals, it does little to provide theory and research with an understanding of the broader range of prejudices in society.

THE NORMATIVE WINDOW

What social psychologists study as prejudice is closely linked to a window of normative acceptability of prejudice—where norms about certain prejudices are changing from acceptable to unacceptable in society (Crandall, Eshleman, & O'Brien, 2002; Pettigrew, 1991; Sherif & Sherif, 1953). We argue that prejudices that are in a narrow window of shifting normative acceptability are the entrée, the main meal, of social psychological research. In general, social psychologists study prejudices (1) that they perceive to be wrong, (2) that appear common in the general population, and (3) that are shifting from normative acceptability to normative unacceptability.

The "normative window" that is studied mostly by social scientists refers to a "window" of time in which social norms are shifting toward the equal treatment, the normalization, and the reduction of stigma and exclusion of a group, but for which the entire process has not yet been completed, and for which complete social agreement about the standing of the group has not yet been achieved. Groups in the normative window are typically social, ethnic, religious, or others that have made strides toward acceptability—and have achieved some movement toward this goal. These groups are thus moving upward in social status, and the stigma and stereotyping toward them should be tending downward.

These are very interesting groups, and social scientists rightly study attitudes toward them. But this is a tiny fraction of the possible targets. While the field has concentrated on interesting prejudices closely connected to social problems, the failure to consider other areas of prejudice narrows the focus and leads us to miss a wide range of phenomena relevant to the process. In Table 3.1, we have identified the most highly cited scholarly works of four different eras. This table represents the five most highly cited articles found in Google Scholar (accessed March 5, 2012), published in four different eras, that included the word "prejudice" in the title. Across the 69 years encompassing the earliest and the most recent of the publications (1935–2003), it is clear that racial and ethnic prejudice predominates in social science research on prejudice. Although some of the earlier contributions also take anti-Semitism seriously, as a research area anti-Semitism has moved out of the spotlight. In the most recent era, gender, disability, and sexual orientation have moved into focus. The top area of social science research remains racial and ethnic issues (and, within that, *Whites' attitudes toward Blacks* predominates as a topic), but the field is diversifying.

Figure 3.1 provides a visual representation of the normative window of prejudice. We describe its fundamental concepts, arguments, and assumptions below.

1. There is a continuum of prejudices in society, ranging from completely unacceptable to all to completely acceptable to all.
2. Whether or not a prejudice is thought to exist (alternatively, whether negative attitudes toward a group are called a prejudice) and is a meaningful subject of study is closely related to its normative status. When negative attitudes are completely acceptable, or when they are largely absent, such feelings are not called a prejudice.
3. We speculate that there is a general tendency for groups to move toward social acceptability. In Figure 3.1, this means that groups that are at the left of the diagram have a tendency to move toward the right of the diagram.
4. As groups pass through a window of normative uncertainty—where attitudes are at the center of social controversy—negative attitudes are labeled a "prejudice," and the interest of social scientists is piqued.
5. If and when a social group obtains general acceptance—the prejudice becomes unacceptable to a dominant social consensus—then negative attitudes toward the group are seen not as prejudice but rather as the idiosyncratic views of an irrational possessor.

If there is an entire range of acceptable and unacceptable prejudices, we might partition them into three kinds: (1) groups universally agreed to be deserving of prejudice ("Unsuppressed Prejudice"), (2) groups universally agreed *not*

TABLE 3.1 Five Most Frequently Cited Articles With "Prejudice" in Their Title, by Era

Year	Title	Author	Publisher/ Journal Title
1900–1950			
1950	*Dynamics of prejudice*	Bettelheim & Janowitz	Harper
1946	Some roots of prejudice	Allport	*Journal of Psychology*
1946	*Problems in prejudice*	Hartley	King's Crown Press
1935	Racial prejudice and racial stereotypes	Katz & Braly	*Journal of Abnormal and Social Psychology*
1947	The evasion of propaganda: How prejudiced people respond to anti-prejudice propaganda	Cooper & Jahoda	*Journal of Psychology*
1951–1975			
1967	Personal religious orientation and prejudice	Allport	*Journal of Personality and Social Psychology*
1958	Race prejudice as a sense of group position	Blumer	*Pacific Sociological Review*
1972	*Prejudice and racism*	Jones	Addison-Wesley
1964	*Social change and prejudice*	Bettelheim & Janowitz	Free Press
1962	Racial prejudice, interpersonal attraction, and assumed dissimilarity of attitudes	Byrne & Wong	*Journal of Abnormal and Social Psychology*
1976–1990			
1979/1954	*The nature of prejudice*	Allport	Addison-Wesley
1989	Stereotypes and prejudice: Their automatic and controlled components	Devine	*Journal of Personality and Social Psychology*
1986	*Prejudice, discrimination, and racism*	Dovidio & Gaertner	Academic Press
1989	*Children and prejudice*	Aboud	Blackwell
1981	Prejudice and politics: Symbolic racism versus racial threats to the good life	Kinder & Sears	*Journal of Personality and Social Psychology*
1991–2012			
1998	Stereotyping, prejudice, and discrimination	Fiske	*Handbook of Social Psychology*
1995	Subtle and blatant prejudice in Western Europe	Pettigrew & Meertens	*European Journal of Social Psychology*
2002	Role congruity theory of prejudice toward female leaders	Eagly	*Psychological Review*
1991	*Pride against prejudice: A personal politics of disability*	Morris	Women's Press
2003	Prejudice, social stress, and mental health in lesbian, gay, and bisexual populations	Meyer	*Psychological Bulletin*

Note: Journal articles are listed with the periodical's title in the publisher's column.

Historical trend for targets from Acceptable → through Controversial → to Unacceptable

SUBSTANTIAL NEGATIVE AFFECT BUT NOT CONSIDERED A PREJUDICE	WINDOW OF PREJUDICE RESEARCH	VERY LITTLE NEGATIVE AFFECT
Rapists, enemy soldiers, terrorists, prostitutes, etc.	Immigrants, gay parents, female CEOs, sex workers, etc.	Farmers, housewives, firemen who died during 9/11, etc.
"Unsuppressed"	*"Normative Window"*	*"True Lows"*

Entirely Socially *Acceptable* Prejudices		Entirely Socially *Unacceptable* Prejudices

Figure 3.1   Defining the limits of acceptable targets of prejudice research.

to be targets of prejudice, where there is a strong consensus that the group does not deserve prejudice and its prevalence among individuals is genuinely low ("True Lows"), and (3) groups for which norms regarding the acceptability of prejudice are ambiguous ("Normative Window"). This region is called normative because the perception of affect as "prejudiced" depends on shifts in prevailing social norms. It is called a window because affect inside the region is viewed as prejudiced, whereas affect outside it is not. The normative window defines whether we perceive a particular negative affect as an instance of prejudice.

Unsuppressed prejudices are groups toward which we have prejudice without suppression, such as terrorists, child molesters, murderers, people convicted of sex crimes, or kids who steal other kids' lunch money. This category represents entirely socially acceptable prejudices that are usually blatantly expressed. Groups for which there is almost no prevailing prejudice, called True Lows, include grandparents, special education teachers, and firefighters who died on 9/11, among many others. This category represents entirely socially unacceptable prejudices and consequently signals idiosyncratic strangeness rather than being considered as prejudice. In everyday language, someone who dislikes puppeteers is a weirdo; they are not described as prejudiced.

Groups that fall "in the window" are the targets of prejudice studied by social scientists. They are groups for which there is normative ambiguity about the acceptability of prejudice; prejudice toward these groups is usually expressed subtly. Examples of these typical targets of prejudice are groups defined by race, religion, ethnicity, physical disability, gender, or sexual orientation, or any group for which there is *not* near complete agreement about the acceptability of prejudice. Researchers study prejudice toward these groups because they matter to others and to them, and because they feel that the prejudice they perceive toward these groups is unwarranted. Groups in the window are marked by changing social norms—they are groups for which a negative consensus used to exist but for which there is currently pressure for greater acceptance.

Two studies from our lab support the three-group hypothesis (Ferguson & Crandall, 2006). In first study, students at the University of Kansas ($N = 226$) rated 42 target groups on a 0–100 feeling thermometer measuring liking/rejection. Factor analysis revealed that these ratings could be divided into three distinct categories reflecting the three clusters of prejudice posited by Figure 3.1: Unsuppressed Prejudices, Normative Window, and True Lows. The list of groups that loaded on each factor is shown in Table 3.2. Among the groups falling into the Normative Window factor grouping, those groups comprising the left column can be considered "typical" targets of prejudice (e.g., Blacks, immigrants, poor people). The groups comprising the right column, by contrast, are all social change agents (e.g., modern artists, feminists; we cannot explain "people from Alaska"—these data were collected prior to Sarah Palin's rise to fame). Those in the latter group are identified as people who are likely to become targets of prejudice in the near future, if they are not already. But it also highlights the potential importance of pushing for social change in determining who is a target of prejudice.

TABLE 3.2   Factor Groupings for Likeability of Target Groups

Factor Name	Groups Loading on Factor	
Normative Window	• Arab Americans • Hispanic Americans • Immigrants • Jews • Asian Americans • Black Americans • Homosexuals raising kids • Poor people • Native Americans • Ugly people	• Feminists • Modern artists • New age religion followers • Librarians • People from Alaska • People who push for social change
Unsuppressed Prejudices	• Liars • People who cheat on spouses • Neglectful parents • People who cheat on exams • People who litter • Pregnant women who drink alcohol • People who cut in line • Drunk drivers	• Wife beaters • Lazy people • Alcoholics • Child abusers • Racists • Members of religious cults • Men who leave their families
True Lows	• Grandparents • Farmers • Pet owners • High-school cheerleaders • Working mothers • Women who stay home to raise children	• Athletes • Doctors • Accountants • Musicians • Bicyclists

In Study 2, participants ($N = 227$) rated 105 groups on 24 different dimensions (e.g., dangerous, under personal control, related to age, gender, sexual, contagious, embarrassing, visible, rare). The means of each rating for each group were calculated, and the 105 groups were treated as "subjects" with 24 variables each. These means were submitted to a cluster analysis and, as in the factor analysis, yielded a three-cluster result: Unsuppressed Prejudice, Normative Window, and True Lows.

These two studies both demonstrate using a large, diverse set of social groups (N's = 42, 105) allowed three clusters of social groups to emerge. One category is the target of unsuppressed negative affect—the normative consensus is that these groups should be rejected. Another category is the target of little negative affect—the normative consensus is that these groups should be accepted. The third category is the subject of social science research; it is the groups within the normative window—there is no prevailing consensus about how the groups should be treated. The prejudices that researchers study do not represent the complete range of prejudices that exist. The most important missing targets are those for which a consensus exists that negative affect is appropriate. The dimensions that differentiate prejudice toward the Unsuppressed groups and toward the Normative Window groups go largely unstudied.

SOCIAL NORMS AND THE ACCEPTABILITY OF PREJUDICE

The social acceptability of prejudice changes over time. Prejudice based on sexual orientation was completely unstudied by social psychologists in the 1950s; it is now a staple of research. Allport (1954) discusses prejudice aimed at Italian- and Irish-American immigrants—there is virtually no focus on these prejudices today and there is reason to believe that they have reduced in the United States. The amount of prejudice changes as a function of a variety of issues, particularly the threat posed by a social group (Stangor & Crandall, 2000): Which groups are immigrating and the target of job competition, the current status of international conflict and economic disputes, changes in sex roles, and disputes over oil all affect which prejudices are acceptable.

Where does social change come from? We have argued that there is a general trend toward reduction in prejudice. There are several reasons to believe that the modern world pushes toward such a trend. Increasing contact, both real and symbolic, is a result of globalization of markets and increased access to information (Friedman, 2000). The ever growing availability and speed of the Internet, continued improvement in world travel, and the globalization of markets lead to increased diversity and contact (Friedman, 2005). In addition to contact and knowledge, other Western and global forces prompting reduced prejudice toward many groups are greater availability of education (Schafer, 1999), pressures toward democracy (Rudra, 2005), increased mass-media access to other groups (Chiu, Gries, Torelli, & Cheng, 2011), and mutual reliance based on shared economies (Archibugi, Koenig-Archibugi, & Marchetti, 2011).

We cannot develop the argument fully here, although we refer the reader to the arguments made by Friedman on globalization (Friedman, 2000, 2005) and by Pinker on the reduction of violence (Pinker, 2011). Figure 3.2 displays how changes based in economic, geographic, or other extra-societal forces can

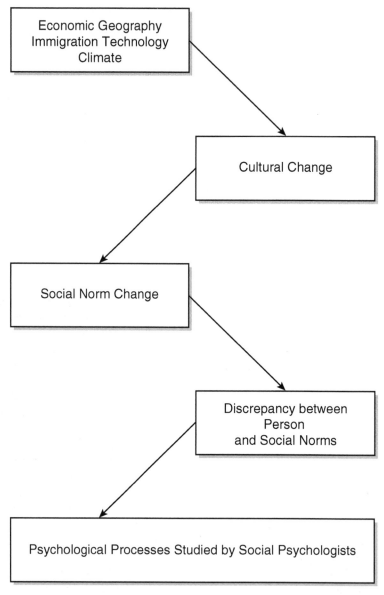

Figure 3.2   Fundamental sources of social change and where social psychology fits into social and cultural change.

translate into culture change, which then entails the shifting landscape of social norms. As social norms change, some people find themselves discrepant from the moving standard of tolerance. It is the people who are behind the times, who fail to adapt easily to shifting standards of decency, whose intolerance of groups reflects patterns of yesterday, that we label "prejudiced." Not all is rosy, of course, but we throw our lot in with Martin Luther King, Jr., who said that "the arc of the moral universe is long but it bends toward justice" (King, 1990, p. 52).

Here is a small thought experiment on the fluidity of social norms about prejudice. How many times have we read that some certain negative attitude toward a group is "the last acceptable prejudice"? We conducted a Google Scholar search (data downloaded March 30, 2011) and found 206 hits for the exact phrase "the last acceptable prejudice," with many articles identifying Catholics, homosexuals, or fat people as the sole remaining targets of prejudice. This is absolutely not the case—there are many delightful opportunities for prejudice, and most people enjoy them reliably. But it is the very idea that there is a category "last acceptable prejudice" that captures, simultaneously, the importance of normative appropriateness, its inherent instability, and the sense that many prejudices are increasingly unacceptable.

The prevalence of prejudice is closely related to social norms about prejudice; the acceptability of prejudice is a close indicator of what prejudices people actually experience. Crandall et al. (2002) showed that people's reports of prejudice are closely related to what is normative. One group ($N = 150$) rated 105 groups on how acceptable prejudice toward each of the groups should be, while another ($N = 121$) indicated their own personal prejudice toward the same groups. The correlation between reported prejudice and acceptability of prejudice was almost perfect ($r = .96$). A follow-up study (Ferguson & Crandall, 2006) obtained a higher correction ($r = .98$). People only report having prejudices that are normatively acceptable.

Social and normative acceptability may determine expression, but it does not define prejudice. Just because a prejudice is common, accepted, or normal does not make it not a prejudice. While one could put this into the definition itself (and much theory and research on prejudice does), this would simply define away a wide range of interesting and relevant psychological phenomena. We must take into account both that prejudices are acquired through our social lives and that definitions of prejudice are embedded in culture. The same forces that determine which prejudices people have are the forces that shape the social world and normative acceptability. For example, based on the standard/ evaluative meaning of prejudice (i.e., prejudice is irrational), one could not say that slave owners' attitudes toward their slaves involved prejudice in a world that completely accepted slavery and characterized slaves as substantially less than full humans. But this makes the definition of prejudice entirely dependent upon the social group in which the attitude is found. In a small and fervent group of Taliban-supported terrorists, lethal anti-American attitudes would not be prejudice; nor would anti-Semitic attitudes at the local KKK rally.

One might complain that these are minority positions, and the larger context of the United States or the world would lead to the definition of such attitudes as prejudiced. But this merely points out the shifting basis of norms and their relations to groups, and the reader may simply be choosing the reference group that supports their particular favored definitions of prejudice. Many American readers' attitudes toward the United States would be strikingly non-normative when the entire world is chosen as the reference group. We argue that negative affect based on group membership should be considered prejudice regardless of normative acceptability. An adequately justified prejudice is still a prejudice.

SOCIAL CHANGE AND THE PREJUDICED PERSONALITY

Several reviews of what characterizes people "high in prejudice" have suggested traits or attributes closely tied to widespread social change (Allport, 1950, 1954; Bettelheim & Janowitz, 1964; Nelson, 2005). The "prejudiced personality" may be based on resistance to the changing norms of social acceptability toward particular groups. Individual differences might be conceptualized as a general orientation to change and stability in society, particularly with respect to status of social groups. Several personality factors in prejudice research can be characterized as the *individual's resistance to change* (e.g., political conservatism, need for closure, certain kinds of religiosity, closed mindedness), *the individual's inability to cope with change* (e.g., need for closure, low levels of education, low income/SES, low need for cognition), and *resistance to social change that upsets status hierarchies* (e.g., political conservatism, social dominance orientation, authoritarianism). Additionally, one might characterize variables that relate to a tolerant personality as an orientation of acceptance of change in society.

Ferguson and Crandall (2006) measured several of these markers, including religion as quest (i.e., open mindedness about religious truth; Batson, Schoenrade, & Ventis, 1993), right-wing authoritarianism (Altemeyer, 1981), social dominance orientation (Pratto, Sidanius, Stallworth, & Malle, 1994), and political conservatism. These personality measures of "change resistance" or "status quo preference" jointly predict rejection of Normative Window targets ($multiple$-R = .40, p < .00001). The personality measures were significantly less reliable for predicting Unsuppressed and True Low prejudices (both $multiple$-R's < .20). These data echo the early findings by Hartley (1946).

Ferguson and Crandall (2006) also had two different groups of students rate 120 social groups. One group (N = 100) rated the groups on the extent to which they must "publicly act more positive toward the group than they really feel" (a measure of prejudice suppression). A different group (N = 78) rated the groups on how they thought "people will feel toward these groups 20 years in the future." The groups that were rated most suppressed were the same groups that people felt would be more tolerated in the future (r = .64). There is a collective sense that groups who are currently in the normative window—and rated as suppressed prejudice—are likely to shift into the realm of normative acceptability sometime in the future.

THE IMPORTANCE OF SOCIAL CHANGE

We identify a historical trend for prejudices to shift from acceptable, to controversial, to unacceptable—in accordance with changing social norms. When Allport published *The Nature of Prejudice* (1954), homosexuals and feminists were part of the Unsuppressed Prejudice category and Italian- and Irish-American immigrants fell squarely within the normative window. More than 50 years later, Italian- and Irish-American immigrants have now shifted into the True Lows category while homosexuals and feminists have moved into the normative window. Our forecast for the future is that homosexuals and feminists will gradually move out of the window and into the category of entirely socially unacceptable prejudices, while some of the groups presently in the Unsuppressed Prejudices category will move into the Normative Window (whichever groups push for social change). We suggest that, even within the confines of this chapter, our example groups will eventually look awkward, foolish, *dated*—and this historical eventuality would confirm the very processes we describe.

The historical trend we identify illustrates that the key component to when a prejudice is recognized is social change. Groups in the Normative Window that are typical targets of prejudice, as we understand it, are moving from Unsuppressed Prejudice, entirely acceptable prejudice, toward True Lows, where prejudice is entirely unacceptable—but they haven't made it there *yet*.

Shifting Positions in the Social Hierarchy

The main theme of this chapter is that prejudice is closely linked to social change, and that labeling negative feeling toward a group as "prejudice" is based substantially on that group's changing position in the social hierarchy. To reiterate this most simply, we argue that:

1. Prejudice research looks primarily at groups which are undergoing social change, which are often pushing for change in the accepted value of their group.
2. People who report the most prejudice are people who are likely to resist social change.
3. People who are described as changing the status quo are lumped together with ethnic minorities, physically disabled—within the normative window.
4. The more that people feel they must suppress a particular prejudice, the more they also feel that prejudice will be reduced toward that particular group in the future.
5. Racism and other prejudices are often expressed in terms of resistance to change—go slow, gradual change, "too demanding in their push for civil rights," or "with all deliberate speed."
6. In times of social change, conflict, and upheaval, prejudice and discrimination increase, from filling out prejudice questionnaires to lynching and race riots.

This sixth point is quite well spelled out in other sources, and, given our focus on the context of psychological rather than sociological processes (not to mention the size of the argument and the weight of the evidence that one must cover), our coverage here is only a brief mention. This should be construed as respect for the complexity of the issue and not our sense of its unimportance (Ellsworth, 1992; Hepworth & West, 1988; cf. Green, Glaser, & Rich, 1998).

Allport (1954) devoted chapter 14 of his book to "Social Structure and Cultural Pattern," which covered the cultural context where "prejudice personalities will be more numerous" (p. 221). Prejudice was thought to be increased by social mobility, rapid social change, and assimilation processes. One of the first studies in prejudice in the social sciences as we know them was Bogardus's (1928) *Immigration and Race Attitudes*, which focuses on the changing pattern of racial groups in America and its effect on racial attitudes. And best known in this domain is Bettelheim and Janowitz's (1964) classic *Social Change and Prejudice*, which takes a social-psychoanalytic look at prejudice as a consequence of people's (in)ability to cope with social mobility, status anxiety, and social change. This area of research is much neglected in social psychology, and deserves more serious attention in the future.

THE PRACTICAL VALUE OF STUDYING MULTIPLE PREJUDICES

The first author's introduction to the prejudice literature came from studying prejudice against fat people (e.g., Crandall & Biernat, 1990; Crandall, 1994). He spent many years comparing racial prejudice and fat prejudice—how they were alike (e.g., based in antipathy and emotion, attributions of responsibility) and how they were different (e.g., levels of acceptability of open expression, the role of stereotyping in justification). This comparison helped generate ideas for a more general approach to prejudice (e.g., Crandall et al., 2002; Crandall & Eshleman, 2003; this chapter).

CONCLUSION

If only there were evil people somewhere insidiously committing evil deeds and it were necessary only to separate them from the rest of us and destroy them. But the line dividing good and evil cuts through the heart of every human being. And who is willing to destroy a piece of his own heart?
(Alexander Solzhenitsyn, *The Gulag Archipelago*)

The very heart of prejudice, as we understand it, is difficulty with and resistance to social change. At the cultural, national, social, and individual level, it is social change and the costs of adapting to it that lead to prejudice, or at least the kinds of prejudice studied by social scientists. Groups that seek change will meet with enmity from groups and individuals that resist change. When social psychologists see a particular prejudice as illegitimate, they become interested in the study of that prejudice. Otherwise, scientists are likely to be mostly silent on the prejudice.

Prejudice is a normal social and psychological process. Its appearance is predictable—as predictable as determining which people will display the most of it. But, despite this inevitability, there is some hope for its reduction. Every social process, social hierarchy, and cultural arrangement was the result of social change at one time, and as new hierarchies become the status quo they are judged more favorably (Eidelman, Crandall, & Pattershall, 2009). Ironically, increases in prejudice toward a group will sometimes be a sign that their lot in society is improving. Prejudice against both homosexuals and Muslims have seen a peak in recent years in the USA, and this has been followed by substantial decreases in the rates of prejudice. Thinking about what makes a prejudice in a social context offers an alternate way of thinking about it and encourages an alternate strategy for researching prejudice—the very kind of social change we prescribe.

REFERENCES

Allport, G. W. (1950). Prejudice: A problem in psychological and social causation. *Journal of Social Issues* (Supplement Series No. 4), 2–23.

Allport, G. W. (1954). *The nature of prejudice*. Cambridge, MA: Addison-Wesley.

Altemeyer, B. (1981). Right-wing authoritarianism. Winnipeg, Canada: University of Manitoba Press.

American Psychological Association. (2006). Resolution on prejudice, stereotypes, and discrimination. *American Psychologist, 62*, 475–481.

Archibugi, D., Koenig-Archibugi, M., & Marchetti, R. (Eds.) (2011). *Global democracy: Normative and empirical perspectives*. Cambridge, UK: Cambridge University Press.

Arkes, H. R., & Tetlock, P. E. (2004). Attributions of implicit prejudice, or "Would Jesse Jackson 'fail' the Implicit Association Test?" *Psychological Inquiry, 15*, 257–278.

Batson, C. D., Schoenrade, P,. & Ventis, W. L. (1993). *Religion and the individual: A social-psychological perspective*. New York: Oxford University Press.

Bettelheim, B., & Janowitz, M. (1964). *Social change and prejudice.* New York: Free Press of Glencoe.

Biernat, M. (2003). Toward a broader view of social stereotyping. *American Psychologist, 58*, 1019–1027.

Bogardus, E. S. (1928) *Immigration and race attitudes*. New York: D. C. Heath.

Chiu, C.-Y., Gries, P., Torelli, C. J., & Cheng, S. Y. Y. (2011). Toward a social psychology of globalization. *Journal of Social Issues, 67*, 1540–4560. Doi: 10.1111/j.1540-4560.2011.01721.x

Crandall, C. S. (1994). Prejudice against fat people: Ideology and self-interest. *Journal of Personality and Social Psychology, 66*, 882–894.

Crandall, C. S., and Biernat, M. R. (1990). The ideology of anti-fat attitudes. *Journal of Applied Social Psychology, 20*, 227–243.

Crandall, C. S., & Eshleman, A. (2003). A justification-suppression model of the expression and experience of prejudice. *Psychological Bulletin, 129*, 414–446.

Crandall, C. S., Eshleman, A., & O'Brien, L. (2002). Social norms and the expression and suppression of prejudice: The struggle for internalization. *Journal of Personality and Social Psychology, 82,* 359–378.

Crandall, C. S., & Ferguson, M.A. (2006). *Prejudice and prejudices: How resistance to social change is at the heart of prejudice.* Paper presented at "Looking Toward the Future: Discrimination and prejudice in the 21st Century," University of Wisconsin, Madison.

Dovidio, J. F. (2001). On the nature of contemporary prejudice: The third wave. *Journal of Social Issues, 57,* 829–849.

Eagly, A. H., & Steffen, V. J. (1984). Gender stereotypes stem from the distribution of women and men into social roles. *Journal of Personality and Social Psychology, 46,* 735–754.

Eidelman, S., Crandall, C. S., & Pattershall, J. (2009). The existence bias. *Journal of Personality and Social Psychology, 97,* 765–775.

Ellsworth, S. (1992). *Death in a promised land: The Tulsa race riot of 1921.* Baton Rouge: Louisiana State University Press.

Ferguson. M. A., & Crandall C. S. (2006, May). *Seeing prejudice through the normative window.* Paper presented at the 78th annual meeting of the Midwestern Psychological Association, Chicago.

Friedman, T. (2000). *The Lexus and the olive tree: Understanding globalization.* New York: Anchor.

Friedman, T. (2005). *The world is flat: A brief history of the twenty-first century.* New York: Farrar, Straus, & Giroux.

Green, D. P., Glaser, J., & Rich, A. (1998). From lynching to gay bashing: The elusive connection between economic conditions and hate crime. *Journal of Personality and Social Psychology, 75,* 82–92.

Hartley, E. L. (1946). *Problems in prejudice.* New York: Octagon.

Hepworth, J. T., & West, S. G. (1988). Lynchings and the economy: A time-series reanalysis of Hovland and Sears (1940). *Journal of Personality and Social Psychology, 55,* 239–247.

King, M. L., Jr. (1990). *A testament of hope.* New York: HarperOne.

Lewin, K. (1951). *Field theory in social science: Selected theoretical papers.* Ed. Dorwin Cartwright. New York: Harper & Row.

Nelson, T. D. (2005). *The psychology of prejudice* (2nd ed.). Boston: Allyn & Bacon.

Pettigrew, T. F. (1991). Normative theory in intergroup relations: Explaining both harmony and conflict. *Psychology & Developing Societies, 3,* 3–16.

Pettigrew, T. F. (2004). The social science study of American race relations in the 20th century. In C. S. Crandall and M. Schaller (Eds.), The social psychology of prejudice: Historical and contemporary issues. Seattle, WA: Lewinian Press.

Pinker, S. (2011). *The better angels of our nature: Why violence has declined.* New York: Viking.

Pratto, F., Sidanius, J., Stallworth, L. M., & Malle, B. F. (1994). Social dominance orientation: A personality variable predicting social and political attitudes. *Journal of Personality and Social Psychology, 67,* 741–763.

Rudra, N. (2005). Globalization and the strengthening of democracy in the developing world. *American Journal of Political Science, 9,* 704–730.

Schafer, M. J. (1999). International nongovernmental organizations and Third World education in 1990: A cross-national study. *Sociology of Education, 72,* 69–88.

Shadish, W. R., Cook, T. D., & Campbell, D. T. (2002). *Experimental and quasi-experimental designs for generalized causal inference*. Boston: Houghton Mifflin.

Sherif, M., & Sherif, C. W. (1953). *Groups in harmony and tension*. New York: Harper.

Stangor, C., & Crandall, C. S. (2000). Threat and the social construction of stigma. In T. F. Heatherton, R. E. Kleck, & M. R. Hebl (Eds.), *The social psychology of stigma* (pp. 62–87). New York: Guilford Press.

Williams, B. A. O. (1993). *Morality: An introduction to ethics*. New York: Cambridge University Press.

4

An Adaptationist Perspective on the Psychology of Intergroup Prejudice

CARLOS DAVID NAVARRETE

Michigan State University

JOSHUA M. TYBUR

University of New Mexico

*H*umans did not evolve to be racist, and racism is not an evolved psychological adaptation. For psychological traits to be considered adaptations, the problems that they are designed to solve must have been recurrent throughout the evolutionary history of the human lineage for long enough to have been shaped by natural selection. This is not likely to have been the case with racism, since only technologies developed relatively recently (in evolutionary time scale) have allowed humans to travel the types of long distances that enable members of differing racial groups to interact (Stringer & McKie, 1997). It is thus unlikely that natural selection shaped the human mind to produce a psychological system that was designed to promote racially biased cognition, attitudes, and behaviors. More plausibly, the mind generates mental representations of the self and others that might be described as racist as an epiphenomenon, or "by-product," of mechanisms evolved to solve other categories of adaptive challenges in our evolutionary past.

But does this mean that understanding the psychology of racism precludes an evolutionary analysis of its origins and maintenance? No, it does not, as the scope of evolutionary approaches to human psychology is not limited to investigations of features of the mind that can plausibly be described as evolved adaptations but also includes the study of traits that might be considered mental epiphenomena of adaptive systems—or, rather, "psychological by-products" of adaptations (Tooby & Cosmides, 1992). As such, there are ways that racism may be fruitfully investigated from an evolutionary perspective. The evolutionary approach we adopt has been referred to as the "adaptationist" perspective, which can be described as one which considers the likely selection pressures that recurred over evolutionary history to frame testable hypotheses regarding human cognition, attitudes, emotion, and behavior (Andrews, Gangestad, & Matthews, 2002; Buss, Haselton, Shackelford, Bleske, & Wakefield, 1998; Tooby & Cosmides, 1992). An adaptationist approach involves a consideration that psychological systems underlying how people think about themselves and others are "for" functional ends—that is, they exist to solve some problem inherent in the human condition. Some such problems reflect unique challenges faced by humans, such as acquiring language; other challenges apply more broadly across several species, and include selecting mates, avoiding infectious disease, managing conflict with intrasexual competitors (by defeating or avoiding them), and acquiring or maintaining access to resources. As one might imagine, functional solutions to each of these problems may require different strategies, and these strategies may be generated from different psychological systems.

With respect to postulating the existence of an evolved psychology that generates racial prejudice as a by-product of other adaptive systems, predictions derived from an adaptationist perspective are informed by a consideration of the kinds of evolved psychological machinery that may be responsible for the social construction of "race," and what kinds of downstream psychological biases may occur as a result. Among such possibilities are psychological mechanisms evolved to identify basic social categories (Cheney & Seyfarth, 1982; Tajfel, 1981), which can then be used to denote coalitional groups (Kurzban, Tooby, & Cosmides, 2001), or norm boundaries that allow for coordination within cultural groups (Gil-White, 2001; Hirschfeld, 1996)—none of which are mutually exclusive.

Whatever combination of basic cognitive processes is responsible for how humans think about race, we believe that a research program that tests hypotheses about when and how racial prejudice is expressed can be enriched by considering the kinds of challenges people face when interacting with individuals from a social group other than their own (hereafter referred to as *outgroups*). When an individual target is categorized as a member of an outgroup, how a person responds to him or her depends on many variables. When studying individual responses to others in intergroup contexts, it is helpful to think of outgroups as posing different kinds of adaptive challenges than do ingroup members. Furthermore, in some domains, the problems posed by outgroup members differ markedly depending on whether the target or the perceiver is male or female. However, in other domains, perhaps men and women may face similar threats from outgroups, regardless of target gender. As such, one might imagine that the psychology of intergroup prejudice differs considerably between men and women in some domains and but not in others. In this chapter, we describe how an adaptationist perspective can be utilized to begin to understand these similarities and differences, and how it can provide both a rich source of theoretical tools for framing interesting hypotheses regarding the psychology and natural history of prejudice and perhaps some insight into why it is so persistent. Across domains in which the sexes differ and converge in their interactions with outgroups, we draw attention to the fact that intergroup bias is a complex phenomenon deeply rooted in our evolutionary history and likely has served functional outcomes for the agents of group-based prejudice and discrimination. An appreciation of this history is crucial to understanding the psychological underpinnings of racism, ethnocentrism, and other forms of xenophobia.

TWO PSYCHOLOGICAL SYSTEMS FOR PREJUDICE: ONE META-THEORY

The first domain we explore is one in which the challenges and solutions reflect different strategies between men and women, and it draws on insights from parental investment and sexual selection theories (Darwin, 1871; Bateman, 1948; Trivers, 1972). Along these lines, we posit that selection has produced psychological systems managing the cognitive processing of the risks and benefits of physical and sexual aggression in intergroup contexts (Thornhill & Palmer, 2000; Tooby & Cosmides, 1988; Navarrete, McDonald, Molina, & Sidanius, 2010), the former being relevant primarily for males as both the agents and the targets, and the latter being relevant primarily for males as the agents and females as the targets.

The second domain is one that reflects greater similarity between men and women in the strategies taken to meet a challenge, and it is informed by the literature on psychological manifestations of disease-avoidance strategies (Curtis & Biran, 2001; Fessler, 2002) more recently characterized as part of an evolved "behavioral immune system" (Schaller & Duncan, 2007; Neuberg, Kenrick, & Schaller, 2011). Within this framework, we suggest that interactions with outgroups pose an adaptive problem that afflicts both sexes relatively equally: that of risking contact with foreign vectors of infectious disease.

In attempting to provide intellectually satisfying accounts of how the psychology of prejudice operates across both these domains, it is perhaps most fruitful to stay true to a broader computational approach shared by psychologists of different stripes and stay away from the language of tired and unproductive discourse such as that of the debates about *nature versus nurture*, *genes versus culture*, or even *personality versus social context*. Such language only distracts from drawing insight from the conceptual gains made across the social sciences in which broad consensus exists, such as the understanding that the workings of the mind could be better understood as the output of computational systems with working mechanisms designed "for" a purpose or goal of the system (e.g., Tooby & Cosmides, 1992). The mechanisms that compose these systems may be understood with little concern as to how much of the design of a given mechanism is owed to genetically versus socially transmitted information, since natural selection is indifferent to whether the information that builds computational systems comes from genes or from environments (Dawkins, 1982). Rather, what matters is that the mechanisms that generate behavior operate on reliable, species-typical decision rules which the laws of selection can then shape, depending on whether the outcomes have effects on survival and reproduction in a given environment. The decision rules themselves may be affected by the experiences and "life history" of the organism, and they may differ considerably between individuals within the same species as a reflection of their adaptive strategies to their unique circumstances (Griskevicius, Tybur, Delton, & Robertson, 2011; Kaplan & Gangestad, 2005). From this broad, computational understanding of psychological systems, the utility of dichotomous thinking regarding even notions such as the relative importance of personality versus social contexts becomes ever less compelling, since one's "personality" or "context" are more rightfully conceptualized as informational inputs into the computational systems of the mind—systems which must yield, as does all of nature, to the forces of natural selection.

EVOLVED SEX DIFFERENCES IN THE PSYCHOLOGY OF PREJUDICE: DIFFERENT ADAPTIVE PROBLEMS YIELDS DIFFERENT PSYCHOLOGIES

The Roots of a Male-Specific Psychology of Prejudice

Sexual selection is a component of natural selection that operates along two pathways (Darwin, 1871; Fisher, 1930; Andersson, 1994)—*intra-* and *inter-*sexual selection. Intrasexual selection involves competition between members of the same sex and produces traits that are useful in competition with same-sex rivals in gaining access to mating opportunities (e.g., elongated teeth and horns, large muscles). Intersexual selection involves a feedback process in which the strategies and preferences of one sex give rise to counter-strategies and preferences in the other. Rather than evolving to subdue same-sex rivals via intrasexual competition, this process typically encourages the evolution of traits that are useful in attracting members of the opposite sex (e.g. plumage, nuptial gifts, etc.).

Parental investment theory begins with the observation that, for most sexually reproducing organisms, the sexes differ in the minimum physiological effort they must exert to produce viable offspring (Clutton-Brock, 1991). Humans are no different in this respect. For example, at minimum, women must bear the costs of gamete production, fertilization, placentation, gestation, birthing, and lactation, whereas men are minimally obligated to invest solely in the energy required for gamete production and fertilization. Given this disparity, the marginal fitness gains from acquiring multiple mates are far greater for men than for women, and the costs of mating with a poor quality mate are far greater for women than for men. That is, women are physically constrained by their reproductive physiology for a relatively lower potential for quantity over their lifespan, and increasing the number of sexual partners does not increase offspring count to the same degree as it does for men. In fact, it can place women at higher risk for harmful consequences of sex, including infection and poor genetic quality of the copulating partner, without the cost offsets of steeply increased offspring number, as is the case for men.

Taken together, insights from sexual selection and parental investment theory suggest that this fundamental difference in reproductive physiology between the sexes produces an asymmetry in the strength of intrasexual competition, with competition for mates operating more strongly on males (Trivers, 1972). For men, risky, aggressive, and dangerous tactics used to subdue, debilitate, or eliminate same-sex competitors can greatly increase reproductive output by signaling dominance and perhaps underlying genetic quality (Griskevicius et al., 2009) or by increasing sexual access to the associated opposite-sex surplus. For women, however, given the constraints of their reproductive physiology, the same risky, potentially dangerous tactics would not significantly increase reproductive output.

The above suggests that, when we apply the principles of sexual selection and parental investment to the problem of human intergroup aggression, we should expect males to be both its primary agents and its targets (Buss & Shackelford, 1997; Daly & Wilson, 1988; Sidanius & Pratto, 1999; Tooby & Cosmides, 1988). This can occur even under conditions of high risk of injury or death, since the formation of coalitions is typically characterized by mechanisms for effective risk management (such as a "veil of ignorance" of who lives or dies) and "winner take all" outcomes that create massive incentives for survivors—incentives that may increase even as casualties mount, since gains rise steeply as the number of survivors drops (Choi & Bowles, 2007; Tooby & Cosmides, 1988). In sum, the wasteful "dysfunction" of intergroup aggression among males persists because the offsetting reproductive gains are potentially immense, and this harsh state of affairs generates the incentive for men to engage in risky and aggressive strategies in order to dominate other groups, as well as to avoid being dominated. With respect to what this means for a male-specific psychology of prejudice, we suspect that it taps into a psychological system for managing intergroup relations designed ultimately to perpetrate and resist intergroup dominance and aggression among males. And, to the extent that racial categories can be mentally represented as group-like entities to the human mind (Kurzban et al., 2001), we submit that the workings of this psychological system should be detectable in empirical investigations of intergroup phenomena—including sex differences in behavior, emotional reactions, attitudes, and cognitive processing.

As expected from this basic theoretical framework, the incidence of "real-world" intergroup aggression differs markedly between the sexes. Across human societies, intergroup aggression is characterized by an asymmetry between men and women as both targets and aggressors, such that lethal aggression in domains ranging from gang fights to regional and geopolitical conflict can be described as primarily "a male affair" (for reviews, see Daly & Wilson, 1988; Keegan, 1993; Wrangham & Peterson, 1996). Archeological, primatological, and genetic studies have affirmed that this is likely to have been the case throughout human evolutionary history (e.g., Keeley, 1996; Kelly,

2005; Makova & Li, 2002; Wrangham & Peterson, 1996). In modern societies, it is men that are primarily involved in most acts of group-based violence, ranging from lynchings to hate crimes, many of which are racially motivated (reviewed in Sidanius & Pratto, 1999).

Data from studies measuring racial attitudes and discrimination support this perspective. Based on the idea that racially prejudiced attitudes can be conceptualized as a type of "low-level" expression of intergroup aggression among males, Sidanius & Veniegas (2000) made two predictions: (1) that men should express greater racial prejudice and discrimination than women and (2) such prejudice should be more strident against males of the racial outgroup. Survey evidence does in fact suggest that men are, on average, more biased than women on explicit measures of race bias (e.g., Ekehammar, 1985; Ekehammar & Sidanius, 1980, 1982; Furnham, 1985; Marjoribanks, 1981; Sidanius, Cling, & Pratto, 1991; Sidanius & Ekehammar, 1980).

Archival and audit studies have provided some support for the second prediction that men are the targets of greater levels of group-based prejudice. Examples are readily found in audit studies in the educational system (Gordon, Piana, & Keleher, 2000), the labor market (Arai & Thoursie, 2009; Aria, Bursell, & Nekby, 2008; Carlsson & Rooth, 2007; Stroh, Brett, & Reilly, 1992), sales pricing of autos (Ayres & Siegelman, 1995), and criminal sentencing (Bushway & Piehl, 2001; Steffensmeier, Ulmer, & Kramer, 1998). Although such outcomes are certainly indicative of "real-world" discrimination, these studies have the limitation that, because the gender of the agent of prejudice is anonymous, it is not clear whether the male-targeted outcomes are the result of greater discrimination among men or whether women also contribute to such negative outcomes for outgroup men.

Some experimental evidence supports the notion of the greater evocative salience of male outgroup targets in engendering biased reactions, as it has been found that men of racial outgroups, relative to female outgroup targets, elicit greater bias with respect to punitive attitudes about criminal sentencing (Haley, Sidanius, Lowery, & Malamuth, 2004), resist extinction of conditioned fear (Navarrete et al., 2009), and facilitate superior detection in visual search tasks akin to the kinds of abilities typically evoked by natural hazards such as snakes or spiders (Ackerman et al., 2006).

Navarrete et al. (2010) tested a more rigorous set of predictions derived from this framework along the following lines. These predictions were informed by a consideration of the specific selection pressures postulated to have shaped the intergroup psychology of men—particularly that the mechanisms that generate racial and ethnic prejudice tap into evolved psychological systems designed to manage aggressive competition among men in high-stakes, risky intergroup contexts. They made two predictions regarding a male-specific psychology of prejudice. These were (1) that discriminatory outcomes would be most strident when men were pitted against other groups of men; and (2) that aggression and social dominance would be the motivation for prejudice more strongly and consistently for men relative to women.

In an experiment using male and female research participants who made decisions regarding fictitious zero-sum outcomes with groups composed of all males or all females, the outcomes were consistent with these predictions. Specifically, when given the option of inflicting a spiteful, costly punishment on another group at the cost of ingroup resources, men choose to punish outgroup male groups but not outgroup female groups, and women choose not to punish any groups. In another series of studies (Studies 2 and 4; Navarrete et al., 2010), men's racial prejudice was found to be related to individual differences in aggression, particularly when the men's goal of intergroup dominance was chronically salient.

In concert with the widely documented sex difference in general prejudice against outgroups, these nuanced patterns of sex-specific relationships among target gender, agent gender, aggression, and the goal of social dominance suggest a meaningful component of racial prejudice may be fundamentally related to recurring intergroup conflict among human males over evolutionary history. However, male–male competition alone does not explain another important aspect of prejudice: that exhibited by women. Although much evidence suggests that women are generally less prejudiced then men, they are clearly not free from bias. In reports where the gender of the outgroup target is manipulated, even though male targets elicit greater biased responses among research participants, levels of bias between male and female participants are sometimes similar (e.g., Haley et al., 2004; Navarrete et al., 2009); in fact women show greater bias than men in some studies (e.g. Owens, Shute, & Slee, 2000; Stets & Straus, 1990; Fisman, Iyengar, Kamenica, & Simonson, 2008). Such findings showing that women demonstrate considerable bias themselves suggest that psychological processes other than those that have evolved to manage intrasexual competition among men may be at work in the psychologies of women.

Below, we describe a *female-specific* psychology that may have evolved in response to the unique problems that women have faced in conflicts of interest with men of other social groups.

Intersexual Selection and Intergroup Conflict

We have argued above that the evolutionary history of aggressive intergroup conflict has been largely a male affair, because the marginal increase in access to the opposite sex via the elimination or domination of same-sex competitors produces greater fitness benefits for men than for women. Of course this should not suggest that women do not have anything to gain in same-sex coalitional conflicts, but rather that the expected reproductive gains are not large enough in women to offset the considerable costs associated with aggressive tactics. Therefore, the psychological systems that potentiate hostile intergroup behavior and generate prejudiced attitudes and emotions toward same-sex outgroup competitors is likely to be muted for women relative to men.

Although women's bias and aggression toward outgroup women may be less severe than men's bias and aggression toward outgroup men, the potential for negative affective or attitudinal biases against outgroup men may be equally possible for women, even if the psychology that generates these biases is not motivated by the same aggression-related motivations applicable to men. This potential for negativity toward outgroup men could have arisen not through the workings of intrasexual competition but, rather, through the forces of inter-sexual conflict operating between the sexes. Although women may have a lower probability of being the agents or victims of lethal intergroup violence, they can nevertheless be the targets of non-lethal violence with the potential for serious fitness consequences.

Across cultures and time, women have often been the victims of brutal sexual aggression in intergroup conflicts (Thornhill & Palmer, 2000; Wrangham & Peterson, 1996; Vikman, 2005). Atrocities in violent political conflicts such as those committed in Bosnia, Rwanda, Darfur, and the U.S. engagements in Vietnam and Iraq highlight the potential for sexual aggression to which women may be subjected during times of war (i.e., intergroup contexts). Acts of sexual aggression are not unique to the human species, as they are common in some animal societies, including some closely related to humans, such as chimpan-zees. Indeed, sexual aggression sometimes reflects a species-typical evolved mating strategy in certain animals and a conditional mating strategy in others (see Thornhill & Palmer, 2000).

For women, two general paternal factors influence the survival prospects of offspring: the genetic quality of the biological father and the amount of invest-ment the father makes in providing for the offspring. Women who mate with low-quality men (i.e., men with genetic predispositions impairing survival pro-spects or the ability to obtain mates) have a higher probability of having low-quality offspring, who themselves may not survive to reproduce or may not be able to obtain mates. Women who conceive but lack any subsequent investment from a father—biological or not—risk not having the nutritional or protective resources necessary for the survival of their offspring. Sexual aggression from strangers poses severe threats across both of these factors. When coerced into intercourse, women lose the opportunity to judge the quality of the aggressor; they essentially risk one of their limited number of lifetime reproductions on a man who may have poor genetic quality. Similarly, women who are aggressed against lose their ability to evaluate a man's investment potential. Moreover, strangers who invade and aggress sexually may be less likely to remain to assist in childcare nine months after conception and beyond.

The costs of aggressing sexually are quite high for men in most contexts (Smith, Borgerhoff Mulder, & Hill, 2001). Men risk both retaliation from the vic-tim and the kin or romantic partner of the victim and loss of social status and alli-ances. Hence, it is not surprising that most men, under most circumstances, do not use sexual aggression as a reproductive strategy. Nevertheless, sexual aggres-sion is markedly more common against outgroups during intergroup conflict than among ingroups in times of peace (Thornhill & Palmer, 2000; Wrangham & Peterson, 1996; Vikman, 2005). At a proximate level, the higher frequency may reflect the lower costs perceived by the perpetrators for harming others during times of intergroup conflict. This may be due to any combination of several social processes, among them de-individuation in group activities, reduced accountability across group boundaries, and ethnocentric double standards in the activation of empathy or when normal rules of moral judgment apply. Regardless of the precise nature of the proximate psychological factors that lead to greater sexual aggression by men in intergroup contexts, it appears that outgroup men have historically posed greater risks of sexual assault against women than familiar men of one's own group. Although sexual aggression and coercion occurs within most societies (e.g., Broude & Greene, 1976; Levinson, 1989), wartime has traditionally provided an even greater affordance of opportunities for sexual aggression as far back as the historical record allows (reviewed in Vikman, 2005). In fact, violent intergroup conflict may have been even more common in prehistoric societies than has been the case in historical societies (Bamforth, 1994; Chagnon, 1996; Daly & Wilson, 1988; Ember, 1978; Ghiglieri, 1999; Keeley, 1996; Knauft, 1987; Krech, 1994; Wrangham & Peterson, 1996). In a recent survey of the history and prehistory of violence, Steven Pinker (2011) has provided convincing evidence that, across cultures and throughout history, physical violence is reliably correlated with other types of antisocial activity, most notably sexual aggression. Taken together, the observations that (a) sexual aggression is not uncommon among our closest primate cousins, (b) warfare and sexual aggression have been tightly linked as far back as recorded history, (c) physical and sexual aggression are reliably linked across space and time, and (d) intergroup violence was much more common in the past than in modern times mean that it is not unreasonable to suspect that women have faced recurring threats of sexual assault throughout our evolutionary history (perhaps threats higher than those encountered in modern Western societies), and that they may have been particularly at risk from men from groups other than their own. Since people are more likely to spend time with persons of their own social groups than with strangers, the threat of sexual assault per interaction with an outgroup male over the course of a lifetime was likely markedly higher than the threat of sexual assault among familiar men controlling for baseline differences in proximity. Given the importance of reproductive choice for women, intersexual selection acting on the conflict of reproductive interests between coercive men and discerning women may have favored a female-specific psychology predisposing women to be vigilant against outgroup men to avoid sexual coercion.

To be sure, by interacting with outgroups, there are potential fitness benefits to broadening the pool of mate choices to include mates of any social group. A wider pool allows for a greater raw number of men of high genetic quality, and it improves the genetic diversity of the mating pool. However, given outgroup men were more likely than ingroup men to compromise female choice via sexual aggression and coercion, selection may favor a negativity bias toward outgroup men under certain conditions.

Although invariant avoidance of outgroup men would drastically decrease the risk of sexual coercion or aggression, women should not be expected strictly to avoid outgroups. Such biases come with their own costs, including diverting attention and energy away from other important tasks and risking losing potentially valuable interactions with outgroups (e.g., non-coercive mating opportunities, trading opportunities). Given that both biases and lack of biases toward outgroups have fitness relevant costs, women's degree of bias should be expected to vary as a function of their appraised vulnerability to lose control of the maintenance of reproductive choices. As such, women who perceive themselves to be more vulnerable to sexual coercion, or who perceive outgroup men as particularly physically formidable (and more likely to overpower them), should be more willing to pay the costs associated with bias (e.g., attention and energy) in order to minimize the probability of sexual aggression and its attendant loss of choice in reproductive partner.

Recent research suggests this may be a productive framework in which to address a female-specific psychology of prejudice. Results from several studies indicate that White women's perceived vulnerability to sexual coercion is positively correlated with negative attitudes toward African Americans (Navarrete, Fessler, Santos Fleischman, & Geyer, 2009; Navarrete et al., 2010, Study 2). One study showed that race prejudice for women was most strongly directed at Black men, not Black women, and that the relationship between perceived vulnerability to sexual coercion and fear toward Black and White men and women was strongest toward Black men (Navarrete et al., 2010, Study 3). Put simply, the degree to which White women were biased against Black men was predicted by how vulnerable White women felt to sexual coercion. Consistent with the notion that a domain-specific link may exist between the avoidance of sexual coercion and the avoidance of outgroup men, this relationship held even when the effect of general fearfulness was statistically controlled.

The relation between inter-individual variation in perceived vulnerability to sexual coercion and bias toward outgroup males suggests that outgroup prejudice may be specifically attuned to the costs of sexual aggression, which are not the same throughout the course of a woman's menstrual cycle. Because the reproductive consequences of sexual aggression are strongest during the peri-ovulatory phase of the menstrual cycle (i.e., the window in which a woman can conceive), women should be especially biased toward outgroup males during the fertile part of their cycle. This should be particularly true for women who perceive themselves to be vulnerable to sexual coercion and who view outgroup men as physically formidable. In a test of these specific theoretically derived predictions, Navarrete, Fessler, Santos Fleischman, & Geyer (2009) report that the relationship between perceived vulnerability to sexual coercion and multiple measures of prejudice toward outgroups grew stronger as fertility increased across the menstrual cycle. These findings are not trivial, given that implicit measures of bias have been shown to correlate more strongly with "real-world" behavior than explicit measures (Greenwald et al., 2009).

McDonald, Asher, Kerr, & Navarrete (2011) replicated and extended these findings by demonstrating a link between conception risk and implicit outgroup prejudice in both racial and non-racial outgroups. In light of the conflict between the potential costs and benefits associated with intergroup interactions, in generating prejudiced evaluations, selection may have favored psychological mechanisms that assess the extent to which outgroup men are perceived as physically formidable, as such traits would increase the effectiveness of a man's attempts physically to overpower and constrain a woman's behavior and, therefore, reproductive choice. McDonald and her colleagues hypothesized that the link between conception risk and implicit intergroup prejudice should be particularly strong for women who associate the outgroup with physical formidability.

Two studies were conducted to test this prediction using both White or Black men as targets, as well as men categorized into arbitrarily bifurcated social groups distinguishable solely by shirt colors. Research participants were assigned to groups based on largely arbitrary preferences for one primary color versus another (e.g., yellow vs. blue), after which they completed implicit association tests measuring the extent to which they readily associated (a) outgroup men as physically formidable ("physicality") relative to ingroup men with (b) the extent to which outgroup men were more negatively/less positively evaluated on affectively charged semantic terms (e.g., horrible, evil, good, etc.) relative to ingroup men. Across both studies, the results revealed that conception risk led to greater prejudice in intergroup evaluations most consistently when outgroup men were associated with physicality. These findings suggest that the psychological system by which women's evaluations of outgroup men become more negative as a function of conception risk does not depend on a specific racial context (e.g., Black vs. White). Instead, the mechanisms within the system likely rely on more basic categorization processes that respond to cues that are dependent not on the race of the target but, rather, on the target's group category—even if largely arbitrary. This is consistent with the points we made earlier that our evolved psychology is likely to have been shaped during a time in our evolutionary history when groups were defined not by race but, rather, by differences in coalitional alliances marked by nonphysical traits such as linguistic accent, dialect, and social customs or norms.

Overall, these results suggest that women may be equipped with flexible psychological mechanisms designed to protect reproductive choice by avoiding outgroup men, who have historically posed the greatest reproductive threat, particularly when (a) a woman perceives herself as particularly vulnerable and (b) the targets are perceived as being most capable of effectively constraining her reproductive choice.

Sex Differences in Prejudice: Summary

We have so far argued that the adaptive problems posed by intergroup conflict have been different for men and women throughout human evolutionary history, and that the manner in which natural and sexual selection has provided ways of dealing with these problems may have set the stage for important psychological differences between the sexes. We think these differences reflect the workings of an evolved psychology designed to provide sex-specific solutions to the unique challenges that are posed by outgroup men to each sex. These problems and solutions have produced psychological sex differences in the expression of intergroup bias likely to have evolved on separate sexually selected

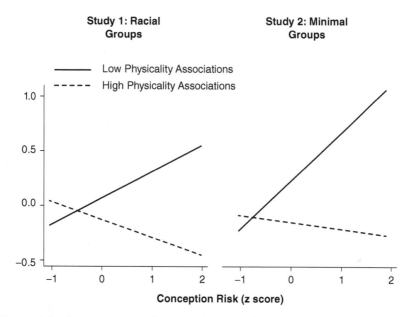

Figure 4.1   Intergroup prejudice as a function of conception risk and physicality associations (1 standard deviation above and below mean physicality) (from McDonald et al., 2011).

avenues of conflict: intrasexual conflict, in which males of separate coalitions have competed with each other for potential access to mates, and intersexual conflict, in which females have attempted to avoid sexually aggressive tactics from outgroup males. These paths to prejudice are psychologically manifested as a predisposition for *aggressive* prejudice for men and greater proneness to *fearful* prejudice for women—both paths directed most strongly toward male exemplars of the outgroup.

We now turn to a domain of prejudice in which men's and women's psychologies may be expected to be more similar than different: the intersection of prejudice and the psychology of pathogen avoidance.

OUTGROUP BIAS AND PATHOGEN AVOIDANCE

Whereas sexual selection refers specifically to the kinds of processes shaped by competition between and within the sexes for access to mating reproductive opportunities, natural selection refers more broadly to processes through which fitness-promoting traits are favored, including what is typically referred to as "survival." With respect to the more general challenge of survival, an additional threat posed by outgroups—one that may have also shaped the evolution of psychological biases—is that of infectious disease.

Humans throughout evolutionary history have consistently faced challenges posed by infectious disease. In fact, infectious parasites posed a threat to multi-cellular organisms well before mammals even evolved. Threats posed by parasitic micro-organisms have motivated a suite of complex adaptations, including sexual recombination, the immune system, and psychological and behavioral strategies designed to mitigate the deleterious effects of infectious disease (Curtis, de Barra, & Aunger, 2011; Hamilton, Axelrod, & Tanese, 1990; Schaller & Duncan, 2007; Tybur, Lieberman, & Griskevicius, 2009). Essentially, a competitive "arms race" occurs between pathogens and hosts, in which larger organisms adapt to counter-threats posed by constantly evolving micro-organisms (Van Valen, 1973). This is sometimes referred to as the *Red Queen Effect*, which describes an evolutionary "arms race" where constant development of counter-strategies are needed just in order to maintain the fitness of an organism relative to the systems with which it is co-evolving (Ridley, 1993). The term is taken from Lewis Carroll's *Through the Looking Glass*, in which the Red Queen comments: "It takes all the running you can do, to keep in the same place." The only method through which to mitigate the deleterious effects of pathogens that vary across time and space is to develop immune responses that are similarly varied across historical and geographic regions.

Like other organisms, the varied immune responses that develop among humans can be conceptualized as a composition of specialized defenses against specific parasites within the local ecology. The immune systems of individuals living in separate groups are often adapted to different parasites, such that some groups possess immunities to parasites to which other groups may be vulnerable (Black, 1975). As a result, groups of individuals can be carriers of pathogens that may produce deleterious symptoms to which they themselves are largely immune, but to which individuals from other groups are not. Thus, for any given individual, interactions with ingroup members whose immune systems are locally adapted are a much safer bet than interactions with outgroup members adapted to different parasite ecologies, and thus may carry parasite that, while relatively innocuous in them, may have debilitating fitness consequences if transmitted to members of other groups.

The lethal spread of smallpox and measles from Europeans to traditional populations possessing no immunity to these diseases provides a dramatic instance of this principle. Although pathogens as virulent as smallpox or measles typically require large population densities with substantial geographic boundaries between them to evolve such devastating effects (see Anderson & May, 1979), small-scale traditional societies nevertheless are adapted to resist local parasites that differ from those encountered by more distant groups (Black, 1975). Pathogen transmission via intergroup contact can occur along multiple routes, including pathways that involve direct personal contact (e.g., shaking hands, sharing food, sexual intercourse), or along contact pathways that may be relatively less personal but are nevertheless not uncommonly associated with intergroup encounters, such as trading pelts, blankets, or other objects, urinating or defecating in the local water supply, and contacting local nonhuman pathogen vectors such as mosquitoes, ticks, or livestock. In sum, as is the case for sexual aggression threats to women, the average interaction with an outgroup member conceivably poses a greater pathogen transmission risk than the average interaction with an ingroup member, all else equal.

It has also been proposed that norms and traditions that vary between groups (e.g., hygiene, food selection, storage, and preparation) may develop in response to specific endemic infectious disease threats (Schaller & Murray, 2008, 2010; Sherman & Billing, 1999). Outgroups may have different cultural practices based on unique parasite threats in their own ecologies. For example, groups living in areas with climates conducive to food-borne bacterial contamination may develop cuisines with certain antimicrobial components. Spices such as garlic, cumin, oregano, and thyme inhibit bacterial growth and may be incorporated into food preparation to prevent food spoilage. Interactions with outgroups may encourage the diffusions of foreign cultural traditions that, while perfectly acceptable in one ecology, may pose disease threats in another (Nettle, 2006; Schaller & Murray, 2008). In this example, transmission of minimally spiced, minimally antimicrobial food preparation from one group with low threats of bacterial contamination to a group with high threats may pose a pathogen threat to the group living in the more microbe-friendly ecology.

If the problems of pathogen transmission across social groups posed significant fitness challenges throughout our evolutionary history, natural selection may have favored the emergence and maintenance of a psychology predisposing us to xenophobic biases in order to mitigate infectious disease threats posed by people from outgroups. Examples of similar "behavioral immune system" responses exist from the animal behavior literature, where potential disease threats are mitigated via prophylactic behavior such as mammalian mothers removing feces from their dens or bees removing decaying material from their hives. In humans, examples of behavioral prophylaxis may be instantiated as biases against ingesting particular foods or mating with certain people evincing cues of increased disease risk, such as pungent odors emanating from the potential food or mating target. Mental representations of such stimuli may be associated with negative emotions, including disgust—a powerful motivator of the avoidance and expulsion of potential sources of contagion (Tybur et al., 2009).

But, as is the case with biases that function to address the problems associated with physical and sexual aggression in intergroup contexts, such biases motivated by pathogen avoidance are not without tradeoffs. Several *benefits* of interactions with outgroups are limited by persistent biases against them, including mating and exchange opportunities, as we have mentioned above. Furthermore, the attentional and energetic resources necessary to avoid members of outgroups can have their own opportunity costs. Hence, a key test of a behavioral immune system approach to the psychology of prejudice may involve examining how bias varies across individuals differing in their vulnerability to infectious disease. Methodologically similar to the individual difference approach to establishing the link between perceived vulnerability to sexual coercion and negativity to outgroup men, it would be expected that the case for a pathogen-avoidance function for biases against outgroups in general would be strengthened if such biases were found to be strongest among those who appraised themselves as being particularly vulnerable to disease.

Several studies have indeed established this link and suggest that outgroup bias does indeed involve a pathogen-avoidance component. Across four studies, Faulkner, Schaller, Park, and Duncan (2004) found consistent evidence that individuals who chronically perceive themselves as more vulnerable to infectious disease also have more negative attitudes toward the immigration of those of ethnically foreign origins. Another two studies showed that experimental manipulations temporarily making pathogens salient were associated with greater negativity toward ethnically foreign immigrants. Navarrete and Fessler (2006) conceptually replicated and extended these results in finding that perceived vulnerability to infectious disease relates to general ethnocentric attitudes among U.S. college students, and that reading about and rating how disgusting are various pathogen risks increased individuals' ingroup favoritism. Navarrete, Fessler, and Eng (2007) found that a bias in favor of a pro-American target vs. an anti-American target is higher among pregnant women relative to non-pregnant women, higher still in the first trimester of pregnancy—both periods of natural increased vulnerability to infectious disease. Finally, using measures similar to those employed by Navarrete et al. (2010) to demonstrate a relationship between women's vulnerability to sexual coercion and bias toward Black men, Tybur, Merriman, Caldwell, McDonald, and Navarrete (2010) found that sensitivity to disgust toward pathogen threats predicts social dominance orientation—endorsement of inequality between groups—equally for both men and women (see also Hodson & Costello, 2007).

Studies of societies' mean levels of traits predicted to buffer against infectious disease are also consistent with a behavioral immune system perspective. Group ecologies differ in their parasite variety and density. Presumably, those societies located in environments with more varied parasites must develop immunities that are specifically attuned to the parasites within their ecology. For individuals in these societies, interactions with outgroups may pose a greater infectious disease threat than would be the case in less parasite-dense and varied ecologies. Thus, groups in parasite-rich ecologies are expected to adapt to such conditions by erecting social barriers against intergroup interactions. Consistent with this perspective, societies' parasite prevalence is strongly related to mean levels of collectivism, which concentrates intragroup interactions and limits intergroup interactions (Fincher, Thornhill, Murray, & Schaller, 2008). Parasite prevalence also predicts societies' number of religions, which may encourage intragroup cohesion and interaction and discourage intergroup interactions (Fincher & Thornhill, 2008; see also Fincher & Thornhill, 2012). Taken together, these studies are not only consistent with the hypothesis that intergroup bias is related to avoiding infectious disease; they also demonstrate a nuanced psychology that adjusts bias based on the infectious disease costs associated with intergroup interactions.

Those aspects of intergroup bias brought about by intrasexual and intersexual competition are by nature gendered phenomena. They involve highly sex-specific psychologies that reflect both gender differences in the costs and benefits of sexual activity and the variances in expected and potential reproductive output. In contrast, aspects of intergroup bias related to pathogen avoidance are not expected to demonstrate clear sex differences. Both men and women must cope with threats posed by infectious disease, and pathogen avoidance may motivate intergroup bias equally for the sexes. Unlike research showing strong sex differences in relations between intergroup bias and endorsement of intergroup competition and dominance (Navarrete et al., 2010), none of the research discussed above on intergroup bias and disease avoidance has reported sex-specific effects. Further, the sex of the outgroup member should not strongly influence the threats posed by infectious disease or the amount of bias motivated by pathogen avoidance. Whereas outgroup men, but not outgroup women, pose a potential threat of sexual aggression and coercion to women specifically, both outgroup sexes presumably pose a similar pathogen-related threat to both ingroup sexes.

DIFFERENTIATING BIASES

All three evolutionary processes discussed in this chapter are posited to contribute to intergroup biases generated by an evolved psychology of prejudice. We have argued that intrasexual selection operating more strongly among men than among women may have produced psychological biases that motivate aggressive competition between males of different groups. Intersexual selection operating on the conflict of mating interests between men and women may have produced biases that motivate women's avoidance of outgroup males when perceived vulnerability to sexual coercion is high. And, lastly, we have argued that natural selection operating on the problems posed by pathogen transmission between groups has produced biases that motivate avoidance of contact with outgroups in general, particularly when appraisals of an individual's vulnerability to pathogen threats are chronically or contextually high.

Because the threats forming the selection pressure vary between all three processes, the nature of bias should also be differentiable. Although considerable evidence now exists for the notion that men of a racial outgroup evoke greater negative reactions among both men and women, the ways in which they are negatively prejudiced differ considerably. As previously noted, men's bias against outgroup males is both more punitive in nature than women's and more readily related to aggression and dominance motives (Navarrete et al., 2010). Women's bias against outgroup males is characterized more by fear and avoidance and is related to chronic concerns about sexual coercion. Both sexes' bias toward outgroups in general appears to relate to pathogen concerns, when it may be characterized by avoidance motivated by disgust, and is predicted by chronic and situational vulnerability to infection.

IMPLICATIONS AND LIMITATIONS

We have described women's bias as targeted primarily toward outgroup men rather than toward ingroup men or outgroup women, because of the costs associated with increased risk of sexual coercion by outgroup men, all else equal. We have also described men's bias as targeted primarily toward outgroup men, because of the gains to be had by eliminating or dominating other male coalitions. And we have posited that a crucial component of group-based prejudice expressed by both men and women is characterized by pathogen-avoidance motives. In marshaling empirical support for these claims, we have described work that exploits the natural variation existing between individuals on the traits relevant to the function of these biases in order to explain variance in the expression of bias. This is because we do not expect that, as a product of evolution by natural selection, the psychology of prejudice should be characterized by built-in preferences or tastes that are not sensitive to environmental input. Instead we posit the existence of dynamic, evolved psychological systems that are sensitive to the costs and benefits of any course of action in the face of uncertain outcomes and incomplete information. The costs of any course of action in response to a given threat are likely to include a *cost risk quotient* that represents one's probability of falling victim to the threat. Highly aggressive and dominant men may feel better able to engage the threat of outgroup men, and therefore express greater prejudice—a syndrome likely to be related to readying oneself for approach-related posturing or violent engagement. On the other hand, women who appraise themselves as highly vulnerable to sexual coercion and people of both sexes who appraise themselves as vulnerable to infection become more prejudiced not because such personality profiles are associated with the need to ready oneself for approach-related contact, but for precisely the opposite reason: Because prejudice is not only about approach-related aggression and dominance, it is about avoiding danger among those individuals who have appraised themselves as not up to the challenge. Thus prejudicial outcomes can arise by opposing strategies.

Although strong, potentially costly responses to threats related to coalitional aggression, sexual aggression and coercion, and infection are not universally experienced on account of their energetically expensive natures, people may nonetheless engage in other, more measured responses to these problems. For example, instead of experiencing fear and engaging in flight and concealment when presented with a threat of sexual aggression, women may avoid costly mating by experiencing disgust and engaging in more measured avoidance (Tybur et al., 2009). Disgust, though typically thought of as functioning to motivate pathogen avoidance (e.g., Curtis & Biran, 2001), is elicited by a number of sexual behaviors that connote costs, including incest, sexual coercion, and behaviors that do not increase reproductive success but do involve potential disease costs (e.g., anal sex). Effectively, the underlying reasons for avoiding such maladaptive sexual interactions are similar to those motivating women's intergroup bias discussed earlier in the chapter. Some women are less biased against outgroups than others, and these individual differences appear to relate to the degree to which women feel vulnerable to sexual coercion. For the same reason that women are not universally biased toward outgroup men (e.g., the attentional and energetic costs of bias and avoidance), they should also not be expected universally to use the same strategies to avoid males who may present threats of coercion. Fear, flight, and concealment are costly strategies of avoidance, and they may not be necessary to avoid suboptimal mates. Instead, disgust, rejection, and mild avoidance (e.g., walking away) may be less costly alternative responses to suboptimal mates who are unlikely successfully to aggress or coerce. Women who perceive relatively low—but still a degree of—vulnerability to sexual coercion may still be biased against outgroup males, but their bias may be qualitatively different from that of women with greater perceived vulnerability. Rather than avoiding outgroup male sexual partner via *fear*, they may engage in avoidance by being *disgusted*. Disgust may motivate general proximal avoidance and distancing from men perceived as potentially sexually aggressive or coercive, but in a less extreme manner than fear. Indeed, we find that sensitivity to *sexual* disgust consistently relates to variables relevant to outgroup bias more strongly than sensitivity to pathogen or moral disgust (Tybur et al., 2010).

Emotional and behavioral responses subsumed between and within biases functioning to neutralize different threats are heterogeneous, but at the same time they should be flexible and responsive to fluctuating threats from a dynamic environment. Although some women may tend to respond to outgroup males with fear, and others with disgust, these responses should vary between contexts with differing probabilities of sexual coercion. A woman faced with a rapidly approaching outgroup male may experience fear and flight regardless of chronic perceptions of vulnerability to sexual coercion, because the situational sexual aggression threat is high and the costs associated with fear and flight are necessary to neutralize the threat. On the other hand, women who feel highly vulnerable to sexual coercion may feel disgust rather than fear toward outgroup males when the probability of coercion is relatively low (e.g., when they are protected by an imposing group of ingroup males). Such questions have yet to be empirically examined.

Although we have focused initially on differentiation within responses to sexual coercion and aggression threats, the emotional and behavioral responses to infection threats posed by outgroups perhaps exhibit the greatest degree of heterogeneities. The pathogen-avoidance hypothesis of intergroup bias was initially motivated partially by observations that outgroups are often compared to disgusting, disease-ridden animals (e.g., cockroaches). Although disgust certainly motivates avoidance of infectious materials and outgroups often elicit disgust (Cottrell & Neuberg, 2005), intergroup conflict is often characterized by interactions that are high pathogen risks. Violent confrontation between groups risks physical contact and inadvertent exchanges of infectious bodily fluids, including blood and saliva. This apparent contradiction between the goal of avoiding pathogens and actions that risk infection could develop under two conditions. First, goals related to avoiding pathogens and dominating other groups may be in competition, and so cross-group domination may win out. In refraining from combat to avoid pathogens, individuals within groups may risk extreme social status costs that are ultimately more harmful to lifetime repro-ductive output than infection itself (Matthew & Boyd, 2011). Second, violent confrontation could ultimately serve the goal of pathogen avoidance despite short-term increases in infection risk. By dominating, intimidating, and even eliminating potentially infectious outgroup members, male coalitions may dis-suade other groups from future interactions that may pose greater disease risks than those involved in conflict.

Although it is perhaps useful for reducing our nuanced approach to the evo-lutionary psychology of prejudice to a few memorable heuristics, one may be tempted to make the following characterizations of our theoretical and empiri-cal claims: Male prejudice is about aggression and dominance, female prejudice is about fear of rape, and general biases among both men and women are about disgust. Such characterizations would not be unfair given the three evolutionary processes we described as important historical forces likely to have shaped the psychology of modern humans. To be sure, we think that sexual selection is extremely important, to the extent that intergroup bias is a gendered phenom-enon, and that disease-avoidance concerns, as a fundamental problem for all life forms on the planet, form the root of a whole host of human biases and pre-ferences, not only those related to group-based prejudice. However, we have been careful to avoid claims that all features of the prejudiced mind are reduci-ble to sexual selection and disease avoidance. There are other problems related to group-based prejudice that have not been treated here, some of which are related fundamentally to gender—such as female coalitional alliances and intra-sexual aggression. A growing body of work suggests that aggression may not be less common among women than among men, only that it may be less explicit and physically violent in nature. As is the case with females of many primate species, coalitions among women and girls against same-sex competitors may be fundamental to the human condition. An evolutionary analysis of such dynamics is waiting to be done and represents a limitation in current theory and research in evolutionary approaches to social psychology, as it is in this present chapter.

Likewise, our current analysis has left out a major thread within the evolu-tionary literature, and one which surely must be a key component of the psy-chological architecture shared by both men and women with respect to thinking about groups: that of the problem of cooperation within groups and how to coordinate collective action. How the problem of cooperation is relevant to the emergence and maintenance of intergroup biases is an under-explored area of inquiry among evolutionary and social psychological researchers (for exceptions, see Brewer, 1999; Gil-White, 2001). Perhaps humankind's most noble social instincts can also lead to between-group preferences—our capacity for compassion for others like ourselves, our willingness to sacrifice our own comfort and safety for the benefit of others, our desire to conform in order to not offend others may all have a dark side to them if their expression is contingent on anything other than unconditional love. The frontiers of the psychological science are ripe for bold perspectives that seek to explain difficult topics— perspectives that cut across disciplinary lines in the search for ever more accurate narratives of topics such as how and why we are so damned tribal.

REFERENCES

Anderson, R. M., & May, R. M. (1979). Population biology of infectious diseases. *Nature*, 280, 361–367.

Andersson, M. (1994). *Sexual selection*. Princeton, NJ: Princeton University Press.

Andrews, Gangestad, & Matthews (2002). To be added on proof.

Arai, M., Bursell, M., & Nekby, L. (2008). *Between meritocracy and ethnic discrimination: The gender difference*. SULCIS Working Papers 2008:2. Stockholm University, Linnaeus Center for Integration Studies.

Arai, M., & Thoursie, P. S. (2009). Renouncing personal names: An empirical examination of surname change and earnings. *Journal of Labor Economics*, 27, 127–147.

Ayres, I., & Siegelman, P. (1995). Race and gender discrimination in bargaining for a new car. *American Economic Review*, 85, 304–321.

Bamforth, D. B. (1994). Indigenous people, indigenous violence: Precontact warfare on the North American Great Plains. *Man*, 29, 95–115.

Bateman, A. J. (1948). Intra-sexual selection in drosophila. *Heredity*, 2, 349–368.

Black, F. L. (1975). Infectious diseases in primitive societies. *Science*, 187, 515–518.

Brewer, M. B. (1999). The psychology of prejudice: Ingroup love or outgroup hate? *Journal of Social Issues. Special Issue: Prejudice and intergroup relations: Papers in honor of Gordon W. Allport's centennial*, 55, 429–444.

Broude, G. J., & Greene, J. (1976). Cross-cultural codes on twenty sexual attitudes and practices. *Ethnology*, 15, 409–430.

Bushway, S. D., & Piehl, A. M. (2001). Judging judicial discretion: Legal factors and racial discrimination in sentencing. *Law & Society Review*, 35, 733–764.

Buss, D. M., Haselton, M. G., Shackelford, T. K., Bleske, A., & Wakefield, J. C. (1998). Adaptations, exaptations, and spandrels. *American Psychologist*, 53, 533–548.

Buss, D. M., & Shackelford, T. K. (1997). Human aggression in evolutionary psychological perspective. *Clinical Psychology Review*, 17, 605–619.

Carlsson, M., & Rooth, D. O. (2007). Evidence of ethnic discrimination in the Swedish labor market using experimental data. *Labour Economics*, 14, 716–729.

Chagnon, N. A. (1996). Chronic problems in understanding tribal violence and warfare. In G. Bock & J. Goode (Eds.), *The genetics of criminal and antisocial behavior*. New York: Wiley.

Cheney, D., and Seyfarth, R. (1982). Recognition of individuals within and between groups of free-ranging vervet monkeys. *American Zoologist*, 22, 519–529.

Choi, J., & Bowles, S. (2007). The coevolution of parochial altruism and war. *Science*, 318, 636–640.

Clutton-Brock, T. (1991). *The evolution of parental care*. Princeton, NJ: Princeton University Press.

Cottrell, C. A., & Neuberg, S. L. (2005). Different emotional reactions to different groups: A sociofunctional threat-based approach to prejudice. *Journal of Personality & Social Psychology*, 88, 770–778.

Curtis, V., & Biran, A. (2001). Dirt, disgust, and disease: Is hygiene in our genes? *Perspectives in Biology and Medicine, 44,* 17–31.

Curtis, V., de Barra, M., & Aunger, R. (2011). Disgust as an adaptive system for disease avoidance behavior. *Philosophical Transactions of the Royal Society B, 366,* 389–401.

Daly, M., & Wilson, M. (1988). *Homicide.* Hawthorne, NY: Aldine de Gruyter.

Darwin, C. (1871). *The descent of man and selection in relation to sex.* London: John Murray.

Dawkins, R. (1982). *The extended phenotype,* Oxford, UK: W. H. Freeman.

Ekehammar, B. (1985). Sex differences in socio-political attitudes revisited. *Educational Studies, 11,* 3–9.

Ekehammar, B., & Sidanius, J. (1980). Negative similarities versus correlational similarities. *Multivariate Behavioral Research, 15,* 95–98.

Ekehammar, B., & Sidanius, J. (1982). Sex differences in socio-political attitudes: A replication and extension. *British Journal of Social Psychology, 21,* 249–257.

Ember, C. (1978). Myths about hunter-gatherers. *Ethnology, 27,* 239–248.

Faulkner, J., Schaller, M., Park, J. H., & Duncan, L. A. (2004). Evolved disease-avoidance mechanisms and contemporary xenophobic attitudes. *Group Processes & Intergroup Relations, 7,* 333–353.

Fessler, D. M. T. (2002). Reproductive immunosuppression and diet: An evolutionary perspective on pregnancy sickness and meat consumption. *Current Anthropology, 43,* 19–39, 48–61.

Fincher, C. L., & Thornhill, R. (2008). Assortative sociality, limited dispersal, infectious disease and the genesis of the global pattern of religion diversity. *Proceedings of the Royal Society B: Biological Sciences, 275,* 2587–2594.

Fincher, C. L., & Thornhill, R. (2012). Parasite-stress promotes in-group assortative sociality: The cases of strong family ties and heightened religiosity. *Behavioral and Brain Sciences, 35,* 61–119.

Fincher, C. L., Thornhill, R., Murray, D. R., & Schaller, S. (2008). Pathogen prevalence predicts human cross-cultural variability in individualism/collectivism. *Proceedings of the Royal Society B: Biological Sciences, 275,* 1279–1285.

Fisher, R. A. (1930). *The genetical theory of natural selection.* Oxford, UK: Oxford University Press.

Fisman, R., Iyengar, S. S., Kamenica, E., & Simonson, I. (2008). Racial preferences in dating. *Review of Economic Studies, 75,* 117–132.

Furnham, A. (1985). Adolescents' sociopolitical attitudes: A study of sex and national differences. *Political Psychology, 6,* 621–636.

Ghiglieri, M. P. (1999). *The dark side of man: Tracing the origins of male violence.* Reading, MA: Perseus Books.

Gil-White, F. J. (2001). Are ethnic groups biological "species" to the human brain? Essentialism in our cognition of some social categories. *Current Anthropology, 42,* 515–554.

Gordon, R., Piana, L. D., & Keleher, T. (2000). *Facing the consequences: An examination of racial discrimination in U.S. public schools.* Oakland, CA: ERASE Initiative, Applied Research Center.

Greenwald, A. G., Poehlman, T. A., Uhlmann, E., & Banaji, M. R. (2009). Understanding and using the Implicit Association Test, III: Meta-analysis of predictive validity. *Journal of Personality and Social Psychology, 97,* 17–41.

Griskevicius, V., Tybur, J. M., Gangestad, S. W., Perea, E. F., Shapiro, J. R., & Kenrick, D. T. (2009). Aggress to impress: Hostility as an evolved context-dependent strategy. *Journal of Personality and Social Psychology, 96,* 980–994.

Griskevicius, V., Tybur, J. M., Delton, A. W., & Robertson, T. E. (2011). The influence of mortality and socioeconomic status on risk and delayed rewards: A life history theory approach. *Journal of Personality and Social Psychology, 100,* 1015–1026.

Haley, H., Sidanius, J., Lowery, B., & Malamuth, N. (2004). The interactive nature of sex and race discrimination: A social dominance perspective. In G. Philogene (Ed.), *Racial identity in context: The legacy of Kenneth B. Clark* (pp. 149–160). Washington, DC: American Psychological Association.

Hamilton, W. D., Axelrod, R., & Tanese, R. (1990). Sexual reproduction as an adaptation to resist parasites. *Proceedings of the National Academy of Sciences of the USA, 87,* 3566–3573.

Hirschfeld, L. A. (1996). *Race in the making: Cognition, culture and the child's construction of human kinds.* Cambridge, MA: MIT Press.

Hodson, G., & Costello, K. (2007). Interpersonal disgust, ideological orientations, and dehumanization as predictors of intergroup attitudes. *Psychological Science, 18,* 691–698.

Kaplan, H. S., & Gangestad, S. W. (2005). Life history theory and evolutionary psychology. In D. M. Buss (Ed.), *Handbook of evolutionary psychology* (pp. 68–95). New York: Wiley.

Keegan, J. (1993). *The history of warfare.* New York: Alfred A. Knopf.

Keeley, L. H. (1996). *War before civilization: The myth of the peaceful savage.* New York: Oxford University Press.

Kelly, R. C. (2005). The evolution of lethal intergroup violence. *Proceedings of the National Academy of Sciences, 102,* 15294–15298.

Knauft, B. (1987). Reconsidering violence in simple human societies. *Current Anthropology, 28,* 457–500.

Krech, S. (1994). Genocide in tribal society. *Nature, 371,* 14–15.

Kurzban, R., Tooby, J., & Cosmides, L. (2001). Can race be erased? Coalitional computation and social categorization. *Proceedings of the National Academy of Sciences, 98,* 15387–15392.

Levinson, D. (1989). *Family violence in cross-cultural perspective.* Newbury Park, CA: Sage.

Makova, K. D., & Li, W.-H. (2002). Strong male-driven evolution of DNA sequences in humans and apes. *Nature, 416,* 624–626.

Marjoribanks, K. (1981). Sex-related differences in socio-political attitudes: A replication. *Educational Studies, 7,* 1–6.

Matthew, S., & Boyd, R. (2011). Punishment sustains large-scale cooperation in prestate warfare. *Proceedings of the National Academy of Sciences of the USA, 108,* 11375–11380.

McDonald, M., Asher, B., Kerr, N., & Navarrete, C. D. (2011). Fertility and intergroup bias in racial and in minimal group contexts: Evidence for shared architecture. *Psychological Science, 22,* 860–865.

Navarrete, C. D., & Fessler, D. M. T. (2006). Disease avoidance an ethnocentrism: The effects of disease vulnerability and disgust sensitivity on intergroup attitudes. *Evolution and Human Behavior, 27,* 270–282.

Navarrete, C. D., Fessler, D. M. T., & Eng, S. J. (2007). Elevated ethnocentrism in the first trimester of pregnancy. *Evolution and Human Behavior, 28,* 60–65.

Navarrete, C. D., Fessler, D. M. T., Santos Fleischman, D., & Geyer, J. (2009). Race bias tracks conception risk across the menstrual cycle. *Psychological Science, 20,* 661–665.

Navarrete, C. D., McDonald, M., Molina, L., & Sidanius, J. (2010). Prejudice at the nexus of race and gender: An out-group male target hypothesis. *Journal of Personality & Social Psychology, 98*, 933–945.

Navarrete, C. D., Olsson, A., Ho, A. K., Mendes, W., Thomsen, L., & Sidanius, J. (2009). Fear extinction to an outgroup face: The role of target gender. *Psychological Science, 20*, 155–158.

Nettle, D. (2006). The evolution of personality variation in humans and other animals. *American Psychologist, 61*, 622–631.

Neuberg, S. L., Kenrick, D. T., & Schaller, M. (2011). Human threat management systems: Self-protection and disease-avoidance. *Neuroscience & Biobehavioral Reviews, 35*, 1042–1051.

Owens, L., Shute, R., & Slee, P. (2000). "Guess what I just heard!": Indirect aggression among teenage girls in Australia. *Aggressive Behavior, 26*, 67–83.

Pinker, S. (2011). *The better angels of our nature: Why violence has declined.* New York: Viking.

Ridley, M. (1993). *The red queen: Sex and the evolution of human nature.* London: Viking.

Schaller, M., & Duncan, L. A. (2007). The behavioral immune system: Its evolution and social psychological implications. In J. P. Forgas, M. G. Haselton, & W. von Hippel (Eds.), *Evolution and the social mind: Evolutionary psychology and social cognition* (pp. 293–307). New York: Psychology Press.

Schaller, M., & Murray, D. R. (2008). Pathogens, personality and culture: Disease prevalence predicts worldwide variability in sociosexuality, extraversion, and openness to experience. *Journal of Personality and Social Psychology, 95*, 212–221.

Schaller, M., and Murray, D. R. (2010). Infectious diseases and the evolution of cross-cultural differences. In M. Schaller, A. Norenzayan, S. J. Heine, T. Yamagishi, and T. Kameda (Eds.), *Evolution, culture, and the human mind* (pp. 243–256). New York: Psychology Press.

Sherman, P. W., & Billing, J. (1999). Darwinian gastronomy: Why we use spices. *BioScience, 49*, 453–463.

Sidanius, J., Cling, B. J., & Pratto, F. (1991). Ranking and linking as a function of sex and gender role attitudes. *Journal of Social Issues, 47*, 131–149.

Sidanius, J., & Ekehammar, B. (1980). Sex-related differences in socio-political ideology. *Scandinavian Journal of Psychology, 21*, 17–26.

Sidanius, J., & Pratto, F. (1999). *Social dominance: An intergroup theory of social hierarchy and oppression.* New York: Cambridge University Press.

Sidanius, J., & Veniegas, R. C. (2000). Gender and race discrimination: The interactive nature of disadvantage. In S. Oskamp (Ed.), *Reducing prejudice and discrimination: The Claremont symposium on applied social psychology* (pp. 47–69). Mahwah, NJ: Erlbaum.

Smith, E. A., Borgerhoff Mulder, M., & Hill, K. (2001). Controversies in the evolutionary social sciences: A guide to the perplexed. *Trends in Ecology and Evolution, 16*, 128–135.

Steffensmeier, D., Ulmer, J., & Kramer, J. (1998). The interaction of race, gender, and age in criminal sentencing: The punishment cost of being young, Black, and male. *Criminology, 36*, 763–797.

Stets, J. E., & Straus, M. A. (1990). Gender differences in reporting of marital violence and its medical and psychological consequences. In M. A. Straus & R. J. Gelles (Eds.), *Physical violence in American families* (pp. 151–165). New Brunswick, NJ: Transaction Books.

Stringer, C., & McKie, R. (1997). *African exodus: The origins of modern humanity*. London: Jonathan Cape.

Stroh, L. K., Brett, J. M., & Reilly, A. H. (1992). All the right stuff: A comparison of female and male mangers' career progression. *Journal of Applied Psychology, 77*, 251–260. Personal author, compiler, or editor name(s); click on any author to run a new search on that name.

Tajfel, H. (1981). *Human groups and social categories*. Cambridge, UK: Cambridge University Press.

Thornhill, R., & Palmer, C. (2000). *A natural history of rape: Biological bases of sexual coercion*. Cambridge, MA: MIT Press.

Tooby, J., & Cosmides, L. (1988). *The evolution of war and its cognitive foundations*. Institute for Evolutionary Studies Technical Report 88(1).

Tooby, J., & Cosmides, L. (1992). The psychological foundations of culture. In J. Barkow, L. Cosmides, & J. Tooby (Eds.), *The adapted mind: Evolutionary psychology and the generation of culture* (pp. 19–136). New York: Oxford University Press.

Trivers, R. L. (1972). Parental investment and sexual selection. In B. Campbell (Ed.), *Sexual selection and the descent of man* (pp. 136–179). Chicago: Aldine-Atherton.

Tybur, J. M, Lieberman, D., & Griskevicius, V. (2009). Microbes, mating, and morality: Individual differences in three functional domains of disgust. *Journal of Personality and Social Psychology, 97*, 103–122.

Tybur, J. M., Merriman, L. A., Caldwell, A. E., McDonald, M. M., & Navarrete, C. D. (2010). Extending the behavioral immune system to political psychology: Are political conservatism and disgust sensitivity really related? *Evolutionary Psychology, 8*, 599–616.

Van Valen, L. (1973). A new evolutionary law. Evolutionary Theory, 1, 1–30.

Vikman, E. (2005). Ancient origins: Sexual violence in warfare, part I. *Anthropology & Medicine, 12*, 21–31.

Wrangham, R. W., & Peterson, D. (1996). *Demonic males: Apes and the origins of human violence*. Boston: Houghton Mifflin.

5

Stereotype Threat

JENESSA R. SHAPIRO

University of California, Los Angeles

JOSHUA ARONSON

New York University

> In the perception of society my athletic talents are genetic; I am a likely mugger/rapist; my academic failures are expected; and my academic successes are attributed to others. To spend most of my life fighting these attitudes levies an emotional tax that is a form of intellectual emasculation.
>
> (Neil de Grasse Tyson, 1991)

De Grasse Tyson's statement about the "emotional tax" he carried with him throughout his education is not uncommon among Black students in the White academy. This observation reflects the pervasive role that stereotypes can play in undermining the intellectual lives of Black students—and, indeed, of anyone who contends with stereotypes that question his or her abilities. Social psychologists have referred to this additional burden as *stereotype threat*—the concern that one's performance or actions can be seen through the lens of a negative stereotype (e.g., Aronson et al., 1999; Shapiro & Neuberg, 2007; Steele, 1997; Steele, Spencer, & Aronson, 2002). Stereotype threat is different than many other theories that often turn to cultural or biological factors to explain the underrepresentation of ethnic minorities in higher education and women in math, science, technology, and engineering fields. Instead, researchers who study stereotype threat focus on the psychological experience of the social structure, exploring how being confronted with negative stereotypes can levy an "emotional tax" that interferes with performance.

For example, in a classic series of studies conducted by Claude Steele and Joshua Aronson (1995), Black students' performance on a SAT-like test was suppressed when situational cues made racial stereotypes salient. In one study, White and Black students were randomly assigned to learn that a SAT-like test was either a good indicator of their underlying intellectual abilities (stereotype threat condition) or a nondiagnostic problem-solving exercise (no-threat condition). Demonstrating the power of the test framing, Black students performed more poorly in the stereotype threat condition relative to the no-threat condition. The difference in the way the test was described had no discernible effect on the White students' performance (see Figure 5.1). In a second study, the researchers had all participants complete the test with the no-threat instructions (nondiagnostic problem-solving exercise). However, half of the students were asked to indicate their race prior to completing the test, thereby making their race salient to them. The simple manipulation asking about race led Black students to perform more poorly on the test compared to when race was not mentioned.

Almost twenty years have passed since these first studies were published. The research conducted in the wake of these seminal findings has uncovered mounting evidence for the pernicious effects of stereotype threat: Women underperform in math and science domains, political contexts, and chess (e.g., Maass, D'Ettole, & Cadinu, 2008; McGlone, Aronson, & Kobrynowicz, 2006; Spencer, Steele, & Quinn, 1999); Latinos underperform on academic tasks (Schmader & Johns, 2003); older adults underperform on memory tests

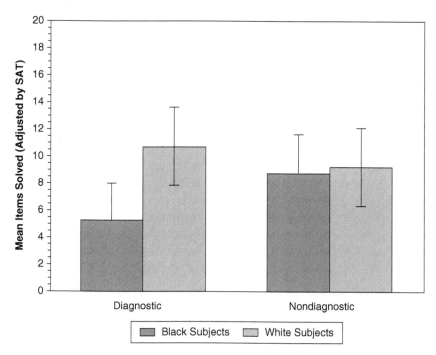

Figure 5.1   Mean test performance by Black and White participants in Study 2 by Steele and Aronson (1995).

(e.g., Levy, 1996); Whites underperform on measures of racism (Frantz, Cuddy, Burnett, Ray, & Hart, 2004; Goff, Steele, & Davies, 2008); and students who have a mental illness underperform on rational thinking tests (Quinn, Kahng, & Crocker, 2004). And this is just a small sample of the groups and domains represented in the stereotype threat literature.

When a negative stereotype exists about a group—any group—to which one belongs, one is at risk for stereotype threat. Indeed, there is some research that suggests an individual need not even possess the negatively stereotyped identity—they just need to believe there is a chance others will categorize them as having this identity. For example, when gay men were asked to disclose their sexual orientation in a childcare context (threatening for gay men in light of stereotypes about gay men posing a risk for children), they appeared more anxious and were judged to have inferior childcare skills compared to gay men who were allowed to conceal their sexual orientation or heterosexual men who revealed their sexual orientation (Bosson, Haymovitz, & Pinel, 2004). However, when *heterosexual men* were *not* able to disclose their sexual orientation—a situation in which they could be mistaken for belonging to the negatively stereotyped group—their behavior mirrored the behavior of the gay male participants in the disclosure condition. That is, when heterosexual men were not able to disclose their sexual orientation (a condition in which they could be mistaken for gay men), they demonstrated increased anxiety and poorer childcare skills (Bosson et al., 2004). These data demonstrate that, in some situations, the possibility of being misclassified as belonging to a negatively stereotyped group can put someone at risk for stereotype threat (see also Bosson, Prewitt-Freilino, & Taylor, 2005).

Most stereotype threat research focuses on its implications for intellectual performance (e.g., math performance among women, IQ performance among Black students). Yet its scope of influence goes beyond test performance. For example, stereotype threat increases self-handicapping behaviors or the self-defeating tendency to put obstacles in the way of one's success (e.g., not studying, staying out late the night before a test). These obstacles provide explanations for one's performance that are not as deprecatory as low ability ("I didn't get any sleep last night" versus "I'm not smart enough"). For example, research suggests that, compared to non-stereotype threatened participants, stereotype threatened participants are likely to spend less time and energy practicing and more time and energy generating excuses for failure, both of which can help people deflect feelings of incompetence (e.g., Brown & Josephs, 1999; Keller, 2002; Steele & Aronson, 1995; Stone, 2002). Stereotype threat also yields reduced self-efficacy (Aronson & Inzlicht, 2004); lowered confidence that one will do well in the stereotyped domain (Stangor, Carr, & Kiang, 1998); lowered aspirations to pursue stereotype-relevant careers (Davies, Spencer, Quinn, & Gerhardstein, 2002; Davies, Spencer, & Steele, 2005); and negative physical and psychological health consequences, including increased general anxiety (Ben-Zeev, Fein, & Inzlicht, 2005; Bosson, Haymovitz, & Pinel, 2004), blood pressure (Blascovich, Spencer, Quinn, & Steele, 2001), and feelings of dejection (Keller & Dauenheimer, 2003).

A SITUATIONAL THREAT

What is particularly striking about the stereotype threat phenomenon is that it is situational: Any cue in the environment that makes negative stereotypes salient can elicit stereotype threat. As a result, there are many aspects common to everyday organizational and academic environments that can produce stereotype threat, from being in the numerical minority (e.g., being the only woman in an engineering class or firm; Inzlicht & Ben-Zeev, 2000; Sekaquaptewa & Thompson, 2003) to interacting with someone who likely holds negative stereotypes (Logel et al., 2009). A particularly noteworthy demonstration of the situational nature of stereotype threat comes from the work of Margaret Shih and her colleagues. These researchers examined the performance of Asian women, who have two identities that carry with them very different implications for math performance. On the one hand, Asians are stereotyped as being good at math. On the other hand, females are stereotyped as having weak abilities in math contexts. Thus, the researchers randomly assigned Asian female participants to complete a demographics prompt that had them focus on either their gender or their race/ethnicity, or neither (a control condition), before completing a math test. The focus of the demographics section influenced participants' performance differentially: Asian women who answered questions about their gender performed more poorly than those in the control condition, whereas those who answered questions about their race performed better than those participants in the control condition (Shih, Pittinsky, & Ambady, 1999).

As another example, consider White males. Across most stereotype threat research examining gender in the context of math, White males are found to be relatively unaffected by stereotype threat manipulations; indeed, given that men are stereotyped as stronger than women in math contexts, they tend to perform *slightly better* on standardized math tests when gender or gender stereotypes are made salient (a phenomenon called "stereotype lift"; Walton & Cohen, 2003). However, Joshua Aronson and his colleagues considered a situation in which White males are stereotyped as weaker in math skills—when they are compared to Asians. In this study, when they were reminded that *Asians* are stereotyped as stronger in math than Whites, White men underperformed on math tests relative to a control condition (Aronson et al., 1999). This particular study highlights the situational nature of stereotype threat because it specifically assesses the performance of a group in a domain in which they are chronically *positively* stereotyped. Regardless of these positive stereotypes, White men were still at risk for stereotype threat when negative stereotypes were made salient. This emphasizes an important component of stereotype threat—that a long history of contending with negative stereotypes is not necessary for a person to experience stereotype threat.

Another impressive example of the role situational factors play in yielding stereotype threat was conducted by Jeff Stone and his colleagues in a domain in which stereotypes can favor White or Black participants depending on the context—sports (Stone, Lynch, Sjomeling, & Darley, 1999). That is, depending on the sport or the player's position in a particular sport, an athletic task can be conceptualized as cerebral (e.g., quarterback) or as drawing on athletic talent (e.g., running back). Stone and his colleagues used a golf-putting task and randomly assigned Black and White male participants to a condition that described the task as (a) diagnostic of sports intelligence, (b) diagnostic of natural athletic ability, or (c) a measure of general sports performance (control). As anticipated, the way the golf test was framed had a significant effect on performance. Black participants underperformed relative to control when the task was described as measuring sports intelligence, whereas White participants underperformed relative to control when the task was described as measuring natural athletic ability. It is important to emphasize that the task was *exactly the same* across conditions—nothing changed except for the description. The findings from the three studies described here—Asian women performing a math task when their Asian or female identity is made salient, White men performing a math task when Asian stereotypes are made salient, and White and Black men performing a sports task described in terms of natural athletic talent or intelligence— underscore the power of the situation in producing stereotype threat effects and the wide-reaching implications of stereotype threat for anyone, regardless of minority group membership or status.

ANTECEDENTS AND CONSEQUENCES OF STEREOTYPE THREAT

What causes decrements in performance when a situational cue triggers stereotype threat? Stereotype threat does not typically lead to decreased motivation in testing situations; indeed, it most often gives rise to a greater desire to do well on a given task and disprove the negative stereotypes (Steele & Aronson, 1995). Indeed, research demonstrates that participants put forth more effort in stereotype-threatening situations (Jamieson & Harkins, 2007, 2009). However, more effort does not always translate into better performance; higher motivation to do well in situations where there are negative expectations can produce intrusive and distracting thoughts (for a review, see Schmader, Johns, & Forbes, 2008). In one study, Cadinu, Maass, Rosabianca, and Kiesner (2005) found that women experiencing stereotype threat were more likely to report negative math-related thoughts (and not other thoughts) compared to women in a no-threat condition. Moreover, the difference in the content of women's thoughts accounted for the lower performance in the stereotype threat condition.

Consistent with these findings, recent models articulating the mechanisms underlying stereotype threat effects argue that, in stereotype-threatening situations, distracting concerns usurp the executive resources needed to complete cognitively demanding tasks successfully (Schmader et al., 2008). Indeed, research directly testing "working memory efficiency" finds that working memory is reduced by stereotype threat (Beilock, Rydell, & McConnell, 2007; Schmader & Johns, 2003). Sian Beilock and her colleagues provided a very clever demonstration of the role of working memory in producing stereotype threat effects. Specifically, participants completed math problems that were either horizontal or vertical with the hypothesis that, when stereotype threat was activated, women's performance would suffer mainly on the math problems presented horizontally. Their reasoning was that horizontal problems rely heavily on verbal working memory resources because they require the verbal maintenance of intermediate steps in one's memory. In contrast, research finds that math problems presented in a vertical format rely more heavily on spatial resources because individuals tend to solve vertical problems in a spatial mental workspace (Trbovich & LeFevre, 2003). As a result, if stereotype threat taxes verbal working memory resources (due to increased verbal thoughts and worries during the experience of stereotype threat), it is performance on the horizontal problems that should suffer the most (Beilock et al., 2007). This is exactly what Beilock and her colleagues found—stereotype threatening situations impaired math performance on the horizontally oriented math problems and not on those vertically oriented. It is also important to note that, regardless of problem orientation, women in the stereotype threat condition reported more worries and performance concerns than women in the no-threat condition. Given that these worries harmed performance only on the horizontal problems, this provides some additional evidence that such worries were specifically contaminating verbal working memory and harming the performance of a task that utilizes verbal working memory resources.

In addition to reducing the efficiency of working memory, intrusive thoughts tend to require management. Michael Inzlicht and his colleagues have found that the exertion of self-control to regulate and manage one's thoughts and emotions consequently depletes many of the resources essential to the effective accomplishment of other tasks that require conscious effort. For example, in one study, Inzlicht, McKay, and Aronson (2006) measured female participants' performance on a handgrip exercise, an exercise that requires maintaining a tight squeeze on a spring-loaded exerciser (the kind bodybuilders use to strengthen their hands and forearms). What is nice about the handgrip task is it requires considerable self-regulation but not working memory, allowing for an assessment of self-control independent of working memory. Before females began the handgrip exercise, they learned they would eventually complete a math or verbal test described either as capable of revealing gender differences (stereotype threat condition) or as being gender fair (no-threat condition). Consistent with a resource depletion account, female participants receiving the stereotype threat instructions when taking the math test let go of the handgrip more quickly (i.e., had impaired self-regulation) than those participants who believed they would take a verbal test. Performance on the handgrip task did not vary in the no-threat condition.

Because working memory and executive control are vital to everyday tasks beyond the classroom (or the weight room, for that matter), recent research reveals the experience of stereotype threat can spill over into stereotype-irrelevant domains that require these resources. For example, Beilock and colleagues (2007) found that women performed worse on a *verbal* task after completing a stereotype-threatening math test. How is this possible given positive stereotypes about girls in a variety of verbal domains (i.e., reading, writing, oral expression) and other research showing that women's verbal performance does not suffer with the typical stereotype threat instructions (e.g., Inzlicht & Ben-Zeev, 2000)? Beilock and her colleagues found that performing a stereotype-threatening math task depleted participants' working memory, a resource essential for verbal problem-solving. Thus, the experience of stereotype threat in a negatively stereotyped domain (e.g., math) can spill over into a subsequent task, even if it is positively stereotyped, and depress performance. Inzlicht and his colleagues have found similar evidence for non-academic tasks that require self-regulation: Stereotype-threatening situations were more likely than non-stereotype-threatening situations to lead female participants to respond aggressively, indulge in unhealthy food, and engage in risky decision-making (Inzlicht & Kang, in press). These spill-over effects are distressing. Such findings demonstrate that stereotype threat can literally tire us out mentally and thereby contribute to unwanted outcomes in a variety of situations, academic or otherwise. Furthermore, as stereotype threat chips away at stereotype-irrelevant domains, such as women's performance on a verbal task, it becomes more difficult to identify stereotype threat as the culprit and therefore more difficult to remediate.

NATURE OF THE THREAT

Stereotype threat emerges in situations where negative stereotypes call into question one's abilities, prompting an additional cognitive burden. This seems fairly straightforward, and the data generally fall in line with this characterization. Yet a more nuanced picture of stereotype threat is emerging as a new generation of researchers examine the causes and consequences of this important and seemingly commonplace phenomenon. A key question is this: What exactly underlies stereotype threat? Do I feel threatened because my performance could prove that the negative stereotypes are true of me, or do I worry that I will make my group look bad? And whose judgment matters? That is, in whose eyes do I worry about confirming the stereotype? Mine? Someone else's? Both at the same time? Aronson and his colleagues raised a similar set of questions over a decade ago:

> Is stereotype threat self-threatening because it arouses a fear of being a bad ambassador of one's group to mainstream society? Or is it more simply the apprehension about appearing incompetent—for the sake of one's own reputation? Or, alternatively, is it merely the result of worrying that one might lack ability? Or is it some combination of these concerns? These are important questions that will have to await the results of future research for answers.
> (Aronson et al., 1999, p. 43)

Although these questions were proposed a little over a decade ago, very little research has addressed them. Recently, Shapiro and Neuberg (2007) argued these distinctions are important, articulating a Multi-Threat Framework consisting of six core stereotype threats. These stereotype threats emerge from the intersection of two dimensions—the target of the threat (Will one's actions reflect upon the self or one's group?) and the source of the threat (Who has the opportunity to use these actions as an indication of ability: the self, outgroup others, or ingroup others?). *Self-Concept Threat* is the fear of seeing oneself as actually possessing the negative stereotypic trait. For example, James, a Black male, might fear that a poor performance in an academic exam will suggest that he is indeed, by virtue of his race, less intelligent than his White classmates. *Own-Reputation Threat (Outgroup, Ingroup)* is the fear of stereotypic characterization in the eyes of others (outgroup or ingroup, respectively). For example, James may fear that a poor performance would enable an employer, teacher, or friend to see him as stereotypic and thereby treat him in an unfavorable manner. *Group-Concept Threat* is the fear of seeing one's group as possessing the negative stereotypic trait. That is, James might fear that an inadequate performance will confirm, in his own mind, the stereotype that Blacks are less intelligent than Whites. Finally, *Group-Reputation Threat (Outgroup, Ingroup)* is the fear of reinforcing negative stereotypes about one's group in the minds of others—the fear of being a bad ambassador for one's group. James's concern here would be that a poor performance in the test would lead others to believe the stereotypes are accurate—that Blacks as a whole are less intelligent than Whites.

Although each of these stereotype threats requires knowledge that the stereotypes exist, a distinct set of factors are proposed to elicit each stereotype threat (Shapiro, 2011; see Shapiro & Neuberg, 2007, for a review). As an example of how one of these factors serves differentially to elicit the stereotype threats, consider Self-Concept Threat. Risk for Self-Concept Threat increases to the extent that someone thinks the stereotype could be true of his or her personal abilities. If Michelle does not believe there is any chance that she is any worse at math because she is a woman, then she should not fear that a math performance could confirm, in her own mind, that she is stereotypic. In contrast, she would not need to believe stereotypes to be at risk for Own-Reputation Threat (Outgroup). Regardless of whether Michelle thinks that girls are good at math, she nonetheless may fear that outgroup others (e.g., men) hold the stereotype and could therefore judge her performance through the lens of this stereotype.

As another example, one's risk for Group-Reputation Threat increases to the extent that one identifies with the negatively stereotyped group, sees this group as central to one's self-concept, or considers the group an important social identity. That is, if Michelle does not see her gender as an important identity, she is unlikely to care about the ramifications of her performance for how others perceive women. However, group identification should be irrelevant to risk for Self-Concept Threat or Own-Reputation Threat (Outgroup). That is, regardless of whether Michelle sees being a woman as central to her self-concept, she can still fear that, because she is a woman, a poor performance in a math test can confirm that she is stereotypic, in her own mind or in the minds of outgroup others.

In addition to the theoretical benefit of differentiating between these stereotype threats, there are important pragmatic implications. As the preceding discussion makes clear, there are a variety of stereotype threats, and failing to distinguish between them ultimately masks the presence of multiple, distinct psychological experiences that can arise from the existence of stereotypes. As a result, researchers, practitioners, and interventionists may believe they are working with one form of stereotype threat when in fact they may indeed be tapping into another. Thus, differentiating between stereotype threats is important to interpreting, extending, and generalizing stereotype threat research and findings (Shapiro, Williams, & Hambarchyan, in press). Although research into multiple stereotype threats is not yet abundant, we believe it holds an important key for advancing our understanding of important interpersonal behavior.

DO STEREOTYPE THREAT EFFECTS EMERGE OUTSIDE THE LAB?

Although hundreds of demonstrations of stereotype threat have been published over the past 15 years, only a handful of these studies examine the presence of stereotype threat outside of the lab. Here we will briefly review evidence demonstrating the presence of stereotype threat in real-world, often high-stakes, achievement settings. In one study, Alter, Aronson, Darley, Rodriguez, and Ruble (2010) had Black children between the ages of nine and 13 complete ten items from a standardized math test either before or after indicating their race on a demographics page. Students who completed the test before indicating their race did over 20% better on the math test (a significant improvement) than students who indicated their race before completing the test. Keller and Dauenheimer (2003) performed a similar study with children (about 15 years old) in a German secondary school taking a math test. Here, the test was administered in the way the students were accustomed to taking tests, with one change: Half of the students learned the test had ostensibly shown gender differences in the past (high stereotype threat condition) whereas the other half learned the test had not shown these differences (no-threat condition). Again, consistent with research conducted in the lab, although the performance of male and female students did not differ in the "no gender differences" condition (no-threat condition), male students performed significantly better than female students in the high stereotype threat condition (see also Good, Aronson, & Harder, 2008, for an identical study in a college calculus class). Neuville and Croizet (2007) found a similar pattern of results among French third graders taking a math test in their classrooms. Before starting a test administered in the way they were accustomed to taking tests, half of the children were assigned to color a picture of a girl with a doll or a boy with a ball (gender salient, high stereotype threat condition) or a picture of a landscape (low threat condition). On the difficult math problems, girls and boys performed similarly when gender was not activated by the coloring task (low stereotype threat condition); however, girls performed worse when their gender was activated (high stereotype threat condition). Similarly, Huguet and Regner (2007; see also Huguet & Regner, 2009) found that middle-school girls (ages 11 to 13) performed significantly worse than boys on a task when it was described as a geometry task (high stereotype threat condition), yet these girls were more successful than the boys on the *same* task when it was described as a drawing task (no-threat condition).

These findings are impressive. Whereas the lab gives researchers a controlled context to explore stereotype threat effects, the field introduces many factors that are not easily brought under a researcher's control. Yet, despite these obstacles, manipulations as subtle as a demographics assessment or coloring a picture of a doll do seem to undermine performance—the sort of performance that has implications for honors placement, grade advancement, and the like. However, it is still unclear whether stereotype threat undermines performance on high-stakes standardized tests—the types of tests that garner the most attention because they often serve as gatekeepers to educational opportunities such as college and graduate school. To address this question, Stricker and Ward (2004) examined the influence of identifying gender before (compared with after) taking the Advanced Placement Calculus Examination and the Computerized Placement Tests. Recently, Danaher and Crandall (2008) revisited these data. Their analyses found that asking for gender after (compared with before) taking the AP Calculus exam led females to pass the test at a rate of about a 6% higher, changing the pass rate advantage enjoyed by men from 16% to 5%. Danaher and Crandall argue that, had gender been asked after, instead of before, the test was administered, this would have translated to 4,763 more women receiving AP credit in 2004.

To add to this emerging focus on how stereotype threat unfolds outside the lab, Walton and Spencer (2009) recently conducted two meta-analyses exploring the robustness of the stereotype threat effect and examining the extent to which standardized measures underestimate the ability of negatively stereotyped groups. Specifically, across lab-based research that manipulates stereotype threat, Walton and Spencer found that, in situations in which stereotype threat was reduced (i.e., no-threat or safe conditions), stereotyped groups performed (a) better than stereotyped groups in stereotype threat conditions and (b) better than the non-stereotyped group in the no-threat conditions. Walton and Spencer's second meta-analysis assessed three field interventions that used random assignment to intervention. Again, these data reveal that Black students receiving stereotype threat-reducing interventions performed (a) better than Black students who did not receive interventions and (b) equivalently to or better than White students (receiving and not receiving interventions).

Although only a small amount of research has explored stereotype threat effects in real-world contexts, these few studies confirm students are at risk for stereotype threat in non-laboratory contexts. Furthermore, there are many reasons to believe findings from field research are underestimating actual effects. First, as noted earlier, research in the field cannot control for many of the variables that are often controlled for in the lab. As a result, there is a great deal of additional noise in data collected in the field. Lab research can also more easily measure important individual difference factors that moderate stereotype threat effects (Nguyen & Ryan, 2008), thereby pinpointing the situations where stereotype threat is most likely to occur and for whom it will be most disruptive. For example, lab studies assessing math performance can look at differences between students who have poor, compared to strong, math skills or poor, compared to strong, working memory (Beilock & DeCaro, 2007), factors that are important because math performance is unlikely to change in stereotype-threatening situations if one's skills in this area are already poor. Field research likely aggregates across such factors. Given that stereotype threat effects have consistently emerged in field research despite these constraints, research is likely underestimating the true phenomenon.

DEVELOPMENTAL AND CROSS-CULTURAL RESEARCH

Developmental and cross-cultural research provides additional support for the role negative stereotypes play in undermining performance. First, when one considers the math performance of boys and girls, girls across all ages tend to perform more strongly than, or equivalently to, boys in math computation and understanding of mathematical concepts. However, after middle school, gender differences tend to emerge in math problem-solving skills, with males performing more strongly than their female classmates (Hyde, Fennema, & Lamon, 1990). It is further the case that, around the age of ten, at about the same time these gender differences begin emerging, the content of gender stereotypes held by children begins to look like the content of gender stereotypes held by adults (e.g., Ruble & Martin, 1998). At around this age children also begin to learn that it is inappropriate to use social categories (such as race and gender) as a means of evaluating others (e.g., Apfelbaum, Pauker, Ambady, Sommers, & Norton, 2008). Thus, developmental research suggests that gender gaps in math performance tend to coincide with the understanding of gender stereotypes. This suggests that it is unlikely a coincidence that research examining stereotype threat effects in classrooms (such as the research reviewed earlier) tends to focus consistently on the performance of middle- and high-school students.

A more explicit test of this hypothesis comes from Nalini Ambady and her colleagues. In this research, Asian-American children in elementary and middle school performed a math test after their gender or race, or neither identity, was made salient. Consistent with the hypothesis that stereotype threat effects tend to track stereotype knowledge, Ambady, Shih, Kim, & Pittinksy (2001) found that upper elementary-school girls (ages eight to ten) performed better in the math test in the gender salience condition compared to the control or Asian salience conditions. In contrast, the older, middle-school girls underperformed in the test when gender was made salient (relative to control and Asian salience). Muzzatti and Agnoli (2007) found a similar pattern of results with Italian students. In two studies, students took a math test after viewing stimuli that consisted of either ten neutral images (e.g., flowers; low stereotype threat condition) or ten famous mathematicians, of which only one was a woman (high stereotype threat condition). In one study, only fifth-grade female students' performance was influenced by this manipulation: Males and females in grades 2 to 4 performed similarly in the high stereotype threat and low stereotype threat conditions. However, in grade 5, female students performed more poorly in the high stereotype threat condition compared to males in both conditions and to females in the low stereotype threat condition. In the second study, the authors looked at grades 3, 5, and 8. Again, the oldest students were the most likely to show stereotype threat effects. In grades 3 and 6, girls and boys performed similarly across conditions. However, whereas eighth-grade girls and boys performed similarly in the low stereotype threat condition, female students in the high stereotype threat condition performed more poorly than male students (regardless of condition) and female students in the low stereotype threat condition.

Cross-cultural research demonstrates a pattern that is similar to that in the developmental literature: underperformance in domains that are negatively stereotyped within that particular culture. For example, in a study looking across cultures and mental rotation abilities, researchers found that differences in male and female mental rotation were correlated positively with gender equity and economic development, suggesting that gender egalitarianism may contribute to fewer stereotype-driven decrements in performance (Lippa, Collar, & Peters, 2010). A similar finding emerged in a study of stereotype threat among Black immigrants. Kay Deaux and her colleagues assessed the performance of first- and second-generation West Indian immigrant college students. Specifically, they anticipated that first-generation immigrants would be buffered from stereotype threat effects because their knowledge of the negative stereotypes endorsed in the United States would be limited. However, they anticipated second-generation West Indian students, given that, by definition, they grew up in U.S. culture surrounded by stereotypes about Black Americans, would be at risk for stereotype threat. Consistent with their predictions, first- and second-generation West Indian students did not differ in their performance in a test described as non-diagnostic (no-threat condition). However, when the test was described as diagnostic (stereotype threat condition), second-generation students performed worse than first-generation students (Deaux et al., 2007).

STEREOTYPE THREAT-REDUCTION STRATEGIES

The excitement and interest surrounding stereotype threat stems in large part from the possibility that its real-world costs are substantial. Lab and field data suggest the experience of stereotype threat may partially account both for the gap in average achievement between Black and Caucasian students and for the relatively low numbers of women in math- and science-based careers. As a result, interventions that reduce the experience of stereotype threat form a powerful tool for influencing an important set of societal problems. Thus, it is no surprise that recent research has turned to developing and testing interventions designed to mitigate the harmful effects of stereotype threats. Importantly, researchers have looked at many of these strategies both in the lab and in the field. Here we review a few approaches from this burgeoning literature, describing first the work conducted in the lab and then work testing these strategies in the field.

One intervention approach that has received a great deal of empirical attention is the no-threat condition in the existing stereotype threat studies. That is, within most studies, there is an identity-safe condition, or a condition that should be stereotype threat-free (or reduced). In general, these conditions are made less threatening by changing the framing of the task and/or situation. For example, no-threat conditions often reduce the salience of the negatively stereotyped identity by removing demographic questions, eliminating one's token status, and the like (e.g., Inzlicht & Ben-Zeev, 2000; Steele & Aronson, 1995; Stricker & Ward, 2004). Other studies change the framing of the task so that it is represented as nondiagnostic of ability (e.g., Steele & Aronson, 1995) or free of bias (e.g., does not yield differences between groups; Davies et al., 2005; Good et al., 2008; Spencer et al., 1999; Quinn & Spencer, 2001). Each of these strategies reduces the likelihood that stereotype threat will emerge. As a result, these conditions offer insight into how interventions might create environments that do not elicit stereotype threat.

Researchers have also examined specific strategies that can be implemented in situations that elicit stereotype threat. One of these strategies is self-affirmation. A self-affirmation task involves reflecting on important aspects of one's life or engaging in an activity that makes salient important values that are different from the threatening domain. Self-affirmation theory proposes that, when people experience a threat to their self-integrity, self-affirmations buffer against the (negative) self-evaluative implications (Aronson, Blanton, & Cooper, 1995; Aronson et al., 1999; Derks, van Laar, & Ellemers, 2009; Sherman & Cohen, 2006; Steele, 1998). Given that stereotype threats tend to challenge self-integrity, self-affirmation is a natural fit as a stereotype threat intervention. In a lab-based study, Martens, Johns, Greenberg, and Schimel (2006) found support for self-affirmation as a way in which to reduce stereotype threat: Stereotype threatened women who affirmed a valued attribute (different from math) performed at levels similar to women in the no-threat condition. In the field, Geoffrey Cohen and his colleagues went into the seventh-grade classrooms of a school that consisted mostly of middle- to lower-middle-class families divided almost evenly between Black and White students. The researchers anticipated stereotype threat might be suppressing the performance of the Black students and that a self-affirmation task might help to buffer against stereotype threat-driven performance decrements. Thus, Cohen, Garcia, Apfel, and Master (2006) randomly assigned children to a self-affirmation condition (writing for

15 minutes about their most important value, selected from a list of values) or a control condition (writing about their least important value). The effects of this simple exercise were surprisingly powerful. Black students in the self-affirmation condition earned significantly higher grades at the end of the term compared with Black students in the control condition, reducing the racial achievement gap by about 40%. A follow-up study two years later with these same children revealed that the affirmation led to an increase of 0.24 points in Black students' grade point average. The lowest performers appeared to benefit the most from the self-affirmations; they had higher grade point average increases and lower rates of grade repetition (Cohen, Garcia, Purdie-Vaughns, Apfel, & Brzustoski, 2009).

Another class of interventions that has received support for reducing the negative effects of stereotype threat is the framing of intelligence as malleable. Carol Dweck (e.g., 1999) has found that people differ in their views regarding the nature of intelligence; some (entity theorists) see their intelligence as fixed, whereas others (incremental theorists) see it as more malleable. Because stereotypes about group differences imply that intelligence is a fixed entity, an intervention that can move students to see intelligence as malleable is another natural fit for reducing the influence of stereotype threat. That is, if one believes one can become smarter, an allegation of lacking intelligence should be less upsetting than if one sees oneself as being as smart as one will ever be. In one study, Aronson, Fried, and Good (2002) increased Black college students' perceptions of the malleability of intelligence by having them act as ostensible pen pals to younger kids. In their role as a pen pals, one group of students wrote letters offering the younger kids encouragement and emphasizing that intelligence is like a muscle, that it is expandable with mental work. Two other groups of students were in control conditions. One control group wrote to pen pals about different types of intelligence and the other group did not have any pen pals. The results of this study revealed that Black students encouraged to view (and write about) intelligence as malleable reported greater enjoyment of the academic process and greater academic engagement, and obtained higher grade point averages than the students in both of the control conditions.

Good, Aronson, and Inzlicht (2003) also examined the utility of teaching about incremental theories of intelligence as a strategy to reduce gender gaps in math performance. In this study, junior high-school students in a largely low-income area took a standardized math test. However, before they began, students were randomly assigned to learn about the expandable nature of intelligence (incremental theories of intelligence condition) or about the perils of drug use (control condition). Although males outperformed females in the control condition, female and male performance did not differ when students learned about incremental theories of intelligence. Blackwell, Trzesniewski, and Dweck (2007) replicated this intervention and found similar results.

A third category of interventions that has received empirical support is teaching about stereotype threat or warning students about the stereotype-driven anxiety they might experience. This research suggests that forewarning students about stereotype threat is important because it allows participants to attribute their anxiety to something other than an indication of poor ability. In the lab, Johns, Schmader, and Martens (2005) had female students complete a GRE-like math test under conditions typical of stereotype threat research, describing the test as either a problem-solving exercise (no-threat condition) or a standardized test assessing gender differences in mathematics performance (stereotype threat condition). However, an additional group of participants received the stereotype threat instructions along with information that they may feel anxious while taking the test—a natural result of stereotypes and nothing to do with their actual ability to perform well on the test. Although males outperformed females in the typical stereotype threat condition, there were no gender differences in the no-threat condition or in the stereotype threat condition in which participants received the additional information about the role of stereotypes in creating anxiety.

McGlone and Aronson (2007) extended this research by considering aspects of forewarning that can backfire, or exacerbate, rather than alleviate the threat. Specifically, forewarning combats a persuasive message by increasing thoughts about negative stereotypes and allowing for the development of counter-arguments to this message. However, this process of becoming distracted by the stereotypes is the way in which stereotype threat serves to undermine performance. Thus, McGlone and Aronson explored the efficacy of providing information about stereotype threat coupled with thought suppression instructions or with a reminder of an identity that is positively stereotyped, such as participants' identity as students at an elite, private, liberal arts university. In this study, participants took a math test that was described as a standardized test. In one condition participants received no additional information (stereotype threat condition). The remaining participants received the testing information and a description of the stereotype threat phenomena. In addition, half of these participants were told they should suppress any thoughts about stereotypes (stereotype threat + suppression condition) and the other half were told they were less vulnerable to stereotype threat because they were students at an elite private college (stereotype threat + positive identity). Female participants who received no additional information (stereotype threat condition) or who were told to suppress stereotype-relevant thoughts (stereotype threat + suppression condition) performed worse in the math test compared to male participants. However, female participants' performance did not differ from males when they were told they were unlikely to be at risk for stereotype threat because they were students at an elite college (stereotype threat + positive identity).

In another set of studies, Johns, Inzlicht, and Schmader (2008) similarly assessed the role of emotion suppression and reappraisal of anxiety. These researchers found that learning about stereotype threat was effective if participants were able to think objectively about the test and reappraise their anxiety as a normal reaction that could, in some circumstances, help their performance. In contrast, learning about stereotype threat was not helpful if participants tried to suppress the thoughts and feelings that arise in stereotype-threatening situations: Suppression led to poorer performance in stereotype threat conditions. In a study conducted in the field, Good et al. (2003) had junior highschool students take a math test in which they were given an attributional outlet for their anxiety—they were taught that most students experience difficulty early in junior high but then go on to succeed—or an anti-drug intervention (control). Consistent with lab research, girls in the attribution condition performed better in their statewide end-of-year math test than those in the control condition.

In addition to the interventions reviewed above, other strategies have been shown to reduce stereotype threat effectively. Some successful intervention techniques have focused on role models (e.g., Marx & Roman, 2002) or similarities between ingroup and outgoup members in the threatened domain (e.g., Rosenthal, Crisp, & Suen, 2007). In contrast, some successful techniques have focused on the individual—for example, by having stereotype-threatened participants think of themselves in terms of their valued and unique characteristics (Ambady, Paik, Steele, Owen-Smith, & Mitchell, 2004) or, as briefly mentioned above, in terms of other (non-stereotyped or positively stereotyped) identities (e.g., identity as a student; McGlone & Aronson, 2006; Rydell, McConnell, & Beilock, 2009).

Thus, although 15 years of research has repeatedly revealed the deleterious consequences that stereotype threat can have on negatively stereotyped groups, more recent intervention research provides an optimistic outlook—that future research may be able to identify strategies that serve to protect against this pernicious phenomenon. Furthermore, most of these interventions involve simple techniques (e.g., teaching about stereotype threat, writing about an important value for 15 minutes) that can be implemented with little to no cost in almost any academic or organizational environment. The studies that have taken these mostly lab-tested strategies into the field show promising results.

FUTURE DIRECTIONS FOR STEREOTYPE THREAT RESEARCH

Stereotype threat provides a compelling account of how negative stereotypes can undermine performance—regardless of whether someone has contended chronically with these negative stereotypes or recently learned of their relevance to an important task. There are several unanswered questions future research could help resolve. First, a better understanding of the nature of the multiple forms of stereotype threats will be important to appreciate fully the stereotype threat phenomenon. Although the structure of the different stereotype threats is outlined in the literature (Shapiro & Neuberg, 2007), there is no research explicitly testing the different forms they can take, the different variables that are necessary to produce such threats, the different factors that serve to moderate these effects, and the like. Answering these questions will be of paramount significance to understanding who is at risk for stereotype threat and when.

Second, only in recent years has research begun to provide evidence of the mechanisms serving to create stereotype threat effects (e.g., working memory, self-regulation). We anticipate future research will continue to explore these mechanisms and how they work individually or in tandem to undermine performance. Understanding these mechanisms will be critical to our ability to intervene successfully. We also anticipate that, with the advent of more sophisticated technologies, more research will use social neuroscience to understand stereotype threat (e.g., Derks, Inzlicht, & Kang, 2008; Forbes, Schmader, & Allen, 2008). In one of the few studies using functional magnetic resonance imaging to assess the effects of stereotype threats, Krendl, Richeson, Kelley, and Heatherton (2008) found that, in non-threatening situations, women showed heightened activation in regions of the brain associated with mathematical learning. However, when reminded about stereotypes (stereotype threat condition), women did not recruit the same regions but showed activation in regions of the brain associated with social and emotional processing (see also Wraga, Helt, Jacobs, & Sullivan, 2007). This study demonstrates that social neuroscience approaches will nicely complement existing behavioral data, helping to piece together how stereotype threat infiltrates important mental processes.

Another direction for future research is the field. Stereotype threat is a phenomenon that was developed with a very specific problem in mind—a problem that emerges in schools, in the workplace, at home, and anywhere people engage in activities that are important to their everyday lives. Thus, future research will benefit immensely from more work that leaves the lab and explores the phenomenon in the field. Furthermore, the majority of stereotype threat research takes place with university-aged students as its participants. University students are an important subject group, but work targeting younger children will provide answers to both interesting theoretical and pragmatic questions. As reviewed earlier, developmental research suggests stereotype threat effects begin to emerge in middle school and early high school, when stereotypes and stereotyping become more salient. Understanding these processes will not only be interesting but may serve as an important and effective point for intervention. Furthermore, because students are likely to experience stereotype threat for a number of years before they arrive to a college setting, these experiences likely shape choices such as college attendance, selection of a major, and the like—all before the typical research participant steps into the traditional stereotype threat study. Thus, appreciating the developmental trajectory of stereotype threat will be an asset to understanding the phenomenon as a whole and will allow researchers to ask questions about its cumulative nature over time.

And, finally, more research on stereotype threat interventions will be essential. As we better understand stereotype threat, this knowledge will fuel stronger, theoretically driven interventions. Although there has been a surge in studies that show effective interventions, very few studies test the mechanisms that account for this success. Knowing why interventions alleviate stereotype threat will be important for comprehending the boundary conditions of these interventions and the extent to which they are generalizable to different stereotypes and/or situations. This is another domain in which field research accompanying lab research will be critical.

IN CONCLUSION

Since Steele and Aronson's initial empirical publication of stereotype threat in 1995, stereotype threat research has escalated. There have been hundreds of studies exploring this phenomenon in different groups contending with different stereotypes in vastly different domains. This research demonstrates the power of simple situational factors that make salient a negatively stereotyped identity. However, it also suggests that, as our understanding of this phenomenon becomes more complete, we should be able to harness the power of these simple situational factors and reduce the pernicious effects of stereotype threats. Indeed, we may be able to do better than this. Stereotype threat may in fact have positive effects. In 1991, Neil de Grasse Tyson received his doctoral degree in astrophysics from Columbia University. He was the seventh African-American astrophysicist out of 4,000 astrophysicists nationwide. Thus, despite his statement that negative expectations were a great burden, he succeeded brilliantly in his field. We believe that, far from emasculating de Grasse Tyson, stereotype threat may have been an important motivator for him, a spur to prove his doubters wrong. There is ample evidence that, when they are confronted by negative stereotypes, individuals get motivated to disprove the stereotype. Sometimes this motivation backfires, spoiling performance, as in many of the studies we have described. But sometimes stereotype threat can lift performance, such as when tasks are well learned, or when the student has adopted a mindset that puts learning before proving his or her intelligence to others. We believe that the most important future research will identify those factors, both psychological and structural, that can help transform debilitating threats into energizing motivators.

REFERENCES

Alter, A. L., Aronson, J., Darley, J. M., Rodriguez, C., & Ruble, D. N. (2010). Rising to the threat: Reducing stereotype threat by reframing the threat as a challenge. *Journal of Experimental Social Psychology, 46*, 166–171.

Ambady, N., Paik, S. K., Steele, J., Owen-Smith, A., & Mitchell, J. P. (2004). Deflecting negative self-relevant stereotype activation: The effects of individuation. *Journal of Experimental Social Psychology, 40*, 401–408.

Ambady, N., Shih, M., Kim, A., & Pittinsky, T. L. (2001). Stereotype susceptibility in children: Effects of identity activation on quantitative performance. *Psychological Science, 12*, 385–390.

Apfelbaum, E. P., Pauker, K., Ambady, N., Sommers, S. R., & Norton, M. I. (2008). Learning (not) to talk about race: When older children underperform in social categorization. *Developmental Psychology, 44*, 1513–1518.

Aronson, J., Blanton, H., & Cooper, J. (1995). From dissonance to disidentification: Selectivity in the self-affirmation process. *Journal of Personality and Social Psychology, 68*, 986–996.

Aronson, J., Fried, C. B., & Good, C. (2002). Reducing the effects of stereotype threat on African American college students by shaping theories of intelligence. *Journal of Experimental Social Psychology, 38*, 113–125.

Aronson, J., & Inzlicht, M. (2004). The ups and downs of attributional ambiguity: Stereotype vulnerability and the academic self-knowledge of African American college students. *Psychological Science, 15*, 829–836.

Aronson, J., Lustina, M. J., Good, C., Keough, K., Steele, C. M., & Brown, J. (1999). When White men can't do math: Necessary and sufficient factors in stereotype threat. *Journal of Experimental Social Psychology, 35*, 29–46.

Beilock, S. L., & DeCaro, M. S. (2007). From poor performance to success under stress: Working memory, strategy selection, and mathematical problem solving under pressure. *Journal of Experimental Psychology: Learning, Memory, and Cognition, 33*, 983–998.

Beilock, S. L., Rydell, R. J., & McConnell, A. R. (2007). Stereotype threat and working memory: Mechanisms, alleviation, and spillover. *Journal of Experimental Psychology: General, 136*, 256–276.

Ben-Zeev, T., Fein, S., & Inzlicht, M. (2005). Arousal and stereotype threat. *Journal of Experimental Social Psychology, 41*, 174–181.

Blackwell, L., Trzesniewski, K., & Dweck, C. S. (2007). Implicit theories of intelligence predict achievement across an adolescent transition: A longitudinal study and an intervention. *Child Development, 78*, 246–263.

Blascovich, J., Spencer, S. J., Quinn, D., & Steele, C. (2001). African Americans and high blood pressure: The role of stereotype threat. *Psychological Science, 12*, 225–229.

Bosson, J. K., Haymovitz, E. L., & Pinel, E. C. (2004). When saying and doing diverge: The effects of stereotype threat on self-reported versus non-verbal anxiety. *Journal of Experimental Social Psychology, 40*, 247–255.

Bosson, J. K., Prewitt-Freilino, J. L., & Taylor, J. N. (2005). Role rigidity: A problem of identity misclassification? *Journal of Personality and Social Psychology, 89*, 552–565.

Brown, R. P., & Josephs, R. A. (1999). A burden of proof: Stereotype relevance and gender differences in math performance. *Journal of Personality and Social Psychology, 76*, 246–257.

Cadinu, M., Maass, A., Rosabianca, A., & Kiesner, J. (2005). Why do women underperform under stereotype threat? Evidence for the role of negative thinking. *Psychological Science, 16*, 572–578.

Cohen, G. L., Garcia, J., Apfel, N., & Master, A. (2006). Reducing the racial achievement gap: A social-psychological intervention. *Science, 313*, 1307–1310.

Cohen, G. L., Garcia, J., Purdie-Vaughns, V., Apfel, N., & Brzustoski, P. (2009). Recursive processes in self-affirmation: Intervening to close the minority achievement gap. *Science, 324*, 400–403.

Danaher, K., & Crandall, C. S. (2008). Stereotype threat in applied settings re-examined. *Journal of Applied Social Psychology, 38*, 1639–1655.

Davies, P. G., Spencer, S. J., Quinn, D. M., & Gerhardstein, R. (2002). Consuming images: How television commercials that elicit stereotype threat can restrain women academically and professionally. *Personality and Social Psychology Bulletin, 28*, 1615–1628.

Davies, P. G., Spencer, S. J., & Steele, C. M. (2005). Clearing the air: Identity safety moderates the effects of stereotype threat on women's leadership aspirations. *Journal of Personality and Social Psychology, 88,* 276–287.

Deaux, K., Bikmen, N., Gilkes, A., Ventuneac, A., Joseph, Y., Payne, Y. A., et al. (2007). Becoming American: Stereotype threat effects in Afro-Caribbean immigrant groups. *Social Psychology Quarterly, 70,* 384–404.

Derks, B., Inzlicht, M., & Kang, S. (2008). The neuroscience of stigma and stereotype threat. *Group Processes & Intergroup Relations, 11,* 163–181.

Derks, B., van Laar, C., & Ellemers, N. (2009). Working for the self or working for the group: How self-versus group affirmation affects collective behavior in low-status groups. *Journal of Personality and Social Psychology, 96,* 183–202.

Dweck, C. S. (1999). *Self-theories: Their role in motivation, personality and development.* Philadelphia: Taylor & Francis/Psychology Press.

Forbes, C. E., Schmader, T., & Allen, J. J. B. (2008). The role of devaluing and discounting in performance monitoring: A neurophysiological study of minorities under threat. *Social Cognitive and Affective Neuroscience, 3,* 253–261.

Frantz, C. M., Cuddy, A. J. C., Burnett, M., Ray, H., & Hart, A. (2004). A threat in the computer: The race implicit association test as a stereotype threat experience. *Personality and Social Psychology Bulletin, 30,* 1611–1624.

Goff, P. A., Steele, C. M., & Davies, P. G. (2008). The space between us: Stereotype threat and distance in interracial contexts. *Journal of Personality and Social Psychology, 94,* 91–107.

Good, C., Aronson, J., & Harder, J. A. (2008). Problems in the pipeline: Stereotype threat and women's achievement in high-level math courses. *Journal of Applied Developmental Psychology, 29,* 17–28.

Good, C., Aronson, J., & Inzlicht, M. (2003). Improving adolescents' standardized test performance: An intervention to reduce the effects of stereotype threat. *Journal of Applied Developmental Psychology, 24,* 645–662.

Huguet, P., & Regner, I. (2007). Stereotype threat among schoolgirls in quasi-ordinary classroom circumstances. *Journal of Educational Psychology, 99,* 545–560.

Huguet, P., & Regner, I. (2009). Counter-stereotypic beliefs in math do not protect schoolgirls from stereotype threat. *Journal of Experimental Social Psychology, 45,* 1024–1027.

Hyde, J. S., Fennema, E., & Lamon, S. J. (1990). Gender differences in mathematics performance: A meta-analysis. *Psychological Bulletin, 107,* 139–155.

Inzlicht, M., & Ben-Zeev, T. (2000). A threatening intellectual environment: Why females are susceptible to experiencing problem-solving deficits in the presence of males. *Psychological Science, 11,* 365–371.

Inzlicht, M. & Kang, S. K. (in press). Stereotype threat spillover: How coping with threats to social identity affects aggression, eating, decision-making, and attention. *Journal of Personality and Social Psychology.*

Inzlicht, M., McKay, L., & Aronson, J. (2006). Stigma as ego depletion: How being the target of prejudice affects self-control. *Psychological Science, 17,* 262–269.

Jamieson, J. P., & Harkins, S. G. (2007). Mere effort and stereotype threat performance effects. *Journal of Personality and Social Psychology, 93,* 544–564.

Jamieson, J. P., & Harkins, S. G. (2009). The effect of stereotype threat on the solving of quantitative GRE problems: A mere effort interpretation. *Personality and Social Psychology Bulletin, 35,* 1301–1314.

Johns, M., Inzlicht, M., & Schmader, T. (2008). Stereotype threat and executive resource depletion: Examining the influence of emotion regulation. *Journal of Experimental Psychology: General, 137,* 691–705.

Johns, M., Schmader, T., & Martens, A. (2005). Knowing is half the battle: Teaching stereotype threat as a means of improving women's math performance. *Psychological Science, 16,* 175–179.

Keller, J. (2002). Blatant stereotype threat and women's math performance: Self-handicapping as a strategic means to cope with obtrusive negative performance expectations. *Sex Roles, 47,* 193–198.

Keller, J., & Dauenheimer, D. (2003). Stereotype threat in the classroom: Dejection mediates the disrupting threat effect on women's math performance. *Personality and Social Psychology Bulletin, 29,* 371–381.

Krendl, A. C., Richeson, J. A., Kelley, W. M., & Heatherton, T. F. (2008). The negative consequences of threat: A functional magnetic resonance imaging investigation of the neural mechanisms underlying women's underperformance in math. *Psychological Science, 19,* 168–175.

Levy, B. (1996). Improving memory in old age through implicit self-stereotyping. *Journal of Personality and Social Psychology, 71,* 1092–1107.

Lippa, R. A., Collar, M. L., & Peters, M. (2010). Sex differences in mental rotation and line angle judgments are positively associated with gender equality and economic development across 53 nations. *Archives of Sexual Behavior, 39,* 990–997.

Logel, C., Walton, G. M., Spencer, S. J., Iserman, E. C., von Hippel, W., & Bell, A. E. (2009). Interacting with sexist men triggers social identity threat among female engineers. *Journal of Personality and Social Psychology, 96,* 1089–1103.

Maass, A., D'Ettole, C., & Cadinu, M. (2008). Checkmate? The role of gender stereotypes in the ultimate intellectual sport. *European Journal of Social Psychology, 38,* 231–245.

Martens, A., Johns, M., Greenberg, J., & Schimel, J. (2006). Combating stereotype threat: The effect of self-affirmation on women's intellectual performance. *Journal of Experimental Social Psychology, 42,* 236–243.

Marx, D. M., & Roman, J. S. (2002). Female role models: Protecting women's math test performance. *Personality and Social Psychology Bulletin, 28,* 1183–1193.

McGlone, M. S., & Aronson, J. (2006). Stereotype threat, identity salience, and spatial reasoning. *Journal of Applied Developmental Psychology, 27,* 486–493.

McGlone, M. S., & Aronson, J. (2007). Forewarning and forearming stereotype-threatened students. *Communication Education, 56,* 119–133.

McGlone, M. S., Aronson, J., & Kobrynowicz, D. (2006). Stereotype threat and the gender gap in political knowledge. *Psychology of Women Quarterly, 30,* 392–398.

Muzzatti, B., & Agnoli, F. (2007). Gender and mathematics: Attitudes and stereotype threat susceptibility in Italian children. *Developmental Psychology, 43,* 747–759.

Neuville, E., & Croizet, J. C. (2007). Can salience of gender identity impair math performance among 7–8 years old girls? The moderating role of task difficulty. *European Journal of Psychology of Education, 22,* 307–316.

Nguyen, H. H. D., & Ryan, A. M. (2008). Does stereotype threat affect test performance of minorities and women? A meta-analysis of experimental evidence. *Journal of Applied Psychology, 93,* 1314–1334.

Quinn, D. M., Kahng, S. K., & Crocker, J. (2004). Discreditable: Stigma effects of revealing a mental illness history on test performance. *Personality and Social Psychology Bulletin, 30,* 803–815.

Quinn, D. M., & Spencer, S. J. (2001). The interference of stereotype threat with women's generation of mathematical problem-solving strategies. *Journal of Social Issues, 57,* 55–71.

Rosenthal, H. E. S., Crisp, R. J., & Suen, M. (2007). Improving performance expectancies in stereotypic domains: Task relevance and the reduction of stereotype threat. *European Journal of Social Psychology, 37,* 586–597.

Ruble, D. N., & Martin, C. (1998). Gender development. In N. Eisenberg (Ed.), *Handbook of child psychology,* Vol. 3: *Personality and social development.* New York: John Wiley & Sons.

Rydell, R. J., McConnell, A. R., & Beilock, S. L. (2009). Multiple social identities and stereotype threat: Imbalance, accessibility, and working memory. *Journal of Personality and Social Psychology, 96,* 949–966.

Schmader, T., & Johns, M. (2003). Converging evidence that stereotype threat reduces working memory capacity. *Journal of Personality and Social Psychology, 85,* 440–452.

Schmader, T., Johns, M., & Forbes, C. (2008). An integrated process model of stereotype threat effects on performance. *Psychological Review, 115,* 336–356.

Sekaquaptewa, D., & Thompson, M. (2003). Solo status, stereotype threat, and performance expectancies: Their effects on women's performance. *Journal of Experimental Social Psychology, 39,* 68–74.

Shapiro, J. R. (2011). Different groups, different threats: A multi-threat approach to the experience of stereotype threats. *Personality and Social Psychology Bulletin, 37,* 464–480.

Shapiro, J. R., & Neuberg, S. L. (2007). From stereotype threat to stereotype threats: Implications of a multi-threat framework for causes, moderators, mediators, consequences, and interventions. *Personality and Social Psychology Review, 11,* 107–130.

Shapiro, J. R., Williams, A. M., & Hambarchyan, M. (in press). Are all interventions created equal? A multi-threat approach to tailoring stereotype threat interventions. *Journal of Personality and Social Psychology.*

Sherman, D. K., & Cohen, G. L. (2006). The psychology of self-defense: Self-affirmation theory. *Advances in Experimental Social Psychology, 38,* 183–242.

Shih, M., Pittinsky, T. L., & Ambady, N. (1999). Stereotype susceptibility: Identity salience and shifts in quantitative performance. *Psychological Science, 10,* 80–83.

Spencer, S. J., Steele, C. M., & Quinn, D. M. (1999). Stereotype threat and women's math performance. *Journal of Experimental Social Psychology, 35,* 4–28.

Stangor, C., Carr, C., & Kiang, L. (1998). Activating stereotypes undermines task performance expectations. *Journal of Personality and Social Psychology, 75,* 1191–1197.

Steele, C. M. (1997). A threat in the air: How stereotypes shape intellectual identity and performance. *American Psychologist, 52,* 613–629.

Steele, C. M. (1998). Stereotyping and its threat are real. *American Psychologist, 53,* 680–681.

Steele, C. M., & Aronson, J. (1995). Stereotype threat and the intellectual test-performance of African-Americans. *Journal of Personality and Social Psychology, 69,* 797–811.

Steele, C. M., Spencer, S. J., & Aronson, J. (2002). Contending with group image: The psychology of stereotype and social identity threat. *Advances in Experimental Social Psychology, 34,* 379–440.

Stone, J. (2002). Battling doubt by avoiding practice: The effects of stereotype threat on self-handicapping in White athletes. *Personality and Social Psychology Bulletin, 28,* 1667–1678.

Stone, J., Lynch, C. I., Sjomeling, M., & Darley, J. M. (1999). Stereotype threat effects on Black and White athletic performance. *Journal of Personality and Social Psychology, 77,* 1213–1227.

Stricker, L. J., & Ward, W. C. (2004). Stereotype threat, inquiring about test takers' ethnicity and gender, and standardized test performance. *Journal of Applied Social Psychology, 34,* 665–693.

Trbovich, P. L., & LeFevre, J. (2003). Phonological and visual working memory in mental addition. *Memory & Cognition, 31,* 738–745.

Walton, G. M., & Cohen, G. L. (2003). Stereotype lift. *Journal of Experimental Social Psychology, 39,* 456–467.

Walton, G. M., & Spencer, S. J. (2009). Latent ability: Grades and test scores systematically underestimate the intellectual ability of negatively stereotyped students. *Psychological Science, 20,* 1132–1139.

Wraga, M., Helt, M., Jacobs, E., & Sullivan, K. (2007). Neural basis of stereotype-induced shifts in women's mental rotation performance. *Social Cognitive and Affective Neuroscience, 2,* 12–19.

6

Cultural Dynamics of Intergroup Relations

How Communications Can Shape Intergroup Reality

YOSHIHISA KASHIMA
University of Melbourne

Consider the following facts.

- Lehman Brothers, one of the most respected financial companies, files for bankruptcy, sending the world economy into a tailspin.
- The UN Copenhagen Climate Change Conference fails to produce decisive action, resulting in a blame game of the developing and the developed countries.
- Worsening financial conditions in some European countries threaten the stability of the European Union.
- The People's Republic of China continues an expansion of its military capability by committing a large portion of its GDP to armed forces.
- Reports continue to come in about the Syrian government's violent crackdown on its own citizens' protests.
- The 2012 election in Russia sees the incumbent, Vladimir Putin, declare his winning presidency amid the accusation of electoral anomalies.

Geographically and psychologically remote as they may be, these global events are inexorably implicated in our everyday life. Not only career diplomats and foreign affairs experts but ordinary citizens are now asked to make decisions about policies with potentially far-reaching global implications. For instance, the U.S. president, Barack Obama, continues to have a dialogue with his Israeli counterpart, Benjamin Netanyahu, about Israel's potential military action against Iran's nuclear facilities. What do you think of this development, even though many of you are unlikely to have direct experience about Iran? This is not a question relevant only to Israelis and Iranians. It is a question critically relevant for the global community.

Globalization has highlighted the social reality that researchers of stereotypes and prejudice must contend with. Arguably the recent research in stereotypes and prejudice has largely presumed firsthand experience—stereotypers are in direct interaction with the targets of the stereotype. It is generally true about the intergroup relations within the United States. In the globalized world, however, equally important intergroup processes unfold through public and private discourse. Whether they be political, economic, environmental, legal, or moral, many a contemporary social issue requires us to deliberate and decide on a course of action based not necessarily on our firsthand experience but on our knowledge about the world, which we acquire mostly secondhand through the mass media, the Internet, and word of mouth. In other words, the question is about how stereotypes conveyed in communication (i.e., cultural information about social groups) shape intergroup relations. It is there that the current social psychology is wanting; there lies a frontier of research in stereotypes and prejudice.

This chapter presents a coherent theoretical perspective on how to conceptualize stereotype dynamics when the impact of socially communicated stereotypes is taken seriously. I call such socially communicated information "cultural information," and I first give a brief description of what stereotypes as cultural information looks like. Starting with a definition of a stereotype and its implications, I make a case for the importance of grounding (Clark, 1996)—collaborative interpersonal communication—as a critical mechanism for cultural dynamics of intergroup relations, then summarize and elaborate on the grounding model of cultural information transmission (Kashima, Klein, & Clark, 2007). In particular, I argue that *the grounding of cultural information about a social group has profound implications for the social construction of intergroup relations*. Put succinctly, it is the cultural dynamics of intergroup relations—stability and change of culture about intergroup relations over time—with which this chapter is concerned.

WHAT IS A STEREOTYPE?

The stereotype concept has been defined in a number of ways (e.g., Stangor & Lange, 1994), and researchers typically adopt a definition in accordance with their theoretical perspective. A stereotype here is defined simply as *information about a social group used by human minds*. Although stereotypes are often measured in terms of the extent to which people attribute to social groups characteristics that are akin to personality traits (e.g., Katz & Braly, 1933), we take a view that information about a social group has much broader meaning. First, information about a social group often includes information about its members as well (e.g., Smith & Zarate, 1992; Kashima, Woolcock, & Kashima, 2000). People can construct the distribution of group members on some dimension, while estimating its central tendency (e.g., mean, mode, etc.), dispersion around the central tendency (e.g., standard deviation, range), and the like (e.g., Judd & Park, 1993). This implies that a standard of comparison for an individual relative to the distribution is also included (e.g., Biernat & Manis, 1996).

Second, information about a social group, at least tacitly, presupposes another group in contrast to which the target group is construed (*contrast group*) within a broader collective that contains both. This broader collective serves as a *frame of reference* (Turner, 1987). For instance, when information about women is considered, it often implies the typical contrast category, men, and also the broader frame of reference in which both women and men are considered—namely, humans. In other words, a stereotype about a group often contains information about *intergroup relations* between the target and contrast groups. Indeed, research by Fiske, Cuddy, and Glick (2007; Fiske, Cuddy, Glick, & Xu, 2002) implies that stereotype contents of warmth and competence about a group are closely associated with the intergroup relations of conflict and status between the target and the contrast group. Kashima et al.'s (2009) research on a folk theory of social change also suggests that a stereotype can contain a temporal dimension, in which a country is seen to develop over time from a warm, but less competent traditional community to a less warm, but more competent modern society. In this case, the current society is tacitly contrasted with its past or future.

A stereotype is therefore a collection of information about a social group, its members, and its relations with other contrast groups. Apart from the possibility that some aspects of stereotyping (i.e., use of a stereotype) and prejudice have genetic bases (e.g., Hirschfeld, 1996), humans can acquire a stereotype through firsthand direct experience with or secondhand hearsay about the target group. The information which is acquired from other people is *cultural* information—any information that is socially transmitted from one person to another. It is distinguished from genetic information transmitted by biological means. Cultural information can be declarative (i.e., ideas or what something is) or procedural (i.e., practices or how something is done) and therefore can inform both thought contents and processes; it can be transmitted in a variety of forms, through language and other symbols, icons, or other semiotic forms, with the proviso that it must take a form that can be registered by human sensory systems.

It is the processing of cultural information about a social group with which this chapter is concerned. In the section to follow, I will first provide a general discussion about the grounding model of cultural transmission—its main concepts and implications—and then examine more specifically the communication of stereotypes as an instance of the general process.

GROUNDING MODEL OF CULTURAL INFORMATION TRANSMISSION

Cultural information is transmitted from one person to another through *grounding* (Kashima et al., 2007; Clark, 1996). Grounding is a coordinated process by which two or more people establish a mutual understanding within a social interaction. To give a general sense of what grounding is, imagine two or more people who are about to interact with each other. They typically do so for some purpose. For instance, you might need to get directions for a shop in an unfamiliar city. In order to achieve this goal, you approach a man and ask for directions. He may tell you to look at that Asian guy standing at the corner— "See that Asian guy? Tall for an Asian, you know"—and then proceed to tell you to turn left there and keep going for a couple of blocks. You need to come to a mutual understanding about who the Asian guy is, where he is, etc., in order for you to achieve the goal of getting to the shop. More generally, people engage in a variety of activities. One of the critical ingredients in all these is to understand each other as to what has been said and done. It is the interactants' coordinated actions to this end that constitute grounding, the process of establishing mutual understandings for the current purposes of the social interaction.

Somewhat more systematically, these social interactions can be thought of as *joint activities* in which the interactants are engaged. A joint activity is a type of action performed by multiple individuals. Typically, it is temporally bounded (it has a beginning and an end), spatially bounded (it takes place in a specific location), purposive (it has a joint goal and approximate processes by which the goal is attained), and role differentiated (it typically defines which role enacts which processes in what order and in coordination with which other roles). To achieve the goal of a joint activity, interactants perform a variety of behaviors using a variety of tools, including language (e.g., Holtgraves & Kashima, 2008). For many joint activities, the transmission of cultural information is *not* their primary goal (although it is for some—for instance, teacher–student interaction in classrooms, lectures at universities); it serves as a subgoal, which needs to be achieved only to the extent necessary for carrying out the primary goal of a joint activity. In other words, cultural information is often transmitted as a *side effect* or an *unintended consequence*.

Grounding involves coordinated actions by the sender of cultural information and its receiver, entailing the sender's *presentation* of the information and the receiver's *acceptance*, in which the receiver provides some evidence of his or her understanding. The latter can take verbal or nonverbal forms (likely to involve both), from a simple nod or an "OK", through a more extensive repetition or rephrasing of the information, to a much more elaborate explication, commentary, or critique. Note that presentation and acceptance are almost never a straightforward exchange of well-formed sentences. The sender often makes false starts, mistakes, and self-repairs; the receiver too often repairs the sender's or his or her own messages, or shows evidence of misunderstanding, which the sender corrects. Throughout, however, the critical process is that the interactants coordinate their linguistic and other types of behaviors so as to establish a mutual understanding of the cultural information for the current purpose of carrying out their joint activity.

There are several implications of the grounding model. First, the transmission of cultural information is almost never complete. The sender's representation of the information and the receiver's representation of it are bound to be different. Furthermore, the sender's initial understanding of given cultural information does not have to be the same as his or her final understanding of it. Through the process of grounding, the sender and the receiver could come to have a very different mutual understanding. In other words, grounding may involve an element of creativity. The upshot of this is that no cultural information is likely to be shared completely by the people involved. This results in *distributed cognition*. That is, a set of information is held not by each individual for its entirety but collectively distributed across multiple individuals.

Second, grounding processes simultaneously generate both a *collective identity* and a *collective representation*, because common ground that they construct contains information about what the mutual understandings are (collective representation) and who the interactants (or who "we") are that share the mutual understandings (collective identity). Depending on who this "we" is construed to be, the generated collective identity could be the particular group of interactants involved in the particular joint activity or a broader ingroup (social category) that includes the interactants. Common ground that is confined to those particular interactants is called *context-specific* common ground; common ground that is extended beyond that particular context of interaction and which includes a temporally continuous broader collective identity is called *generalized* common ground. Using a variety of semiotic tools, a context-specific common ground can be transfigured into a generalized common ground, which is spatially expansive, temporally extended, and socially broad (Kashima et al., 2007). This then may become a communal common ground of a large-scale social group.

The grounding model of cultural information transmission is located at the intersection of neo-diffusionist culture meta-theory (Kashima, 2008; Kashima, Peters, & Whelan, 2008) and socially situated cognition (Smith & Semin, 2004, 2007). On the one hand, neo-diffusionism is a meta-theoretical perspective that regards culture as a collection of socially transmitted information (i.e., cultural information) held in a population, and takes the view that its dynamics is critically determined by the diffusion of cultural information. The more often cultural information is transmitted, the more prevalent it becomes. The frequency of transmission of given cultural information, however, is likely to depend on its adaptiveness—it is more likely communicated if it is adaptive for some reason (see Kashima et al., 2008, for a more detailed discussion).

However, most neo-diffusionist theories take a relatively simple view of cultural transmission (cf. Sperber, 1996; see Kashima et al., 2008, on this point). The perspective of socially situated cognition complements this shortcoming by regarding cognitive processes as strongly embedded in social situations in which they take place. In particular, it regards cognition as an embodied, adaptive mechanism for action regulation, which emerges out of the dynamic interaction between the agent and the environment. It also regards cognition as distributed across brains and the environment and across social agents (Smith & Semin, 2004, 2007). The grounding model reflects a socially situated cognitive perspective in the domain of culture by treating cultural transmission as a profoundly social psychological process which is both dynamic and socially coordinated embodied interaction *in situ*.

All in all, the grounding model takes the view that cultural transmission does not happen in a social vacuum. Cultural information is typically transmitted not for its own sake but often as a side effect of engaging in a joint activity for the purpose of carrying out some other task. The insistence on this point makes the grounding model particularly compatible with the program of cultural psychology inspired by Vygotsky (e.g., Cole, 1996; Rogoff, 2003; Wertsch, 1991) and also G. H. Mead's (1934) symbolic interactionism.

Antecedents of Grounding

There are two main antecedents of grounding: *common ground* and *joint activity*. In this section, the general properties of these theoretical concepts are discussed, and more specific implications for stereotype communication are taken up later.

Joint Activity   A joint activity provides a context in which grounding and the evolution of common ground takes place. The goal of a joint activity can vary from mostly task goals, such as seeking advice at work or discussing a holiday plan at home, to relational goals, such as getting to know someone, mending a relationship after a quarrel, or deepening one's relationship from friendship to something more romantic (or perhaps ending one, as the case may be). Nonetheless, the main purpose of a joint activity—however the interactants understand it—plays a significant role in determining the type of cultural information likely to be grounded.

This point is well illustrated by one of the most consistent findings in the stereotype communication literature. When the task of a joint activity is to tell a story, participants focus on communicating about the central part of the story, where the plot unfolds, and avoid communicating its peripheral part, i.e., interesting, but irrelevant detail. In other words, what is communicated is central—more task-relevant—information rather than peripheral information (Clark & Kashima, 2007; Kashima, 2000; Lyons & Kashima, 2001, 2003, 2006). It is perhaps an obvious point, but it often seems overlooked, and its importance cannot be overstated.

Common Ground   *Common ground* is information that the interactants actually share and also presuppose that they share. This includes information available to the interactants directly from their surroundings and from their past interaction, if any (*personal common ground*—e.g., today's weather), and information available from their shared cultural background (*communal common ground*—e.g., language, commonsense). The latter is the type of information that people who belong to a certain social category (e.g., gender, ethnic, national, occupational) tend, and are presumed, to share. Interactants start with *initial common ground* when they begin their joint activity; they use the initial common ground as a semiotic resource to ground their new mutual understandings, which are further added to the common ground in the course of their joint activity; and they finish with *terminal common ground*. Thus, common ground is a dynamic configuration. It emerges and evolves as interactants engage in their joint activity, at the end of which some aspects of the terminal common ground are left in the interactants' memory systems.

When interactants meet for the first time, their common ground needs to be discovered and constructed to carry out their joint activity. That they do so is illustrated by the well-known finding of Stasser and his colleagues (Stasser & Titus, 1985, 1987; Stasser, Taylor, & Hanna, 1989) about conversational sharing of shared information in small groups. Generally in these studies, each interactant is given some information about target people; however, some information is shared among all interactants, but other information is known only by one interactant. Note that the interactants are not told about this distribution of information within the group, but they must discover who knows what in order to carry out their task of selecting the most suitable person for a job. Consistent findings from this research are that interactants tend to talk more about the information that they already share in common than the unshared information. Whereas this does not make for efficient information sharing, it is a necessary step from the perspective of the grounding model.

Common ground provides primary semiotic resources with which the interactants ground their mutual understandings. Wu and Keysar (2007) showed that those who share a greater common ground can ground information more efficiently. Indeed, Fast, Heath, and Wu (2009) found this to be the case even in the domain of professional baseball players. They showed that well-known baseball players (those in common ground) are more often talked about (grounded in the Internet) and became even more prominent (attracting more All-Star votes). Common ground enables grounding, which in turn further expands the common ground. Thus, common ground evolves with grounding (e.g., Clark & Wilkes-Gibbs, 1986; Krauss & Weinheimer, 1964, 1967).

Common ground sets the immediate enabling and constraining conditions for the grounding of new cultural information by determining (1) how *informative* given cultural information is and (2) how *fluently* (i.e., with how few social and psychological resources) it can be grounded. First, if given information is easy to infer from the current common ground, the interactants do not need to be told about it. It is when the information goes beyond what is mutually known that it is likely to inform. Second, if given information is difficult to infer from the mutual knowledge, the sender may need to explain it more. Especially if it is contrary to common ground (i.e., non-conventional), the sender is likely to need not only to explain it, but also to justify it in an argument. All this makes for less smooth interaction. All in all, the more easily given cultural information can be inferred from the current common ground, the less informative it is, and the more easily it can be grounded. There is an inherent *informativeness-groundability dilemma*; given a certain common ground, there is a likely trade-off between how informative one can be and how fluently one can interact.

How one resolves this dilemma can have a significant implication for the regulation of social relationships. If informative cultural information is grounded, the interactants can potentially benefit from greater mutual under-standing, which may help the interactants successfully carry out their joint activ-ities; however, there is a risk of prolonged and inefficient communication, misunderstanding, and awkwardness in the process of the social interaction because they may have to engage in an extended explanation, justification, or even argumentation. Furthermore, information that is closely aligned with common ground can be used to "claim common ground"—that is, to communi-cate and ground the common collective identity that the common ground implies (Brown & Levinson, 1987). Taken together, cultural information that is very distant from the interactants' common ground (i.e., non-conventional information) may be beneficial for the task goal but costly for their social rela-tionship and connectivity.

Grounding Stereotypes in Joint Activities

Stereotypes are often part of the common ground already. People believe that others in their general community not only share the stereotypes but also endorse them (Devine, 1989). This makes stereotypes a fertile ground for test-ing the implications of the grounding model. Much of the subsequent discus-sion revolves around the grounding of information that is consistent with a stereotype (stereotype-consistent, SC, information) and information that is inconsistent with it (stereotype-inconsistent, SI, information).

First and foremost, the grounding model predicts that the task goal of a joint activity would determine whether SC or SI information is likely to be grounded. In particular, the grounding model predicts that SC information is more likely discussed when interactants have consensus goals than when they do not. This is because SC information would be seen to be more useful for reaching a consensus than SI information, as SC information is perceived to be already shared and taken for granted (i.e., common ground). This prediction was borne out by research by Ruscher, Hammer, and Hammer (1996). They manipulated dyads to have a joint goal to reach a consensus or not, gave them information about a stimulus person that contained SC and SI information, and examined the amount of time the interactants spent on discussing it. Their find-ings were consistent with the prediction of the grounding model.

Whereas their 1996 study explicitly manipulated the task goal of consensus formation, Ruscher and Hammer's (1994) experiments arguably manipulated a tacit task goal to form a consensus in dyads (see Ruscher & Hammer, 2006, for this interpretation of their experiment). For instance, in their Experiment 2, they showed SC and SI information that described a stimulus person in two different conditions and observed the participants' dyadic discussions about the target. In the baseline condition, the target person's group membership (alcoholic) was presented first, followed by his SC and SI behavioral descriptions; the participants then discussed the target, but they were told that there was no need for them to form a consensus. This was followed by a second presentation of the target's SC and SI information and a second dyadic discussion. In the other condition, participants were first given the behavioral information without being told the target's group membership, followed by a first dyadic discussion. It was in the second set of stimulus presentation that the target's group membership was revealed, together with a different set of SC and SI information. Ruscher and Hammer called the latter condition "disrupted condition," where the interactants' impressions about the target were disrupted by the surprising group membership—he is an alcoholic! Although the participants were told there was no need to form a consensus in all conditions, they spent more time discussing SC information only after their impressions were disrupted. This seems to suggest that whatever impressions were grounded in the first discussion were disrupted by the surprising group membership information, which then generated a tacit goal to ground this disrupting information—i.e., tacit consensual goal. This joint goal appears to have increased the tendency for the interactants to discuss SC information.

In addition, the grounding model is consistent with existing research about how interactants form impressions about a new social group for which they have no prior common ground. As discussed earlier in relation to work by Stasser and his colleagues (e.g., Stasser & Titus, 1985), the grounding model suggests that interactants should first attempt to discover their common ground. In the domain of stereotype communication, Klein, Jacobs, Gemoets, Licata, and Lambert (2003) found evidence consistent with this prediction. Their design is rather complex but, for the purpose of exposition, a simplified conceptual description is given. Basically, they gave interactants some information about groups that was shared among them and other information that was unshared. Consistent with the grounding model, they found that the interactants discussed more shared information than unshared information, presumably with the purpose of discovering and constructing their common ground. In Experiment 2, however, they gave expectations about the groups, so that shared information was consistent or inconsistent with their shared expectations. They also included a condition in which no expectation was provided. Here, the interactants whose shared information was inconsistent with their shared expectations did not discuss shared information preferentially, although they tended to discuss shared information more than unshared information in the other conditions. This finding can be interpreted in line with the grounding model. It appears that, in the inconsistent condition, shared information was seen to be less likely to provide common ground, reducing the likelihood for the interactants to present it in their discussion.

In a related study, Brauer, Judd, and Jacquelin (2001) manipulated the actual sharedness of information. In their experiments, interactants were given the same amount of information about a new social group in two different conditions. In the shared condition, all the interactants shared similar information about the group, receiving information that implied certain characteristics (e.g., selfish, cowardly) more than their opposites. In the unshared condition, however, two interactants shared similar information about the group (i.e., more information that implied certain characteristics than their opposites), but one interactant did not share this (i.e., equal amount of information for the given characteristics and their opposites). When interactants actually have shared information, they should find it easier to discover their common ground and to discuss their shared information more; however, when interactants do not share information, this should hamper the discovery of common ground. Consistent with this prediction, the interactants spent more time discussing shared information in the shared condition than in the unshared condition. Intriguingly, the discussion in the shared condition made the shared impressions about the group more extreme, suggesting that they grounded their shared stereotypes about the group in their common ground.

Relational and Task Goals Relate to SC and SI Communication   The grounding model suggests that task and relational goals in joint activities should have significant implications for communication of stereotype-relevant information. This is because, *assuming that given stereotypes are in common ground* (taken for granted to be shared and endorsed), SC information is likely to be perceived to be less *informative*, but more socially *connective*, than information inconsistent with SI information (Clark & Kashima, 2007). This is a special case of the informativeness groundability dilemma discussed earlier. Consistent with this reasoning, Clark and Kashima found that people rated gender SI information as more informative (i.e., informative, relevant, surprising, and unexpected, requiring explanation and justification) but less connective (socially bonding, friendly, likable, entertaining) than gender SC information. Although their finding presents initial evidence, the veridicality of this general proposition needs to be tested with a wider range of stereotypes. It is quite possible that SC and SI information for some of the protected stereotypes (i.e., those stereotypes about which cultural norms dictate that people should refrain from speaking negatively) is not seen to perform social connective functions.

The grounding model predicts that, when the joint activity presumes a goal to form or strengthen social relationships, connective SC information is more likely communicated than when it does not. There are at least two lines of work that support this prediction. First, Ruscher, Cralley, and O'Farrell (2005) showed this to be the case in dyadic face-to-face communication. They manipulated a same-sex dyad's motivation to strengthen their relationship by getting them to share their answers to some personal questions (vs. writing them without sharing them). In the condition where answers were shared (i.e., stronger motivation to form a good relationship), dyads reported greater attractions to each other and spent more time discussing SC information and less time discussing SI information than in the control condition.

Ruscher, Santuzzi, and Hammer's (2003) findings are also in line with this reasoning. The researchers examined existing dyads' impressions about a stimulus person after their face-to-face discussion. They also measured the closeness of the pairs: some were very close to each other with longstanding relationships, whereas others were relatively recent acquaintances. They found that those with longstanding relationships tended to develop more complex impressions of the target person, which presumably incorporated both SC and SI information, than those without such strong relationships. This suggests that dyads that do not have a need to strengthen their relationships may have been more likely to ground SI information than those who did. Presumably, dyads with strong relational ties did not need to strengthen their relationships further, and therefore they were able to afford to engage in the more socially costly communication of SI information.

A second line of support comes from *serial reproduction* experiments in which a stimulus is transmitted from one person to another, who in turn transmits it to a third person, and so on, in a communication chain. It is like the party game of Chinese whispers (Allport & Postman, 1947; Bartlett, 1932). This experimental paradigm simulates people who are engaged in public activities, where they tell a story to someone who is not personally well known to them but who is in the same general community (e.g., university). Using this experimental paradigm, Kashima and his colleagues (Kashima, 2000; Kashima & Kostopoulos, 2004; Lyons & Kashima, 2001, 2003, 2006) showed that SC information is more likely to persist than SI information (cf. Goodman, Webb, & Stewart, 2009).

In typical experiments, Kashima and his colleagues constructed a story in which a protagonist engaged in both SC and SI behavior, gave it to the first person in a serial reproduction chain, had their participants retell the story to another participant in writing, and observed what type of information was retained in the story as it was passed on from the first to the last person. In these studies, the participants were students at a university and expected fellow students to be receiving their story. There was little difference in the reproduction of SC and SI information initially (in fact, in Kashima, 2000, SI information was more likely to be reproduced than SC information in the first two positions), but SC information was more likely to be retained than SI information in later reproductions. A story became more stereotypical as it was transmitted in communication chains (see Figure 6.1). Clark and Kashima (2007) showed that this stereotype consistency bias in serial reproductions was likely due to the social connective nature of SC information. They found that SC information was seen to be more socially connective than SI information and that social connectivity of information predicted the perceived communicability (ease of communication), which in turn predicted the actual communication (i.e., how many steps in the communication chain the information was transmitted).

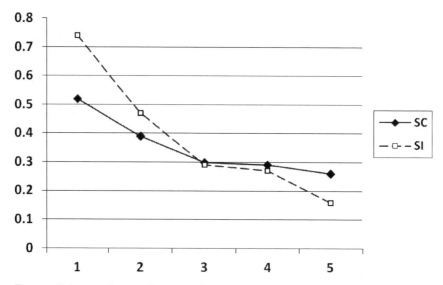

Figure 6.1   Serial reproduction of stereotype-consistent (SC) and stereotype-inconsistent (SI) information. Based on story reproduction data in Kashima (2000).

Furthermore, Clark and Kashima (2007) found that this SC bias in serial reproduction seems explicable at least in part by the social connective implication of SC information. SC information can be socially connective because stereotypes are seen to be in people's common ground. Indeed, they found that social connectivity of information predicted the number of steps in serial reproductions it was passed on: the more connective it is, the more likely it survived in the communication chain and was passed on to people later in the chain.

Nevertheless, if there is a good reason to suspect that the stereotypes may not be taken for granted, and may not be endorsed as part of their common ground, SC information may not be seen to be so socially connective (because there is a chance that someone may object to it), and that this may make it less likely for people to communicate SC information. This implication of the grounding model was borne out by the findings of Lyons and Kashima (2003) and Clark and Kashima (2007). These researchers manipulated the perceived endorsement of stereotypes (artificially created stereotypes in the case of the former and existing stereotypes in the latter) in the participants' general community, and observed whether this affected the tendency to communicate SC information. When the participants were led to believe their general community might not endorse the stereotypes, the communication of SC information was reduced more than when they were led to believe the community endorsed them. Thus, a reduction in connectivity of SC information resulted in a lesser amount of SC communication.

However, it is important to recognize that the grounding model suggests that SI information may be communicated more than SC information if the task goal of the joint activity makes SI information more task relevant. Ruscher and Duval's (1998) findings seem to be in line with this reasoning. They had same-sex dyads who were previously acquainted communicate to their mutual acquaintance their impressions about a target person who exhibited both SC and SI behaviors. In one condition, dyads had (and knew they had) the same information, whereas in the other condition they had (and knew they had) different information. Dyads who had different information spoke about SI information more than dyads who had the same information. This is because the dyads who had different information were more motivated to communicate accurate information than those who had the same information. Apparently, the shared goal of communicating accurate information made SI information more task relevant; consequently, the participants communicated more SI information.

Goodman et al.'s (2009) recent findings, where SI information was more likely passed on in serial reproductions, may be interpreted in terms of the task relevance of SI information. They conducted serial reproduction experiments using a newspaper article whose main point was to inform the public that (1) a scientific study has found that some heroin users can have as productive lives as non-users, and that (2) a drug addiction group has condemned the finding. They found that people tended to retain more SI information (e.g., a new study found that heroin can be taken without damaging health) than SC information (e.g., heroin is not a safe drug). It is obvious that the main point of the article is the counter-stereotypical scientific finding that heroin may not be harmful. Given the obvious importance in the task of communicating this SI information, the participants communicated it more than SC information. It is worth noting that the communication of SI information was not influenced by whether participants believed the newspaper article to be fake or genuine, suggesting that its informative value was not the reason for the greater communication of SI information.

Finally, the grounding model predicts that the extent to which SI information is seen to be informative should affect its transmission. In particular, the sender's perception of the receiver's knowledge state should be a significant factor. Note that SI information is informative only when the relevant stereotypes are already part of the sender and receiver's common ground, and therefore seen to be known to the receiver. If the receiver is *completely ignorant* about the stereotypes (i.e., they are not part of personal common ground), which are otherwise part of the sender's communal common ground, SI information is perhaps seen as not particularly informative. In contrast, if the receiver is known to have *complete knowledge* about the stereotypes, the sender is likely to regard SI information as particularly informative. In other words, when senders regard the receivers to be knowledgeable about stereotypes, they are more likely to communicate SI information than when they regard the receivers to be ignorant about the stereotypes. Lyons and Kashima (2003) found supportive evidence for this hypothesis.

Using an existing stereotype of engineers, Klein, Demoulin, Licata, and Lambert (2004) reported a finding consistent with this reasoning. They manipulated the sender's perception of the receiver's knowledge state by telling the sender that the receiver did or did not know a target person's group membership. When the receiver knows about the target's group membership relative to when the receiver does not know about it, SI information should be seen to be more informative, and therefore the sender should communicate it more. Indeed, this is what was found.

All in all, the existing literature on stereotype communication is consistent with the grounding model of cultural information transmission in the intergroup arena. Generally, the joint activity in which communication takes place—especially its goal—and whether stereotypes constitute an aspect of common ground are critical factors that influence the communication of SC or SI information. Provided that a stereotype is part of the interactants' communal common ground, the task goal of forming a consensus and the relational goal of strengthening interpersonal relationships (or at least not jeopardizing them) can both increase the likelihood of communicating SC information, because it is more likely to be seen to help them reach a consensus and to enhance social connectivity. However, a particular receiver's knowledge state—whether the stereotype is in their personal common ground—can affect the communication of SI information. If the receiver is completely ignorant about the stereotype, this reduces the informative value of SI information, which then in turn can reduce the likelihood of SI communication.

Grounding SC and SI Information with Different Lexicon—Linguistic Category Model

Linguistic category model (LCM; Semin & Fiedler, 1988) and associated research suggests that different styles of language use may go with the grounding of SC and SI information. According to LCM, different types of predicates can be used to describe the behaviors at different levels of abstraction: descriptive action verbs (e.g., "run") at a descriptive level, which does not involve much evaluative inference; interpretive action verbs (e.g., "exercise") at a more abstract level that implies some interpretation (e.g., someone may be running because he wants to exercise or because he is late for an appointment); state verbs (e.g., "like to stay fit") as relatively stable psychological states; and trait adjectives (e.g., "athletic") as stable dispositions at the most abstract level. More recent research by Carnaghi et al. (2008) has shown that nouns (e.g., "an athlete") are even more abstract than adjectives. With increasing abstraction, a behavior is characterized in a more stable and less contextualized manner.

There is a well-known tendency, called an intergroup linguistic bias, in which people tend to use more abstract words to describe an outgroup's negative behavior and their ingroup's positive behavior (e.g., Maass, 1999; Maass & Arcuri, 1996; Maass, Milesi, Zabbini, & Stahlberg, 1995; Maass, Salvi, Arcuri, & Semin, 1989). One of the causes of this tendency is a linguistic expectancy bias (Wigboldus, Semin, & Spears, 2000), where information that is consistent with expectations is likely to be described abstractly. People tend to have positive expectations about their ingroup but negative ones about their outgroup; these differential expectations could produce the intergroup linguistic bias. Indeed, Wigboldus et al. (2000) showed that SC information is described more abstractly than SI information. Whether this tendency is due to strategic language use (e.g., Douglas & Sutton, 2003) or automatic processes (e.g., Wenneker, Wigboldus, & Spears, 2005; Wenneker & Wigboldus, 2008) may have important implications for subsequent cognitive processes.

Consequences of Grounding Cultural Information About Social Groups

Grounding of cultural information about social groups has profound implications for intergroup processes—in particular, the cultural dynamics of intergroup relations. This section examines the consequences of grounding for the senders, the receivers, and finally the collective that includes both the senders and the receivers.

Consequences for Senders   When the sender has a good reason to believe that cultural information about a social group has been grounded with the receiver, the sender is likely to strengthen the sense of *shared reality* about the stereotype (e.g., Echterhoff, Higgins, & Levine, 2009; Hardin & Higgins, 1996) concerning the target group. Hausmann, Levine, and Higgins (2008) extended the "Saying is Believing" paradigm (e.g., Higgins & Rholes, 1978; Echterhoff, Higgins, & Groll, 2005) to group targets. In one condition, they led their participants to believe that their descriptions of a group enabled the receiver to identify the group correctly, thereby providing evidence that a mutual understanding about the target group was established. This condition essentially constitutes a successful grounding of a particular view about the group. A successful grounding resulted in the message sender's biased "recall." In particular, their memory was biased in the direction of their message content, suggesting that their sense of the reality about the group was shifted toward the grounded cultural information.

Kashima et al. (in press) provided further suggestive evidence that successful grounding about the senders' impressions about a social group strengthens their sense of shared reality. In particular, Kashima et al. found in three studies that people who have more extensively grounded their impressions about a social group tended not only to strengthen their impressions but also to essentialize the group. Essentialism is people's belief in the unchangeable essence of objects in the world; when applied to a social group, it includes a belief that the essence that determines group membership is unchangeable (e.g., Haslam, Rothschild, & Ernst, 2000). People often essentialize social groups in their discourse (Verkuyten, 2003; Wagner, Holtz, & Kashima, 2009), implying the unalterable reality of the groups' characters. Kashima et al.'s finding shows that such discursive tendencies have psychological consequences. That the sender believes in the unalterability of the group's character suggests that the sender regards the group to be more firmly grounded in reality as well.

Consequences for Receivers   Grounding has psychological consequences in the receiver by constituting a significant component of the receiver's information environment. First, the receiver's memory system is likely to encode grounded cultural information as a true representation *unless a contrary psychological response is encoded with it*. Gilbert and his colleagues (Gilbert, Krull, & Marone, 1990; Gilbert, Tafarodi, & Marone, 1993) showed that the cognitive system regards encoded information as true unless it is explicitly encoded as false. When cultural information is grounded as a means to attain the primary goal of a joint activity (as we argued is usually the case), it is unlikely to be counter-argued or encoded as false but, rather, likely to be taken for granted, albeit tentatively. This then may be cumulated in the receiver's memory system as a true representation of the world. Consistent with this line of reasoning, Stukas, Bratanova, Peters, Kashima, and Beatson (2010) found that the receiver formed a stereotype about a group in line with the communicated cultural information *unless* they felt no shared reality was established. When they felt no shared reality was established with the sender of cultural information, the cultural information had no effect on the receiver's stereotypes.

Intriguingly, cultural information about an individual member of a stereotyped group is often generated and interpreted in light of the standard associated with the distribution of individuals in the group (Biernat & Manis, 1996). Given someone's academic skills, he or she could be characterized as "good" or "bad" depending on the comparison group. As a university student, an individual may be "bad," but, as an African American, he or she might be considered to be "good." Collins, Crandall, and Biernat (2006) found that a counter-stereotypical description of a member of a stereotyped group (e.g., an African American student as academically good) may be interpreted using a narrower stereotyped group as the standard of comparison (i.e., he's good *as an African American man*). Collins, Biernat, and Eidelman (2009) showed that this can have an intriguing effect when the sender and the receiver used the same standard associated with a stereotyped group in a two-way communication. Given the same performance, the sender described the target person more academically positively when he was an African American than when he was a Caucasian or when his racial background was not mentioned; however, the receiver interpreted the more positively described African-American student as performing more poorly. The tacitly shared rule of conversation seems to result in an ironic misunderstanding and even a stereotype-confirming inference.

Second, the receiver is likely to regard the grounded cultural information as part of the collective representation contained in the common ground. Recall that grounding cumulates common ground, which contains both a collective identity and a collective representation. Consequently, the cultural information is likely to constitute what the receiver takes for granted as information shared and presumed to be shared by the collective *unless a contrary psychological response is encoded with it*. Put somewhat differently, the receivers of cultural information acquire their representations about their own ingroup and its members' shared knowledge through the grounded cultural information. One example of this process is the acquisition of an ingroup norm. As Verkuyten (2001) noted, conversations about an outgroup often ground the target group's abnormality, which by implication defines the presumed norm of their own ingroup. Thus, grounding of cultural information about a social group may inform the receivers' representations about their own ingroup. Although we are not aware of direct evidence for this proposition, it seems to be a reasonable conjecture.

Collective Consequences   Finally, grounding has collective implications for the group that includes both the sender and the receiver as its members. As noted earlier, this group can be understood by the interactants either as a group of those particular individuals who are engaged in the joint activity or as a group that is greater than those and extends to a broader category of individuals. Regardless, a collective representation and a collective identity of that group are constructed as part of their common ground.

If biased information about a social group is grounded, it is likely to bias the collective representation about the group in the absence of any contrary information. Schaller and Conway (1999) found that, when people were surreptitiously led to communicate more positive or negative information to one another, this led them to form a positive or negative collective representation, respectively. Furthermore, secondhand information often lacks information about the variability within a group. Consistent with this, Thompson, Judd, and Park (2000) showed that, when secondhand information is passed on from one triad to the next triad in a communication chain, where increasingly more biased information is communicated to others later in the chain, people evaluated the group as increasingly more homogeneous and in a more biased manner. Brauer et al. (2001) also found that more biased grounding of information resulted in more extreme and stereotyped impressions about a group. These stereotyped impressions may be further circulated through social networks in a broader society. However this occurs, once stereotypes are so widely circulated that they become part of the common ground of the society at large, SC information may be disseminated through social networks (e.g., serial reproduction chains), as discussed earlier (e.g., Kashima, 2000); this is likely to contribute to the maintenance of the existing stereotypes.

This line of thinking can explain an intriguing paradox between the stability of stereotypes within a society at the aggregated level (i.e., stereotypes that people generate on the average at one point in time to another) and the relative instability of stereotypes at the individual level (i.e., stereotypes that one person generates at one point in time to another). On the one hand, a series of studies of ethnic stereotypes in the United States from the 1930s to the 1990s (Katz & Braly, 1933; Gilbert, 1951; Karlins, Coffman, & Walters, 1969; Dovidio & Gaertner, 1986; Devine & Elliot, 1995) showed that, despite some trends (Dovidio & Gaertner, 1986), there is a significant stability in at least what people regard is stereotypically believed by the general public about African

Americans across more than half a century (Devine & Elliot, 1995). On the other hand, Garcia-Marques, Santos, and Mackie (2006) found that stereotypes that Portuguese participants generated at two different occasions differed a great deal, suggesting that the stereotypes were not so stable over time at the individual level. This paradox may be explicable in terms of the grounding model of cultural information transmission. A number of events that occur randomly may influence each individual's stereotypes, which may result in the fluctuation of stereotypes at the individual level; however, cultural information circulated within the population may remain relatively stable, and this is likely to stabilize the stereotypes at the aggregate level. Consistent with this line of reasoning, Schaller, Conway, and Tanchuk (2002) showed that those characteristics which are more communicable (i.e., easy to communicate and therefore more likely to circulate in community) tended to remain in the stereotypes of those groups that are more often talked about. In particular, the communicability of characteristics and their stereotypicality were positively correlated consistently over decades especially for African Americans because this group is often a target of communication.

Furthermore, when the grounded cultural information pertains to a social group, the collective representation can include not only information about the target group *per se*, but also information about the ingroup defined by the collective identity and information about the intergroup relation between the target group and the ingroup. This is a straightforward implication of the previous discussion about information about a social group—it *describes* intergroup relations. And psychological consequences of grounding do not stop at the construction of collective representations about the intergroup relations, but may extend to the construction of the social reality that they purport to represent. There is evidence to suggest that grounded cultural information—especially when it has an emotive content—may *construct* the very intergroup relations that the cultural information implies. Peters and Kashima (2007) manipulated the likelihood with which the receiver grounded the sender's emotional reaction to cultural information about a social group, and examined its effects on the formation of an ingroup bonding between the sender and the receiver as well as the action tendencies of this ingroup toward the target group. They found that grounding facilitated the ingroup formation as well as the coordination between the sender and the receiver in engaging with the action tendencies implied by the emotion toward the target group.

Consistent with this line of reasoning, some findings suggest that the grounding of SC information about an outgroup facilitates the maintenance of the ingroup's social integration. Castelli and his colleagues (Castelli, Vanzetto, Sherman, & Arcuri, 2001; Castelli, Zogmaister, & Arcuri, 2003) showed that people said they disliked those who have expressed negative stereotypes about an outgroup, but tended to conform to them more than to those who expressed positive counter-stereotypical views about the outgroup. This implies that, despite explicit disliking, they may exhibit greater social cohesion with stereotyping ingroup members. More recently, Castelli, Pavan, Ferrari, and Kashima

(2009) showed that people tended to mimic those who expressed more stereo-typical views about an outgroup than those who expressed counter-stereotypical views. If mimicry is an indicator of social connection, as Lakin, Jefferis, Cheng, & Chartrand (2003) propose, these findings suggest that the grounding of an outgroup stereotype may not only be seen to be socially connective (Clark & Kashima, 2007) but it also enhances social connectivity among ingroup members at an implicit level, thereby enhancing the integration of the ingroup as a whole.

All in all, the grounding of cultural information about a social group has profound implications for intergroup relations. The senders of the information can strengthen their sense of shared reality about the target group and intergroup relations with the receivers; the receivers strengthen their representations not only about the target group and their ingroup's intergroup relations with the target, but also their ingroup's norm; and the ingroup collective identity and collective representations, which are constructed as part of the common ground that the sender and receiver build, may be turned into the social reality of the intergroup relations that the collective representations purport to describe. To the extent that the grounding of cultural information is the engine of cultural dynamics—stability and change of culture over time—and the construction of social reality, cultural dynamics of intergroup relations is a critical influence on the social construction of intergroup relations.

POTENTIAL AREAS OF FUTURE RESEARCH AND CONCLUDING COMMENTS

Cultural dynamics of intergroup relations are products of intrapersonal as well as interpersonal processes. This section will point to a number of areas that require further research in each of these domains.

A Variety of Questions about Firsthand and Secondhand Information

Once the acquisition of cultural information from others is taken seriously, there emerge two sets of obvious and critical questions. First of all, we acquire cultural information from a number of different sources. When different types of information are presented by different people, how do we integrate them? If there are numerous episodes of cultural information presentation, it may be a reasonable approximation to treat each episode equally; however, it is intuitively obvious that different information sources are treated differently. The literature on social influence gives us a compendium of source variables such as status, expertise, ingroup membership, etc., etc., but an intriguing question is how different information sources are integrated together. A classical work by Birnbaum and Stegner (1979) addressed some of the issues, although there seems to remain a large and fertile ground for further exploration.

The second set of questions has to do with the interaction of secondhand and firsthand information. That is, how do people treat secondhand information if it is combined with firsthand information acquired through their direct experience? It is a question about social learning and individual learning (Boyd & Richerson, 1985). Firsthand information may be more risky to acquire but is likely to be more accurate; secondhand information may be biased or inaccurate, but it is less costly and may have withstood the test of time already. People may rely more on firsthand or secondhand information depending on their personality and individual difference characteristics, the social situations in which they find themselves, and the characteristics of the information that is to be acquired. I am not aware of any systematic investigation of this issue.

Stereotype Communication and Cognition

One obvious question is about the relation of stereotype communication to cognition. That is, how do communicative and cognitive processes interact? Imagine you are talking about your recent trip to a foreign country—its people, clothes, food, street vendors, and touts. You are communicating about your past experience. This information must come from the cognitive processes involving memory—especially recall. There is a large body of research on stereotypes and memory (for a review, see Fyock & Stangor, 1994; Kashima, 2000; also Rojahn & Pettigrew, 1992; Stangor & McMillan, 1992), but its link to communication is yet to be explored. Namely, how does recall affect communication? Obviously, what is communicated must be recalled; however, not all that is recalled is communicated. Of all the information recalled, how do people select what to communicate?

A variety of motives—some directly relevant to the topic, others not so directly relevant—can influence the choice about presenting what is recalled. Impression management goals (e.g., Schaller & Conway, 1999) can affect the communication of stereotypes about protected groups (those groups about which there is a strong norm not to speak negatively). In particular, self-censorship— choosing not to mention information that has negative bearing on the group—is a distinct possibility. However, what may be the cognitive implications of suppressing some negative information about the group? Research (Wenzlaff & Wegner, 2000, for a review) suggests the suppressed information may have a rebound effect—but does it? If it does, self-censorship can have a detrimental effect on potential transformation of cultural stereotypes through ironic and insidious processes akin to Freudian suppression.

On the other hand, the act of communication itself may affect what is recalled. For instance, the interaction partner's interest can play a major role. Talking about your trip to an epicurean (or to an equestrian), you might end up recalling (and perhaps reconstructing) information about food (or a horse) a lot more than otherwise. This is because, when the joint activity has the goal of "entertainment," information that interests one's partner is critically relevant to the goal. Here, the partner's interest may act as a cue to probe one's memory system; if it is not the kind of memory cue that one typically uses, this may enable one to retrieve information that does not otherwise come to mind. More generally, what role do stereotypes play in this type of reconstructive communication? Do we recall SC or SI information, or do we modify stereotype-neutral or inconsistent information into a more stereotypical form when communicating?

Furthermore, linguistic practices (Holtgraves & Kashima, 2008)—typical styles of language use—in communication can play an important role in the interaction between stereotype communication and cognition. For instance, whether people choose to use more abstracting (e.g., adjectives) or more contextualizing (e.g., verbs) linguistic practices can affect subsequent memory. Goodman et al. (2009) reported an intriguing finding that complements the grounding model explanation of SC communication. In their Experiment 4, using a newspaper article, they found that there was an SC bias in serial reproductions when information about a person was described at an abstract level, although no SC bias was found when information was described at a concrete level. This is consistent with Stangor and McMillan's (1992) meta-analysis, which showed that people tend to recall expectancy-consistent information better than expectancy-inconsistent information when it is abstract trait information, but this is reversed for concrete behavior information. Applying this insight to the communication of SC and SI information, it is possible that, in their communication, people may redescribe someone's SC behavior more abstractly but their SI behavior more concretely, and this may result in a greater tendency for people to communicate SC than SI information. This is because of Wigboldus et al.'s (2000) linguistic expectancy bias, according to which people tend to describe an SC behavior, which is consistent with a stereotype-based expectancy about a group, at a more abstract level than an SI behavior. Although Goodman et al. did not test this possibility directly, their findings are suggestive and can be tested empirically.

The grounding of cultural information may result in shared reality in the communicator (Hardin & Higgins, 1996), as we noted earlier. However, what if the grounded information does not agree with the sender's or the receiver's personal belief? That is, what if grounded information turned out to be something that they do not personally endorse? Under what circumstances would they *express* a disclaimer or a disagreement? *How* do they do so? Directly or indirectly? What if they do not do so? Would this generate cognitive dissonance and result in a modification of personal beliefs? There are a number of potential complex intrapersonal implications—cognitive, affective, or motivational—of stereotype communication which we know very little about.

Stereotype Communication in Intergroup Contexts

Much of the research on stereotype communication has examined only a limited type of intergroup context of communication—namely, when people are communicating about their outgroup. Nevertheless, there are a great many other types of intergroup contexts in which cultural information about a group can be communicated. It is intuitively and theoretically likely that different types of stereotype communication occur in different intergroup contexts. With

TABLE 6.1   Intergroup Communication Context

Type	Groups	Description
I	T = S = R	Ingroups talking about ingroup
II	T ≠ S = R	Ingroups talking about outgroup
III	T = S ≠ R	Sender talking about ingroup to outgroup
IV	T = R ≠ S	Sender talking about outgroup to the outgroup

T = Target Group; S = Sender's Group; R = Receiver's Group.

TABLE 6.2   Intergroup Communicative Motives

Target	Motive	Strategy	Tactic
Ingroup	Protection	Direct	Avoid ingroup negative information
		Indirect	Avoid outgroup positive information
	Enhancement	Direct	Prefer ingroup positive information
		Indirect	Prefer outgroup negative information
Outgroup	Protection	Direct	Avoid outgroup negative information
		Indirect	Avoid ingroup positive information
	Enhancement	Direct	Prefer outgroup positive information
		Indirect	Prefer ingroup negative information

the exception of Freytag (2008) and Kwok, Wright and Kashima (2007), I am not aware of any systematic work done on this obvious, but important, area of research. To facilitate further discussion, I present both a typology of different types of intergroup contexts with regard to stereotype communication and theoretical conjectures about these contexts.

In communicating cultural information about a social group, three groups are critically involved: the sender's group (S), the receiver's group (R), and the target group (T) about which the sender presents the cultural information to the receiver. Table 6.1 presents four different types of intergroup communication contexts. Extending Brown and Levinson's (1987) notion of interpersonal facework, Kwok et al. (2007) suggested that intergroup facework is likely played out in these cases, where the ingroup's face and outgroup's face are protected or enhanced. In total, there may be four types of motives: ingroup face protection, ingroup face enhancement, outgroup face protection, and outgroup face enhancement. Each motive is associated with preference for or avoidance of positive or negative information about the ingroup and the outgroup, as shown in Table 6.2. So, for instance, to enhance ingroup face, the sender can directly present ingroup positive information, or indirectly present outgroup negative information, and so on.

Each context is likely to make different types of sender and receiver social identities salient (Tajfel & Turner, 1986; Turner, 1987), and, depending on the norm associated with the activated social identity and the joint activity in which the sender and receiver are engaged, different types of motives (e.g., ingroup enhancement or protection) are likely to be in operation. This then results in different types of information choice in the sender's presentation and the receiver's acceptance or endorsement of the presented information. All in all, I am not aware of a systematic investigation of the interplay among intergroup context, intergroup communicative motives, and stereotype communication. This is an obvious gap in knowledge waiting to be filled.

An intriguing line of research is now emerging in which a variety of speech acts that occur in intergroup contexts and their effects are examined. For instance, Hornsey (2005, for a review) investigated the effect of criticism directed to a group. Apparently, people take more seriously a criticism directed to their ingroup if they come from other ingroup members than if they come from outgroups. Whether this is due to social identity processes or other mechanisms associated with what is seen to be appropriate (Sutton, Douglas, Elder, & Tarrant, 2008) is an issue that awaits further investigation. Philpot and Hornsey (2008) investigated the effect of intergroup apologies, where an offending group offers an apology to another group that has been subjected to some discrimination, oppression, or violation. It was found that an intergroup apology does not have much effect on forgiveness. Many types of speech acts other than criticism and apology are possible in people's active attempts at shaping and reshaping intergroup relations. More research attention can be directed here in the future.

Stereotype Communication in News, Mass Media, and Other Cultural Artifacts

The discussion so far has concentrated on the situation in which people communicate cultural information about social groups. An obvious omission is cultural artifacts—namely, a variety of human-made objects that carry cultural information about social groups. In fact, the portrayal of members of social groups in mass media (e.g., news, TV programs, advertisements) and other cultural artifacts (e.g., computer games) has been examined extensively, and the current research suggests that, despite some historical changes, subtly biased representations of groups are produced not only in primetime entertainments (e.g., Signorelli & Bacue, 1999) but also in news media (e.g., Gilens, 1996; Zuckerman & Kieffer, 1994), as well as in other forms of new media (e.g., computer games; Dill & Thill, 2007; see Ruscher, 2001; Dill, 2009, for general reviews). Obviously, people have direct experience of interaction with women, and therefore, even though these media are not the only information sources, exposure to biased media portrayals appears to influence the individual viewer cognitions (e.g., Hurtz & Durkin, 2004).

This type of work has been directed at disadvantaged social groups (e.g., women, African Americans) in societies with whom people typically have direct interactions. Mass-media coverage of foreign countries, with whose members people do not have direct experience, may have a profound effect on their stereotypes about those countries and people living in them. For example, Yang, Ramasubramanian, and Oliver (2008) found that Koreans who view American television programs more often have a more exaggerated, stereotypical view of Americans as being materially affluent (e.g., % of U.S. households having swimming pools, owning luxury cars, yachts), and this stereotypical view was associated with their dissatisfaction with their own country. Lim and Seo (2009) suggest that U.S. newspaper representations of North Korea (*New York Times*) were closely associated with a shift in public opinion about North Korea in the United States. Media portrayal of a foreign country may have a significant effect on people's stereotypes about the country.

Not only do mass media directly affect individuals, they can in fact significantly influence interpersonal communication. When a culturally significant event is reported in mass media (e.g., September 11 attacks), people obviously spend time talking about them in groups and dyads (e.g., Mehl & Pennebaker, 2003). What are the effects of such interpersonal communications that implicate some social groups? More generally, how does cultural information available in mass media and other cultural artifacts interact with interpersonal stereotype communication? One potential effect is that interpersonal communication may extend the reach of mass-media communication. That is, even if people do not obtain information directly from mass media, they may obtain it through other people, as Lazarsfeld, Berelson, and Gaudet's (1968) classical two-step flow model suggests. Another potential effect is that mass media may provide common ground for interpersonal communication; to the extent that people do not directly disendorse the media-presented information, interpersonal communication and grounding may further strengthen the media effect (e.g., Dunlop, Wakefield, & Kashima, 2008; Morton & Duck, 2001; Hafstad & Aaro, 1997; Hafstad, Aaro, & Langmark, 1996).

Concluding Comments

Because of globalization, the entire world today is the community in which people's actions have potential impacts on others who live on the other side of the planet. Even if we do not have direct interaction with them, our views and decisions about them can have profound implications for their well-being. Stereotype dynamics in these social circumstances take on a dimension that departs from those that the previous generations of social psychologists have imagined in the past. Here, transmission of cultural information about social groups plays a fundamental role; the current social psychology is ill-equipped to analyze this fundamental shift in the global circumstance. Although there are many relevant theoretical and empirical insights that are available in the literature, they are distributed across disparate areas. This chapter has attempted to provide some preliminary theorizing and to review the existing literature that bears on this profound shift. It is my hope that it provides an impetus to the furthering of this research in social psychology.

REFERENCES

Allport, G. W., & Postman, L. F. (1947). *The psychology of rumor.* New York: Russell & Russell.

Bartlett, F. C. (1932). *Remembering: A study in experimental and social psychology.* Cambridge, UK: Cambridge University Press.

Biernat, M., & Manis, M. (1996). Shifting standards and stereotype-based judgments. *Journal of Personality and Social Psychology, 66,* 5–20.

Birnbaum, M. H., & Stegner, S. E. (1979). Source credibility in social judgment: Bias, expertise, and the judge's point of view. *Journal of Personality and Social Psychology, 37,* 48–74.

Boyd, D., & Richerson, P. J. (1985). *Culture and the evolutionary process.* Chicago: University of Chicago Press.

Brauer, M., Judd, C. M., & Jacquelin, V. (2001). The communication of social stereotypes: The effects of group discussion and information distribution on stereotypic appraisals. *Journal of Personality and Social Psychology, 81,* 463–475.

Brown, P., & Levinson, S. C. (1987). *Politeness: Some universals in language usage.* Cambridge, UK: Cambridge University Press.

Carnaghi, A., Maass, A., Gresta, S., Bianchi, M., Cadinu, M., & Arcuri, L. (2008). *Nomina sunt omina:* On the inductive potential of nouns and adjectives in person perception. *Journal of Personality and Social Psychology, 94,* 839–859.

Castelli, L., Pavan, G., Ferrari, E., & Kashima, Y. (2009). The stereotyper and the chameleon: The effects of stereotype use on perceiver's mimicry. *Journal of Experimental Social Psychology, 4,* 835–839.

Castelli, L., Vanzetto, K., Sherman, S. J., & Arcuri, L. (2001). The explicit and implicit perception of ingroup members who use stereotypes: Blatant rejection but subtle conformity. *Journal of Experimental Social Psychology, 37,* 419–426.

Castelli, L., Zogmaister, C., & Arcuri, L. (2003). Perceiving ingroup members who use stereotypes: Implicit conformity and similarity. *European Journal of Social Psychology, 33,* 163–175.

Clark, A. E., & Kashima, Y. (2007). Stereotype consistent information helps people connect with others: Situated-functional account of stereotype communication. *Journal of Personality and Social Psychology, 93,* 1028–1039.

Clark, H. H. (1996). *Using language.* New York: Cambridge University Press.

Clark, H. H., & Wilkes-Gibbs, D. (1986). Referring as a collaborative process. *Cognition, 22,* 1–39.

Cole, M. (1996). *Cultural psychology: A once and future discipline.* Cambridge, MA: Harvard University Press.

Collins, E. C., Biernat, M., & Eidelman, S. (2009). Stereotypes in the communication and translation of person impressions. *Journal of Experimental Social Psychology, 45,* 368–374.

Collins, E. C., Crandall, C. S., & Biernat, M. (2006). Stereotypes and implicit social comparison: Shifts in comparison-group focus. *Journal of Experimental Social Psychology, 42,* 452–459.

Devine, P. G. (1989). Stereotypes and prejudice: Their automatic and controlled components. *Journal of Personality and Social Psychology, 56,* 5–18.

Devine, P. G., & Elliot, A. J. (1995). Are racial stereotypes really fading? The Princeton trilogy revisited. *Personality and Social Psychology Bulletin, 21,* 1139–1150.

Dill, K. E. (2009). *How fantasy becomes reality: Seeing through media influence*. New York: Oxford University Press.

Dill, K. E., & Thill, K. P. (2007). Video game characters and the socialization of gender roles: Young people's perceptions mirror sexist media depictions. *Sex Roles, 57,* 851–864.

Douglas, K. M., & Sutton, R. M. (2003). Effects of communication goals and expectancies on language abstraction. *Journal of Personality and Social Psychology, 84,* 682–696.

Dovidio, J. F., & Gaertner, S. L. (1986). Prejudice, discrimination, and racism: Historical trends and contemporary approaches. In J. F. Dovidio & S. L. Gaertner (Eds.), *Prejudice, discrimination, and racism* (pp. 1–34). New York: Academic Press.

Dunlop, S., Wakefield, M., & Kashima, Y. (2008). The contribution of anti-smoking advertising to quitting: Intra- and inter-personal processes. *Journal of Health Communication, 13,* 250–266.

Echterhoff, G., Higgins, E. T., & Groll, S. (2005). Audience-tuning effects on memory: The role of shared reality. *Journal of Personality and Social Psychology, 89,* 257–276.

Echterhoff, G., Higgins, E. T., & Levine, J. M. (2009). Shared reality: Experiencing commonality with others' inner states about the world. *Perspectives on Psychological Science, 4,* 496–521.

Fast, N. J., Heath, C., and Wu, G. (2009). Common ground and cultural prominence: How conversation reinforces culture. *Psychological Science, 20,* 904–911.

Fiske, S. T., Cuddy, A. J. C., & Glick, P. (2007). Universal dimensions of social cognition: Warmth and competence. *Trends in Cognitive Sciences, 11,* 77–83.

Fiske, S. T., Cuddy, A. J. C., Glick, P., & Xu, J. (2002). A model of (often mixed) stereotype content: Competence and warmth respectively follow from perceived status and competition. *Journal of Personality and Social Psychology, 82,* 878–902.

Freytag, P. (2008). Sender-receiver constellations as a moderator of linguistic abstraction biases. In Y. Kashima, K. Fiedler, & P. Freytag (Eds.), *Stereotype dynamics* (pp. 213–237). New York: Erlbaum.

Fyock, J., & Stangor, C. (1994). The role of memory biases in stereotype maintenance. *British Journal of Social Psychology, 33,* 331–343.

Garcia-Marques, L., Santos, A. S. C., & Mackie, D. M. (2006). Stereotypes: Static abstractions or dynamic knowledge structures? *Journal of Personality and Social Psychology, 91,* 814–831.

Gilbert, D. T., Krull, D. S., & Malone, P. S. (1990). Unbelieving the unbelievable: Some problems in the rejection of false information. *Journal of Personality and Social Psychology, 59,* 601–613.

Gilbert, D. T., Tafarodi, R. W., & Malone, P. S. (1993). You can't not believe everything you read. *Journal of Personality and Social Psychology, 65,* 221–233.

Gilbert, G. M. (1951). Stereotype persistence and change among college students. *Journal of Personality and Social Psychology, 46,* 245–254.

Gilens, M. (1996). Race and poverty in America: Public misperceptions and the American news media. *Public Opinion Quarterly, 60,* 515–541.

Goodman, R. L., Webb, T. L., & Stewart, A. J. (2009). Communicating stereotype-relevant information: Is factual information subject to the same communication biases as fictional information? *Personality and Social Psychology Bulletin, 35,* 836–852.

Hafstad, A., & Aaro, L. E. (1997). Activating interpersonal influence through provocative appeals: Evaluation of a mass media-based anti-smoking campaign targeting adolescents. *Health Communication, 9*, 253–272.

Hafstad, A., Aaro, L. E., & Langmark, F. (1996). Evaluation of an anti-smoking mass media campaign targeting adolescents: The role of affective responses and interpersonal communication. *Health Education Research, 11*, 29–38.

Hardin, C. D., & Higgins, E. T. (1996). Shared reality: How social verification makes the subjective objective. In R. M. Sorrentino & E. T. Higgins (Eds.), *Handbook of motivation and cognition* (Vol. 3, pp. 28–84). New York: Guilford Press.

Haslam, N., Rothschild, L., & Ernst, D. (2000). Essentialist beliefs about social categories. *British Journal of Social Psychology*, 39: 113–127.

Hausmann, L. R. M., Levine, J. M., & Higgins, E. T. (2008). Communication and group perception: Extending the "saying is believing" effect. *Group Processes and Intergroup Relations, 11*, 539–554.

Higgins, E. T., & Rholes, W. S. (1978). "Saying is believing": Effects of message modification on memory and liking for the person described. *Journal of Experimental Social Psychology, 14*, 363–378.

Hirschfeld, L. A. (1996). *Race in the making: Cognition, culture, and the child's construction of human kinds*. Cambridge, MA: MIT Press.

Holtgraves, T., & Kashima, Y. (2008). Language, meaning and social cognition. *Personality and Social Psychology Review, 12*, 73–94.

Hornsey, M. J. (2005). Why being right is not enough: Predicting defensiveness in the face of group criticism. *European Review of Social Psychology, 16*, 301–334.

Hurtz, W., & Durkin, K. (2004). The effects of gender-stereotyped radio commercials. *Journal of Applied Social Psychology, 34*, 1974–1992.

Judd, C. M., & Park, B. (1993). Definition and assessment of accuracy in social stereotypes. *Psychological Review, 100*, 109–128.

Karlins, M., Coffman, T. L., & Walters, G. (1969). On the fading of social stereotypes: Studies in three generations of college students. *Journal of Personality and Social Psychology, 13*, 1–16.

Kashima, Y. (2000). Maintaining cultural stereotypes in the serial reproduction of narratives. *Personality and Social Psychology Bulletin, 26*, 594–604.

Kashima, Y. (2008). A social psychology of cultural dynamics: How cultures are formed, maintained, and transformed. *Social and Personality Psychology Compass, 2*, 107–120.

Kashima, Y., Bain, P., Haslam, N., Peters, N., Laham, S., Whelan, J., Bastian, B., Loughnan, S., Kaufmann, L., & Fernando, J. (2009). Folk theory of social change. *Asian Journal of Social Psychology, 12*, 227–246.

Kashima, Y., Kashima, E. S., Bain, P., Lyons, A., Tindale, R. S., Robins, G., Vears, C., & Whelan, J. (in press). Communication and essentialism: Grounding the shared reality of a social category. *Social Cognition*.

Kashima, Y., Klein, O., & Clark, A. E. (2007). Grounding: Sharing information in social interaction. In K. Fiedler (Ed.), *Social communication* (pp. 27–77). New York: Psychology Press.

Kashima, Y., & Kostopoulos, J. (2004). Cultural dynamics of stereotyping: Interpersonal communication may inadvertently help maintaining auto-stereotypes too. *Cahiers de Psychologie Cognitive/Current Psychology of Cognition, 22*, 445–461.

Kashima, Y., Peters, K., & Whelan, J. (2008). Culture, narrative, and human agency. In R. Sorrentino & S. Yamaguchi (Eds.), *Handbook of motivation and cognition across cultures* (pp. 393–421). San Diego, CA: Academic Press.

Kashima, Y., Woolcock, J., & Kashima, E. (2000). Group impressions as dynamic configurations: The tensor product model of group impression formation and change. *Psychological Review, 107*, 914–942.

Katz, D., & Braly, K. (1933). Racial stereotypes in one hundred college students. *Journal of Abnormal and Social Psychology, 28*, 280–290.

Klein, O., Demoulin, S., Licata, L., & Lambert, S. (2004). "If you know he is an engineer, I don't need to tell you he is smart": The influence of stereotypes on the communication of social knowledge. *Cahiers de Psychologie Cognitive/Current Psychology of Cognition, 22*, 463–478.

Klein, O., Jacobs, A., Gemoets, S., Licata, L., & Lambert, S. M. (2003). Hidden profiles and the consensualization of social stereotypes: How information distribution affects stereotype content and sharedness. *European Journal of Social Psychology, 33*, 755–777.

Krauss, R. M., & Weinheimer, S. (1964). Changes in the length of reference phrases as a function of social interaction: A preliminary study. *Psychonomic Science, 1*, 113–114.

Krauss, R. M., & Weinheimer, S. (1967). Effects of referent similarity and communication mode on verbal encoding. *Journal of Verbal Learning and Verbal Behavior, 6*, 359–363.

Kwok, W.-W., Wright, B., & Kashima, Y. (2007). Constructing intergroup relationships in social communication. *Japanese Psychological Research, 49*, 121–135.

Lakin, J. L., Jefferis, V. E., Cheng, M. C., & Chartrand, T. L. (2003). The chameleon effect as social glue: Evidence for the evolutionary significance of nonconscious mimicry. *Journal of Nonverbal Behavior, 27*, 145–162.

Lazarsfeld, P. E., Berelson, B., & Gaudet, H. (1968). *The people's choice: How the voter makes up his mind in a presidential election* (3rd ed.). New York: Columbia University Press.

Lim, J., & Seo, H. (2009). Frame flow between government and the news media and its effects on the public: Framing of North Korea. *International Journal of Public Opinion Research, 21*, 204–223.

Lyons, A., & Kashima, Y. (2001). The reproduction of culture: Communication processes tend to maintain cultural stereotypes. *Social Cognition, 19*, 372–394.

Lyons, A., & Kashima, Y. (2003). How are stereotypes maintained through communication? The influence of stereotype sharedness. *Journal of Personality and Social Psychology, 85*, 989–1005.

Lyons, A., & Kashima, Y. (2006). Maintaining stereotypes in communication: Investigating memory biases and coherence-seeking in storytelling. *Asian Journal of Social Psychology, 9*, 59–71.

Maass, A. (1999). Linguistic intergroup bias: Stereotype perpetuation through language. *Advances in Experimental Social Psychology, 31*, 79–121.

Maass, A., & Arcuri, S. (1996). Language and stereotyping. In C. N. Macrae, C. Stangor, & M. Hewstone (Eds.), *Stereotypes and stereotyping* (pp. 193–226). New York: Guilford Press.

Maass, A., Milesi, A., Zabbini, S., & Stahlberg, D. (1995). The linguistic intergroup bias: Differential expectancies or in-group protection? *Journal of Personality and Social Psychology, 68*, 116–126.

Maass, A., Salvi, D., Arcuri, L., & Semin, G. (1989). Language use in intergroup contexts: The linguistic intergroup bias. *Journal of Personality and Social Psychology, 57*, 981–993.

Mead, G. H. (1934). *Mind, self, and society*. Chicago: University of Chicago Press.

Mehl, M. R., & Pennebaker, J. W. (2003). The social dynamics of a cultural upheaval: Social interactions surrounding September 11, 2001. *Psychological Science, 14*, 579–585.

Morton, T. A., & Duck, J. M. (2001). Communication and health beliefs: Mass and interpersonal influences on perception of risk to self and others. *Communication Research, 28*, 602–626.

Peters, K. O., & Kashima, Y. (2007). From social talk to social action: Shaping the social triad by emotion sharing. *Journal of Personality and Social Psychology, 93*, 780–797.

Philpot, C. R., & Hornsey, M. J. (2008). What happens when groups say sorry: The effect of intergroup apologies on their recipients. *Personality and Social Psychology Bulletin, 34*, 474–487.

Rogoff, B. (2003). *The cultural nature of human development*. Oxford, UK: Oxford University Press.

Rojahn, K., & Pettigrew, T. F. (1992). Memory for schema-relevant information: A meta-analytic resolution. *British Journal of Social Psychology, 31*, 81–109.

Ruscher, J. B. (2001). *Prejudiced communication: A social psychological perspective*. New York: Guilford Press.

Ruscher, J. B., Cralley, E. L., & O'Farrell, K. J. (2005). How newly acquainted dyads develop shared stereotypic impressions through conversation. *Group Processes and Intergroup Relations, 8*, 259–270.

Ruscher, J. B., & Duval, L. L. (1998). Multiple communicators with unique target information transmit less stereotypical impressions. *Journal of Personality and Social Psychology, 74*, 329–344.

Ruscher, J. B., & Hammer, E. D. (1994). Revising disrupted impressions through conversation. *Journal of Personality and Social Psychology, 66*, 530–541.

Ruscher, J. B., & Hammer, E. D. (2006). The development of shared stereotypic impressions in conversation: An emerging model, methods, and extensions to cross-group settings. *Journal of Language and Social Psychology, 25*, 221–243.

Ruscher, J. B., Hammer, E. Y., & Hammer, E. D. (1996). Forming shared impressions through conversation: An adaptation of the continuum model. *Personality and Social Psychology Bulletin, 22*, 705–720.

Ruscher, J. B., Santuzzi, A. M., & Hammer, E. Y. (2003). Shared impression formation in the cognitively interdependent dyad. *British Journal of Social Psychology, 42*, 411–425.

Schaller, M., & Conway, L. G., III. (1999). Influence of impression-management goals on the emerging contents of group stereotypes: Support for a social-evolutionary process. *Personality and Social Psychology Bulletin, 25*, 819–833.

Schaller, M., Conway, L. G., III, & Tanchuk, T. L. (2002). Selective pressures on the once and future contents of ethnic stereotypes: Effects of the communicability of traits. *Journal of Personality and Social Psychology, 82*, 861–877.

Semin, G. R., & Fiedler, K. (1988). The cognitive functions of linguistic categories in describing persons: Social cognition and language. *Journal of Personality and Social Psychology, 54*, 558–568.

Signorelli, N., & Bacue, A. (1999). Recognition and respect: A content analysis of prime-time television characters across three decades. *Sex Roles, 40*, 527–544.

Smith, E. R., & Semin, G. R. (2004). Socially situated cognition: Cognition in its social context. *Advances in Experimental Social Psychology, 36*, 53–117.

Smith, E. R., & Semin, G. R. (2007). Situated social cognition. *Current Directions in Psychological Science, 16*, 132–135.

Smith, E. R., & Zarate, M. A. (1992). Exemplar-based model of social judgment. *Psychological Review, 99*, 3–21.

Sperber, D. (1996). *Explaining culture*. Oxford, UK: Blackwell.

Stangor, C., & Lange, J. E. (1994). Mental representations of social groups: Advances in understanding stereotypes and stereotyping. *Advances in Experimental Social Psychology, 26*, 357–416.

Stangor, C., & McMillan, D. (1992). Memory for expectancy-congruent and expectancy-incongruent information: A review of the social and social-developmental literatures. *Psychological Bulletin, 111*, 42–61.

Stasser, G., Taylor, L. A., & Hanna, C. (1989). Information sampling in structured and unstructured discussions of three- and six-person groups. *Journal of Personality and Social Psychology, 57*, 67–78.

Stasser, G., & Titus, W. (1985). Pooling of unshared information in group decision making: Biased information sampling during discussion. *Journal of Personality and Social Psychology, 48*, 1467–1478.

Stasser, G., & Titus, W. (1987). Effects of information load and percentage of shared information on the dissemination of unshared information during group discussion. *Journal of Personality and Social Psychology, 53*, 81–93.

Stukas, A. A., Bratanova, B., Peters, K., Kashima, Y., & Beatson, R. M. (2010). Confirmatory processes in attitude transmission: The role of shared reality. *Social Influence, 5*, 1–17; iFirst. DOI: 10.1080/15534510903384916.

Sutton, R. M., Douglas, K. M., Elder, T. J., & Tarrant, M. (2008). Social identity and social convention in responses to criticisms of groups. In Y. Kashima, K. Fiedler, & P. Freytag (Eds.), *Stereotype dynamics* (pp. 339–365). Mahwah, NJ: Erlbaum.

Tajfel, H., & Turner, J. C. (1986). The social identity theory of social behavior. In S. Worchel & W. G. Austin (Eds.), *Psychology of intergroup relations* (2nd ed., pp. 7–24). Chicago: Nelson-Hall.

Thompson, M. S., Judd, C. M., & Park, B. (2000). The consequences of communicating social stereotypes. *Journal of Experimental Social Psychology, 36*, 567–599.

Turner, J. C. (1987). *Rediscovering the social group: A self-categorization theory*. Oxford, UK: Blackwell.

Verkuyten, M. (2001). "Abnormalization" of ethnic minorities in conversation. *British Journal of Social Psychology, 40*, 257–278.

Verkuyten, M. (2003). Discourses about ethnic group (de-)essentialism: Oppressive and progressive aspects. *British Journal of Social Psychology, 42*, 371–391.

Wagner, W., Holtz, P., & Kashima, Y. (2009). Constructing and deconstructing essence in representing social groups: Identity projects, stereotyping, and racism. *Journal for the Theory of Social Behavior, 39*, 363–383.

Wenneker, C., & Wigboldus, D. (2008). A model of biased language use. In Y. Kashima, K. Fiedler, & P. Freytag (Eds.), *Stereotype dynamics* (pp. 165–188). New York: Lawrence Erlbaum Associates.

Wenneker, C. P. J., Wigboldus, D. H. J., & Spears, R. (2005). Biased language use in stereotype maintenance: The role of encoding and goals. *Journal of Personality and Social Psychology, 89*, 504–516.

Wenzlaff, R. M., & Wegner, D. M. (2000). Thought suppression. *Annual Review of Psychology, 51*, 59–91.

Wertsch, J. (1991). *Voices of the mind*. London: Harvester Wheatsheaf.

Wigboldus, D. H. J., Semin, G. R., & Spears, R. (2000). How do we communicate stereotypes? Linguistic bases and inferential consequences. *Journal of Personality and Social Psychology, 78,* 5–18.

Wu, S., & Keysar, B. (2007). The effect of information overlap on communication effectiveness. *Cognitive Science, 31,* 169–181.

Yang, H., Ramasubramanian, S., & Oliver, M. B. (2008). Cultivation effects on quality of life indicators: Exploring the effects of American television consumption on feelings of relative deprivation in South Korea and India. *Journal of Broadcasting and Electronic Media, 52,* 247–267.

Zuckerman, M., & Kieffer, S. C. (1994). Race differences in face-ism: Does facial prominence imply dominance? *Journal of Personality and Social Psychology, 66,* 86–92.

7

Stereotypes and Prejudice from an Intergroup Relations Perspective

Their Relation to Social Structure

FELICIA PRATTO

University of Connecticut

KRISTIN E. HENKEL

Western Connecticut State University

I-CHING LEE

National Chengchi University

*I*ntergroup relations are the warp, or substructure, of the fabric of hierarchical societies. But the weft—stereotypes and prejudice—gives the fabric its color, texture, and feel, and so these are more often noticed than the substructure of intergroup relations. The warp and weft must be suited to each other, or the fabric does not hold. This chapter examines how stereotypes and prejudice are interwoven with intergroup relations in hierarchical societies. In general, processes give structural integrity to the fabric. Particular aspects of intergroup relations give rise to compatible stereotypes and prejudices (Cottrell & Neuberg, 2005). Stereotypes and prejudice stabilize social structure by encouraging group discrimination (e.g., Pratto, 1999). For this reason, to change either social structure or stereotypes and prejudice, one is likely to have to invoke change in the other. Conversely, change in either warp or weft of societies may be limited by the other. The close associations between stereotypes and prejudices and the social structures of societies have not been fully addressed in research. For example, few studies consider stereotypes and prejudice from the point of view of both targets and perpetrators, and there is considerable confusion about what aspects of intergroup relations (e.g., status, contact, power) matter for stereotypes and prejudices. Likewise, very little work has demonstrated experimentally how particular aspects of intergroup relations give rise to particular kinds of prejudice or stereotypes, and even less research has demonstrated the social or psychological processes about how stereotypes legitimize social structure or how prejudice leads people to behave in ways to change or reproduce social structure. For this reason, this chapter considers intergroup relations within societies as a context for understanding stereotypes and prejudice. The first section outlines the basic aspects of intergroup relations which may give rise to stereotypes and prejudice, and the second section details how the use of stereotypes and prejudice may perpetuate aspects of intergroup relations.

STRUCTURAL ASPECTS OF INTERGROUP RELATIONS

Varieties of Intergroup Relations

The fact that many aspects of group membership (e.g., power, status, ethnic category) are confounded makes it challenging to name exactly what aspect of the structure of intergroup relations (e.g., status, power, segregation, numerosity) is pertinent to stereotype contents, stereotyping processes, and prejudice. Ideally, researchers should use terms that characterize the aspects of intergroup relations that are important to their work. Our first aim is to delineate aspects of intergroup relations that may be pertinent to stereotypes and prejudice so that the study of the two can be theoretically clear. Another problem is that sometimes researchers label only the group experiencing *problems* from stereotyping and prejudice, without naming the groups relatively free of such problems. For example, the reader might consider what terms for groups would contrast with "stigmatized" or "denigrated." Explicating these contrasts (e.g., "unmarked," "respected") may help researchers specify the relevant structural conditions of the groups. For example, as women are seldom minorities, the historical tendency to view prejudice and stereotypes about women versus men as deriving from the same processes relevant to ethnic minorities and majorities was incomplete. Another common omission is failing to name the *agents* of stereotyping, prejudice, and discrimination by using passive language (e.g., "Blacks are disliked." "Women are objectified.") This practice fails not only to explain whose actions matter and why, but also to explicate the *process*, which it may even linguistically normalize. Our second aim, which comes from our focus on *inter*group relations, is to show that the conditions, processes, and experiences of *all* relevant groups should be studied to understand how stereotypes and prejudice pertain to social structure. Table 7.1 provides terms for

TABLE 7.1 Paired Complementary Group Labels and Relevant Dimension of Intergroup Relations

Complementary Group Labels		Dimension of Intergroup Relation
Majority	Minority	Numerical representation in a population
Ingroup	Outgroup	Group inclusion/exclusion from own stance
Mainstream	Marginalized	Group inclusion/exclusion from societal stance
In-crowd	Ostracized	Group inclusion/exclusion and acceptability
Normative	Non-normative	Implicit normative status
Unmarked	Marked	Explicitly designated normative status
Esteemed	Denigrated	Group-linked prestige
High-status	Low-status	Group-linked prestige *or* income level
Respectable	Stigmatized	Social acceptability
Advantaged	Disadvantaged	Power, privilege, *or* material wealth
Dominant, privileged	Subordinate, oppressed	Power (general)
Ruling class	Working class	Material, political, and ideological power (Marxist)
Secure	Threatened	Group-linked risk
Focal	Forgotten	Amount of social attention typically received

complementary groups that reflect particular aspects of their intergroup relation. We first describe aspects of intergroup relations that are pertinent to stereotypes and prejudice. We distinguish two primary groupings noted by social dominance theory (e.g., Sidanius & Pratto, 1999) as being associated with power differences in all heterogeneous societies: Gender pertains to roles and expectations about men and women, but it also includes the nature of their sexuality and sexual and non-sexual family relationships. Arbitrary set groups are social distinctions constructed collectively; often they are said to be defined by ethnicity, race, religion or sect, class, tribe, region of origin, or nationality status—a non-comprehensive list which indicates the arbitrary nature of their definition (Sidanius & Pratto, 1999, p. 33). We then argue that power permeates all kinds of intergroup relations and that, by understanding power in intergroup relations, we are able to understand other aspects of intergroup relations (e.g., numerosity, segregation) that instigate stereotype contents, stereotype processes, and various kinds of prejudice. We will show that stereotypes and prejudice do not constitute just an intra- and inter-individual phenomenon but are essential aspects of enacting many kinds of group power.

Gender   Understanding gender is necessary for understanding how societies perpetuate themselves because gender roles are practiced and learned in the family, the basic social unit of societies that enables the transmission of culture. Many social practices outside the family also concern gender, such as what kinds of paid work men and women do, who has public legitimacy, and who uses violence.

Because gender is fundamentally linked to the distribution of necessities and obligations, it is strongly associated with power. Pratto and Walker (2004) distinguished four basic kinds of power (i.e., violence, material resources, relationship obligation, and ideology) that differ for men and women. First, men use and are victimized by most forms of violence more than women. Second, in modern societies, men control access to material resources more than women. Third, women are more obliged than men to care for others without equal reciprocal obligations. Within many families, women may be recognized as having certain kinds of authority or expertise (e.g., over emotional work or food), but being more obliged to do so than others is fundamentally disempowering. Fourth, men are advantaged more than women by cultural ideologies such as sexism and status prescriptions. Moreover, the kinds of power used most by men (resources, violence, ideologies) can more readily be used to gain other kinds of power than the kinds of power used most by women (relationships). One must also consider how gender intersects with another important social group distinction, described next.

Arbitrary Set Groups   Societies have groups that are culturally recognized as distinct, usually because they have different histories and practices and hold different amounts of power. These groups can be socially constructed by race (e.g., in the United States), religious affiliation (e.g., in Northern Ireland), caste system (e.g., in India), social class (e.g., in China), tribal clans (e.g., in Somalia), or nationality (e.g., immigrants in Germany). The fact that different societies rely on different distinctions (e.g., language, accent, ancestral origin, physical appearance, name) and collectively constructed groups, such as ethnicity, tribe, race, nationality, and caste, highlights their arbitrary and social construction. Such social groups are called arbitrary set categories in social dominance theory (e.g., Sidanius & Pratto, 1999). In most nations, there is at least one arbitrary set group (e.g., Whites in the United States, Protestants in Northern Ireland) that enjoys more of the good things in life—pleasant living conditions, access to resources, health, positive social attention, reputation, and other things people value—than at least one other arbitrary set group (e.g., people with Turkish ethnicity in Germany). The unequal distribution between such groups of the things people value versus the things they do not—such as unemployment, dangerous living conditions, stigma, mistreatment by the legal system—is not due to chance; it results from and re-creates differential power. Thus, the arbitrary set distinction is one of the most general ways of distinguishing social groups with different power. Before detailing how power regarding groups is enacted, we explain how numerosity and segregation differ from power and are related to stereotypes and prejudice.

Numerosity: Majorities, Minorities, and Pluralities

Whether groups are majorities or minorities is sometimes assumed to stand for whether they have greater or lesser power. For example, scholars often use the term "cultural minority" to denote groups with little power (e.g., those of low status or low education). Not only does this fail to specify the structural dimension of interest, it overgeneralizes different cultural minorities who differ substantially from one another in education level, power, and status (Ogbu, 1990).

Groups with greater numbers do not generally have more power. For example, Blacks, although mostly enslaved, outnumbered Whites in much of the antebellum American South. Ruling elites are small—consider any monarchy, White rule in apartheid South Africa, colonial rule, the British class system, and Communist Party rule in China. All these are cases in which a small minority had/have considerably more power than the majority (see Gramsci, 1971, on political elites). However, majorities can make themselves more powerful through political processes—for example, they can construct political systems that allow them greater power (e.g., majority rule). Even if one kind of arbitrary dominant group (e.g., race or religion) constitutes a majority, the true ruling elite is often a tiny subset of that group and may even include subordinate group members (e.g., in the United States, Black women Cabinet members). This may make elite rule more hidden and more popular. Democratic governments can establish political processes that temper majoritarianism, such as parliamentarianism and election by ward. One should not assume, then, that majority status makes groups more powerful but, rather, that political and identity processes may.

Numerosity is, however, an appropriate dimension to consider regarding prejudice and stereotyping for minority influence and contact theory. Research on intragroup dynamics appropriately refers to numerosity concerning *opinion* minorities or majorities (e.g., Aebischer, Hewstone, & Henderson, 1984). Although opinion majorities are often more influential, opinion minorities can sometimes persuade others to change their views (e.g., Aebischer et al., 1984), especially by promoting tolerance for alternative views (Prislin & Filson, 2009). Majority members can sometimes be ostracized if they are seen as deviating too much from the group—the "black sheep" effect (e.g., Marques, Abrams, & Serôdio, 2001).

Except for isolated groups, minorities are far more likely to have contact, both interpersonally and through the media, with majorities than majorities are with minorities. Majorities' infrequent contact with minorities allows prejudice and culturally transmitted stereotypes to go unchecked. For majority members, intergroup contact may increase empathy for minority members and reduce prejudice (especially fear) and reliance on stereotypes of the minority group (Pettigrew & Tropp, 2008). However, contact with majority group members is not altogether positive for minority group members because they can perceive intergroup contact as an impediment to social change (Hopkins & Kahani-Hopkins, 2006) and find it aversive (Shelton, 2003). Minorities reduce their prejudice toward majorities less than majorities do following contact (Tropp & Pettigrew, 2005). Further, African Americans' contact with other African Americans provides psychological protection that contact with Whites does not (Cole & Yip, 2008; Postmes & Branscombe, 2002). The different processes and outcomes of contact for majority and minority members constitute one reason why we emphasize that researchers should consider the perspectives and conditions of people in different group positions, rather than assuming that the psychology of dominant groups pertains equally to all (e.g., Dixon, Durrheim, & Tredoux, 2005; Hopkins & Kahani-Hopkins, 2006).

Taking asymmetries concerning numerosity and power into account provides more accurate and useful information about how contact might affect intergroup relations. For example, extended contact with people from other cultures can reduce anxiety about how to interact with such people (e.g., Stephan & Stephan, 1992) and change explanations for their behavior from mostly internal to mostly external (Vollhardt, 2010). However, these effects of intercultural contact and the development of greater intercultural competency are stronger for majorities than for minorities (e.g., Kim & van Dyne, 2012). Thus, cultural training programs for employees of international companies, study abroad and foreign students' programs, and tourism programs may benefit by being sensitive to these asymmetries.

The intergroup perspective highlights that, although contact may improve majority group members' attitudes and beliefs, costs can arise for minorities. A longitudinal study of roommate dyads showed that Whites' concerns over appearing prejudiced toward Black roommates corresponded to Whites' anxiety levels (Shelton, West, & Trail, 2010), but their anxiety provoked anxiety in their Black roommates (West, Shelton, &Trail, 2009). When existing or experimentally created disadvantaged groups have or anticipate contact with advantaged groups focusing on intergroup commonalities, they develop expectations for power-sharing and equality that are not enacted by advantaged groups (Saguy, Tausch, Dovidio, & Pratto, 2009) and cease attributing their lack of power to discrimination (Saguy & Chernyak-Hai, 2012). For individual emotional experience and for collective outcomes such as collective action and ingroup solidarity, intergroup contact serves majorities and more powerful groups better than it does minorities and less powerful groups, at least in the short run.

Intergroup Segregation and Integration

Physical segregation limits the chances for intergroup contact and is an important aspect of intergroup relations for several reasons. First, as already mentioned, segregation helps to sustain stereotypes and prejudice because it prevents intergroup contact (Pettigrew, 1998). Second, segregation is often a *de facto* way that dominant groups control access to social and natural resources (Clark, Chein, & Cook, 1952/2004). For example, the United States used warfare and forced drives to banish Native Americans to reservation land that held little economic possibility. Third, groups that are segregated are more likely to maintain intergroup boundaries because they are less likely to develop integrated friendships and families. Even when their societies' official policies have changed toward equality and desegregation, group members segregate themselves in informal settings such as on beaches and in school cafeterias because of discomfort with outgroup members (e.g., Dixon & Durrheim, 2003; Tatum, 1997). Segregation, then, helps maintain group distinctions across generations, so that intergroup boundaries appear stable.

Well-known examples of arbitrary set segregation, such as apartheid, Jim Crow practices, and economic segregation by neighborhood, highlight that the physical segregation of groups ferments prejudice and allows stereotypes to go unchecked by personal experience. However, there are other relevant but overlooked forms of segregation. Men and women are often together in households but segregated at work into different jobs (e.g., Cotter, Hermsen, & Vanneman, 2004), different institutions, or different divisions of organizations (e.g., Tomaskovic-Devey, 1993). Members of subordinate groups often perform subservient work for members of dominant groups in private spaces (e.g., homes, hotel rooms) and concerning intimate aspects of people's lives (e.g., Jureidini, 2009). For example, servants care for sick people, launder undergarments, witness family interactions, and sometimes serve as confidants. Dominants in such situations may trust but neither respect nor empower subordinates, who must work to maintain psychological distance (Jackman, 1994; Pratto & Walker, 2000). Thus, dominants and subordinates can have frequent and even intimate contact and still be highly segregated *psychologically and by role*. Psychological segregation, wherein outgroup members are not recognized as having equivalent value to oneself or one's ingroup, enables prejudice (e.g., Bar-Tal, 1989; Pratto & Glasford, 2008). Segregation by role also provides information on which people may rely to create stereotypes of groups playing those roles (e.g., Conway, Pizzamiglio, & Mount, 1996; Eagly & Steffen, 1984; Hoffman & Hurst, 1990). Thus, although some stereotypes and kinds of prejudice are quite outlandish (e.g., that particular races are the offspring of unions with the devil), some of them may be based in observations and the kinds of relationships members of different groups have (or lack) with one another (e.g., women as nurturers).

Examining Intergroup Relations from the Perspective of Power

Having discussed how numerosity, segregation, and integration pertain to prejudice and stereotyping, we now turn to how power dynamics in intergroup relations pertains to stereotypes and prejudice. Here is where we must imagine the warp (or structure) and weft (or stereotypes and prejudice) of societies, deciding how to weave the one into the other. Group power determines how much its members are affected by stereotyping and prejudice. More dynamically, power is what enables groups to monopolize resources, to attack or ignore other groups, to privilege (their) ways of living, to set agendas, and to live luxurious rather than marginal lives. Various kinds of power (e.g., violence, money) can be changed via social interaction. Power, then, is dynamic and is often a *potential* rather than an absolute (Pratto, Pearson Lee, & Saguy, 2008).

Power and Freedom Power is associated with, but not the same as, freedom of choice. Nearly everyone has some degree of agency or ability to act (Dijke & Poppe, 2006; Russell, 1938). Only in cases of absolute constraint would a person be prevented from acting (Wartenberg, 1990). Even when constrained, people retain some choices (e.g., over some of their thoughts), even if those choices are not attractive (e.g., to go on hunger-strike), and so power should not be understood as something one has or does not have (i.e., as absolute). Rather, the degree of one's power is reflected in the scope and desirability of one's choices (Lewin, 1951; Thibaut & Kelley, 1959). In fact, people in more powerful positions have more varied choices and behavior than people in less powerful positions (Guinote, Judd, & Brauer, 2002).

Group membership, such as one's gender or arbitrary set group, often delineates one's alternatives. For example, women may choose genital cutting because it is their best way of obtaining social recognition, material security, and community belonging (Tietjens Meyers, 2000). Similarly, whether one's food options are healthy depends substantially on one's neighborhood, which is related to one's race and income level (e.g., Zenk et al., 2005). Subordinate groups often are surrounded by a "circle of oppression" in that their choices are limited by institutional discrimination in each arena of their lives, whereas dominant groups find that their societies often afford their every desire (Sidanius & Pratto, 1999). Further, the circle of oppression can "ripple." For example, low income constrains one's choices of where to live, so a deficit in one kind of power (e.g., money) can contribute to deficits in other kinds of power (e.g., health and safety).

To account for these social dynamics and profound differences in whether different groups can meet their survival needs or realize their desires, Pratto, Lee, Tan, and Pitpitan (2011) offer an ecological definition of power in Power Basis Theory: A person's power to meet survival needs stems from the confluence among his or her capabilities, sensitivities, and local environment. That is, if the person is sensitive to his or her own needs and capable of finding how those needs can be met in the environment, and the environment affords meeting those needs, the person is empowered. A person with the same sensitivity to needs and capabilities would not be empowered in an environment lacking the means to meet needs, nor would a person in an environment replete with survival resources be able to meet needs without being sensitive to those needs and how to use survival resources. According to Power Basis Theory, constructive power is the means of meeting survival needs, and destructive power is the ability to prevent others from meeting their needs. Unlike definitions of power that view it as entirely relational (e.g., Fiske & Berdahl, 2007), in that one agent's power is always relative to that of another agent, Power Basis Theory defines power as the means of meeting or preventing the meeting of survival needs and views power as a function of the relationship between an agent's environment and his or her sensitivity and motivational systems. Other people and groups may be part of a person or a group's environment, but a given agent's power is defined in relation to that agent's meeting of survival needs, not a comparison with the power of other agents. This conception of power is closer to empowerment than to relational power as specified by interdependence theory (Thibault & Kelley, 1959). Power Basis Theory and its definition of power offer several implications for intergroup relations. First, the reason particular kinds of power arise repeatedly in intergroup relations (e.g., violence, controlling access to resources) is that they address specific survival needs (e.g., need for wholeness, need to consume) that are common (Pratto et al., 2011). In other words, the basis of power is need. Any group that manages to restrict another group's ability to meet its own needs, such as by monopolizing material resources, violent attacks, excluding it from useful exchanges with other groups, reneging on its obligations to the group, delegitimizing the group, providing false information or restricting the flow of truthful knowledge, destroying group continuity or cultural transmission, or even preventing the other group from using what power it has to gain other forms of power, will have hampered the other group's power, whether or not this results in greater odds of survival and well-being for the perpetrator. Second, because power can be both constructive and destructive, groups and individuals will strive to gauge who is safe and who is not, and so they monitor others' trustworthiness or beneficence to assure their own well-being. This, we posit, is why trust or morality or beneficence are recurrent dimensions in person-perception and group stereotypes. Third, dynamics in intergroup relations often hinge on how groups transform one kind of power into another kind through intergroup interaction. For example, to confer that a nation has lost legitimacy, other nations may impose economic sanctions. Groups may also *de facto* change their relations toward other groups when monopolizing one kind of power (e.g., lucrative jobs) to increase other kinds of power (e.g., political influence).

However, according to Power Basis Theory, power is dynamically social not because having power necessitates *control over* (Fiske & Berdahl, 2007) or *affiliation with* (Turner, 2005) others, but because social interaction is the main route to transforming kinds of power, and because people share their ecology with others who have the same survival needs. The next sections show how several aspects of intergroup relations can be understood by considering how they relate to particular kinds of power that Power Basis Theory delineates as meeting survival needs (Pratto et al., 2011).

Group Status   The need to belong is met by legitimacy or acceptance in a community. One marker of legitimacy is "group status" or a group's relative social standing. High-status groups bring their members respect, *de facto* acceptance, authority, and access to useful social networks (e.g., Lin, 2000). Because it can be used to gain desired goods, control, efficacy, influence, etc., status is a highly fungible kind of power. But, unlike inclusive acceptance or unconditional respect for persons (Lalljee, Tam, Hewstone, Laham, & Lee,

2009), which could allow everyone to have their need to belong met, group status is hierarchical and status competitions are mainly zero sum. Status therefore implies that some will not have their need to belong met. We argue that the primary social function of denigrating stereotypes and prejudice is to mark which groups can be excluded from a community or from access to power (Pratto & Pitpitan, 2008). For example, belonging to a denigrated group (e.g., African Americans) can make one feel "under suspicion" (Steele, 1987), and high-status groups often exclude or omit low-status groups (e.g., the handicapped, immigrants, lesbians) from social discourse.

Violence and Coercion   Violence directed against oneself is antithetical to one's need for wholeness or health. A group's use of force or violence often communicates the threat of harm, which may induce another group to do something it would not otherwise choose to do (e.g., giving their own necessities to the other group). This is coercion (Dahl, 1957; Raven, 1965). Coercive power constrains choice for others. Although coercion may occur directly and interpersonally, as in a mugging, it can also occur indirectly due to the involved parties' group membership. Learning that similar others have been harmed, as in cases of publicized rape, intimate partner violence, and other kinds of terrorism, produces fear in potential targets, so that coercion can vicariously constrain choices. For example, newspaper descriptions of cadavers of Guatemala's death-squad victims communicated to readers that the victims had been tortured and raped, and that similar fates could be expected for others who opposed the government (Torres, 2005). When police, vigilantes, or other official or unofficial agents of the dominant group exercise violence against subordinate group members, this coercion can be considered terror, a means of maintaining oppression and intergroup dominance (e.g., in social dominance theory; Sidanius & Pratto, 1999, Chapter 8).

Resource Control, Expropriation and Exploitation   Humans' need for water, food, shelter and other material necessities makes control of access to resources a kind of power. Groups may restrict physical access, ownership, employment, and remuneration to themselves or may coerce other groups by offering limited access. In theory, exchanges concerning resources could be egalitarian in the sense of having complementary interdependence. For example, if a landowner pays a fair wage to tenant farmers so that the farmers and the landowner all are advantaged by the relation, or if a husband and wife divide the paid and unpaid work of family life so that their needs and freedoms are equal, the parties might have a balance of power (Becker, 1981). However, egalitarian interdependence between groups is rare (Sidanius & Pratto, 1999).

Group membership, especially subordinate group membership, often limits life choices, and, coupled with people's need to obtain material necessities, such limits enable *expropriation*. Expropriation is taking the fruits of others' labor without adequate compensation (e.g., Jackman, 2001). This includes underpaying a group compared to what another group earns, or to their own needs, and uncompensated work, such as that performed by the estimated tens of millions of contemporary slaves (e.g., Bales, 1999). More broadly, exploitation can mean taking any valued aspect of another (dignity, privacy, or work), for one's own benefit or pleasure. Exploitation dehumanizes people by reducing them to chattel, to laborers, to sex objects, to sources of amusement, or to some other diminution of their totality as human beings. For example, sexual objectification can erase a woman's non-sexual senses of self (Saguy, Dovidio, Quinn, & Pratto, 2010). Members of subordinate groups experience such treatment more frequently than members of dominant groups, due both to material conditions (e.g., Bales, 1999) and to shared prejudice and stereotypes (e.g., Swim, Hyers, Cohen, & Ferguson, 2001).

Obligations: Paternalism/Maternalism and Transformative/Facilitative Power

In infancy, infirmity, and illness, humans require the care of others, and families and other care-giving relationships (e.g., teacher–student) have the purpose of survival and development. In *paternalism* or *maternalism*, junior members depend on senior members, and the senior is obliged to care for the junior. Some such relationships are *facilitative* or *transformative*, in that the senior will use her greater power to help the other to develop and become more self-empowered (Wartenberg, 1990). Such power relations are asymmetric but not exploitative. But maternalistic/paternalistic relations may be exploitative when the senior defines the interests of the junior in a way that serves the senior more than the junior (Pratto & Walker, 2000). Several intergroup and international relations throughout history fit this description, and they are justified by prejudicial ideologies such as apologies for colonization ("the White man's burden"), "benevolent" sexism, and economic rules imposed by the International Monetary Fund (see Jackman, 1994).

Implications of Intergroup Power for Stereotype Contents

Groups who are able to meet their own needs are empowered whether or not they influence or exploit other groups, and even if they are segregated from other groups (Henry & Pratto, 2010). When one group is more powerful than another, the more powerful group more easily meets its own needs and has a broader alternative set. Because power has life-and-death consequences, people try to gauge who will likely harm or benefit them. One fundamental judgment people make of groups is whether groups are trustworthy or beneficent (e.g., Leach, Minescu, Poppe, & Hagendoorn, 2008), depending on whether they share compatible goals (Alexander, Brewer, & Livingston, 2005) or compete against their own group (Fiske, Xu, Cuddy, & Glick, 1999). People also judge how much power groups generally have, but make this judgment for specific kinds of power. This implies that stereotypes of groups will include a trustworthiness component and also components corresponding to each major kind of power: violence (traits concerning forcefulness), resource control (wealth), asymmetric obligations (dominance), and legitimacy (popularity).

To test these predictions, we asked 24 U.S. undergraduates to rate groups on a number of personality traits that reflect different types of power and trust. Among the groups were some commonly studied in U.S. stereotyping research (e.g., White women, White men, Black women, Black men) and others we thought represented high or low levels of power in meeting different needs: violence (soldiers, peace activists), resources (rich people, welfare recipients), obligations (housewives, children), or legitimacy (judges, convicts). Other stimulus groups were terrorists, working poor, politicians, human rights workers, chief executive officers, parents, retarded people, career women, white-collar criminals, and nuns. Different orders of these groups were randomly assigned to different participants.

As in much research in person- and group-perception, a discriminant function analysis produced a two-factor space (general power and trustworthiness) for the groups. For example, CEOs and rich people were rated high in power and moderate in trustworthiness; Black women, children, and retarded people were rated low in power and moderate in trustworthiness. The two discriminant functions, however, classified only 35% of the groups correctly. In our view, this is because the power–trust model does not explain why perceivers derive such stereotype contents of the groups, such as through the perceptions of the *kinds* of power groups wield. For example, although white-collar criminals and politicians were rated high on general power but low on general trust, they may be perceived to exercise different kinds of power. When we examined the trait dimensions more specific to particular *kinds* of power, we were able to distinguish these two groups (as well as groups within each quadrant of the discriminant function space). Results of these repeated measures analyses of variance by group and trait dimensions (popularity pertaining to legitimacy, forcefulness pertaining to violence, wealth pertaining to resources, and dominance pertaining to obligations) showed that groups could be distinguished by their signature patterns of kinds of power. For example, terrorists were rated much higher on forcefulness and lower on wealth than politicians (see Figure 7.1). Other experiments show that people make these kinds of trait inferences based on the kinds of power people use (Pratto & Lee, 2010).

These results highlight the importance of theorizing carefully about the nature of intergroup relations when examining stereotypes and prejudice. Here, we have shown that considering particular *types* of power, instead of labeling everything status or warmth, helps us distinguish among stereotype contents of different groups Other studies of stereotyping have fruitfully considered how roles held by different groups influence stereotype contents (e.g., Eagly, 1987), and image theory (Herrmann, 1985) has addressed how goal-compatibility, power, and cultural dominance between nations influences countries' stereotypes of and attitudes toward one another and why they are not symmetric (e.g., Alexander, Brewer, & Livingston, 2005; Alexander, Levin, & Henry, 2005). Instead of focusing just on the contents of stereotypes and form of prejudice, we can understand why they have the texture and color they do by attending to the underlying warp, the structure into which they are woven.

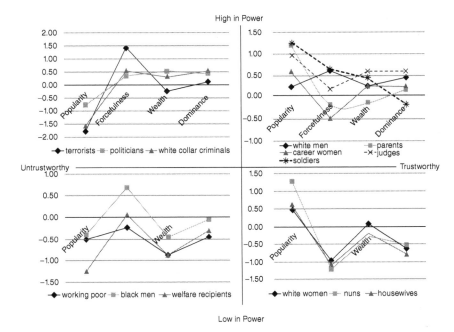

Figure 7.1   Standardized mean ratings of various groups by power-typed traits (popularity, forcefulness, wealth, dominance) arranged by whether a group was rated low or high in overall power and trustworthiness.

Intergroup Relations are Enculturated and Institutionalized

Finally, the intergroup perspective on stereotypes and prejudice emphasizes that intergroup relations are not just interpersonal relations between members of different groups. Often, stable power relations between groups are both enculturated and institutionalized (e.g., Jones, 1997; Pratto, 1999). Intergroup relations are enculturated in structuring particular cultures and in instantiating and being supported by culturally shared worldviews. Further, the actions of groups and their members are interpreted through cultural meaning systems. For example, most popular accounts of U.S. history begin not with Native American peoples but with European pilgrims and colonizers, whose desires for freedom and prosperity, respectively, are the progenitors of "American" cultural values. Origin myths often establish who are the "true" people of the culture (and who is excluded). Reminders of such cultural stories are readily found in symbols, linguistic expressions, and other cultural artifacts. For example, Sardinia's flag depicts the heads of four Moors blindfolded for execution, to symbolize the conquest of Sardinia over its previous rulers.

Even when intergroup relations change, or when particular events or actions make them seem to change, these new events are often interpreted through cultural lenses. For example, the editorial cartoonist Tom Toles quoted

Thomas Jefferson's phrase from the Declaration of Independence "that all men are created equal" in his cartoon declaring that this foundational cultural sentiment was ratified the day Barack Obama was elected as president. The cartoon situates Obama's election as the culmination of American principles while pointing out the long history of failure to enact those principles. The embeddedness of intergroup relations within culture constrains the direction and pace of change in intergroup relations (see also Johnson, 1994; Pratto, 1999).

People in different group positions and with different cultural stances may interpret the same action or event through different cultural lenses. The different interpretations may create or sustain stereotypes and prejudice. For example, the cross erected by Catholics at Auschwitz, where Nazis murdered many Jews, might be interpreted through a Catholic lens as a way of making sacred ground where profound sin was committed and of honoring the innocent, who suffered and died like Christ. But, through a Jewish lens, this cross can be interpreted as an erasure of the Jewishness of the murder victims, a misguided attempt to redeem a people who have always been God's people, or even a sign that Christian bigotry has in fact conquered Europe's Jews (see Carroll, 2001). Intercultural misunderstandings can lead to profound injury, as in this example.

Further, people can use other people's cultural meanings to act in ways that deliberately humiliate, defile, and even provoke violence. For example, Americans relied on knowledge of Islamic sensibilities to torture and humiliate prisoners in Abu-Ghraib and Guantánamo Bay prisons, Romans defiled bodies by leaving them on crucifixes until they were eaten by carrion in offense against Jewish burial customs, and Ariel Sharon set off the Second Intifada by visiting the Al-Aqsa Mosque. The multiplicity of cultural worldviews when groups interact suggests that stereotypes and prejudice should be understood from more than one group's perspective.

Institutionalization means that the ordinary ways that institutions behave often reflect and even reinforce the tenor of intergroup relations. For example, laws concerning heterosexual marriage allow corporations and governments not to recognize the relationships of gay men and lesbian partners. But, just as institutional practices can reinforce intergroup inequality, changing the operation of institutions can readily change intergroup relations. For example, President Truman's executive order to racially integrate the U.S. armed forces prompted a major reduction of Whites' racism against Blacks (Moskos, 1966). Institutional changes can also beget cultural changes. For example, to attract women settlers, the Western U.S. states were among the first to allow women to own property in their own names; these same states were also the first to grant women suffrage (Matsuda, 1985). Full appreciation of intergroup relations should consider how institutions and cultural meaning systems and symbols interface with those relations, as they provide the larger context for stereotyping and prejudice. One means of doing so is to replicate different intergroup, cultural, or historical institutional conditions in the laboratory. Another method is to examine stereotypes and prejudice in organizations before and after changes in their internal practices. A third method is to compare regional or societal outcomes by comparing societies with different laws or cultural norms or societies undergoing change.

Summary

The first section explained aspects of intergroup relations (e.g., numerosity, segregation) and argued that power in intergroup relations results in asymmetries in stereotypes and prejudice. The next section shows how stereotypes and prejudice affect individuals to get them to act in ways that reproduce culture and social structure. We organize the research with regard to how structural features influence stereotyping and prejudice and how these influence aspects of social structure, including asymmetries in which groups get stereotyped, discrimination, segregation, social stability, and social change.

WHO GETS STEREOTYPED?

Whereas aspects of intergroup relations give rise to stereotypes and prejudice, stereotypes and prejudice also maintain social structure by targeting which groups get stereotyped and peculiarized. Powerful groups are overrepresented in the media, and this makes them common exemplars in people's minds, which leads to the implicit sense that they are "normal" (Pratto, Hegarty, & Korchmaros, 2007). As norm theory (Kahneman & Miller, 1986) predicts, exemplars who differ from implicit cognitive norms, such as subordinate group members, attract attention, and people explain their "difference" from the implicit norm using stereotypes (Hegarty & Pratto, 2001), which are often communicated to others (Pratto et al., 2007). This leads to stereotypes of less powerful groups being communicated more broadly and more frequently, so they continue to be more cognitively accessible than stereotypes of powerful groups.

The implicit contrast between those who differ from a hidden norm leads to "otherization" or an implicit exclusion from general or dominant social categories. For example, Americans associate U.S. symbols with White Americans more than with non-White Americans (e.g., Devos & Banaji, 2005). Barlow, Taylor, and Lambert (2000) found that, even though Black Americans felt American, they were not perceived as such by White Americans. Cultural and mental group dominance contributes to stereotyping and prejudice. This asymmetrical instigation of stereotyping and "othering" maintains the power structure by freeing members of powerful groups from the burden of stereotyping and prejudice. For example, in the United States, a White male walking down the street rarely attracts attention as non-normative. He will most likely not be stopped by the police or catcalled—experiences that are not uncommon for Black and Hispanic Americans (American Civil Liberties Union, 2009) and women (Fairchild & Rudman, 2008), respectively.

WHO STEREOTYPES OTHERS?

People in positions of authority can control others' outcomes and can also stereotype. When told that they would have an influence over a hiring decision, participants in a laboratory study paid more attention to stereotype-consistent information about a Hispanic job applicant than when they were told that they would have no influence over the decision (Goodwin, Operario, & Fiske, 1998). Of course, such inattention might not only harm the target but also leads the stereotyper to make non-optimal decisions by relying on stereotypical information. Glaser (2006) showed that, when institutions engage in stereotyping—for instance, when police departments use "racial profiling" to decide whom to pull over—they increase racial disparities in who goes to prison. Fortunately, institutional controls can also help curb stereotyping and the discrimination that can result from this. For example, although people high on social dominance orientation often use race or gender rather than competence to decide whom to hire, when they are given explicit directions from legitimate authorities to use job-relevant criteria, they cease discriminating (Umphress, Simmons, Boswell, & Triana, 2008).

STEREOTYPES, PREJUDICE, AND VARIETIES OF ATTENTION

Stereotypes and associated prejudice help to maintain the social structure because they produce different outcomes for groups with different kinds of power. In some cases, stereotypes and prejudice lead to vigilance, in some they lead to patronizing prejudice, and in some they lead to a lack of attention, or social invisibility.

Vigilance: Danger Stereotypes and Fearful Prejudice

Stereotypes concerning a group's threat to one's wholeness can lead people to be vigilant (Schaller, Faulkner, Park, Neuberg, & Kenrick, 2004). The type of attention paid to young Black males in the United States exemplifies this vigilance: young Black males are stereotyped as criminal and violent (e.g., Welch, 2007), and this dangerous portrayal induces fear, which can be characterized as prejudice (e.g., Cottrell & Neuberg, 2005). Both the stereotype and the prejudice are communicated, such as when the media described Black survival tactics after Hurricane Katrina as "looting" (e.g., Henkel, Dovidio, & Gaertner, 2006) and when White parents pull their children closer when a Black individual approaches (Sears, 1988). Similarly, in the Western media, the incessant association between terrorists and Arabs has Arabs stereotyped as violent terrorists, which leads to a fearful emotional response. Bar-Tal (1996) found that, among Jewish children in Israel, the term "Arab" was learned very early, and, even though it was accompanied by little knowledge, the children described Arabs by referring to violent and aggressive behaviors. Perceived threat exacerbates such prejudice. For example, Schaller and Abeysinghe (2006) found that, when Sinhalese students in Sri Lanka were made to feel like a numerical minority relative to Tamils, their attitudes and beliefs about the Tamils were more demonizing and they were less conciliatory than when they were made to feel like the numerical majority.

Prurience: Grotesque Stereotypes and Disgusted Prejudice

Stereotypes concerning group status and violation of group norms pertain to the need to belong and can lead to another type of vigilant prejudice: a disgusted emotional reaction (e.g., Haidt, Rozin, McCauley, & Imada, 1997), resulting in avoidance and distancing. This type of reaction can come from perceived flaws of character or body such as sexual deviance or uncleanliness. People who are overweight experience this type of discrimination, especially in individualistic cultures, because their "failure to control their weight" is perceived as a moral flaw, with negative consequences for their careers, friendships, and physical and mental health (e.g., Crandall, Nierman, & Hebl, 2009). A disgusted emotional reaction may also characterize responses to people who are "unclean" in some cultures, such as Orthodox Judaism or Islam, in which some group members are excluded from religious practices because they are unclean by nature (e.g., women) or by ritual (e.g., those who have not ritually cleansed themselves). An extreme example of discrimination fed by such prejudice is the stoning of alleged female adulterers.

Paternalism/ Maternalism: Incompetent Stereotypes and Pitying Prejudice

Stereotypes reflecting a failure to fulfill obligations can lead to patronizing attention. Groups stereotyped as unable to provide and care for themselves adequately experience patronizing prejudice, characterized by pity, expressed concern, paternalism or maternalism, vigilance to protect, and power-limiting "protection" (Fiske et al., 1999). Among groups that receive this kind of attention are women, children, the elderly, the handicapped, and people from the developing world. Such dependency maintains the power structure. On an individual level, the type of help offered to outgroup members depends on one's intergroup orientation, such that people who are high in social dominance orientation (Pratto, Sidanius, Stallworth, & Malle, 1994) offer dependency-oriented help rather than empowering help to outgroup members (Halabi, Dovidio, & Nadler, 2008).

Invisibility: Lack of Attention

Groups unable to meet others' needs or to prevent such needs from being met can lead to a profound *lack* of attention, or social invisibility. This occurs when a group gets little to no attention or acknowledgement in the media, public policy, and even research in stereotyping and prejudice. Social invisibility is experienced on a group and an individual level. For example, Yeh, Kim, Pituc, and Atkins (2008) found that, for Chinese immigrant youth, feeling invisible was a major concern for adjustment to living in the United States. There are several reasons why groups may be rendered invisible by normative group members or by themselves.

Groups may be rendered invisible to hide ongoing injustice, because they are marginalized by institutions, because they lack legal standing, or because their agency is not apparent. The U.S. treatment of Native Americans is a strong case in point. Their near physical and legal banishment is reflected in the national narrative that renders contemporary Native Americans invisible—they are part of the national story, but only in a historical context, which freezes them in the past and prevents their visibility as present-day people (e.g., Brayboy & Searle, 2007; Fryberg & Townsend, 2008). Being conquered in perpetuity, or not performing visible work, makes groups seem powerless and groups themselves disappear. Care and maintenance work and work out of the public eye, such as janitorial work, farm work, housework, eldercare, and child-care, seems mostly invisible. Such work is often performed by women, immigrants, and rural people, contributing to the social invisibility of these groups..

Due to historically experienced prejudice and discrimination, groups whose stigma can be concealed may purposely hide, anticipating stigma or discrimination if their identity becomes known. To other groups, these groups may not exist. For example, the work done by illegal immigrants is often hidden, and specific numbers of illegal immigrants are difficult to document (e.g., Bean, Corona, Tuiran, Woodrow-Lafield, & Van Hook, 2001) because discovery of an individual's illegal status may mean deportation. Historically, gay men and lesbians have been invisible because they were not represented in the media (e.g., Gross, 2002), and gay men and lesbians do not reveal their sexual orientation because homosexuality was/is considered a crime or sin. More recently, gay men and lesbians have begun to gain attention by publicly acknowledging their sexual orientation, but the "coming out" process can be dangerous, difficult, and painful (e.g., Herek, 2009).

Some groups may be rendered invisible because they do not fit into standard category schemes. For example, Black women do not receive attention in the civil rights movement because they are female and do not receive attention in the women's rights movement because they are Black (Purdie-Vaughns & Eibach, 2008). They are neither "normatively" Black nor "normatively" female, which renders them invisible in both categories. Similarly, lesbians are not included in the category of "gay" because they are not men and not included in the category of "women" because they are not straight (Blackwood & Wieringa, 2003; Hegarty & Pratto, 2004). In the United States, race is thought of primarily in terms of Black and White, which groups different ethnicities together in one of these categories and excludes others, such as Native Americans, Arab Americans, Asian Americans, Hispanics, and multiracial people. Not all those who are denigrated have elaborated cultural stereotypes about their groups. A major unanswered research question, then, is exactly what influences when stereotypes of groups develop and when they do not. The experiences of people in denigrated and often stereotyped groups and in denigrated "invisible" social categories may be different, and the means of reducing prejudice against either type of group may also differ.

STEREOTYPES AS PRESCRIPTIVE SOCIAL DEVICES

Stereotypes can allege what group members are like. In addition to describing, stereotypes can *prescribe* (Prentice & Carranza, 2002)—implying how groups *should* be. For example, because of the stereotype of all women as nurturing and compassionate, women are expected to *be* nurturing and compassionate. It is this prescriptive nature of stereotypes that makes them ideological and not just descriptive or expectations (e.g., Jost & Banaji, 1994; Pratto, 1999).

Because stereotypes are prescriptive, those who do not fit the stereotypes about them often face negative consequences. For example, Rudman and Glick (2001) found support for the *backlash effect* (Rudman, 1998) when they examined evaluations of women in a hiring setting. They described the available job in either feminine or masculine terms, and the applicants for that job were described as either androgynous or agentic. When students made hiring decisions, agentic women were discriminated against because they were not "nice" enough. Participants' stereotypes formed implicit standards women failed to meet, leading to hiring discrimination. In aggregate, these effects of stereotypes feed back into the social structure, punishing women who do not meet stereotyped expectations and preventing them from becoming more powerful.

In addition, when a particular group's needs violate the perceptions of what that group *should* need, those needs often go unmet. For centuries, American pundits claimed that women did not need education, and Victorians promoted the idea that exercise and sport were bad for women, with discriminatory consequences. At present, the stereotype of Asian Americans as academic high achievers prevents them from receiving the attention and assistance that they may need in an academic setting (Wong, Lai, Nagasawa, & Lin, 1998). These examples show that prescriptive stereotypes can lead to discrimination.

In some cases, the stereotypes of dominants may be the expectation, or prescription, for everybody's character and behavior. For example, it is not uncommon to hear remarks about subordinate groups that reflect an expectation for those groups to be "more like us," the dominant group. Hispanic immigrants are told, "Learn English!" Gay men and Black men are told to show sexual self-restraint. Young girls are told to "throw like boys," and women are expected to fit into the workplace in the same way that men do.

While such remarks may make it seem as if dominant group members want subordinate group members to be more like them, the reality is often very different. African Americans who are well educated and demand respect are derided as "uppity" (e.g., Bell, 2004). Women who speak up and have power are called "bitchy" (e.g., Rudman, 1998). It is the attempt of subordinate group members to match the dominant group prescription that evokes backlash from dominant group members (e.g., Rudman & Glick, 2001). Further, subordinate group members who try to conform to dominant norms can experience negative reactions from their own group members. When subordinate group members try to be like the dominants, their authenticity as a fellow group member is often called into question (e.g., Fordham & Ogbu, 1986). Native Americans call their peers who are good in school "apples"—red on the outside but white on the inside (Garrett & Pichette, 2000). "Oreo" is one parallel slur for good Black students (e.g., Cook & Ludwig, 1997). Boys who are not judged sufficiently masculine are described in feminine terms or called gay (e.g., Martin, 1990). Girls demean each others' attractiveness as females by calling each other "manly" or "ugly" and each others' sexual virtue by using words like "slut" (e.g., Renold, 2002). Subordinate group members who violate stereotype expectations receive negative attention and prejudice from within and from outside their group.

HOW STEREOTYPES AND PREJUDICE LEGITIMIZE THE SOCIAL STRUCTURE

One of the effects of stereotype prescriptions is that they legitimize existing inequality within societies. One means of legitimizing inequality is to delegitimize certain groups (e.g., Bar-Tal, 1990). For example, stereotypes can portray groups as inhuman or subhuman, justifying their extermination (Castano & Giner-Sorolla, 2006), or as completely immoral, and therefore outside the scope of moral concern (e.g., Hubbard, 1998). Another means is that stereotypes and prejudice legitimize discrimination, which then allows for the justification of differential outcomes between groups (e.g., Reyna, Brandt, & Viki, 2009). In addition, stereotypes can legitimize or delegitimize specific groups' use of different types of power (Pratto & Pitpitan, 2008). Taken together, these processes maintain power structures within societies.

Whereas the prescriptive nature of stereotypes allows dominant group members to use power, stereotype prescriptions also prevent subordinate group members from using or gaining power. Sometimes, the content of the stereotypes of subordinate groups directly delegitimizes use of power. For example, a stereotype of African Americans and Latinos is that they are incompetent (e.g., Fiske, Cuddy, Glick, & Xu, 2002); therefore they should not be allowed or be able to use power. Other times, the content of the stereotypes of subordinate groups indirectly delegitimizes use of power, such as when they call into question a group's deservingness. For example, a stereotype of women is that they are materialistic and want to marry for money, calling into question the legitimacy of women who do have financial resources. Similarly, African Americans are stereotyped as criminal (e.g., Devine & Elliot, 1995), which calls into question the legitimacy of the financial success of African Americans; when they appear to have money (e.g., nice cars), they are suspected of being criminals (e.g., Dottolo & Stewart, 2008).

In addition to granting (or limiting) the use of power for dominant (or subordinate) groups, stereotypes and prejudice often legitimize violence against subordinate groups. For example, Bar-Tal (1998) has described an ideology called an "ethos of conflict" in societies where there seems to be intractable conflict. This set of beliefs, woven into the social structure, maintains the state of conflict and justifies the group's purpose in conflict (e.g., security, ethnocentrism, victimhood mentality, patriotism, and unity) while delegitimizing the opposing group and questioning its humaneness. Ideologies and stereotypes change people's interpretation and evaluation of new information (e.g., Iyengar & Ottati, 1994) to be consistent with the ethos of conflict. For example, Bar-Tal, Raviv, Raviv, and Dgani-Hirsch (2009) found that, when Israeli Jews evaluated photographs of the Israeli–Palestinian conflict, their endorsement of the ethos of conflict predicted their perceptions of the Palestinians as more aggressive, assigning blame to Palestinians, attributing the conflict to internal and stable causes on the Palestinian side (as opposed situational factors), and increased endorsement of negative stereotypes of Palestinians. In this case, within an ethos of conflict, the Israeli Jews' stereotype of Palestinians as aggressive, threatening, and violent legitimizes Israel's violence against them.

Stereotyping can lead to discrimination in hiring and law enforcement as well. The stereotype of women as incompetent may lead a manager in a corporation to perceive the women in the office as less competent than the men or as less competent than they actually are (e.g., Heilman, Block, Martell, & Simon, 1989). When it comes time to consider employees for promotion, that manager may overlook qualified women, instead promoting the men. Because the manager perceives the women as less competent, the discriminatory promotion decision is legitimized and justified. Similarly, the stereotype of African Americans as criminal may lead law-enforcement officers to perceive an African-American driver as suspect or potentially criminal. The officers may pull over an African-American driver and believe that they are justified in doing so, even if that driver was doing nothing criminal. The stereotype of African Americans as criminal legitimizes the discriminatory act of "racial profiling" (e.g., Welch, 2007).

SOCIAL STRUCTURE, STEREOTYPES, AND PREJUDICE AS A DYNAMIC SYSTEM

Stereotypes and prejudice change to match and legitimize the social structure—they are legitimizing myths (e.g., Pratto et al., 1994). In a world with prejudice and lots of negative stereotypes, change may seem like a good thing. However, stereotype content may change only to reinforce the harmful ways that subordinate groups are treated and to continue to legitimize the social structure.

Because much research on White racism has focused only on late 20th-century U.S. racism, we will use Whites' stereotypes of Blacks to illustrate this point. Stereotypes about Blacks have changed over time to "match" the nature of relations between dominant Whites and subordinate Blacks (e.g., Geist &

Nelson, 1992). During the Antebellum period, slave-holding Whites were economically dependent on their slaves, and many had Black slaves or servants in their houses or worked alongside Blacks in their fields, making the two groups somewhat intimate. The patronizing and sometimes brutal treatment of Black people was justified because White leaders stereotyped Blacks as child-like, stupid, ignorant, and bestial. These stereotypic "traits" justified slavery because slavery was "good for them" (Jackman, 1994).

When slavery was abolished, the relationship between Blacks and Whites changed, and so did Whites' stereotypes of Blacks (e.g., Helg, 2000). Following a brief post-war period in which Blacks earned wages and elected Black governors and Black majority legislatures in Southern states, Whites found other ways to reassert their dominance. Stereotypes of Black people as immoral, dangerous, and conniving justified Whites' blatantly discriminatory and brutal treatment during this period. Examples of such treatment include the poll tax, Jim Crow laws, and "vigilante" terrorism (destruction of Black property, newspapers, and widespread lynching; Davis, 1983).

Once White hegemony was re-established, Blacks posed less of a power threat to Whites, and so their stereotypes of Black people changed once again, from their being immoral and conniving to a romanticized version where they were simple and quaint, yet still irresponsible, stupid, and lazy (Lemons, 1977). Their alleged incompetence and laziness justified practices of institutional discrimination through segregation, preventing them from holding good jobs. During this period, the comic Black man, known as Step 'n Fetchit, became both a common figure in popular entertainment (vaudeville and musical revue) and a national joke, further dehumanizing and humiliating Black people (Lemons, 1977).

During and after the civil rights movement, however, when Black people demanded equal treatment and respect, the relationship between Blacks and Whites changed again. Whites viewed Blacks as competing for public goods and legitimacy and so felt threatened. Whites' stereotypes changed again to fit the new interracial relations, such that Black people were portrayed as lazy and loud, obnoxious, criminal, and uppity. These stereotypes justify discriminatory treatment of Black people through excessive surveillance, criminalization, and marginalization (e.g., Welch, 2007).

CONCLUSION

In studying stereotyping and prejudice, it is critical to take into account the broader context of intergroup relations. This is because stereotypes and prejudice can occur in individuals, but they both arise from the structural conditions of intergroup relations and work to influence those relations. A purely individualistic social psychology of stereotypes and prejudice omits the important fact that discrimination is exercised largely by institutions, and stereotypes and prejudice are learned from cultural socialization (e.g., Pratto, 1999). Further, power inequalities between groups affect the contents of stereotypes, the frequency of stereotyping, and the flavor of prejudice. Stereotypes, prejudice, and discrimination on an individual level affect and are affected by the broader social structure within which they exist, including enculturated stereotypes, power dynamics, and institutional discrimination. In addition, using precise terms to identify the nature of the intergroup relationship (e.g., "power" rather than "status," "dominant" rather than "majority") helps both researchers and readers to be theoretically clear.

By considering stereotyping and prejudice in the context of intergroup relations, we can address important practical issues: How can contexts be changed so that stereotypes and prejudice occur less often? How can values for tolerance and justice be brought to bear in promoting public acceptance of institutional change? What processes can ameliorate inequality and exclusion without being unfair to other groups? What is it that enables certain societies to hold stereotypes and prejudice relatively in check, whereas other societies use prejudice and stereotypes to excuse their responsibilities or even to justify genocide? Remembering the broader social context allows social psychologists and other researchers to begin to answer such questions.

REFERENCES

Aebischer, V., Hewstone, M., & Henderson, M. (1984). Minority influence and musical preference: Innovation by conversion not coercion. *European Journal of Social Psychology, 14*, 233–333.

Alexander, M. G., Brewer, M. B., & Livingston, R. W. (2005). Putting stereotype content in context: Image theory and interethnic stereotypes. *Personality and Social Psychology Bulletin, 31*, 781–794.

Alexander, M. G., Levin, S., & Henry, P. J. (2005). Image theory, social identity, and social dominance: Structural characteristics and individual motives underlying international images. *Political Psychology, 26*, 27–45.

American Civil Liberties Union. (2009). *The persistence of racial and ethnic profiling in the United States: A follow-up report to the U.N. Committee on the Elimination of Racial Discrimination*. New York: ACLU.

Bales, K. (1999). *Disposable people: New slavery in the global economy*. Berkeley: University of California Press.

Barlow, K. M., Taylor, D. M., & Lambert, W. E. (2000). Ethnicity in America and feeling "American." *Journal of Psychology: Interdisciplinary and Applied, 134*, 581–600.

Bar-Tal, D. (1989). Delegitimization: The extreme case of stereotyping and prejudice. In D. Bar-Tal, C. F. Graumann, A. W. Kruglanski, & W. Stroebe (Eds.), *Stereotyping and prejudice: Changing conceptions* (pp. 169–182). New York: Springer.

Bar-Tal, D. (1990). Causes and consequences of delegitimization: Models of conflict and ethnocentrism. *Journal of Social Issues, 46*, 65–81.

Bar-Tal, D. (1996). Development of social categories and stereotypes in early childhood: The case of "the Arab" concept formation, stereotype and attitudes by Jewish children in Israel. *International Journal of Intercultural Relations, 20*, 341–370.

Bar-Tal, D. (1998). Societal beliefs in times of intractable conflict: The Israeli case. *International Journal of Conflict Management, 9*, 22–50.

Bar-Tal, D., Raviv, A., Raviv, A., & Dgani-Hirsch, A. (2009). The influence of the ethos of conflict on Israeli Jews' interpretation of Jewish–Palestinian encounters. *Journal of Conflict Resolution, 53*, 94–118.

Bean, F. D., Corona, R., Tuiran, R., Woodrow-Lafield, K. A., & Van Hook, J. (2001). Circular, invisible, and ambiguous migrants: Components of difference in estimates of the number of unauthorized Mexican migrants in the United States. *Demography, 38*, 411–422.

Becker, G. (1981). *A treatise on the family*. Cambridge, MA: Harvard University Press.

Bell, E. L. (2004). Myths, stereotypes, and realities of Black women: A personal reflection. *Journal of Applied Behavioral Science, 40*, 146–159.

Blackwood, E., & Wieringa, S. E. (2003). Sapphic shadows: Challenging the silence in the study of sexuality. In L. D. Garnets & D. C. Kimmel (Eds.), *Psychological perspectives on lesbian, gay, and bisexual experiences* (2nd ed., pp. 410–434). New York: Columbia University Press.

Brayboy, B. M. J., & Searle, K. A. (2007). Thanksgiving and serial killers: Representations of American Indians in schools. In S. Books (Ed.), *Invisible children in the society and its schools* (3rd ed., pp. 173–192). Mahwah, NJ: Lawrence Erlbaum Associates.

Carroll, J. (2001). *Constantine's sword: The Church and the Jews*. Boston: Houghton Mifflin.

Castano, E., & Giner-Sorolla, R. (2006). Not quite human: Infra-humanization as a response to collective responsibility for intergroup killing. *Journal of Personality and Social Psychology, 90*, 804–818.

Clark, K. B., Chein, I., & Cook, S. A. (1952/2004). The effects of segregation and the consequences of desegregation. *American Psychologist, 59*, 495–501.

Cole, E. R., & Yip, T. (2008). Using outgroup comfort to predict Black students' college experience. *Cultural Diversity and Ethnic Minority Psychology, 14*, 57–66.

Conway, M., Pizzamiglio, M. T., & Mount, L. (1996). Status, communality, and agency: Implications for stereotypes of gender and other groups. *Journal of Personality and Social Psychology, 71*, 25–38.

Cook, P. J., & Ludwig, J. (1997). Weighing the "burden of 'acting White'": Are there race differences in attitudes toward education? *Journal of Policy Analysis and Management, 16*, 256–278.

Cotter, D. A., Hermsen, J. M., & Vanneman, R. (2004, April 4). *Gender inequality at work*. New York: Russell Sage Foundation. Retrieved from http://www.bsos. umd.edu/socy/vanneman/papers/Cotter_etal.pdf

Cottrell, C. A., & Neuberg, S. L. (2005). Different emotional reactions to different groups: A sociofunctional threat-based approach to "prejudice." *Journal of Personality and Social Psychology, 88*, 770–789.

Crandall, C. S., Nierman, A., & Hebl, M. (2009). Anti-fat prejudice. In T. Nelson (Ed.), *Handbook of prejudice, stereotyping, and discrimination* (pp. 469–487). New York: Psychology Press.

Dahl, R. (1957). The concept of power. *Behavioral Science, 2*, 201–215.

Davis, A. Y. (1983). *Women, race, and class*. New York: Random House.

Devine, P. G., & Elliot, A. J. (1995). Are racial stereotypes really fading? The Princeton Trilogy revisited. *Personality and Social Psychology Bulletin, 21*, 1139–1150.

Devos, T., & Banaji, M. R. (2005). American = White? *Journal of Personality and Social Psychology, 88*, 447–466.

Dijke, M. van, & Poppe, M. (2006). Striving for personal power as a basis for social power dynamics. *European Journal of Social Psychology, 36,* 537–556.

Dixon, J., & Durrheim, K. (2003). Contact and the ecology of racial division: Some varieties of information segregation. *British Journal of Social Psychology, 42,* 1–23.

Dixon, J., Durrheim, K., & Tredoux, C. (2005). Beyond the optimal contact strategy: A reality check for the contact hypothesis. *American Psychologist, 60,* 697–711.

Dottolo, A. L., & Stewart, A. J. (2008). "Don't ever forget now, you're a Black man in America": Intersections of Race, Class and Gender in Encounters with the Police. *Sex Roles, 59,* 350–364.

Eagly, A. H. (1987). *Sex differences in social behavior: A social-role account.* Hillsdale, NJ: Lawrence Erlbaum Associates.

Eagly, A.H., & Steffen, V. J. (1984). Gender stereotypes stem from the distribution of men and women into roles. *Journal of Personality and Social Psychology, 46,* 735–754.

Fairchild, K., & Rudman, L. A. (2008) Everyday stranger harassment and women's objectification. *Social Justice Research, 21,* 338–357.

Fiske, S. T., & Berdahl, J. (2007). Social power. In A. W. Kruglanski & E. T. Higgins (Eds.), *Social psychology: Handbook of basic principles* (2nd ed., pp. 678–692). New York: Guilford Press.

Fiske, S. T., Cuddy, A. C., Glick, P., & Xu, J. (2002). A model of (often mixed) stereotype content: Competence and warmth respectively follow from perceived status and competition. *Journal of Personality and Social Psychology, 82,* 878–902.

Fiske, S. T., Xu, J., Cuddy, A. C., & Glick, P. (1999). (Dis)respecting versus (dis)liking: Status and interdependence predict ambivalent stereotypes of competence and warmth. *Journal of Social Issues, 55,* 473–489.

Fordham, S., & Obgu, J. U. (1986). Black students' school success: Coping with the "burden of acting white." *Urban Review, 18,* 176–206.

Fryberg, S. A., & Townsend, S. S. M. (2008). The psychology of invisibility. In G. Adams, M. Biernat, N. R. Branscombe, C. S. Crandall, & L. S. Wrightsman, (Eds.), *Commemorating Brown: The social psychology of racism and discrimination* (pp. 173–193). Washington, DC: American Psychological Association.

Garrett, M. T., & Pichette, E. F. (2000). Red as an apple: Native American acculturation and counseling with or without reservation. *Journal of Counseling and Development, 78,* 3–13.

Geist, C. D., & Nelson, A. M. S. (1992). From the plantation to *Bel-Air*: A brief history of Black stereotypes. In J. Nachbar & K. Lause (Eds.), *Popular culture: An introductory text* (pp. 262–276). Bowling Green, OH: Popular Press.

Glaser, J. (2006). The efficacy and effect of racial profiling: A mathematical simulation approach. *Journal of Policy Analysis and Management, 25,* 395–416.

Goodwin, S. A., Operario, D., & Fiske, S. T. (1998). Situational power and interpersonal dominance facilitate bias and inequity. *Journal of Social Issues, 54,* 677–698.

Gramsci, A. (1971). *Selections from the prison notebooks.* New York: Wishart.

Gross, L. (2002). *Up from invisibility: Lesbians, gay men, and the media in America.* New York: Columbia University Press.

Guinote, A., Judd, C. M., & Brauer, M. (2002). Effects of power on perceived and objective group variability: Evidence that more powerful groups are more variable. *Journal of Personality and Social Psychology, 82,* 708–721.

Haidt, J., Rozin, P., McCauley, C., & Imada, S. (1997). Body, psyche, and culture: The relationship between disgust and morality. *Psychology and Developing Societies, 9,* 107–131.

Halabi, S., Dovidio, J. F., & Nadler, A. (2008). How and when do high status group members offer help: Effects of social dominance orientation and status threat. *Political Psychology, 29,* 841–858.

Hegarty, P. J., & Pratto, F. (2001). The effects of social category norms on explanations for intergroup differences. *Journal of Personality and Social Psychology, 80,* 723–735.

Hegarty, P. J., & Pratto, F. (2004). The differences that norms make: Empiricism, social constructionism, and the interpretation of group difference. *Sex Roles, 50,* 445–453.

Heilman, M. E., Block, C. J., Martell, R. F., & Simon, M. C. (1989). Has anything changed? Current characterizations of men, women, and managers. *Journal of Applied Psychology, 74,* 935–942.

Helg, A. (2000). Black men, racial stereotyping, and violence in the U.S. south and Cuba at the turn of the century. *Comparative Studies in Society and History, 42,* 576–604.

Henkel, K. E., Dovidio, J. F., & Gaertner, S. L. (2006). Institutional discrimination, individual racism, and Hurricane Katrina. *Analyses of Social Issues and Public Policy, 6,* 99–124.

Henry, P. J., & Pratto, F. (2010). Power and racism. In A. Guinote & T. Vescio (Eds.), *The social psychology of power.* New York: Guilford Press.

Herek, G. (2009). Hate crimes and stigma-related experiences among sexual minority adults in the United States: Prevalence estimates from a national probability sample. *Journal of Interpersonal Violence, 24,* 54–74.

Herrmann, R. K. (1985). *Perceptions and behavior in Soviet foreign policy.* Pittsburgh: University of Pittsburgh Press.

Hoffman, C., & Hurst, N. (1990). Gender stereotypes: Perceptions or rationalizations? *Journal of Personality and Social Psychology, 58,* 197–208.

Hopkins, N., & Kahani-Hopkins, V. (2006). Minority group members' views of intergroup contact: A case study of British Muslims' conceptualizations of "Islamophobia" and social change. *British Journal of Social Psychology, 45,* 245–264.

Hubbard, P. (1998). Sexuality, immorality and the city: Red-light districts and the marginalisation of female street prostitutes. *Gender, Place and Culture, 5,* 55–76.

Iyengar, S., & Ottati, V. (1994). Cognitive perspective in political psychology. In R. S. Wyer Jr., & T. K. Srull (Eds.), *Handbook of social cognition* (pp. 143–187). Hillsdale, NJ: Lawrence Erlbaum Associates.

Jackman, M. R. (1994). *The velvet glove: Paternalism and conflict in gender, class and race relations.* Berkeley: University of California Press.

Jackman, M. R. (2001). License to kill: Violence and legitimacy in expropriative social relations. In J. T. Jost & B Major (Eds.), *The psychology of legitimacy* (pp. 437–467). Cambridge, UK: Cambridge University Press.

Johnson, W. R. (1994). *Dismantling Apartheid: A South African town in transition.* Ithaca, NY: Cornell University Press.

Jones, J. M. (1997). *Prejudice and racism* (2nd ed.). New York: McGraw-Hill.

Jost, J. T., & Banaji, M. R. (1994). The role of stereotyping in system-justification and the production of false-consciousness. *British Journal of Social Psychology, 33,* 1–27.

Jureidini, R. (2009). In the shadows of family life: Toward a history of domestic service in Lebanon. *Journal of Middle East Women's Studies, 5*, 74–101.

Kahneman, D., & Miller, D. T. (1986). Norm theory: Comparing reality to its alternatives. *Psychological Review, 93*, 136–153.

Kim, Y. J., & van Dyne, L. (2012). Cultural intelligence and international leadership potential: The importance of contact for members of the majority. *Applied Psychology: An International Review, 61*, 272–294.

Lalljee, M., Tam, T., Hewstone, M., Laham, S., & Lee, J. (2009). Unconditional respect for persons and the prediction of intergroup action tendencies. *European Journal of Social Psychology, 39*, 666–683.

Leach, C. W., Minescu, A., Poppe, E., & Hagendoorn, L. (2008). Generality and specificity in stereotypes of out-group power and benevolence: Views of Chechens and Jews in the Russian Federation. *European Journal of Social Psychology, 38*, 1165–1174.

Lemons, J. S. (1977). *Black stereotypes as reflected in popular culture, 1880–1920*. Baltimore: Johns Hopkins University Press.

Lewin, K. (1951). *Field theory in social science*. New York: Harper & Brothers.

Lin, N. (2000). Inequality in social capital. *Contemporary Sociology, 29*, 785–795.

Marques, J. M., Abrams, D., & Serôdio, R. G. (2001). Being better by being right: Subjective group dynamics and derogation of ingroup deviants when generic norms are undermined. *Journal of Personality and Social Psychology, 81*, 436–447.

Martin, C. L. (1990). Attitudes and expectations about children with nontraditional and traditional gender roles. *Sex Roles, 22*, 151–165.

Matsuda, M. J. (1985). The West and the legal status of women: Explanations of frontier feminism. *Journal of the West, 24*, 47–56.

Moskos, C. C. (1966). Racial integration in the armed forces. *American Journal of Sociology, 72*, 132–148.

Ogbu, J. U. (1990). Minority education in comparative perspective. *Journal of Negro Education, 59*, 45–57.

Pettigrew, T. F. (1998). Intergroup contact theory. *Annual Review of Psychology, 48*, 65–85.

Pettigrew, T. F., & Tropp, L. R. (2008). How does intergroup contact reduce prejudice? Meta-analytic tests of three mediators. *European Journal of Social Psychology, 38*, 922–934.

Postmes, T., & Branscombe, N. R. (2002). Influence of long-term racial environment composition on subjective well-being in African-Americans. *Journal of Personality and Social Psychology, 83*, 735–751.

Pratto, F. (1999). The puzzle of continuing group inequality: Piecing together psychological, social, and cultural forces in social dominance theory. In M. P. Zanna (Ed.), *Advances in experimental social psychology* (Vol. 31, pp. 191–263). San Diego, CA: Academic Press.

Pratto, F., & Glasford, D. E. (2008). Prospect theory, ethnocentrism, and the value of a human life. *Journal of Personality and Social Psychology, 95*, 1141–1428.

Pratto, F., Hegarty, P. J., & Korchmaros, J. D. (2007). How communication practices and category norms lead people to stereotype particular people and groups. In Y. Kashima, F. Klaus, & P. Freytag (Eds.), *Stereotype dynamics: Language-based approaches to the formation, maintenance, and transformation of stereotypes* (pp. 293–313). New York: Psychology Press.

Pratto, F., & Lee, I. (2010). *Stereotype contents derive from the form and use of power*. Unpublished manuscript, University of Connecticut.

Pratto, F., Lee, I., Tan, J., & Pitpitan, E. (2011). Power basis theory: A psycho-ecological approach to power. In D. Dunning (Ed.), *Social motivation*. New York: Psychology Press.

Pratto, F., Pearson, A. R., Lee, I., & Saguy, T. (2008). Power dynamics in an experimental game. *Social Justice Research, 21,* 377–407.

Pratto, F., & Pitpitan, E. V. (2008). Ethnocentrism and sexism: How stereotypes legitimize six types of power. *Social and Personality Psychology Compass, 2,* 2159–2176.

Pratto, F., Sidanius, J., Stallworth, L. M., & Malle, B. F. (1994). Social dominance orientation: A personality variable predicting social and political attitudes. *Journal of Personality and Social Psychology, 67,* 741–763.

Pratto, F., & Walker, A. (2000). Dominance in disguise: Power, beneficence, and exploitation in personal relationships. In A. Lee-Chai & J. A. Bargh (Eds.), *The use and abuse of power: Multiple perspectives on the causes of corruption* (pp. 93–114). Philadelphia: Psychology Press.

Pratto, F., & Walker, A. (2004). The bases of gendered power. In A. H. Eagly, A. Beall, & R. Sternberg (Eds.), *The psychology of gender* (2nd ed., pp. 242–268). New York: Guilford Press.

Prentice, D. A., & Carranza, E. (2002). What men and women should be, shouldn't be, are allowed to be, and don't have to be: The contents of prescriptive gender stereotypes. *Psychology of Women Quarterly, 26,* 269–281.

Prislin, R., & Filson, J. (2009). Seeking conversion versus advocating tolerance in the pursuit of social change. *Journal of Personality and Social Psychology, 97,* 811–822.

Purdie-Vaughns, V., & Eibach, R. P. (2008). Intersectional invisibility: The distinctive advantages and disadvantages of multiple subordinate-group identities. *Sex Roles, 59,* 377–391.

Raven, B. H. (1965). Social influence and power. In I. D. Steiner & M. Fishbein (Eds.), *Current studies in social psychology* (pp. 371–382). New York: Holt, Rinehart, & Winston.

Renold, E. (2002). Presumed innocence: (Hetero)sexual, heterosexist, and homophobic harassment among primary school girls and boys. *Childhood: A Global Journal of Child Research, 9,* 415–434.

Reyna C., Brandt, M., & Viki, G. T. (2009). Blame it on hip-hop: Anti-rap attitudes as a proxy for prejudice. *Group Processes and Intergroup Relations, 12,* 361–380.

Rudman, L. A. (1998). Self-promotion as a risk factor for women: The costs and benefits of counterstereotypical impression management. *Journal of Personality and Social Psychology, 74,* 629–645.

Rudman, L. A., & Glick, P. (2001). Prescriptive gender stereotypes and backlash toward agentic women. *Journal of Social Issues, 57,* 743–762.

Russell, B. (1938). *Power: A new social analysis*. New York: W. W. Norton.

Saguy, T., & Chernyak-Hai, L. (2012). Intergroup contact can undermine disadvantaged group members' attributions to discrimination. *Journal of Experimental Social Psychology, 48,* 714–720.

Saguy, T., Dovidio, J., Quinn, D., & Pratto, F. (2010). Interacting like a body: Objectification can lead women to narrow their presence in social interactions. *Psychological Science, 21,* 178–182.

Saguy, T., Tausch, N., Dovidio, J. F., & Pratto, F. (2009). The irony of harmony: Intergroup contact can produce false expectations for equality. *Psychological Science, 20,* 114–121.

Schaller, M., & Abeysinghe, A. M. N. D. (2006). Geographical frame of reference and dangerous intergroup attitudes: A double-minority in Sri Lanka. *Political Psychology, 27*, 615–631.

Schaller, M., Faulkner, J., Park, J. H., Neuberg, S. L., & Kenrick, D. T. (2004). Impressions of danger influence impressions of people: An evolutionary perspective on individual and collective cognition. *Journal of Cultural and Evolutionary Psychology, 2*, 231–247.

Sears, D. O. (1988). Symbolic racism. In P. A. Katz & D. A. Taylor (Eds.), *Eliminating racism: Profiles in controversy*. New York: Plenum Press.

Shelton, N. J. (2003). Interpersonal concerns in social encounters between majority and minority group members. *Group Processes and Intergroup Relations, 6*, 171–185.

Shelton, J. N., West, T. V., & Trail, T. E. (2010). Concerns with appearing prejudiced: Implications for anxiety during daily interracial interactions. *Group Processes and Intergroup Relations, 13*, 329–344.

Sidanius, J., & Pratto, F. (1999). *Social dominance: An intergroup theory of social hierarchy and oppression*. New York: Cambridge University Press.

Steele, C. M. (1987). A threat in the air: How stereotypes shape intellectual identity and performance. *American Psychologist, 52*, 613–629.

Stephan, C. W., & Stephan, W. (1992). Reducing intercultural anxiety through intercultural contact. *International Journal of Intercultural Relations, 16*, 89–106.

Swim, J. K., Hyers, L. L., Cohen, L. L., & Ferguson, M. J. (2001). Everyday sexism: Evidence for its incidence, nature, and psychological impact from three daily diary studies. *Journal of Social Issues, 57*, 31–53.

Tatum, B. D. (1997). *Why are all the Black kids sitting together in the cafeteria?* New York: Basic Books.

Thibaut, J. W., & Kelley, H. H. (1959). The social psychology of groups. Oxford, UK: Wiley.

Tietjens Meyers, D. (2000). Feminism and women's autonomy: The challenge of female genital cutting. *Metaphilosophy, 31*, 469–491.

Tomaskovic-Devey, D. (1993). *Gender and racial inequality at work: The sources and consequences of job segregation*. Ithaca, NY: ILR Press.

Torres, M. G. (2005). Bloody deeds/Hechos sangrientos: Reading Guatemala's record of political violence in cadaver reports. In C. Menjívar & N. Rodríguez (Eds.), *When states kill: Latin America, the U.S., and technologies of terror* (pp. 143–169). Austin: University of Texas Press.

Tropp, L. R., & Pettigrew, T. F. (2005). Relationship between intergroup contact and prejudice among minority and majority status groups. *Psychological Science, 16*, 951–957.

Turner, J. C. (2005). Explaining the nature of power: A three-process theory. *European Journal of Social Psychology, 35*, 1–22.

Umphress, E. E., Simmons, A. L., Boswell, W. R., & Triana, M. C. (2008). Managing discrimination in selection: The influence of directives from an authority and social dominance orientation. *Journal of Applied Psychology, 93*, 982–993.

Vollhardt, J. R. (2010). Enhanced external and culturally sensitive attributions after extended intercultural contact. *British Journal of Social Psychology, 49*, 363–383.

Wartenberg, T. E. (1990). *The forms of power*. Philadelphia: Temple University Press.

Welch, K. (2007). Black criminal stereotypes and racial profiling. *Journal of Contemporary Criminal Justice, 23*, 276–288.

West, T. V., Shelton, J. N., & Trail, T. E. (2009). Relational anxiety in interracial interactions. *Psychological Science, 20*, 289–292.

Wong, P., Lai, C. F., Nagasawa, R., & Lin, T. (1998). Asian Americans as a model minority: Self-perceptions and perceptions by other racial groups. *Sociological Perspectives, 41*, 95–118.

Yeh, C. J., Kim, A. B., Pituc, S. T., & Atkins, M. (2008). Poverty, loss, and resilience: The story of Chinese immigrant youth. *Journal of Counseling Psychology, 55*, 34–48.

Zenk, S. N., Schulz, A. J., Israel, B. A., James, S. A., Bao, S., & Wilson, M. L. (2005). Neighborhood racial composition, neighborhood poverty, and the special accessibility of supermarkets in metropolitan Detroit. *American Journal of Public Health, 95*, 660–667.

8

From Prejudiced People to Prejudiced Places

A Social-Contextual Approach to Prejudice

MARY C. MURPHY

Indiana University

GREGORY M. WALTON

Stanford University

> We often consider prejudice as a psychological condition lodged in single individual minds. To understand the total psychosocial complex of prejudice we need also to take into account situational and society factors.
>
> Gordon Allport (1966)

Imagine Karen's first day as a newly minted assistant professor—arriving at her office in the math department at a prestigious university. Filled with excitement, she unpacks her boxes and organizes the space. A few hours in, she walks down the hall toward the women's restroom—but she can't find it. She stops at the administrative assistant's office and is told that, while there is a men's restroom on every floor, the only women's restroom is in the basement, two floors down. How should she interpret this? Why is there only one restroom for women? And, of all places, why is it in the basement?

One interpretation is that people in the math department are sexist—that they don't value women in the field. The lack of women's restrooms may be especially threatening because it exists alongside cultural stereotypes that impugn women's abilities in math and the historical underrepresentation and exclusion of women in math and science fields. In light of these facts, this physical cue may seem to confirm the worst—a prejudice against women. Embedded in this attribution is an assumption that discriminatory circumstances—such as requiring women to go out of their way to use the restroom—betray prejudiced attitudes within individuals.

But this is not the only possible interpretation. A little research might reveal that the math building is one of the oldest on campus—built in the late 1800s when the original campus was constructed. At the time, there were *no* women faculty members. The only women who worked in the math department were secretaries, and they worked in the basement. So including a women's restroom there—and only there—was logical and sensible. The local and historical context surrounding the cue provides a different perspective—one of practicality and pragmatism that does not require an attribution of prejudice or animus against women. Today, the department would be well advised to accommodate the changing needs of faculty and staff. But the existence of this identity-threatening cue may not necessarily signal prejudice on the part of people currently working in the math department.

Surprisingly, social psychology—a field that has at its core the press of the situation in shaping human behavior (Asch, 1952; Ross & Nisbett, 1991)—tends to locate prejudice in individuals' internal attitudes and evaluations. When people behave in a prejudiced manner, we tend to view the act as reflecting a bias within them, which is relatively stable across interaction partners and situations. To investigate this bias, we have developed state-of-the-art tools to measure individual differences in prejudice—from subtle explicit measures, to implicit reaction time measures, to brain and hormonal responses. Thus, we can assess how much explicit, implicit, and perhaps even unconscious prejudice a person carries with them. Social psychologists have further investigated how people's scores on prejudice measures predict their thoughts, emotions, and behavior in intergroup settings (e.g., Greenwald, Poehlman, Uhlmann, & Banaji, 2009). When researchers strive to create interventions to reduce bias and discrimination, the typical goal is to reduce the amount of prejudice that exists within individuals—for instance, by re-creating approach tendencies toward minority groups (e.g., Kawakami, Dovidio, Moll, Hermsen, & Russin, 2000). Only rarely considered is how situations give rise to, facilitate, or prevent acts of prejudice or how reshaping environments could reduce or eliminate them.

Research that locates prejudice within individuals is unquestionably important. But, we suggest, an exclusive focus on individual differences neglects a broader view of prejudice. This broader view would place more emphasis on the perspectives and experiences of targets of prejudice. From a majority perspective, problems of prejudice may seem to stem from "prejudiced people" who stereotype or discriminate against minority group members. Who is racist? How can their racism be reduced or eliminated? From this perspective, identifying the psychological and biological mechanisms that underlie a person's level of prejudice is a "natural" means toward reducing prejudice and promoting a more just society.

But, from the perspective of targets of prejudice (often minority group members), biology and reaction times matter less than whether one is treated with dignity and respect. These experiences derive both from people and from situations. Extant research has shown that settings can—purposefully or incidentally—create disparate experiences and treatments for some social groups relative to others. Drawing in part on stereotype and social identity threat research (Steele, Spencer, & Aronson, 2002), we argue that our current state of knowledge, built over decades of careful study, allows us to specify particular kinds of contexts and environments as "prejudiced." By this we mean that certain contexts have the predictable effect of creating and re-creating inequality of experience and outcomes based on individuals' social group membership—advantaging people from some social groups and disadvantaging people from other social groups.

Consistent with this framework, we argue for a conceptualization of prejudice as something that people and contexts *do*, not just the type of person someone *is* (Markus & Moya, 2010). This interpretation shifts our view of prejudice from a static and fixed property of individuals to one that is active, dynamic, and sourced both from people (e.g., their attitudes and beliefs) and from the contexts that they inhabit. In fact, according to the social-contextual model of prejudice, to understand fully the effect that people's attitudes have on others, one must consider the contexts within which the actor and the target are embedded.

This conceptualization is more in line with how targets actually experience prejudice. From the target's perspective, prejudice is a dynamic process of interaction—of treatment, exclusion, or disrespect—that occurs against a cultural, historical, and situational background (Markus & Moya, 2010). Privileging one source of prejudice to the neglect of others prevents a full and complete understanding of how and why group disparities persist. We suggest that, if one ultimate goal of stereotyping and prejudice research is better to understand and to remedy barriers to equal opportunity and access, then a broader view of the antecedents of prejudice is helpful—one that considers how both people *and* places differently shape the experiences and opportunities of majority and minority group members.

This social-contextual approach differs from approaches that conceptualize prejudice as an attitude and discrimination as the behavior that stems from such prejudiced attitudes. While the "prejudice-as-attitude" model is important for understanding individual differences, we suggest that it can nevertheless forestall a serious consideration of the social context as an antecedent of discriminatory outcomes. First, by highlighting prejudiced attitudes as the primary antecedent of discriminatory behavior, the attitude model forgoes the possibility that discriminatory outcomes can occur without prejudiced individuals—a point to which we will return later. Second, with a primary focus on attitudes as the source of prejudice, it is easy to forget that targets do not actually experience actors' attitudes per se. For example, a target does not experience an actor's IAT score. It is only within particular contexts that those attitudes become linked to behavior—and it is the resulting behavior that affects targets. Third, when the attitude model considers the role of situations, the latter are thought either to provide opportunities for acting on prejudiced attitudes or to serve as a barrier to prevent this. Relative to this model, we argue for a much richer role of situations. According to the social-contextual model of prejudice, environments don't just create or prevent opportunities for the expression of prejudice; they can also create bias all on their own. In this chapter, we are concerned with exploring how and when individuals can receive differential treatment or have differential social and psychological experiences as a consequence of their membership in a social group. We contend that such unequal outcomes stem from both people and places.

A contextual theory of prejudice invites us to consider person, situation, and person-by-situation predictors of biased behaviors and biased outcomes. From this perspective, individual attitudes matter, but they should be considered in context. Prejudice can result from individuals' attitudes when they are linked with behavior and also from settings that are set up in ways that produce disparities between social groups. Conceptualizing prejudice—even more subtle, implicit, and unconscious forms of prejudice—as something that exists within individuals without recognizing the role of context risks committing a version of the fundamental attribution error. It risks giving undue weight to people's internal attitudes and dispositions in shaping their behavior to the neglect of important situational variables.

In this chapter, we first discuss some of the pitfalls of considering prejudice and discrimination as emanating solely from individuals and advocate for a broader consideration of the role of situations as causes of inequality. We provide several key examples of prejudiced contexts—situations that predictably produce systematically biased outcomes along social group lines. Finally, we draw from the literature to suggest how consideration of situations could inform novel remedies—changes in social environments—to reduce or eliminate discriminatory outcomes.

PREJUDICE IN INDIVIDUALS

Many contemporary social and political commentators argue that attitudinal prejudice is a thing of the past—no longer an important social issue (e.g., Taranto, 2010; The Economist, 2008; Remnick, 2008). Some express exasperation in general with social scientists and in particular with social psychologists, who, it seems, focus their research agendas on discovering new and ever more subtle forms of bias within individuals, even as indicators show that prejudice has declined sharply over time. While it is clear to us that people continue to hold prejudiced attitudes at the explicit and implicit levels and that, under certain conditions, these attitudes result in overt and subtly biased behavior, we believe that this critique has some merit. Indeed, social psychology has shifted from the macro to the molecular in the study of bias. While once we took what people had to say at face value—via self-report measures of prejudice and stereotyping—today we employ extraordinarily covert methods to detect prejudice. From reaction time tasks to cardiovascular, hormonal, and brain activation measures, our methods reflect not only the development of dual-process models of attitudes (Chaiken & Trope, 1999; Cunningham, Preacher, & Banaji, 2001; Wilson, Lindsey, & Schooler, 2000) but also the assumption that what people say may not be fully accurate—that self-reports, especially those related to sensitive topics like prejudice, are polluted by political correctness concerns—and that indirect evaluations provide better assessments of the "real" levels of prejudice within a person (Crosby, Bromley, & Saxe, 1980; Nosek & Hansen, 2008; Uhlmann, Poehlman, & Nosek, 2012). There is no doubt that this approach has yielded important dividends in understanding and predicting human behavior (e.g., Dasgupta, 2004; Greenwald et al., 2009; McConnell & Leibold, 2001; Ziegert & Hanges, 2005). But the emphasis on covert attitudinal measures, especially in the absence of attention to contextual factors, represents a doubling-down of the field's bet on an individual-difference approach to prejudice. We worry that this primary focus obscures a potentially larger truth—that many people sincerely want to be non-prejudiced and, in important ways, are non-prejudiced (Plant & Devine, 2009). In many cases, addressing the situations that yield prejudiced behavior may be a more effective means for understanding and reducing social inequality than further efforts to detect and mitigate covert prejudicial attitudes.

Social psychology has long conceptualized prejudice as a property of individuals. In the early and middle part of the 20th century, most American psychologists considered prejudice a defect of personality fueled by beliefs about the biological inferiority of racial minorities and manifested in blatant and overt expressions of racial animus (e.g., Adorno, Frenkel-Brunswik, Levinson, & Sanford, 1950; Bogardus, 1928; Katz & Braly, 1935). Ironically, this view coincided with the laws and structures of Jim Crow America, where situations systematically disadvantaged racial minorities. Over the past 50 years, the United States has seen a dramatic reduction in self-reports of explicit prejudice (Schuman, Steeh, Bobo, & Krysan, 1997; Hochschild, 1981, 1995). As the endorsement of prejudice and racial stereotypes began to decline, social and cognitive psychologists started to suggest that prejudice was, in fact, a normal feature of human social cognition and thus potentially present in all people (Allport, 1954). Indeed, social identity researchers demonstrated that intergroup biases emerged even in minimal group contexts—where group membership was randomly assigned and essentially meaningless (e.g., Tajfel, 1970; Tajfel, Billig, Bundy, & Flament, 1971).

As self-reports of explicit prejudice declined further, social psychologists aiming to explain enduring racial disparities suggested that people's negative racial attitudes had not disappeared but had, instead, taken a more subtle and nuanced form (Duckitt, 1992; Pettigrew & Meertens, 1995). For instance, modern racism theorists have suggested that certain conservative political views often serve as cover for prejudiced attitudes (McConahay, 1986; Sears, 1988). Today, most Americans espouse egalitarian ideals regarding race and consider themselves to be non-prejudiced (Dovidio, 2001). But psychologists have demonstrated that aversive and implicit forms of racism persist, in which people espouse egalitarian beliefs but remain ambivalent toward racial minorities, ostensibly because they harbor implicit, and potentially unconscious, negative attitudes toward people of color (Son Hing, Li, & Zanna, 2002; Dovidio & Gaertner, 1986; Katz & Hass, 1988). There is no doubt that it is critical to understand these subtle forms of racism, as they likely affect social interactions, experiences, and outcomes of racial minorities today (Pager & Shepherd, 2008; Smedley, Stith, & Nelson, 2003).

While there are several theories of contemporary racial bias, all posit that, as society has become less tolerant of blatant or overt prejudice, people have become motivated to appear unbiased on explicit racial attitude scales. Thus more subtle and implicit measures have been created to index this modern conceptualization of racial attitudes (Fazio, Jackson, Dunton, & Williams, 1995; Banaji & Greenwald, 1995; Jones & Sigall, 1971). However, when we conceptualize prejudice as hidden within individuals, the way to create an egalitarian society is to detect the prejudice, sort biased from non-biased people, and change the biased people or remove them altogether from the environments that we assume are themselves unbiased. This seems a suboptimal strategy if we want to achieve a fully integrated, egalitarian society. As noted above, we do not doubt that people possess modern, ambivalent, and implicit forms of prejudice and that these forms have important consequences. But we contend that the contemporary focus on internal attitudes—whether explicit or implicit—as a cause of biased behavior and biased outcomes limits our understanding of the causes of inequality. What are some of the limits of the prejudice-as-attitude model?

First, extant research shows that attitudes are weak predictors of behaviors, especially when they are highly general and not tied to the specific behavior at hand (see Ajzen & Fishbein, 2005, for a review). Prejudice, as measured in much contemporary research—for example, through feeling thermometers or implicit reaction time measures—is a paradigmatic example of a generalized, unspecified attitude. We should be impressed when individual-difference measures of generalized prejudice predict specific forms of bias even modestly or inconsistently (Greenwald et al., 2009).

It is because of the weakness of attitudes as predictors of behavior in general that, in many other contexts, social psychologists have emphasized the role of the situation. Indeed, classic studies in our field pit individual differences against situational forces to illustrate the relative power of situations (e.g., Darley & Batson, 1973). Drawing on this intellectual tradition, social psychology's contribution to the understanding and solution of major social problems often emphasizes situational variables. Consider, for example, Americans' environmental awareness and recycling behavior. Do Americans recycle now more than ever (EPA, 2010) because clever marketers have persuaded them to be tree-hugging environmentalists? Far from it. Instead, descriptive norms have become established in local communities and, at the same time, channel factors facilitate the desired behaviors (e.g., Allcott, 2011; Laskey & Kavazovic, 2010). Some channel factors are financial incentives and penalties such as "pay-as-you-throw" programs that charge households for the weight of their garbage while recycling services remain free. Others, such as city-funded recycling receptacles and free pick-up services, have reduced the barriers and inconveniences of recycling (Bator & Cialdini, 2000; Cialdini, 2003; Cialdini, Reno, & Kallgren, 1991; Davis, 2011; EPA, 2012).

Researchers have argued that the rise of anti-prejudice norms has similarly reduced the expression of prejudiced attitudes and behaviors (Crandall & Eshleman, 2003; Crandall & Stangor, 2005). Likewise, research that manipulates prejudice norms can bring significant benefits to attitudes and behavior (e.g., Crandall, Bahns, Warner, & Schaller, 2011; Crandall, Eshleman, & O'Brien, 2002). However, as people conform to these norms in public, it is possible that many will internalize them and that they will become part of people's identities, potentially with lasting effects (Newcomb, Koenig, Flacks, & Warwick, 1967; Plant & Devine, 2009; Walton & Cohen, 2011b). Indeed, research suggests that *appearing* non-prejudiced may not be the central motivation of many people—rather, many are genuinely motivated to *be* non-prejudiced (Plant & Devine, 1998, 2009). Even without an audience and when they report their motivations anonymously, people have largely internalized anti-prejudice norms and endorse anti-prejudice views. In addition, those who are internally motivated to be non-prejudiced are eager to eliminate racial bias within themselves or their behavior even if others won't be privy to these efforts (Plant & Devine, 2009). If leveraged properly, perhaps contextual norms coupled with appropriate channel factors could dampen or extinguish the outward expression of prejudiced behavior and facilitate the internalization of non-prejudiced identities and behaviors even further.

A second limit of conceptualizing prejudice as a quality of individuals is that it can obscure situations in which biased outcomes occur in the absence of prejudicial attitudes. One of the lessons of stereotype threat (Steele, 1997; Steele et al., 2002) is that members of negatively stereotyped groups can experience psychological threat and suffer along important and socially meaningful dimensions as a consequence of subtle situational cues—and this can occur even when other people in a setting are not prejudiced. A White experimenter who represents a test as evaluative of students' intellectual ability can cause a Black student to experience stereotype threat while holding no animus against Blacks (see Steele, 1997; Steele & Aronson, 1995). Similarly, locating the women's restroom in the basement of a math department can cause women to feel that they don't belong in that environment, even if others in the department hold no animus against women. Thus, seemingly neutral situations can trigger threatening or hostile meanings for some groups but not others, causing inequality in important outcomes. Well-meaning individuals—even people who endorse egalitarian attitudes—can create such situations without awareness of the unequal effects the settings produce or how to remedy such a bias. The absence of attitudinal prejudice does not mitigate the real harm caused to minority individuals—the harms of stereotype threat are no less real by virtue of the fact that they can be caused by non-prejudiced (as well as by prejudiced) people.

Understanding prejudice as something that can attach to environments and contexts as well as to people may open our eyes to these forms of bias and suggest novel, theory-based remedies for mitigating inequality.

Third, as mentioned above, primary emphasis on prejudicial attitudes as the cause of bias readily leads people (often majority group members) to be labeled as "prejudiced" or "racist" and to be apprehensive about this prospect. While the threat of such a stigmatizing label may keep some prejudiced individuals "in check," it relies on external motivators such as guilt and shame, which are relatively ineffective in inducing positive long-term behavior change (e.g., Thomaes, Bushman, Stegge, & Olthof, 2008; Tangney, Wagner, Hill-Barlow, Marschall, & Gramzow, 1996; Hooge, Nelissen, Breugelmans, & Zeelenberg, 2011; Kochanska, Barry, Jimenez, Hollatz, & Woodard, 2009). And, while guilt and shame certainly play a role in behavior change (Amodio, Devine, & Harmon-Jones, 2007; Monteith, Mark, & Ashburn-Nardo, 2010), relying primarily on these motivators can backfire by increasing intergroup anxiety and causing people to avoid intergroup contact altogether (Barlow, Louis, & Terry, 2010; Goff, Steele, & Davies, 2008; Plant & Devine, 2003). Indeed, during interracial contact, a significant concern of White individuals is being labeled racist (Richeson & Shelton, 2007; Goff et al., 2008). This concern is exacerbated by a conception of prejudice as an internal, stable property of individuals. Indeed, one significant consequence of this mainstream, fixed theory of prejudice is the avoidance of intergroup contact. The belief that those who "have" prejudice cannot easily change it reduces people's motivation to seek opportunities for interracial interaction (Carr, Dweck, & Pauker, 2012). Revealingly, Carr and colleagues call these avoidant behaviors "prejudiced behavior without prejudice," because the effect occurs regardless of people's scores on measures of racial prejudice (Carr et al., 2012).

Acknowledging how prejudice can adhere to contexts as well as to people may reduce majority group members' fears of being labeled during interracial interactions and facilitate more positive intergroup interactions. Teaching people about contexts that produce biased outcomes may expand their definition of prejudice and encourage greater perspective-taking and improvement in intergroup attitudes and behaviors (see Dweck, 2000; Murphy, Richeson, & Molden, 2011). Indeed, a focus on how environments can be changed may provide a common goal among well-meaning White individuals and ethnic minorities to create unbiased settings. Given the power of self-consistency processes such as cognitive dissonance, these behaviors themselves may lead to reductions in prejudicial attitudes, creating a self-sustaining cycle of egalitarian behaviors and attitudes (see Allport, 1954; Brannon & Walton, in press).

PREJUDICE IN CONTEXTS: A SOCIAL-CONTEXTUAL APPROACH TO PREJUDICE

Of course, not all social-psychological theories of prejudice and discrimination focus on individual differences; several highlight the power of context. Realistic group conflict theory (Duckitt, 1994; Sherif, 1966) and relative deprivation theory (Merton, 1938; Pettigrew et al., 2008) posit that prejudice is contingent on situational and economic factors. According to these models, limited resources increase the likelihood that prejudice will emerge as people compete and experience feelings of scarcity and relative deprivation. Other theories contend that the outward expression of prejudice is guided by social norms in the local context. For example, the justification-suppression model of prejudice (Crandall & Eshleman, 2003) posits that, to understand when and why prejudice emerges, one must examine the local context to decipher prevailing social norms regarding the appropriateness of negative attitudes and expressions toward particular groups. Likewise, Devine's automatic and controlled theory of prejudice (1989) suggests that, while people internalize knowledge of group-based stereotypes through cultural socialization, local norms and individuals' motivation and resources can modulate the use of stereotypes in people's judgment and behavior. While these theories posit that prejudice is a characteristic of individuals, they also contend that the expression of prejudice depends on situational factors. An implication of these theories is that changing situations may reduce the incidence of bias.

Like these theories, we believe that individuals can hold biases and stereotypes that influence their judgment and behavior when the situation permits their expression. But our argument goes beyond these theories by suggesting that environments can cause inequality without the presence of prejudiced people. Next, we point to some illustrative examples of prejudiced contexts that directly and systematically disadvantage some groups relative to others.

One way that contexts can be prejudiced is that they present different, more threatening meaning and construals for some social groups, but not for others. Because of these different meanings, some groups must engage more effortful psychological processes than others, which in turn can hamper their outcomes. As mentioned above, research on stereotype and social identity threat has found that women and people of color routinely face situations where their group is negatively stereotyped or numerically underrepresented. These situational cues create a sense of psychological and physiological vigilance (Murphy, Steele, & Gross, 2007) and tune attention toward other cues of inclusion and belonging in social environments, often at the expense of sustained motivation and performance (Walton & Cohen, 2007, Cheryan, Plaut, Davies, & Steele, 2009). Men and Whites simply do not face such negative and pervasive stereotypes; as a consequence, they do not grapple with the same psychological burdens. We consider situations like these to be prejudiced. They systematically disadvantage individuals from one social group relative to others—exerting a greater psychological burden and influencing basic psychological processes that, in turn, cause group-based differences on such important outcomes as motivation, test performance, and career aspirations. Aspects of the environment such as the number of identity mates in a setting, or the degree to which people in the environment befriend newcomers, may have a greater meaning for people concerned about potential exclusion or isolation due to stigmatized social group membership. While it may not be prejudiced—in the traditional sense of the word—to benefit from having people from your ingroup dominate a setting, it nonetheless creates inequality in construal, experience, and psychological functioning along group lines.

Another way contexts can be prejudiced is if they require members of one group to give up, change, or conceal aspects of themselves in order to be accepted. Imagine being a woman in a computer science class comprised mostly of men. The examples provided in class and the topics of conversation in study groups center on things of interest to the majority of the class—bonding experiences such as all-night coding binges, forgetting to shower, and being a geek. And, while men and women attend the exact same class—a class that, on its face, has nothing to do with gender, the situation can produce disparate experiences for men and women and affect their performance and persistence in the field (Cheryan et al., 2009; Margolis & Fisher, 2002). To belong in an environment like this, women may need to sacrifice part of their feminine identity; similar sacrifices are not necessary for men to "fit in" (Pronin, Steele, & Ross, 2004). Men's identity simply "fits" the field—as though the field were constructed for them. Women might not call their classmates or professor prejudiced, but they might feel that the environment is not a good, fair, or comfortable place for them and, as a consequence, suppress their feminine identity or leave the field (Cheryan et al., 2009; Margolis & Fisher, 2002). In our view, places that allow some people but not others to be true to all parts of themselves are prejudiced (see also Walton, Paunesku, & Dweck, 2012).

A third type of prejudiced context is created when the local context interacts with a person's prejudiced attitude to create disparate outcomes or experiences for some social groups relative to others. For example, in the context of judging criminals, certain attitudes and associations can produce disparate effects that change outcomes for racial minority group members. Implicit associations between African Americans and apes, once thought to be a relic of the past, continue to persist in American society, with grave consequences in criminal justice settings. In an archival study of news articles, researchers found that articles about Blacks convicted of capital crimes were more likely to contain ape-relevant language than articles about Whites convicted of the same crimes. Moreover, individuals portrayed as more apelike were more likely to be executed than those who were not (Goff, Eberhardt, Williams, & Jackson, 2008). The researchers argue that a cultural association between "Black" and "ape" finds voice in popular representations of criminals—such as metaphors, cartoons, visual imagery, and other popular media—and continues to affect life and death outcomes, reinforcing group-based inequities in convictions and death penalty rates (Goff et al., 2008). A less fatal, but nonetheless consequential example occurs in the context of promotions. Research shows that, through cultural and historical representations, a link exists in the United States between the concept of "man" and the concept of "leader" (Eagly & Carli, 2007). This link makes it more likely that men will be perceived as having the characteristics of a leader relative to women. Within the context of promotions, when management looks to identify leaders to promote, this link causes men to be identified and promoted at rates higher than equally qualified women (Eagly & Carli, 2007; see also Biernat, Collins, Katzarska-Miller, & Thompson, 2009; Uhlmann & Cohen, 2005).

Other prejudiced situations are those that employ practices, policies, or decision-making procedures that seem neutral from an observer's perspective but in practice disadvantage some social groups relative to others (Crosby, Iyer, Clayton, & Downing, 2003). Consider a historical example regarding college admissions decisions within the University of California system (Crosby et al., 2003). For decades, admission decisions were based on a "points" system, with extra points being awarded to students for good grades in advanced placement courses. From an observer's perspective, this practice seemed to reward fairly students who performed well on advanced college preparatory material. However, Chancellor Tien of the University of California, Berkeley, abolished this practice when he realized that it systematically disadvantaged students from underfunded high schools that had few advanced placement courses.

Termed "selective system bias," prejudiced situations like these occur when the between-group difference on the "gating mechanism" used to identify candidates is larger than the between-group difference on the criterion (Jencks, 1998; Crosby, 2004). For example, selective system bias can exist for standardized tests, such as the SAT, used in college admissions and scholarship decisions. If racial group differences on the SAT are larger than the between-group differences on the criterion (e.g., students' actual grades in college)—presumably because the lower performing group has other areas of relative strength unmeasured by the SAT—then basing admission decisions on the SAT will effectively discriminate against the lower performing group. Again, this situational factor can cause prejudiced outcomes without there being prejudiced people or prejudicial attitudes.

Another factor that creates prejudiced situations involves the weighing of criteria in selection decisions in ways that may—intentionally or not—discriminate against individuals from certain social groups. Linda Wightman's (1998) discussion of law school admissions provides a clear example. Traditionally, law was considered the domain of men. Today, women still remain significantly underrepresented in law, making up approximately 31.5% of all lawyers (Bureau of Labor Statistics, 2011). Why might this be? Do prejudiced admission officers actively discriminate against women? Is this a problem of people or situations?

Admission decisions by most accredited American law schools are based primarily on two factors: applicants' LSAT scores—usually weighted at about 60%—and their undergraduate grade point averages—weighted at about 40% (Wightman, 1998; Crosby et al., 2003). These weights are applied equally to all students who seek admission—a neutral procedure on its face. The problem emerges when one considers an effect of the weights. Women, on average, do significantly worse on the LSATs than men, but they have better undergraduate grades. By overweighting LSAT scores relative to grades, law schools disadvantage women (Crosby et al., 2003). Furthermore, research has demonstrated

that the use of the LSAT may not be justified if the aim of law schools is to produce effective lawyers at graduation. Indeed, a large-scale study of the predictors of successful lawyering found that LSAT scores are "not particularly
useful" in predicting effectiveness as defined through individual interviews,
focus groups and surveys of practicing lawyers, law faculty, law students, judges,
and legal clients throughout the United States (Shultz & Zedeck, 2008; 2011).
As with the example of the women's restroom in the basement of the math
department, majority group members might not even register a problem with
longstanding practices such as these. As with the predominant view within psychology, their construal may not include an understanding that prejudice could
stem from situations or procedures. As long as the people making the admission
decisions are unbiased, they assume that the outcomes will be unbiased.

Another procedure that creates prejudice is when people continue to accept
measures of merit at face value when those measures are systematically biased
against certain social groups (Walton, Spencer, & Erman, in press). Research
finds that stereotype threat causes grades and standardized test scores assessed
in common academic environments to underestimate the ability and academic
potential of women and minorities (Walton & Spencer, 2009). Accepting
these scores at face value—by, for example, treating a 1,200 SAT score from a
White student and a Black student as reflecting the same level of ability and
potential—would discriminate against the Black student, because the Black student earned that score in the face of stereotype threat. Thus, on average, a
Black student's SAT score reflects a higher level of ability and potential than the
same score from a White student. Not taking this situational variable into
account in making admissions decisions will result in discrimination against
racial and ethnic minority students and women (Walton et al., in press) and do
so even when individual decision-makers are non-prejudiced.

HOW DO ENVIRONMENTS BECOME
PREJUDICED?

There are several ways environments can become prejudiced. Often, they do
not involve prejudiced people at the helm. As we have seen from the examples
above, a common way environments can become prejudiced is when they do
not adequately take into account differences in the way that majority and minority group individuals construe them or how those construals can lead to disparate experiences and outcomes. Because their group membership is linked to
longstanding historical and cultural contexts of stereotyping and prejudice, minority group members bring with them concerns about being the target of
stereotyping and prejudice. These concerns engender a sense of vigilance and
tune their attention to cues that are less important to majority group members.
These cues include such things as test diagnosticity, demographic queries,
subtle cues to nonbelonging, numerical underrepresentation, colorblind diversity ideologies, and fixed representations of intelligence. When majority and
minority group members work in environments that contain such cues—even

though it is the same objective environment—the cues cause threat and under-performance for minority group members but boost performance and psychological wellbeing for majority group members (Murphy & Taylor, 2012; Walton & Cohen, 2003).

Majority group members come from a different cultural and historical perspective that engenders vigilance to a different set of situational cues—often related to changes in the status quo. As the United States undergoes demographic change, groups that have been historically advantaged are tuned to cues that suggest population shifts, changes in attitudes regarding intergroup relations, uncertainties in group status and hierarchy, and economic decline. Research shows that, when demographic changes are salient, racial tensions are likely to emerge as people characterize resources in a zero-sum fashion (Norton & Sommers, 2011). As environments become laden with cues regarding the status quo, prejudice and intergroup tension is likely to emerge.

Another way that environments can become places of prejudice is when local norms suggest that prejudice against particular groups is acceptable (Crandall et al., 2002). When it is common to use group-based stereotypes as heuristics in making judgments and decisions about individuals—even when the focus is on the group's strengths or aptitudes—the stage is set for prejudice and discrimination. For example, when women in a workplace are assigned care-giving roles like coordinating birthday celebrations or an African-American employee is asked to DJ the office holiday party, it doesn't necessarily mean that individuals in the workplace are prejudiced. But it does send a signal that group-based stereotypes are acceptable heuristics to use during social interaction in that setting. Within such environments, it would be unsurprising if the use of stereotypes generalized over time to more consequential interactions such as using stereotypical guides to identify who to promote or commend as a leader in the workplace (Biernat, Fuegen, & Kobrynowicz, 2010; Biernat & Vescio, 2002; Eagly & Carli, 2007; Vescio, Gervais, Snyder, & Hoover, 2005).

Behavioral models of prejudice are also powerful in shaping environments (Donnerstein & Donnerstein, 1978; Glaser & Gilens, 1997). One study showed that, when an audience laughed at racist jokes about people from the Middle East compared to when they remained silent, a more negative implicit norm toward people from the Middle East was formed, which, in turn, led observers to discriminate against the targeted group (Yoshida, Peach, Zanna, & Spencer, 2012). Indeed, groups or individuals can create environments of prejudice through modeling. In fact, research shows that a single individual who expresses benign acceptance of racist acts can affect not only public acceptance but also private acceptance by observers—creating a self-perpetuating cycle of prejudiced norms (Blanchard, Crandall, Brigham, & Vaughn, 1994). While a norms-based approach posits that prejudiced situations like these encourage the expression of individuals' prejudiced attitudes which in turn strengthens those attitudes, the social-contextual model of prejudice extends that prediction by suggesting that prejudiced norms and behavioral models may compel people to behave in prejudiced ways without, in any traditional sense, becoming more prejudiced themselves. Similar to more automatic processes, observing a prejudiced situational norm or behavioral model might automatically activate a prime to behavior link, causing individuals to behave in prejudiced ways.

HOW DO ENVIRONMENTS BECOME UNPREJUDICED?

How might we create egalitarian environments in which social groups are not systematically disadvantaged in their psychological experiences or outcomes? Extant research has shown that people do best in identity-safe settings—settings where they feel that all aspects of their social identities are valued and respected by others and where they are confident that they will be treated as individuals, rather than as token group members (Davies, Spencer, & Steele, 2005; Steele et al., 2002). Within these environments, vigilance processes are relaxed and people feel they will not be perceived, treated, or evaluated based on their group membership (Davies et al., 2005; Murphy et al., 2007).

One way to create identity-safe environments is to introduce situational cues that account for majority and minority differences in construal and allay people's identity-based concerns. For example, stigmatized group members are concerned about being seen to belong or "fit" within valued environments such as schools and workplaces. Several studies reveal that messages that target the belonging concerns of minority group members can buffer the negative psychological experiences and underperformance associated with them without affecting the outcomes of majority group members, who don't grapple with the same concerns (Walton & Cohen, 2007, 2011a; see also Walton & Carr, 2012). Another situational intervention could be undertaken regarding demographic queries that typically precede national standardized tests such as the SAT and the GRE. Research shows that asking students to indicate their racial, ethnic, or gender group membership prior to taking these exams causes women and students of color significantly to underperform, but has no effect on men and White individuals (Danaher & Crandall, 2008). Placing demographic queries after the tests should reduce concerns among those disadvantaged by group-based intellectual stereotypes without affecting majority group members.

Similarly, research shows that both minority and majority group members are concerned that their identities may be liabilities in their pursuit of success within social or professional environments—but for different reasons. While stigmatized groups might be concerned about discrimination, majority group members might be concerned that their majority group membership might place them at a disadvantage when settings aim to "diversify" (Norton & Sommers, 2011). Environments can allay these identity-based concerns by including situational cues that clearly delineate how an individual's success within a setting will be evaluated and how rewards will be distributed (Laurin, Fitzsimmons, & Kay, 2011). These types of situational cues may reduce people's concerns that their social group membership will be a factor that limits or blocks their attainment of important goals within an environment because the criteria for evaluation and promotion are publicly and clearly specified.

Members of majority and minority groups want to be treated with dignity and respect as individuals, but they also want to feel that their group, in a general sense, is viewed with respect. Research reveals that environments differ in the extent to which they cultivate norms of group-based respect. Group-based respect is an indicator of the extent to which an institution acknowledges, accepts, and values each subgroup that makes up the whole (Huo & Molina, 2006). Particularly in racially diverse settings, when they feel that their group membership is respected and valued by an institution or environment, minorities show more positive evaluations of outgroup members as well as greater engagement and motivation (Derks, Van Laar, & Ellemers, 2007; Huo, Molina, Binning, & Funge, 2010). In addition to fostering group-based respect, studies have shown that promoting a cultural value of empathy and compassion is important to reducing prejudice within settings. When an environment explicitly values tolerance, acceptance, and empathy, it may cause people to reconsider the appropriateness of prejudice and discrimination (Aronson, 2000; Crandall & Eshleman, 2003; Galinsky & Moskowitz, 2000; Wilson et al., 2000).

Another way environments can be structured to reduce prejudice is to create opportunities for groups to work together toward common goals. The jigsaw classroom (Aronson & Bridgeman, 1979) is one example of an environment structured around cooperation and collaboration that reduces prejudice and facilitates learning. When all people in an environment are responsible for mastering an aspect of the whole and communicating it to others, each individual—regardless of their group membership—is essential for full understanding. Each person garners respect in the role of expert and each is needed to achieve a maximally positive solution. Relying on and respecting the contribution of each individual, cooperative environments reduce the likelihood that peers will reduce one another to group-based stereotypes. Similarly, the common ingroup identity model (Gaertner & Dovidio, 2000) suggests that, when environments foster superordinate identities that are inclusive and that create connections across subgroups, the meaning and function of these narrower subgroup memberships, such as race, gender, and ethnicity, become less important in intergroup interactions (Gaertner, Dovidio, Nier, Ward, & Banker, 1999; Gaertner, Mann, Murrell, & Dovidio, 1989). Broadening people's conceptions about who belongs to their ingroup fosters more positive, respectful attitudes and behaviors toward individuals formerly perceived as outgroup members. Such common ingroup identities have been shown to provide a foundation for the development of intergroup friendships (West, Pearson, Dovidio, Shelton, & Trail, 2009).

Finally, powerful members often have the cultural capital to shift local norms and create non-prejudiced environments. Within companies, for example, senior management who model appropriate behavior and clearly state expectations of respect and equal treatment influence the way their subordinates interact (Pearson, Andersson, & Porath, 2000). Using case studies and research findings, organizations could educate workers about how policies, procedures, and practices that seem neutral on their face may limit the outcomes or experiences of some social groups. In this way, it may be possible to broaden people's construal of what it means to be prejudiced from a problem of people to a problem of people and environments. By broadening people's construal about how settings produce bias, organizations may be able to leverage the good will of those who truly wish to be egalitarian, encouraging them to work actively toward creating and maintaining non-prejudiced environments. Finally, because vigilance to and processing of bias may have egocentric or ethnocentric components to it (Clayton & Crosby, 1992; Rutte, Diekmann, Polzer, Crosby, & Messick, 1994), encouraging individuals anonymously and confidentially to report their perceptions of biased outcomes and experiences on a regular basis will help environments identify problematic policies or procedures and allocate attention where it is needed. Research shows that, when outcomes or experiences are found to differ by social group membership, managers should take prompt action to address the disparities in order to maintain a culture of equality and respect (Pearson et al., 2000; Pearson & Porath, 2004).

CONCLUSION

While social psychology has a long history of emphasizing the role of the situation in affecting behavior and important outcomes, in the context of stereotyping and prejudice the dominant research emphasis has been on the assessment of individual differences in prejudice, whether explicit or implicit. This approach has yielded a rich understanding of how attitudinal processes contribute to discrimination. In this chapter, we call for a broader consideration of the role of the context in the study of prejudice. We describe research that demonstrates that much is known about aspects of environments that are likely to produce prejudice and discrimination. We hope that more focused attention to environments, and their role in perpetuating and remedying prejudice, will produce novel interventions and solutions to pursue further the ideal of equal opportunity. One lesson of the history of civil rights was that changing laws can change minds by changing behavior first (Pettigrew, 1966). So we hope that identifying and restructuring prejudiced environments will lead to greater equality between groups.

REFERENCES

Adorno, T., Frenkel-Brunswik, E., Levinson, D., & Sanford, R. N. (1950). *The authoritarian personality*. New York: Harper.

Ajzen, I., & Fishbein, M. (2005). The influence of attitudes on behavior. In D. Albarracín, B. T. Johnson, & M. P. Zanna (Eds.), *The handbook of attitudes* (pp. 173–221). Mahwah, NJ: Erlbaum.

Allcott, H. (2011). Social norms and energy conservation. *Journal of Public Economics*, 95, 1082–1095.

Allport, G. W. (1954). *The nature of prejudice*. Cambridge, MA: Addison-Wesley.

Allport, G. W. (1966). Prejudice and the individual. In J. P. Davis (Ed.), *The American Negro reference book* (p. 706). Englewood Cliffs, NJ: Prentice Hall.

Amodio, D. M., Devine, P. G., & Harmon-Jones, E. (2007). A dynamic model of guilt: Implications for motivation and self-regulation in the context of prejudice. *Psychological Science, 18*, 524–530.

Aronson, E. (2000). *Nobody left to hate: Teaching compassion after Columbine*. New York: W. H. Freeman.

Aronson, E., & Bridgeman, D. (1979). Jigsaw groups and the desegregated classroom: In pursuit of common goals. *Personality and Social Psychology Bulletin, 5*, 438–446.

Asch, S. E. (1952). *Social psychology*. Englewood Cliffs, NJ: Prentice Hall.

Banaji, M. R., & Greenwald, A. G. (1995). Implicit gender stereotyping in judgments of fame. *Journal of Personality and Social Psychology, 68*, 181–198.

Barlow, F. K., Louis, W. R., and Terry, D. J. (2010). Minority report: Social identity, cognitions of rejection and intergroup anxiety predicting prejudice from one racially marginalized group towards another. *European Journal of Social Psychology, 40*, 805–818.

Bator, R. J., & Cialdini, R. B. (2000). The application of persuasion theory to the development of effective proenvironmental public service announcements. *Journal of Social Issues, 56*, 527–541.

Biernat, M., Collins, E. C., Katzarska-Miller, I., & Thompson, E. R. (2009). Race-based shifting standards and racial discrimination. *Personality and Social Psychology Bulletin, 35*, 16–28.

Biernat, M., Fuegen, K., & Kobrynowicz, D. (2010). Shifting standards and the inference of incompetence: Effects of formal and informal evaluation tools. *Personality and Social Psychology Bulletin, 36*, 855–868.

Biernat, M., & Vescio, T. K. (2002). She swings, she hits, she's great, she's benched: Implications of gender-based shifting standards for judgment and behavior. *Personality and Social Psychology Bulletin, 28*, 66–77.

Blanchard, F. A., Crandall, C. S., Brigham, J. C., & Vaughn L. A. (1994). Condemning and condoning racism: A social context approach to interracial settings. *Journal of Applied Psychology, 79*, 993–997.

Bogardus, E. S. (1928). *Immigration and race attitudes*. Oxford: Heath.

Brannon, T. N., & Walton, G. M. (in press). Enacting cultural interests: How intergroup contact reduces prejudice by sparking interest in an outgroup's culture. *Psychological Science*.

Bureau of Labor Statistics. (2011). Current population survey: Table 11: Employed persons by detailed occupation, sex, race, and Hispanic or Latino ethnicity. *Annual Averages 2010*. Retrieved from http://www.bls.gov/cps/cpsaat11.pdf

Carr, P. B., Dweck, C. S., & Pauker, K. (2012). *Prejudiced behavior without prejudice? Beliefs about the malleability of prejudice affect interracial interactions*. Unpublished manuscript.

Chaiken, S., & Trope, Y. (1999). *Dual-process theories in social psychology*. New York: Guilford Press.

Cheryan, S., Plaut, V. C., Davies, P., & Steele, C. M. (2009). Ambient belonging: How stereotypical environments impact gender participation in computer science. *Journal of Personality and Social Psychology, 97*, 1045–1060.

Cialdini, R. B. (2003). Crafting normative messages to protect the environment. *Current Directions in Psychological Science, 12*, 105–109.

Cialdini, R. B., Reno, R. R., & Kallgren, C. A. (1990). A focus theory of normative conduct: Recycling the concept of norms to reduce littering in public places. *Journal of Personality and Social Psychology, 58*, 1015–1026.

Clayton, S. D., & Crosby, F. J. (1992). *Justice, gender, and affirmative action*. Ann Arbor: University of Michigan Press.

Crandall, C. S. Bahns, A., Warner, R., & Schaller, M. (2011). Stereotypes as justifications of prejudice. *Personality and Social Psychology Bulletin, 37*, 1488–1498.

Crandall, C. S., & Eshleman, A. (2003). A justification-suppression model of the expression and experience of prejudice. *Psychological Bulletin, 129*, 414–446.

Crandall, C. S., Eshleman, A., & O'Brien, L. T. (2002). Social norms and the expression and suppression of prejudice: The struggle for internalization. *Journal of Personality and Social Psychology, 82*, 359–378.

Crandall, C. S., & Stangor, C. (2005). Conformity and prejudice. In J. F. Dovidio, P. Glick, & L. A. Rudman (Eds.), *On the nature of prejudice: Fifty years after Allport* (pp. 295 – 309). Malden, MA: Blackwell.

Crosby, F. J. (2004). *Affirmative action is dead: Long live affirmative action*. New Haven, CT: Yale University Press.

Crosby, F., Bromley, S., & Saxe, L. (1980). Recent unobtrusive studies of black and white discrimination and prejudice: A literature review. *Psychological Bulletin, 87*, 546–563.

Crosby, F. J., Iyer, A., Clayton, S., & Downing, R. (2003). Affirmative action: Psychological data and the policy debates. *American Psychologist, 58*, 93–115.

Cunningham, W. A., Preacher, K. J., & Banaji, M. R. (2001). Implicit attitude measures: Consistency, stability, and convergent validity. *Psychological Science, 12*, 163–170.

Danaher, K., & Crandall, C. S. (2008). Stereotype threat in applied settings re-examined. *Journal of Applied Social Psychology, 38*, 1639–1655.

Darley, J., & Batson, C. D. (1973). From Jerusalem to Jericho: A study of situational and dispositional variables in helping behaviour. *Journal of Personality and Social Psychology, 27*, 100–108.

Dasgupta, N. (2004). Implicit ingroup favoritism, outgroup favoritism, and their behavioral manifestations. *Social Justice Research, 17*, 143–169.

Davies, P. G., Spencer, S. J., & Steele, C. M. (2005). Clearing the air: Identity safety moderates the effects of stereotype threat on women's leadership aspirations. *Journal of Personality and Social Psychology, 88*, 276–287.

Davis, M. (2011). Behavior and energy savings: Evidence from a series of experimental interventions. *Environmental Defense Fund*. Retrieved from http://opower.com/uploads/library/file/5/edf_behavior_and_energysavings.pdf

Derks, B., Van Laar, C., & Ellemers, N. (2007). The beneficial effects of social identity protection on the performance motivation of members of devalued groups. *Social Issues and Policy Review, 1*, 217–256.

Devine, P. (1989). Stereotypes and prejudice: Their automatic and controlled components. *Journal of Personality and Social Psychology, 56*, 5–18.

Donnerstein, M., & Donnerstein, E. (1978). Direct and vicarious censure in the control of interracial aggression. *Journal of Personality, 46*, 162–175.

Dovidio, J. F. (2001). On the nature of contemporary prejudice: The third wave. *Journal of Social Issues, 57*, 829–849.

Dovidio, J. F., & Gaertner, S. L. (1986). Prejudice, discrimination, and racism: Historical trends and contemporary approaches. In J. F. Dovidio & S. L. Gaertner (Eds.), *Prejudice, discrimination, and racism* (pp. 1–34). New York: Academic Press.

Duckitt, J. (1992). Psychology and prejudice: A historical analysis and integrative framework. *American Psychologist, 47*, 1182–1193.

Duckitt, J. (1994). *The social psychology of prejudice*. Westport, CT: Praeger.

Dweck, C. S. (2000). *Self-theories: Their role in motivation, personality, and development*. Philadelphia: Psychology Press.

Eagly, A. H., & Carli, L. L. (2007). *Through the labyrinth: The truth about how women become leaders*. Boston: Harvard Business School Press.

The Economist (2008, January 24). The cooks spoil Obama's broth. [Editorial]. *The Economist*. Retrieved from http://www.economist.com/node/10566696.

EPA. (2010). Municipal solid waste generation, recycling, and disposal in the United States: Facts and figures for 2010. United States Environmental Protection Agency. Retrieved from http://www.epa.gov/osw/nonhaz/municipal/pubs/msw_2010_rev_factsheet.pdf

EPA. (2012). Pay-as-you-throw. United States Environmental Protection Agency. Retrieved from http://www.epa.gov/osw/conserve/tools/payt/

Fazio, R. H., Jackson, J. R., Dunton, B. C., & Williams, C. J. (1995). Variability in automatic activation as an unobtrusive measure of racial attitudes: A bona fide pipeline? *Journal of Personality and Social Psychology, 69*, 1013–1027.

Gaertner, S. L., & Dovidio, J. F. (2000). *Reducing intergroup bias: The common ingroup identity model*. Philadelphia: Psychology Press.

Gaertner, S. L., Dovidio, J. F., Nier, J. A., Ward, C. M., & Banker, B. S. (1999). Across cultural divides: The value of a superordinate identity. In D. Prentice & D. Miller (Eds.), *Cultural divides: Understanding and overcoming group conflict* (pp.173–212). New York: Russell Sage Foundation.

Gaertner, S. L., Mann, J. A., Murrell, A. J., & Dovidio, J. F. (1989). Reduction of intergroup bias: The benefits of recategorization. *Journal of Personality and Social Psychology, 57*, 239–249.

Galinsky, A. D., & Moskowitz, G. B. (2000). Perspective-taking: Decreasing stereotype expression, stereotype accessibility, and in-group favoritism. *Journal of Personality and Social Psychology, 78*, 708–724.

Glaser, J. M. and Gilens, M. (1997). Inter-regional migration and political resocialization: A study of racial attitudes under pressure. *Public Opinion Quarterly, 61*, 72–86.

Goff, P. A., Eberhardt, J. L., Williams, M., & Jackson, M. C. (2008). Not yet human: Implicit knowledge, historical dehumanization, and contemporary consequences. *Journal of Personality and Social Psychology, 94*, 292–306.

Goff, P. A., Steele, C. M., & Davies, P. G. (2008). The space between us: Stereotype threat and distance in interracial contexts. *Journal of Personality and Social Psychology, 94*, 91–107.

Greenwald, A. G., Poehlman, T. A., Uhlmann, E., & Banaji, M. R. (2009). Understanding and using the Implicit Association Test, III: Meta-analysis of predictive validity. *Journal of Personality and Social Psychology, 97*, 17–41.

Hochschild, J. (1981). *What's fair?* Cambridge, MA: Harvard University Press.

Hochschild, J. (1995). *Facing up to the American dream: Race, class and the soul of the nation*. Princeton, NJ: Princeton University Press.

Hooge, I. E. de, Nelissen, R. M. A., Breugelmans, S. M., & Zeelenberg, M. (2011). What is moral about guilt? Acting "prosocially" at the disadvantage of others. *Journal of Personality and Social Psychology, 100*, 462–473.

Huo, Y. J., & Molina, L. E. (2006). Is pluralism a viable model for diversity? The benefits and limits of subgroup respect. *Group Processes and Intergroup Relations, 35*, 237–254.

Huo, Y. J., Molina, L. E., Binning, K. R., & Funge, S. P. (2010). Subgroup respect, social engagement, and well-being: A field study of an ethnically diverse high school. *Cultural Diversity and Ethnic Minority Psychology, 16*, 427–436.

Jencks, C. (1998). Racial bias in testing. In C. Jencks & M. Phillips (Eds.), *The Black–White test score gap* (pp. 55–85). Washington, DC: Brookings Institution.

Jones, E. E., & Sigall, H. (1971). The bogus pipeline: A new paradigm for measuring affect and attitude. *Psychological Bulletin, 76*, 349–364.

Katz, D., & Braly, K. (1935). Racial prejudice and racial stereotypes. *Journal of Abnormal and Social Psychology, 30*, 175–193.

Katz, I., & Hass, R. G. (1988). Racial ambivalence and American value conflict: Correlational and priming studies of dual cognitive structures. *Journal of Personality and Social Psychology, 55*, 893–905.

Kawakami, K., Dovidio, J. F., Moll, J., Hermsen, S., & Russin, A. (2000). Just say no (to stereotyping): Effects of training in the negation of stereotypic associations on stereotype activation. *Journal of Personality and Social Psychology, 78*, 871–888.

Kochanska, G., Barry, R. A., Jimenez, N. B., Hollatz, A. L., & Woodard, J. (2009). Guilt and effortful control: Two mechanisms that prevent disruptive developmental trajectories. *Journal of Personality and Social Psychology, 97*, 322–333.

Laskey, A., & Kavazovic, O. (2010). OPOWER: Energy efficiency through behavioral science and technology. *XRDS, 17*, 47–51.

Laurin, K., Fitzsimons, G. M., & Kay, A. C. (2011). Social disadvantage and the self-regulatory function of justice beliefs. *Journal of Personality and Social Psychology, 100*, 149–171.

Margolis, J., and Fisher, A. (2002). *Unlocking the clubhouse: Women in computing.* Cambridge, MA: MIT Press.

Markus, H. R., & Moya, P. M. L. (2010). *Doing race: 21 essays for the 21ˢᵗ century.* New York: W. W. Norton.

McConahay, J. B. (1986). Modern racism, ambivalence, and the Modern Racism Scale. In J. F. Dovidio & S. L. Gaertner (Eds.), *Prejudice, discrimination, and racism* (pp. 91–125). New York: Academic Press.

McConnell, A. R., & Leibold, J. M. (2001). Relations among the Implicit Association Test, discriminatory behavior, and explicit measures of racial attitudes. *Journal of Experimental Social Psychology, 37*, 435–442.

Merton, R. K. (1938). Social structure and anomie. *American Sociological Review, 3*, 672–682.

Monteith, M. J., Mark, A. Y., & Ashburn-Nardo, L. (2010). The self-regulation of prejudice: Toward understanding its lived character. *Group Processes and Intergroup Relations, 13*, 183–200.

Murphy, M. C., Richeson, J. A., & Molden, D. C. (2011). Leveraging motivational mindsets to foster positive interracial interactions. *Personality and Social Psychology Compass, 5*, 118–131.

Murphy M. C., Steele, C. M., & Gross, J. J. (2007). Signaling threat: How situational cues affect women in math, science, and engineering settings. *Psychological Science, 18*, 879–885.

Murphy, M. C., & Taylor, V. J. (2012). The role of situational cues in signaling and maintaining stereotype threat. In M. Inzlicht & T. Schmader (Eds.), *Stereotype threat: Theory, process, and applications.* New York: Oxford University Press.

Newcomb, T. M., Koenig, K. E., Flacks, R., & Warwick, D. P. (1967). *Persistence and change: Bennington College and its students after twenty-five years*. New York: John Wiley & Sons.

Norton, M. I., & Sommers, S. R. (2011). Whites see racism as a zero-sum game that they are now losing. *Perspectives on Psychological Science*, 6, 215–218.

Nosek, B. A., & Hansen, J. J. (2008). The associations in our heads belong to us: Searching for attitudes and knowledge in implicit evaluation. *Cognition and Emotion, 22*, 553–594.

Pager, D., & Shepherd, H. (2008). The sociology of discrimination: Racial discrimination in employment, housing, credit and consumer markets. *Annual Review of Sociology, 34*, 181–209.

Pearson, C. M., Andersson, L. M., & Porath, C. L. (2000). Assessing and attacking workplace incivility. *Organizational Dynamics, 29*, 123–137.

Pearson, C. M., & Porath, C. L. (2004). On incivility, its impact, and directions for future research. In R. W. Griffin & A. M. O'Leary-Kelly (Eds.), *The dark side of organizational behavior* (pp. 403–425). San Francisco: Jossey-Bass.

Pettigrew, T. F. (1966). Prejudice and the situation. In J. P. Davis (Ed.), *The American Negro reference book*. Englewood Cliffs, NJ: Prentice Hall.

Pettigrew, T. F., Christ, O., Wagner, U., Meertens, R. W., van Dick, R., & Zick, A. (2008). Relative deprivation and intergroup prejudice. *Journal of Social Issues, 64*, 385–401.

Pettigrew, T. F., & Meertens, R. W. (1995). Subtle and blatant prejudice in Western Europe. *European Journal of Social Psychology, 57*, 57–75.

Plant, E. A., & Devine P. G. (1998). Internal and external motivation to respond without prejudice. *Journal of Personality and Social Psychology, 75*, 811–832.

Plant, E. A., & Devine, P. G. (2003). Antecedents and implications of interracial anxiety. *Personality and Social Psychology Bulletin, 29*, 790–801.

Plant, E. A., & Devine, P. G. (2009). The active control of prejudice: Unpacking the intentions guiding control efforts. *Journal of Personality and Social Psychology, 96*, 640–652.

Pronin, E., Steele, C., & Ross, L. (2004). Identity bifurcation in response to stereotype threat: Women and mathematics. *Journal of Experimental Social Psychology, 40*, 152–168.

Remnick, D. (2008, November 17). The Joshua generation: Race and the campaign of Barack Obama. *The New Yorker*. Retrieved from http://www.newyorker.com/reporting/2008/11/17/081117fa_fact_remnick?currentPage=all

Richeson, J. A., & Shelton, J. N. (2007). Negotiating interracial interactions: Costs, consequences, and possibilities. *Current Directions in Psychological Science, 16*, 316–320.

Ross, L., & Nisbett, R. E. (1991). *The person and the situation: Perspectives of social psychology*. New York: McGraw-Hill.

Rutte, C. G., Diekmann, K. A., Polzer, J. T., Crosby, F. J., & Messick, D. M. (1994). Organizing information and the detection of gender discrimination. *Psychological Science, 5*, 226–231.

Schuman, H., Steeh, C., Bobo, L., & Krysan, M. (1997). *Racial attitudes in America: trends and interpretations* (rev. ed.) Cambridge, MA: Harvard University Press.

Sears, D. O. (1988). Symbolic racism. In P. Katz & D. Taylor (Eds.), *Eliminating racism: Profiles in controversy* (pp. 53–84). New York: Plenum Press.

Sherif, M. (1966). *In common predicament: Social psychology of intergroup conflict and cooperation*. Boston: Houghton-Mifflin.

Shultz, M. M., & Zedeck, S. (2008). *Identification, development, and validation of predictors for successful lawyering*. Retrieved from http://www.law.berkeley.edu/files/LSACREPORTfinal-12.pdf

Shultz, M. M., & Zedeck, S. (2011). Predicting lawyer effectiveness: Broadening the basis for law school admission decisions. *Law and Social Inquiry, 36*, 620–661.

Smedley, B. D., Stith, A. Y., & Nelson, A. R. (2003). *Unequal treatment: Confronting racial and ethnic disparities in health care*. Washington, DC: National Academies Press.

Son Hing, L. S., Li, W., & Zanna, M. P. (2002). Inducing hypocrisy to reduce prejudicial responses among aversive racists. *Journal of Experimental Social Psychology, 38*, 71–78.

Steele, C. M. (1997). A threat in the air: How stereotypes shape intellectual identity and performance. *American Psychologist, 52*, 613–629.

Steele, C. M., & Aronson, J. (1995). Stereotype threat and the intellectual test performance of African-Americans. *Journal of Personality and Social Psychology, 69*, 797–811.

Steele, C. M., Spencer, S. J., & Aronson, J. (2002). Contending with group image: The psychology of stereotype threat and social identity threat. In L. Berkowitz (Ed.), *Advances in Experimental Social Psychology* (Vol. 34, pp. 379–440). San Diego, CA: Academic Press.

Tajfel, H. (1970). Experiments in intergroup discrimination. *Scientific American, 223*, 96–102.

Tajfel, H., Billig, M. G., Bundy, R. P., & Flament, C. (1971). Social categorization and intergroup behaviour. European Journal of Social Psychology, 1, 149–177.

Tangney, J., Wagner, P. E, Hill-Barlow, D., Marschall, D. E., & Gramzow, R. (1996). Relation of shame and guilt to constructive versus destructive responses to anger across the lifespan. *Journal of Personality and Social Psychology, 70*, 797–809.

Taranto, J. (2010, August 13). The carnival police: Joe Conason waxes nostalgic for racism. *Wall Street Journal*. Retrieved from http://online.wsj.com.

Thomaes, S., Bushman, B. J., Stegge, H., & Olthof, T. (2008). Trumping shame by blasts of noise: Narcissism, self-esteem, shame, and aggression in young adolescents. *Child Development, 79*, 1792–1801.

Uhlmann, E. L., & Cohen, G. L. (2005). Constructed criteria: Redefining merit to justify discrimination. *Psychological Science, 16*, 474–480.

Uhlmann, E. L., Poehlman, T. A., & Nosek, B. (2012). Automatic associations: Personal attitudes or cultural knowledge? In J. D. Hanson (Ed.), *Ideology, psychology, and law*. New York: Oxford University Press.

Vescio, T. K., Gervais, S. J., Snyder, M., & Hoover, A. (2005). Power and the creation of patronizing environments: The stereotype-based behaviors of the powerful and their effects on female performance in masculine domains. *Journal of Personality and Social Psychology, 88*, 658–672.

Walton, G. M., & Carr, P. B. (2012). Social belonging and the motivation and intellectual achievement of negatively stereotyped students. In M. Inzlicht & T. Schmader (Eds.), Stereotype threat: *Theory, processes, and application* (pp. 89–106). New York: Oxford University Press.

Walton, G. M., & Cohen, G. L. (2003). Stereotype lift. *Journal of Experimental Social Psychology, 39*, 456–467.

Walton, G. M., & Cohen, G. L. (2007). A question of belonging: Race, social fit, and achievement. *Journal of Personality and Social Psychology, 92,* 82–96.

Walton, G. M., & Cohen, G. L. (2011a). A brief social-belonging intervention improves academic and health outcomes of minority students. *Science, 331,* 1447–1451.

Walton, G. M., & Cohen, G. L. (2011b). Sharing motivation. In D. Dunning (Ed.), *Social motivation* (pp. 79–101). New York: Psychology Press.

Walton, G. M., Paunesku, D., & Dweck, C. S. (2012). Expandable selves. In M. R. Leary & J. P. Tangney (Eds.), *Handbook of self and identity* (2nd ed., pp. 141–154). New York: Guilford Press.

Walton, G. M., & Spencer, S. J. (2009). Latent ability: Grades and test scores systematically underestimate the intellectual ability of negatively stereotyped students. *Psychological Science, 20,* 1132–1139.

Walton, G. M., Spencer, S. J., & Erman, S. (in press). Affirmative meritocracy. *Social Issues and Policy Review.*

West, T. V., Pearson, A. R., Dovidio, J. F., Shelton, J. N., & Trail. T. E. (2009). Superordinate identity and intergroup roommate friendship development. *Journal of Experimental Social Psychology, 45,* 1266–1272.

Wightman, L. (1998). An examination of sex differences in LSAT scores from the perspective of social consequences. *Applied Measurement in Education, 11,* 255–277.

Wilson, T. D., Lindsey, S., & Schooler, T. (2000). A model of dual attitudes. *Psychological Review, 107,* 101–126.

Yoshida, E., Peach, J. M., Zanna, M. P., & Spencer, S. J. (2012). Not all automatic associations are created equal: How implicit normative evaluations are distinct from implicit attitudes and uniquely predict meaningful behavior. *Journal of Experimental Social Psychology, 48,* 694–706.

Ziegert, J. C., & Hanges, P. J. (2005). Employment discrimination: The role of implicit attitudes, motivation, and a climate for racial bias. *Journal of Applied Psychology, 90,* 553–562.

9

Social Psychological Approaches to Understanding Small-Group Diversity

The Flexibility of Cognitive Representations

JULIA D. O'BRIEN

University of Maryland

CHARLES STANGOR

University of Maryland

*T*he study of diversity in social groups has gained importance as a topic in social psychology as it has in other related domains (e.g. Bodenhausen, 2010; van Knippenberg, De Dreu, & Homan, 2004). The interest is timely, given the shifting ethnic diversity of U.S. society and the impact that can have on the effectiveness of organizations and work groups. Social psychological research has much to contribute to the topic, as the questions of interest relate in large part to the development and application of intergroup attitudes.

In this chapter, we focus on ethnic and racial diversity in work groups. We briefly review the existing findings on the outcomes related to diversity in organizational settings and the social psychological research on the cognitive representations of diverse groups. We argue that research on ethnic majority and minority preferences for common ingroup identities vs. dual identities is particularly informative and offers important insights for research on small groups. We extend this research to small work-group settings and present preliminary data from our lab demonstrating that, in these settings, the work group becomes the relevant superordinate group such that the within-group majority or minority status of one's ethnicity, rather than the status of one's ethnicity in society, is more predictive of how one processes the work-group setting.

OUTCOMES OF DIVERSITY

In terms of the influence of racial and ethnic diversity within working groups, prior research has demonstrated both consistent and contradictory effects, depending in part on whether the outcome of interest is intergroup attitudes or group performance and in part on whether the variables are assessed for majority or minority group members. In a recent meta-analysis, Joshi and Roh (2009) found that racial diversity had a small, but negative, overall effect on a variety of performance measures in small groups.

In terms of attitudes, perhaps the most important general principle is attraction similarity. People prefer those who are similar to themselves (Byrne, 1971). Thus they are better able to work with similar others and are more likely to be committed to those they see as sharing their basic beliefs and values (Triandis, 1959; Tsui, Egan, & O'Reilly, 1992). Members of culturally dissimilar groups are less likely to be attracted to one another and have more difficulty communicating with one another than do members of more homogeneous groups.

There is also the danger that diverse groups will experience status conflicts that are exacerbated by stereotypes and prejudice. Ethnic diversity may therefore have a negative impact on social integration, communication, and conflict in groups (Chatman, Polzer, Barsade, & Neale, 1998; Jehn, Northcraft, & Neale, 1999; Pelled, Eisenhardt, & Xin, 1999; Watson, Kumar, & Michaelsen, 1993).

Diversity provides contact settings between ethnicities which in many cases improves intergroup attitudes (Pettigrew & Tropp, 2000). However, this contact does not always lead to positive outcomes or evaluations in diverse groups (Bacharach, Bamberger, & Vashdi, 2005). When working groups are diverse, it may be harder for individuals to identify with the group, at least for those who do not value diversity (van Knippenberg, Haslam, & Platow, 2007). Extreme differences in backgrounds and perspectives make it difficult for group members to find common ground and communicate (Zenger & Lawrence, 1989) and can lead to decreased commitment to group goals (Tsui et al., 1992). Diverse groups may also arouse threat and anxiety, which can then lead to further negative outcomes, such as dismissiveness and avoidance (Shelton, Richeson, Salvatore, & Trawalter, 2005).

In addition to the negative outcomes to the group as a whole, diverse settings carry burdens for group minorities. Being a minority group member can reduce feelings of identity safety (see Davies, Spencer, & Steele, 2005). Heightened distinctiveness due to ethnic minority status within a group often causes minority members to feel as though their behavior and characteristics displayed in the group context will be applied to all members of their ethnic group, giving them the burden of representing their entire ethnicity (Pollak & Niemann, 1998; Sekaquaptewa, Waldman, & Thompson, 2007).

Sekaquaptewa and her colleagues (2007) found that, when participants were solo ethnic minorities in groups, Black participants rated ethnicity as more central to their identity than when they were not solo minorities and compared to White solo minorities. These Black solo participants also reported feeling responsible for their ethnicity's reputation, which hindered their performance through self-handicapping. In addition, Black solo minorities feel the effects chronically, whereas White solo minorities feel the effects acutely (Pollak & Niemann, 1998).

Being a member of a small minority group is even more difficult when minority status is based on two categories that are both stigmatized in a given setting. For instance, Yoder and Aniakudo (1997) found that Black female firefighters reported feeling socially ostracized by other firefighters. White males dominate the profession; therefore White females shared ethnicity and Black males shared gender with the dominant group. The Black female firefighters felt doubly stigmatized because they did not share either category with the majority employees.

Despite the numerous negative outcomes associated with diverse groups, diversity can improve group performance in some contexts (Bantel & Jackson, 1989; Eisenhardt & Bourgeois, 1988; Hambrick, Cho, & Chen, 1996). Having diverse viewpoints within a group can increase cognitive conflict, which can improve creativity (Levine, Resnick, & Higgins, 1993). Heterogeneous groups have been shown to outperform homogeneous groups on tasks that require novel insights and solutions (Nemeth, 1986; Stasser, Stewart, & Wittenbaum, 1995; Watson et al., 1993).

Phillips, Liljenquist, and Neale (2009) found that newcomers to groups who do not share ingroup membership with existing group members helped produce better group decisions, and Cunningham and Sagas (2004) found that athletic teams with more racially diverse coaches had better seasons than those with more homogeneous leadership. Diversity may therefore facilitate learning (Gibson & Vermeulen, 2003) and increase creativity and coordination within the group (Nemeth, 1986; Schruijer & Mostert, 1997; Leung, Maddux, Galinsky, & Chiu, 2008).

In a study with mock juries, Sommers (2006) manipulated the extent to which juries were ethnically diverse and found that the diverse juries tended to be more lenient toward Black defendants. He observed improved performance by these groups as their members shared more information. Interestingly, Sommers also found that, when White participants expected to participate in a diverse jury, they made more accurate statements during deliberation. White jury members also appeared to process information more carefully in these diverse juries than when they were working in all-White juries.

Given the wealth of both positive and negative effects of diverse groups, it is no surprise that major reviews and meta-analyses of the literature (Bowers, Pharmer, & Salas, 2000; Jackson, Joshi, & Erhardt, 2003; Milliken & Martins, 1996; O'Reilly, Williams, & Barsade, 1998) find little evidence that diversity is linked to increased group performance overall. The small overall effect of diversity on group performance may be due to the inconsistent findings regarding the positive and negative effects of diversity. These inconsistent findings may also be because the positive effects of diversity are usually found only under very narrow conditions. For instance, Kooij-de Bode and her colleagues (Kooij-de Bode, van Knippenberg, & van Ginkel, 2010) found that diverse groups that were specifically instructed to share information outperformed homogeneous groups. But, without these specific instructions, they shared less information than homogeneous groups, thus hindering their success.

COGNITIVE REPRESENTATIONS OF DIVERSE GROUPS

One limitation of much prior research and theorizing regarding diversity in organizations and small working groups is that it has taken a linear approach, typically examining the degree or amount of diversity in the group, without much concern for what actually happens in terms of the psychological processes within groups. This can be informed by social psychological research on ethnic diversity at the societal level. Research examining the impact of cognitive representations for intergroup relations is particularly informative.

For a group that has at least a moderate amount of diversity, there are four basic ways that one could categorize its members: as separate individuals, as members of distinct subgroups, as members of one superordinate group, or as members of both the subgroups and the superordinate group (Gaertner & Dovidio, 2000; Dovidio, Gaertner, & Saguy, 2007; Dovidio, Gaertner, & Saguy, 2009). Early intergroup relations researchers proposed decategorization as a method of improving evaluations of outgroup members in intergroup contact settings (Brewer & Miller, 1984). The theory was that, if outgroup members could be categorized as separate individuals instead of as members of specific outgroups, then individuals could become personally acquainted and judge one another on individual characteristics rather than on group stereotypes.

This process of individuation and decategorization can happen naturally in friendships between members of different ethnicities, as individuals focus on traits that are not directly linked to ethnicity. Ely and Thomas (2001) found that acknowledging individual identities and unique qualities led to improved group performance and learning, suggesting that allowing people to express their identities in a manner that is comfortable can improve group interactions. However, decategorization and individuation could be problematic if individuals underestimate the importance of category memberships or try to ignore social categories altogether. Such colorblind approaches to diversity can cause prejudice to rebound after group boundaries are suppressed (Correll, Park, & Smith, 2008), which can subsequently deplete the cognitive resources of minority interaction partners (Holoien & Shelton, 2012).

Decategorization and individuation have the potential to overcome some of the barriers to success in diverse groups (namely the application of negative stereotypes). However, several lines of research suggest that an overemphasis on individual characteristics may not always be preferable. For instance, optimal distinctiveness theory (Brewer, 1991) implies that individuals desire to maximize the joint profit of both their individual and their group memberships. It might therefore be expected that group members would not want to be too isolated within a diverse group because they would feel too "individual" and not sufficiently integrated into the "collective." Supporting this idea, group tokens and minorities are known to suffer from performance deficits (Kanter, 1977; Lord & Saenz, 1985; Stangor, Carr, & Kiang, 1998).

Extending the theory of decategorization and individuation, the Common Ingroup Identity model (Gaertner and Dovidio, 2000; Gaertner, Dovidio, Anastasio, Bachman, & Rust, 1993) proposes that shifting category boundaries can improve intergroup relations. Unlike decategorization, the Common Ingroup Identity model proposes that new inclusive category boundaries should be made salient. According to this theory, intergroup relations should improve if members of different social categories are able to think of themselves as belonging to one larger inclusive social category rather than to smaller subgroups. For instance, in a diverse work team that had White and Black workers, members would be encouraged to think of themselves as team members rather than as White people and Black people. If team members think mainly of their ethnicities as their ingroups, then they would consider some of their team members to be outgroup members. However, if members think of their team as their ingroup, then those who are ethnic outgroup members would become "team" ingroup members.

A wide range of diversity researchers have argued that focusing on a common ingroup is an especially useful strategy (Roberge & van Dick, 2010). Emphasizing a common ingroup reduces the threat between subgroups that is often present during intergroup settings (Riek, Mania, Gaertner, McDonald, & Lamoreaux, 2010) and can lead to better group outcomes than when gender and racial categories are more salient (Homan et al., 2008). A common ingroup identity can improve the helping behavior of individual Whites toward Blacks (Nier et al., 2001) and can also improve group satisfaction (Cunningham, 2005). An intervention that broadened children's ingroup boundaries led to their being more likely to select another child of a different race as a preferred playmate (Houlette et al., 2004), just as a common ingroup identity among roommate pairs of different races lead to longer-lasting friendships (West, Pearson, Dovidio, Shelton, & Trail, 2009). In a similar line of research, Chatman and her colleagues (Chatman and Spataro, 2005; Chatman et al., 1998) have argued that collectivist cultures in diverse groups reduce the salience of subcategory boundaries and lead to better group performance.

From a theoretical standpoint, it is intuitive that emphasizing a shared superordinate group identity should improve relations between former outgroups. This argument is also consistent with research demonstrating that, when multiple social categories are salient, evaluations are more positive when a target shares at least one social category (vs. none; e.g., Crisp & Hewstone,

1999; Migdal, Hewstone, & Mullen, 1998). However, there is some existing research that suggests that a common ingroup identity is not always preferable (e.g., Gómez, Dovidio, Huici, Gaertner, & Cuadrado, 2008). Furthermore, Dynamic Social Influence theory (Latané & Bourgeois, 1996; Latané & L'Herrou, 1996), predicts that, when given the opportunity, groups will spontaneously form into smaller clusters of individuals who have features in common, such as attitudes or (presumably) social categories. Indeed, studies have found that people in working groups, and particularly within-group minorities, tend to spend time with others who share their gender and ethnic group memberships (Carley, 1991; Ibarra, 1992; Mollica, Gray, & Trevino, 2003).

Given that people are often attracted to similar others (Byrne, 1971), a cognitive representation that fosters a connection with similar others within the superordinate group may be preferable. A dual-identity representation, or categorization at both the subgroup and the superordinate group level, allows a group member to maintain identity and connections at the subgroup level while also identifying with the superordinate, or "common," group. Gaertner and his colleagues (Gaertner, Rust, Dovidio, Bachman, & Anastasio, 1996) found that a dual identification in a multi-ethnic high school (racial and high-school identification) led to decreased bias, and González & Brown (2003, 2006) found experimentally that a dual identity decreased bias toward an outgroup.

The inconsistent findings regarding the relative benefits of either type of cognitive representation of diverse groups can be explained, in part, by the divergent preferences of majority and minority group members. There is a growing body of evidence to support the notion that ethnic majorities prefer common ingroup representations whereas minorities prefer dual-identity representations (see Dovidio et al., 2007, 2009). For example, Dovidio, Gaertner, and Kafati (2000) found that, for ethnic minorities, a dual-identity representation increased organizational commitment but that, for ethnic majorities, a common ingroup representation increased organizational commitment. Furthermore, these divergent preferences for dual identities or common ingroup identities are polarized during times of intergroup threat (Dovidio et al., 2007).

Dovidio and his colleagues (2009) have argued that the divergent preferences for common ingroup identities vs. dual identities by majority and minority groups are likely due to the distinct needs and goals of each group within diverse cultures. Ethnic minorities are usually non-dominant. They may be motivated to have contact with majority groups, but they are also often motivated to maintain their cultures and to seek equality (van Oudenhoven, Prins, & Buunk, 1998; Verkuyten, 2006). These motivations lead them to prefer multicultural or integration approaches to diversity that lead to an appreciation of the unique differences between groups (see Verkuyten, 2006). Because multicultural or integration approaches to diversity keep social category boundaries salient (without creating isolated groups that are not in contact), Dovidio and his colleagues (2009) argue that these approaches to diversity signal a dual-identity cognitive representation of the different ethic groups. The contact between ethnic groups promotes a salient superordinate identity, whereas the maintained culture of the subgroups promotes a salient subgroup identity as well.

Within ethnically diverse societies, majority group members may be motivated to maintain the dominance of their culture over minority cultures. Therefore, ethnic majorities tend to prefer assimilation approaches to diversity, as these blur the social category boundaries and, in essence, cause all groups to take on the norms, language, and customs of the ethnic majority (Wolsko, Park, & Judd, 2006; Verkuyten, 2005). Because assimilation approaches to diversity signal only the superordinate category, Dovidio and his colleagues (2009) argue that they lead to common ingroup representations.

In addition, Dovidio et al. (2009) argue that these divergent majority and minority preferences are due specifically to power and status differences, and that the various types of cognitive representations each serve a specific power-related function. They maintain that it should be functional for majorities to endorse a one-group identity, as it would serve to maintain their dominance and the status quo, whereas a one-group identity would be dysfunctional for minority group members, as it would blur group boundaries and thus reduce the salience of group disparities. They assert that a dual identity is thus preferable for minority group members because it maintains group boundaries.

Dixon, Tropp, Durrheim, and Tredoux (2010) have presented a similar argument as to the functionality of a dual identity for minorities. Although a common ingroup identity may lead to improved intergroup evaluations, it may also serve to maintain the status quo and group disparities. With a more salient superordinate group and less salient subgroup boundaries, minority members will be less inclined to view the (now favorable) majority as perpetrating injustices. A dual-identity representation, on the other hand, makes group disparities more salient to both majority and minority group members (Dovidio et al., 2004).

High-status groups should be less motivated to consider group differences, whereas low-status groups should more likely to consider group differences specifically because they seek changes in the status hierarchy (Saguy, Dovidio, & Pratto, 2008). For instance, compared to a dual-identity condition, under a common ingroup identity condition, minority members overestimated the generosity of majority group members (Saguy, Tausch, Dovidio, & Pratto, 2009). Thus, a common ingroup identity may not be functional for improving the position of a low-status minority group.

Some more recent evidence demonstrates the direct link between cognitive representations of diversity and group equality efforts. Glasford & Dovidio (2011) found that a common ingroup identity can in fact hamper social change intentions and motivations, whereas a dual identity does not. A dual identity still had the potential to improve ingroup members' evaluations of outgroups, as it increased motivations for contact and caused participants to recognize shared values between groups. Importantly, a dual identity did not interfere with social change motivations, whereas a common ingroup identity promoted optimism about the future of relations between groups, which subsequently reduced motivations for social change.

COGNITIVE REPRESENTATIONS WITHIN SMALL WORK GROUPS

Much of the research on preferences for, and outcomes of, different cognitive representations of diversity has considered motivations and implications that are relevant for larger organizations or society as a whole (e.g., attitudes toward ethnic groups or social change motivations) and has not been considered specifically in the context of small work groups. Work groups may frequently be comprised of ethnic majorities and minorities; however, the relative status of an ethnicity within a work group may not always match the relative status of the ethnicity within society. Thus, in a small-group context, the relative status of one's ethnicity within the group, rather than within society, may determine one's preferred cognitive representation and subsequent group outcomes.

One can point to motivations within small work groups that are similar to the motivations of ethnicities in society that lead to divergent majority and minority preferences for cognitive representations. The power struggles relative to the work of the small diverse group may become more salient and important than the social change motivations related to one's ethnicity within a larger organization or within society. For example, one could imagine a diverse work group where the within-group majority is Black and the within-group minority is White. It is quite possible that, under this condition, the White within-group minority may be concerned more with inclusion and fairness than the within-group majority that is Black (and an ethnic minority). The White within-group minority may demonstrate a preference for a dual identity within the group, just as ethnic minorities demonstrate preferences for dual identities within society, because the small work group becomes the important superordinate group in that context. Similarly, the Black majority may prefer a common ingroup identity if the work group is the salient superordinate group. Thus, we expect that a within-group majority should prefer a common ingroup representation of the group, just as a within-group minority should prefer a dual identity representation of the group. We expect these preferences regardless of either group's ethnicity or majority status within society.

General group dynamics research supports the expectation that within-group majorities should prefer a common ingroup representation whereas within-group minorities should prefer a dual-identity representation. From the perspective of a within-group minority, in order to be most influential, minorities should be able to communicate with one another (Wood, Lundgren, Ouelette, Busceme, & Blackstone, 1994; Moscovici, Lage, & Naffrechoux, 1969). To maintain consistency and unanimity, minority groups would be best served by a dual-identity representation, as this type of representation should foster the necessary lines of communication within subgroup categories.

Within-group majorities should be more dominant in small groups. If the majority wishes to maintain their dominance in the group setting, the best strategy should be to separate the minority members to reduce their influence. This would be best achieved by decreasing ethnic category salience so that minorities are focused less on communicating within their minority group. Thus within-group majorities should prefer a common ingroup identity.

If the preferences for cognitive representations are due to similar motivations as have been proposed and supported for ethnic majorities and minorities within society (i.e., maintaining power and working for change or equality), then any diverging majority or minority preferences within small work groups should be found only in groups where the status or power of an individual's ethnicity has meaningful implications for each member. For instance, one should find more divergent preferences in groups where the success of the individual group member is directly tied to the success of the whole group than in groups where the success of the group is unrelated to the success of its members.

We tested our hypotheses through two experiments. In both experiments we manipulated the within-group status (majority or minority) of participants' ethnicities and the extent to which the groups were personally important to participants. In both experiments we used the physical structure of groups to signal either a common ingroup representation or a dual-identity representation.

Using the physical arrangement of group members is one experimental method that has been used to manipulate cognitive representations (e.g., Gaertner, Mann, Murrell, & Dovidio, 1989; González & Brown, 2006) and is something that could be used by organizations. To the extent that physical distance signals psychological distance (see Fujita, Henderson, Eng, Trope, & Liberman, 2006), the physical arrangement of individuals may be a particularly important factor in small diverse groups, as it should shape each member's cognitive representation of the group. This is potentially a fruitful method of encouraging one cognitive representation over another.

Given two groups with a similar physical structure, a group in which the majority and minority members are *dispersed* should signal a common ingroup. Such a group would have members of the same ethnicity physically distant from one another, or spread out. A group in which the majority and minority members are *clustered* should signal a dual identity. Such a group would have members of the same ethnicity physically close to one another. That is, in a *dispersed* group arrangement, subgroup boundaries should be blurred, as they would be with a common ingroup identity representation. In a *clustered* group, subgroup boundaries should be salient, but the superordinate group would still be salient, as with a dual-identity representation.

Given the specific motivations of group majorities and minorities laid out above, we expect then that, when a group setting is important to the individual, within-group majorities will prefer dispersed arrangements that signal a common ingroup identity over clustered arrangements, and within-group minorities will prefer clustered arrangements that signal a dual identity over dispersed arrangements. That is, we expect that preferences for clustering or dispersion will vary as a function of the majority or minority status of each individual's ethnicity within the small group rather than the majority or minority status of their ethnicity within society.

Experiment 1

Participants in Experiment 1 viewed a series of paired images of small diverse groups. One group in each pair was clustered and one group was dispersed (see Figure 9.1). Participants were asked to indicate their preference for one of the two groups. Each of the groups contained members of two ethnicities (consisting of Whites and Blacks, Blacks and Asians, or Asians and Whites), and each group was unbalanced such that there were four members of one ethnicity and two members of another. Thus, we were able to test the influence of within-group status on preferences for arrangements because each participant's own ethnicity was pictured as either the group majority or the minority, or was not pictured at all.

Because we expected that preferences for group arrangements would depend on the extent to which group outcomes are tied to personal outcomes, we manipulated the type of settings associated with the groups. To represent a context where personal outcomes are not tied to group outcomes, some participants were given instructions that did not specify that they should think of themselves as group members. The remaining participants were instructed to think of themselves as group members. Of these participants, some were instructed to think of the groups as social groups and others to think of the groups as working groups. Social ties are important in social groups; however, one can freely leave a social group, and one's future outcomes are not directly dependent on the success of a social group as they are in work groups. Therefore, we reasoned that work-group settings would have the highest association between personal outcomes and group outcomes, and would therefore be the most personally important to participants.

Figure 9.1 Participant view of clustered and dispersed groups in Experiment 1. The group on the left is physically clustered and the group on the right is physically dispersed.

Participants were 69 undergraduates (18 male, 51 female; 13 Asian, 13 Black, 43 White) from the University of Maryland, who took part in exchange for course credit. They all completed the study independently on a computer, and all were told that they would view a series of pairs of groups and that their task was to indicate which group they preferred. Participants in the *non-member condition* were simply instructed to indicate the groups they preferred and not specifically told to think of themselves as group members. Participants in the *social group condition* were instructed to think of the groups as representing people with whom they would spend free time (e.g., watch movies, eat dinner) and to select the group with whom they would prefer to become close friends. Participants in the *working group condition* were instructed to think of the group as representing people with whom they would work on an important school project that would make up a large portion of their grade in a course.

After reading the instructions, participants were asked to indicate which of the two groups they preferred by typing the "A" key for the group on the left of the screen or the "L" key for the group on the right of the screen. Participants then viewed the series of paired groups in a random order. Each pair appeared on the screen until the participant indicated which group they preferred.

On each trial, participants saw two groups composed of the same set of six faces (see Figure 9.1). Each group was presented in an oval shape with an equal distance between each face, and the images appeared in color. On each trial the faces from both groups were either all male or all female.

On one side of the screen, the group was clustered by ethnicity such that the two minority faces appeared next to each other in the group. On the other side of the screen, the group was dispersed by ethnicity, such that the two minority members were placed on opposite sides of the group, with two majority members between them on either side. Each male and female pair of groups was presented four times, such that the clustered arrangement appeared on the right two times and on the left two times. This led to a total of 12 pairs for each gender, for a total of 48 paired groups.[1]

We calculated the average preferences for each type of ethnic majority/minority group combination from the four presentations of each pair. To avoid potential confounds with gender, we analyzed only the trials in which the group members were the same gender as the participant. We then collapsed across the particular outgroups presented with each participant's ethnicity (White, Black, or Asian) such that the dependent variable became the preference for

---

1 Because it would not be possible to present the faces visually without either a clustered or a dispersed arrangement, half of the faces were presented in a clustered manner and half were presented in a dispersed manner. To reduce the salience of these arrangements, the faces were presented in random (not circular) patterns with as much distance between faces as was feasible given the size of the page. To control for order effects, we manipulated the order in which participants viewed the clustered and dispersed faces. We included these variables in our analyses, but they did not qualify the results that we report.

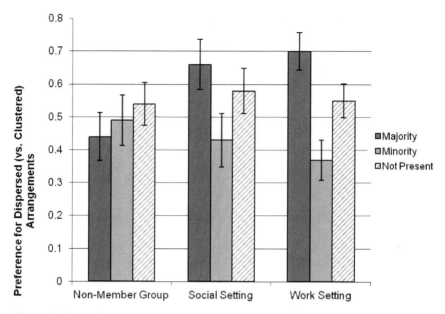

Figure 9.2 Within-Group Status × Group Setting Interaction. Significant preferences for clustering (vs. dispersion) were found for group minorities in both the workgroup and the social-group conditions.

arrangements of groups in which the participant's own ethnicity had majority status or minority status, or was not present at all. The dependent measure was the proportion of group choices for the dispersed (vs. clustered) arrangement. We calculated averages across all trials such that a higher number would indicate a general preference for dispersion and a lower number would indicate a general preference for clustering.

We analyzed the arrangement choice variable using a 3 (Within-Group Status: Majority, Minority, Not Present) × 3 (Group Setting: Non-Member Group, Social Group, Work Group) × 3 (Participant Ethnicity: Asian, Black, White) repeated-measures ANOVA with Participant Ethnicity as a between-subjects variable. Because participant gender did not produce any meaningful interactions or main effects, this factor was removed from subsequent analyses.

We found the predicted main effect for within-group status, $F(2,120) = 5.17$, $p < .01$, such that participants were more likely to prefer clustered group arrangements when their ingroup was pictured in the minority ($M = 0.43$, $SD = .80$) compared to when their ingroup was pictured in the majority ($M = 0.60$, $SD = .26$) and when their ingroup was not pictured at all ($M = 0.56$, $SD = .24$). Follow-up comparisons among the three cell means showed that preferences for clustering were significantly stronger when participants' own ethnicities were pictured in the minority in comparison to when they were in the majority, $F(1,120) = 9.49$, $p.01$, and when their ethnicity was not pictured at all, $F(1,120) = 5.37$ $p < .05$.

The main effect of within-group status was also qualified by a within-group status × group setting interaction, F (4,120) = 2.324, p = .06. As shown in Figure 9.2, in both the working group and the social group conditions, participants were more likely to prefer clustered arrangements when their ethnicity was in the minority ($M_{WorkGroup}$ = .37, SD = .33; $M_{SocialGroup}$ = .43, SD = .27) compared to the majority ($M_{WorkGroup}$ = .70, SD = .25; $M_{SocialGroup}$ = .66, SD = .27), $F_{WorkGroup}$ (1,120) = 17.41, p <.0001 and $F_{SocialGroup}$ (1,120) = 4.75, p <.05. Consistent with our expectations, in the non-member condition there was no significant difference in clustering preferences between within-group majority (M = .44) and minority (M = .49) status, F < 1, p = .37.

These findings confirm our expectation that within-group, but not societal, majority/minority status would influence preferences. Asian, Black, and White participants showed the same patterns of preferences. Neither the Participant Ethnicity × Within-Group Status × Group Setting interaction nor any other main effects or interactions with participant ethnicity were significant. Thus, it appears that, in personally relevant small groups, the small group may be the more salient superordinate group such that the status of one's ethnicity within the group determines one's preferred cognitive representation.

Experiment 2

Experiment 1 provided general support for our hypothesis. Participants who imagined being part of a group showed the preferences that we predicted, whereas participants who did not think of themselves as group members did not. However, because Experiment 1 used a forced-choice paradigm, the participants may have become aware of our interest in the structure of diverse groups. Although it is unlikely that participants guessed our specific hypotheses, Experiment 2 was conducted as a conceptual replication of Experiment 1 and used a less direct measure of group preferences. Furthermore, Experiment 2 used a more direct manipulation of the personal importance variable.

In Experiment 2, all participants were instructed to think of the groups as working groups. We manipulated the personal importance of the groups by telling participants that they should think of themselves as members of some groups and as non-members of others. We measured preferences for clustering and dispersion by presenting participants with six diverse faces and instructing them to create their own preferred group arrangements. We again expected that participants would be more likely to create clustered arrangements when their own ethnicities were pictured as the group minority and to create dispersed arrangements when their own ethnicities were pictured as the group majority, but that this pattern would be stronger when participants were instructed to think of themselves as group members.

Sixty-nine undergraduate students (30 male, 39 female; 14 African American, 55 White) from the University of Maryland completed this study in exchange for course credit.

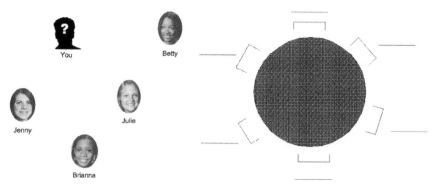

Figure 9.3   Participant view of diverse group of faces in Experiment 2. The blank face with a question mark represents the participant as a member of the group.

They all took part in the paper-and-pencil survey in groups ranging from one to five members, completing first a packet with the images of groups and then a demographics questionnaire. Each packet contained an introduction page instructing participants to think of each group of faces as a working group and to assign each person in the group a seat around a table. To manipulate the personal importance of the groups, they were further instructed that in some groups they would see a blank face with a question mark labeled "You," and that they should think of themselves as members of these groups. Each subsequent page of the survey contained six named faces on the left side of the page and the outline of a table with six blank lines on the right side of the page (see Figure 9.3) where participants could write the names of each group member around the table. For groups that included blank faces with question marks, participants were instructed to write "Me" where they wished to sit.

Participants viewed images only of groups that were of their own gender and that included their own ethnicity. In half of the groups, the participant's ethnicity was the within-group majority, and in the other half the participant's ethnicity was the within-group minority. For White participants the groups contained either White and Black faces or White and Asian faces. For Black participants, the groups contained either Black and White faces or Black and Asian faces.

Each type of diverse group was presented once as a group of low personal importance and once as a group of high personal importance. In the former there were simply two within-group minority and four within-group majority faces. In the latter, where the participant's ethnicity was the majority, there was one blank face to represent the participant, three faces of the participant's ethnicity, and two outgroup faces. All faces were presented with as much distance between them as the page would allow so as not to suggest a particular pattern of faces. However, as a control, we manipulated the arrangement of the faces that were to be arranged such that they were presented in either a clustered or a dispersed arrangement. Therefore, each participant viewed 16 groups and created 16 arrangements.

We coded the types of arrangements participants created based on the number of majority members placed between minority members. Groups in which the minority members were placed next to each other would be maximally clustered and were coded a "0." Groups in which one majority member was placed between minority members were coded a "1." Groups in which two majority members separated the minority members were maximally dispersed and were coded a "2." Thus, a higher number indicates a greater preference for dispersion. Because the specific outgroups paired with each participant's ingroup varied for the two participant ethnicities, we collapsed across the groups and computed average scores for groups where participants' ethnicities comprised the majority and the minority.

To test our hypothesis, we conducted a 2 (Participant Ethnicity: White, Black) × 2 (Within-Group Status: Majority, Minority) × 2 (Personal Importance: High, Low) repeated-measures ANOVA with Participant Ethnicity as a between-subjects factor. Because participant gender did not produce any meaningful interactions or main effects, this factor was removed from subsequent analyses.

There was a significant main effect for Within-Group Status, $F(1,65) = 22.92$, $p < .001$, such that participants were more likely to create clustered arrangements when their own ethnicity was pictured in the minority ($M = .70$, $SD = .65$) vs. the majority ($M = 1.04$, $SD = .67$).

As expected, this main effect was qualified by a significant Within-Group Status × Personal Importance interaction, $F(1,65) = 5.92$, $p < .05$ (see Figure 9.4). When participants imagined themselves as group members, they were more likely to create dispersed arrangements when their ethnicity represented the majority ($M = 1.12$, $SD = .70$) compared to when their ethnicity represented the minority ($M = .59$, $SD = .65$), $F(1,65) = 27.09$, $p < .001$. When participants were not pictured as group members, participants were also more likely to create dispersed arrangements when their ethnicity represented the majority ($M = .97$, $SD = .64$) compared to when their ethnicity represented the minority ($M = .81$, $SD = .64$), but this difference was not significant, $F(1,65) = 2.43$, $p = .12$. Again, there were no other meaningful main effects or interactions.[2]

In sum, Experiment 2 provided a conceptual replication of our hypothesis using a different dependent variable and a more direct manipulation of personal relevance. We again found that preferences for clustering by minorities and dispersion by majorities were more pronounced in groups that were higher in personal importance. Furthermore, because participants in Experiment 2 indirectly indicated their preferences for clustered and dispersed groups by creating

---

2 We found a significant Within-Group Status × Participant Ethnicity interaction, $F(1,65) = 7.92$, $p < .01$, such that Black participants demonstrated a stronger preference for dispersion in the majority compared to White participants. However, both Black and White participants demonstrated the same expected pattern of preferring clustering in the minority and dispersion in the majority.

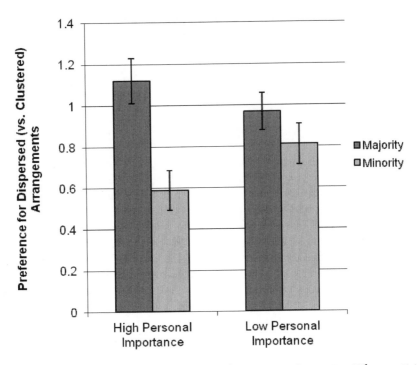

Figure 9.4   Within-Group Status × Personal Importance Interaction. When participants were instructed to think of themselves as members (vs. non-members) of the
groups, they were more likely to create clustered groups when their ingroup was pictured in the minority and to create dispersed groups when their ingroup was pictured in
the majority.

their own group arrangements rather than by making a forced choice, their
decisions represent more closely those that might be made in an actual diverse
group setting. With this method of measuring arrangement preferences, it is
also highly unlikely that participants guessed our hypotheses or even realized
that we were examining clustered vs. dispersed group arrangements.

CONCLUSIONS AND FUTURE DIRECTIONS

Our experiments support our hypothesis that within-group majorities and
minorities have distinct preferences regarding the physical structure of diverse
groups. We argued and found that, in groups of high personal importance,
these preferences are driven by the relative status of one's ethnicity within the
group rather than the status of one's ethnicity within society.

   In line with research examining ethnic majorities' and minorities' preferences for different cognitive representations within society, we reasoned that
small-group minorities should be motivated to gain influence and fairness and
should therefore prefer clustered arrangements that maintain salient subgroup

categories within the superordinate work group. Furthermore, we reasoned that within-group majorities should be concerned more with maintaining dominance in groups, and should therefore prefer dispersed arrangements that reduce the saliency of subgroup categories. Because we reasoned that these preferences would come directly from motivations related to the specific group setting, we expected this pattern of preferences only in group settings that signaled more importance to individual participants. Indeed, in both experiments we found that group majorities preferred dispersed arrangements whereas group minorities preferred clustered arrangements when groups were high in personal importance. When groups were low in personal importance, these preferences were not as pronounced.

This research has several important implications. For one, because both experiments used within-subjects designs, we found that the same participants preferred clustering in some cases and dispersion in other cases. The benefit of using a within-subjects design here demonstrates the flexibility of individuals' cognitive representations. Based on this preliminary evidence, it appears that both ethnic majorities and minorities choose whichever cognitive representation is most beneficial to them in any given context. This finding supports Dovidio et al.'s (2009) argument that the different cognitive representations provide specific functionality to ethnic majorities and minorities.

The present research also demonstrates the potential utility of applying to small work groups social psychological research that has generally been conducted in the interest of improving broader intergroup relations. As the demographics of the United States continue to shift, it is increasingly important to understand the impact of diversity at both the broader societal level and the small-group level. Because most intergroup interactions occur in small-group settings, it is critical that we understand how majority and minority motivations play out in these contexts. Considering the large proportion of time individuals spend at work, and the importance of work-related outcomes, it is especially important to understand how psychological processes related to diversity influence work-group functioning.

This research sheds light on the distinct preferences of majority and minority members of ethnically diverse small groups and the ease with which one could potentially create a work-group environment that is desirable to group members (i.e., through the physical arrangement of members). Dovidio et al. (2009) caution against reaching broad conclusions as to the relative superiority of one cognitive representation over another. However, in a practical sense, it may be wiser to focus on the needs of within-group minorities, because one can only expect to benefit from the diversity in a group if within-group minorities are active group members (e.g., De Dreu & West, 2001). Given that a dual identity is generally preferable to group minorities, organizations could focus efforts on creating environments that allow for these. For instance, organizations could promote group structures that facilitate (but do not mandate) closeness between minorities—perhaps through mentoring programs or by allowing newcomers to choose the location of their workspaces.

We believe that this research offers multiple avenues for future study, which might test these observed patterns in more realistic settings and examine the extent to which cognitive representations influence small-group dynamics and productivity. For instance, researchers should examine the effect of cognitive representations on information sharing. One might predict that within-group minorities would be more inclined to share information in group settings if they felt more secure in their subgroup identities. This research should also extend beyond ethnic diversity to examine other social category diversity, such as gender or age. If the same basic majority and minority preferences appear across various types of social categories within groups, then the research has immense potential to improve the overall functioning of small diverse work groups.

REFERENCES

Bacharach, S., Bamberger, P., & Vashdi, D. (2005). Diversity and homophily at work: Supportive relations among White and African-American peers. *Academy of Management Journal*, 48, 619–644.

Bantel, K. A., & Jackson, S. E. (1989). Top management and innovations in banking: Does the composition of the top team make a difference? *Strategy Management Journal*, 10, 107–124.

Bodenhausen, G. V. (2010). Diversity in the person, diversity in the group: Challenges of identity complexity for social perception and social interaction. *European Journal of Social Psychology*, 40, 1–16.

Bowers, C. A., Pharmer, J. A., & Salas, E. (2000). When member homogeneity is needed in work teams: A meta-analysis. *Small Group Research*, 31, 305–327.

Brewer, M. B. (1991). The social self: On being the same and different at the same time. *Personality and Social Psychology Bulletin*, 17, 475–482.

Brewer, M. B., & Miller, N. (1984). Beyond the contact hypothesis: Theoretical perspectives on desegregation. In N. Miller & M. B. Brewer (Eds.), *Groups in contact: The psychology of desegregation* (pp. 281–302). Orlando, FL: Academic Press.

Byrne, D. (1971). *The attraction paradigm*. New York: Academic Press.

Carley, K. (1991). A theory of group stability. *American Sociological Review*, 56, 331–354.

Chatman, J. A., Polzer, J. T., Barsade, S. G., & Neale, M. A. (1998). Being different yet feeling similar: The influence of demographic composition and organizational culture on work processes and outcomes. *Administrative Science Quarterly*, 43, 749–780.

Chatman, J. A., & Spataro, S. E. (2005). Using self-categorization theory to understand relational demography-based variations in people's responsiveness to organizational culture. *Academy of Management Journal*, 48, 321–331. doi:10.5465/AMJ. 2005.16928415

Correll, J., Park, B., & Smith, J. (2008). Colorblind and multicultural prejudice reduction strategies in high-conflict situations. *Group Processes & Intergroup Relations*, 11, 471–491. doi:10.1177/1368430208095401

Crisp, R. J., & Hewstone, M. (1999). Differential evaluation of crossed category groups: Patterns, processes, and reducing intergroup bias. *Group Processes & Intergroup Relations*, 2, 307–333. doi:10.1177/1368430299024001

Cunningham, G. B. (2005). The importance of a common in-group identity in ethnically diverse groups. *Group Dynamics: Theory, Research, and Practice, 9,* 251–260. doi:10.1037/1089-2699.9.4.251

Cunningham, G. B., & Sagas, M. (2004). Group diversity, occupational commitment, and occupational turnover intentions among NCAA Division IA football coaching staffs. *Journal of Sport Management, 18,* 236–254.

Davies, P., Spencer, S., & Steele, C. (2005). Clearing the air: Identity safety moderates the effects of stereotype threat on women's leadership aspirations. *Journal of Personality and Social Psychology, 88,* 276–287.

De Dreu, C., & West, M. (2001). Minority dissent and team innovation: The importance of participation in decision making. *Journal of Applied Psychology, 86,* 1191–1201.

Dixon, J. A., Tropp, L. R., Durrheim, K., & Tredoux, C. (2010). "Let them eat harmony": Prejudice-reduction strategies and attitudes of historically disadvantaged groups. *Current Directions in Psychological Science, 19,* 76–80.

Dovidio, J. F., Gaertner, S. L., & Kafati, G. (2000). Group identity and intergroup relations: The Common In-Group Identity model. In S. R. Thye, E. J. Lawler, M. W. Macy, & H. A. Walker (Eds.), *Advances in group processes* (Vol. 17, pp. 1–34). Stamford, CT: JAI Press.

Dovidio, J. F., Gaertner, S. L., & Saguy, T. (2007). Another view of "we": Majority and minority group perspectives on a common ingroup identity. *European Review of Social Psychology, 18,* 296–330. doi:10.1080/10463280701726132

Dovidio, J. F., Gaertner, S. L., & Saguy, T. (2009). Commonality and the complexity of "we": Social attitudes and social change. *Personality and Social Psychology Review, 13,* 3–20.

Dovidio, J. F., ten Vergert, M., Stewart, T. L., Gaertner, S. L., Johnson, J. D., Esses, V. M., et al. (2004). Perspective and prejudice: Antecedents and mediating mechanisms. *Personality and Social Psychology Bulletin, 30,* 1537–1549.

Eisenhardt, K. M., & Bourgeois, L. J. (1988). Politics of strategic decision making in high-velocity environments: Toward a midrange theory. *Academy of Management Journal, 31,* 737–770.

Ely, R. J., & Thomas, D. A. (2001). Cultural diversity at work: The effects of diversity perspectives on work group processes and outcomes. *Administrative Science Quarterly, 46,* 229–273.

Fujita, K., Henderson, M., Eng, J., Trope, Y., & Liberman, N. (2006). Spatial distance and mental construal of social events. *Psychological Science, 17,* 278–282.

Gaertner, S., & Dovidio, J. (2000). *Reducing intergroup bias: The Common Ingroup Identity model.* New York: Psychology Press.

Gaertner, S. L., Dovidio, J. F., Anastasio, P. A., Bachman, B. A., & Rust, M. C. (1993). The common ingroup identity model: Recategorisation and the reduction of intergroup bias. In W. Stroebe & M. Hewstone (Eds.), *European review of social psychology* (Vol. 4. pp. 1–26). New York: John Wiley & Sons.

Gaertner, S. L., Mann, J., Murrell, A., & Dovidio, J. F. (1989). Reducing intergroup bias: The benefits of recategorization. *Journal of Personality and Social Psychology, 57,* 239–249. doi:10.1037/0022-3514.57.2.239

Gaertner, S. L., Rust, M. C., Dovidio, J. F., Bachman, B. A., & Anastasio, P. A. (1996). The contact hypothesis: The role of a common ingroup identity on reducing intergroup bias among majority and minority group members. In J. L. Nye & A. M. Brower (Eds.), *What's social about social cognition?* (pp. 230–260). Newbury Park, CA: Sage.

Gibson, C., & Vermeulen, F. (2003). A healthy divide: Subgroups as a stimulus for team learning behavior. *Administrative Science Quarterly, 48,* 202–239.

Glasford, D. E., & Dovidio, J. F. (2011). E pluribus unum: Dual identity and minority group members' motivation to engage in contact, as well as social change. *Journal of Experimental Social Psychology, 47,* 1021–1024. doi:10.1016/j.jesp.2011.03.021

Gómez, Á., Dovidio, J. F., Huici, C., Gaertner, S. L., & Cuadrado, I. (2008). The other side of we: When outgroup members express common identity. *Personality and Social Psychology Bulletin, 34,* 1613–1626. doi:10.1177/0146167208323600

González, R., & Brown, R. (2003). Generalization of positive attitude as a function of subgroup and superordinate group identification in inter-group contact. *European Journal of Social Psychology, 33,* 195–214.

González, R., & Brown, R. (2006). Dual identities in intergroup contact: Group status and size moderate the generalization of positive attitude change. *Journal of Experimental Social Psychology, 42,* 753–767. doi:10.1016/j.jesp.2005.11.008

Hambrick, D. C., Cho, T. S., & Chen, M.-J. (1996). The influence of top management team heterogeneity on firms' competitive moves. *Administrative Science Quarterly, 41,* 659–684.

Holoien, D., & Shelton, J. (2012). You deplete me: The cognitive costs of colorblindness on ethnic minorities. *Journal of Experimental Social Psychology, 48,* 562–565. doi:10.1016/j.jesp.2011.09.010

Homan, A. C., Hollenbeck, J. R., Humphrey, S. E., Van Knippenberg, D., Ilgen, D. R., & Van Kleef, G. A. (2008). Facing differences with an open mind: Openness to experience, salience of intragroup differences, and performance of diverse work groups. *Academy of Management Journal, 51,* 1204–1222. doi:10.5465/AMJ.2008.35732995

Houlette, M., Gaertner, S. L., Johnson, K. M., Banker, B. S., Riek, B. M., & Dovidio, J. F. (2004). Developing a more inclusive social identity: An elementary school intervention. *Journal of Social Issues, 60,* 35–56.

Ibarra, H. (1992). Homophily and differential returns: Sex differences in network structure and access in an advertising firm. *Administrative Science Quarterly, 37,* 422–447.

Jackson, S. E., Joshi, A., & Erhardt, N. L. (2003). Recent research on team and organizational diversity: SWOT analysis and implications. *Journal of Management, 29,* 801–830.

Jehn, K. A., Northcraft, G. B., & Neale, M. A. (1999). Why differences make a difference: A field study of diversity, conflict, and performance in workgroups. *Administrative Science Quarterly, 44,* 741–763.

Joshi, A., & Roh, H. (2009). The role of context in work team diversity research: A meta-analytic review. *Academy of Management Journal, 52,* 599–628.

Kanter, R. M. (1977). Some effects of proportions on group life: Skewed sex ratios and responses to token women. *American Journal of Sociology, 82,* 965–990.

Kooij-de Bode, H. J. M., van Knippenberg, D., & van Ginkel, W. P. (2010). Good effects of bad feelings: Negative affectivity and group decision making. *British Journal of Management, 21,* 375–392.

Latané, B., & Bourgeois, M. J. (1996). Experimental evidence for dynamic social impact: The emergence of subcultures in electronic groups. *Journal of Communication, 46,* 35–47.

Latané, B., & L'Herrou, T. (1996). Spatial clustering in the conformity game: Dynamic social impact in electronic groups. *Journal of Personality & Social Psychology, 70,* 1218–1230.

Leung, K. Y., Maddux, W. W., Galinsky, A. D., & Chiu, C. Y. (2008). Multicultural experience enhances creativity: The when and how. *American Psychologist, 63,* 169–181.

Levine, J. M., Resnick, L. B., & Higgins, E. T. (1993). Social foundations of cognition. *Annual Review of Psychology, 44*, 585–612.

Lord, C., & Saenz, D. (1985). Memory deficits and memory surfeits: Differential cognitive consequences of tokenism for tokens and observers. *Journal of Personality and Social Psychology, 49*, 918–926.

Migdal, M. J., Hewstone, M., & Mullen, B. (1998). The effects of crossed categorization on intergroup evaluations: A meta-analysis. *British Journal of Social Psychology, 37*, 303–324. doi:10.1111/j.2044-8309.1998.tb01174.x

Milliken, F. J., & Martins, L. L. (1996). Searching for common threads: Understanding the multiple effects of diversity in organizational groups. *Academy of Management Review, 21*, 402–403.

Mollica, K. A., Gray, B., & Trevino, L. K. (2003). Racial homophily and its persistence in newcomers' social networks. *Organization Science, 14*, 123–136.

Moscovici, S., Lage, E., & Naffrechoux, M. (1969). Influence of a consistent minority on the responses of a majority in a color perception task. *Sociometry, 32*, 365–380.

Nemeth, C. J. (1986). Differential contributions of majority and minority influence. *Psychological Review, 93*, 23–32.

Nier, J. A., Gaertner, S. L., Dovidio, J. F., Banker, B. S., Ward, C. M., & Rust, M. C. (2001). Changing interracial evaluations and behavior: The effects of a common group identity. *Group Processes & Intergroup Relations, 4*, 299–316.

O'Reilly, C. A., III, Williams, K. Y., & Barsade, S. (1998). Group demography and innovation: Does diversity help? In D. H. Gruenfeld (Ed.), *Research on managing groups and teams* (Vol. 1, pp. 183–208). Stamford, CT: JAI Press.

Pelled, L. H., Eisenhardt, K. M., & Xin, K. R. (1999). Exploring the black box: An analysis of work group diversity, conflict, and performance. *Administrative Science Quarterly, 44*, 1–28.

Pettigrew, T. F., & Tropp, L. R. (2000). Does intergroup contact reduce prejudice? Recent meta-analytic findings. In S. Oskamp (Ed.), *Reducing prejudice and discrimination* (pp. 93–114). Mahwah, NJ: Lawrence Erlbaum Associates.

Phillips, K., Liljenquist, K., & Neale, M. (2009). Is the pain worth the gain? The advantages and liabilities of agreeing with socially distinct newcomers. *Personality and Social Psychology Bulletin, 35*, 336–350.

Pollak, K., & Niemann, Y. (1998). Black and White tokens in academia: A difference of chronic versus acute distinctiveness. *Journal of Applied Social Psychology, 28*, 954–972.

Riek, B. M., Mania, E. W., Gaertner, S. L., McDonald, S. A., & Lamoreaux, M. J. (2010). Does a common ingroup identity reduce intergroup threat? *Group Processes & Intergroup Relations, 13*, 403–423. doi:10.1177/1368430209346701

Roberge, M., & van Dick, R. (2010). Recognizing the benefits of diversity: When and how does diversity increase group performance? *Human Resource Management Review, 20*, 295–308. doi:10.1016/j.hrmr.2009.09.002

Saguy, T., Dovidio, J. F., & Pratto, F. (2008). Beyond contact: Intergroup contact in the context of power relations. *Personality and Social Psychology Bulletin, 43*, 432–445.

Saguy, T., Tausch, N., Dovidio, J. F., & Pratto, F. (2009). The irony of harmony: Intergroup contact can produce false expectations for equality. *Psychological Science, 20*, 114–121.

Schruijer, S., & Mostert, I. (1997). Creativity and sex composition: An experimental illustration. *European Journal of Work and Organizational Psychology, 6*, 175–182.

Sekaquaptewa, D., Waldman, A., & Thompson, M. (2007). Solo status and self-construal: Being distinctive influences racial self-construal and performance apprehension in African American women. *Cultural Diversity and Ethnic Minority Psychology, 13,* 321–327.

Shelton, J., Richeson, J., Salvatore, J., & Trawalter, S. (2005). Ironic effects of racial bias during interracial interactions. *Psychological Science, 16,* 397–402.

Sommers, S. R. (2006). On racial diversity and group decision making: Identifying multiple effects of racial composition on jury deliberations. *Journal of Personality and Social Psychology, 90,* 597–612.

Stangor, C., Carr, C., & Kiang, L. (1998). Activating stereotypes undermines task performance expectations. *Journal of Personality and Social Psychology, 75,* 1191–1197.

Stasser, G., Stewart, D. D., & Wittenbaum, G. M. (1995). Expert roles and information exchange during discussion: The importance of knowing who knows what. *Journal of Experimental Social Psychology, 31,* 244–265. doi:10.1006/jesp.1995.1012

Triandis, H. C. (1959). Cognitive similarity and interpersonal communication in industry. *Journal of Applied Psychology, 43,* 321–326.

Tsui, A. S., Egan, T. D., & O'Reilly, C. A. (1992). Being different: Relational demography and organizational attachment. *Administrative Science Quarterly, 37,* 549–579.

van Knippenberg, D., De Dreu, C. K. W., & Homan, A. C. (2004). Work group diversity and group performance: An integrative model and research agenda. *Journal of Applied Psychology, 89,* 1008–1022.

van Knippenberg, D., Haslam, S., & Platow, M. J. (2007). Unity through diversity: Value-in-diversity beliefs, work group diversity, and group identification. *Group Dynamics: Theory, Research, and Practice, 11,* 207–222. doi:10.1037/1089-2699.11.3.207

van Oudenhoven, J., Prins, K. S., & Buunk, B. P. (1998). Attitudes of minority and majority members towards adaptation of immigrants. *European Journal of Social Psychology, 28,* 995–1013. doi:10.1002/(SICI)1099-0992(1998110)28:6 < 995::AID-EJSP908 > 3.0.CO;2-8

Verkuyten, M. (2005). Ethnic group identification and group evaluation among minority and majority groups: Testing the multiculturalism hypothesis. *Journal of Personality and Social Psychology, 88,* 121–138.

Verkuyten, M. (2006). Multicultural recognition and ethnic minority rights: A social identity perspective. *European Review of Social Psychology, 17,* 148–184. doi:10.1080/10463280600937418

Watson, W. E., Kumar, K., & Michaelsen, L. K. (1993). Cultural diversity's impact on interaction process and performance: Comparing homogeneous and diverse task groups. *Academy of Management Journal, 36,* 590–602.

West, T. V., Pearson, A. R., Dovidio, J. F., Shelton, J., & Trail, T. E. (2009). Superordinate identity and intergroup roommate friendship development. *Journal of Experimental Social Psychology, 45,* 1266–1272. doi:10.1016/j.jesp.2009.08.002

Wolsko, C., Park, B., & Judd, C. M. (2006). Considering the Tower of Babel: Correlates of assimilation and multiculturalism among ethnic minority and majority groups in the United States. *Social Justice Research, 19,* 277–306. doi:10.1007/s11211-006-0014-8

Wood, W., Lundgren, S., Ouellette, J., Busceme, S., & Blackstone, T. (1994). Minority influence: A meta-analytic review of social influence processes. *Psychological Bulletin, 115,* 323–345.

Yoder, J., & Aniakudo, P. (1997). "Outsider within" the firehouse: Subordination and difference in the social interactions of African American women firefighters. *Gender & Society, 11*, 324–341.

Zenger, T. R., & Lawrence, B. S. (1989). Organizational demography: The differential effects of age and tenure distributions on technical communication. *Academy of Management Journal, 32*, 353–376.

10

Group Identification and Prejudice Distribution
Implications for Diversity

CHERYL R. KAISER

University of Washington

KERRY E. SPALDING

University of Washington

> Diversity on the bench is critical. As practitioners, you need judges who "get it!" We need judges who understand what discrimination feels like. We need judges who understand what inequality feels like. We need judges who understand the subtleties of unfair treatment and who are willing to call it out when they see it!
>
> Debbie Wasserman-Schultz

When Debbie Wasserman-Schultz, a member of the U.S. House of Representatives, delivered this call for greater judicial diversity, she was guided by the assumption that members of groups that are devalued in society share two commonalities—namely, consensually acknowledging the prevalence of discrimination and behaving in ways that eliminate this injustice. At first glance, Wasserman-Schultz's assumptions seem reasonable and are in fact shared by many people in society, scientists and lay people alike. In this chapter, we draw upon contemporary research on discrimination to explore these assumptions about members of devalued groups. We will argue that these assumptions are both part right and part wrong. Specifically, we explore why some members of devalued groups perceive widespread prejudice and advocate on behalf of their own group and why others do not. We further explore the implications of these assumptions for efforts to increase diversity and eliminate injustice.

Investigating the two assumptions underlying Wasserman-Schultz's statement requires an understanding of the concept of group identification. Group identification, the importance of one's group to one's self-concept (Luhtanen & Crocker, 1992; McCoy & Major, 2003; Turner, Hogg, Oakes, Reicher, & Wetherell, 1987), has long been of interest to scholars studying the experiences of members of devalued social groups. It has been investigated in many roles, including as a lens for detecting discrimination (Major, Quinton, & Schmader, 2003; Operario & Fiske, 2001; Sellers & Shelton, 2003), as a source of vulnerability and resilience when faced with discrimination (Branscombe, Schmitt, & Harvey, 1999; McCoy & Major, 2003; Quinn & Chaudoir, 2009), and as a precursor to collective action aimed at remedying discrimination (Klandermans, 2002; Van Zomeren, Postmes, & Spears, 2008). Across all these contexts, group identification has been conceptualized as something that exclusively shapes the internal workings of one's mind; that is, group identification is an intrapersonal phenomenon that acts like a psychological compass guiding the individual through the social world.

More recently, scholars have begun to recognize that the level of group identification of devalued group members also shapes the minds of other people with whom those group members interact. That is, group identification is interpersonal, in that other individuals react differently to members of devalued groups who vary in their level of group identification. In this chapter we describe emerging research on the interpersonal nature of group identification and then explore the implications of this perspective for understanding why members of disadvantaged groups vary in their perceptions of discrimination and their propensity to engage in behaviors that eliminate injustice and increase diversity.

GROUP IDENTIFICATION AND PERCEIVED DISCRIMINATION

The assumption that members of devalued groups consensually perceive discrimination is at odds with empirical research showing that there is great variability with respect to such perceptions. In explaining this variability, scholars have frequently turned toward examining the role of group identification. This research reveals that members of socially devalued groups who are strongly identified with their group report experiencing more prejudice and discrimination than their weakly identified counterparts (see Major, Quinton, & McCoy, 2002; Schmitt & Branscombe, 2002, for reviews). This positive relationship between group identification and prejudice perceptions has been observed among a wide variety of devalued groups, including ethnic minorities, women, lesbians, and the elderly (see Major, Quinton, & McCoy, 2002, for a review). To explain this relationship between group identification and prejudice, scholars have adopted two primary theoretical perspectives.

One explanation, offered by Gordon Allport more than 50 years ago, reasoned that simply being devalued would cause members of these groups to band together to cope with prejudice, resulting in enhanced identification with the group. Allport (1954, p. 148) asserted that "misery finds balm through the closer association of people who are miserable for the same reason. Threats drive them to seek protective unity within their common membership." More recently, Branscombe et al. (1999) developed and tested this rationale in their Rejection-Identification Model, which has shown, for example, that group identification increases when people are exposed to information arguing that their group experiences prejudice relative to when they are exposed to information conveying that their group experiences positive treatment (Jetten, Branscombe, Schmitt, & Spears, 2001; see also Leach, Mosquera, Vliek, & Hirt, 2010).

The other explanation for the relationship between group identification and perceiving prejudice is grounded in social cognitive models of construct activation (Higgins, King, & Mavin, 1982) and argues that people who experience more chronic activation of their group identification are more apt to interpret ambiguous events through the lens of their group membership relative to people who do not experience such chronic activation (Major et al., 2003; Operario & Fiske, 2001; Sellers & Shelton, 2003; Shelton & Sellers, 2000). For example, after experiencing an ambiguous negative interaction with Whites, strongly identified ethnic minorities were more likely to label that experience as prejudice compared to their less identified counterparts (Operario & Fiske, 2001).

PREJUDICE DISTRIBUTION PERSPECTIVE

Both of these prevailing explanations for the relationship between group identification and prejudice fall under the broad rubric of internal psychological processes, arguing that prejudice perceptions result from the inner workings of one's mind. Although these explanations account for important parts of the relationship between group identification and perceived prejudice, they leave unexamined the possibility that strongly identified members of devalued groups actually experience more bias than the weakly identified. This may be the case because other people objectively express more prejudice and discrimination toward the former group. We and others have begun devoting theoretical and empirical attention to addressing this interpersonal explanation for the relationship between group identification and perceived prejudice.

Recently, we introduced a theoretical account, which we refer to as the *prejudice distribution perspective*, which places the relationship between group identification and perceived prejudice squarely within the realm of interpersonal processes (see Kaiser & Pratt-Hyatt, 2009; Kaiser & Wilkins, 2010, for reviews of this perspective). The prejudice distribution perspective asserts that the relationship between group identification and prejudice occurs, in part, because majority group members direct more prejudice toward strongly identified members than weakly identified members of devalued groups.

In the first set of experiments to test this hypothesis (Kaiser & Pratt-Hyatt, 2009), White participants evaluated members of ethnic minority groups (i.e., Black Americans and Latino Americans) who varied in their level of group identification. Group identification was manipulated in numerous ways across studies, including showing participants the ethnic minority target's varying score on a measure of group identification (specifically, the centrality subscale of Luhtanen & Crocker's (1992) Collective Self-Esteem Scale) or by communicating that the target belonged to either an ethnic minority-serving social organization or a general student organization. Across these six experiments, White participants evaluated strongly identified minorities more negatively than moderately or weakly identified minorities (See Figure 10.1 for data from Experiment 2 in this series). Thus, these data provide initial evidence that some of the relationship between group identification and perceived prejudice stems from processes occurring entirely outside of the minds of members of devalued groups. These studies suggest that strongly and weakly identified minorities live in social environments that differ in the presence of prejudice and discrimination.

Other recent findings in the literature are also consistent with the prejudice distribution perspective. For example, in one experiment (Dovidio, Gaertner, Shnabel, Saguy, & Johnson, 2010), White university students expressed more positive attitudes and empathy, and were more helpful toward a Black American who defined himself with a superordinate identity shared with Whites (fellow student at their university), compared to when he defined himself through either a separate identity (Black) or a dual identity (Black student at the university). These effects may have occurred because the superordinate self-description conveyed that the student viewed his racial identity as less

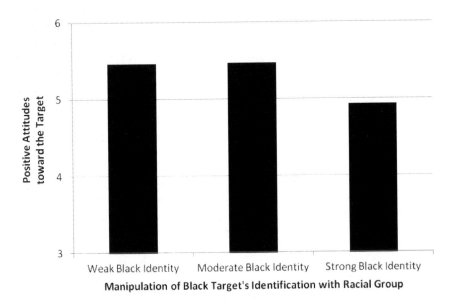

Figure 10.1   Whites express less positive attitudes toward Blacks who identify strongly with their race compared to Blacks who identify moderately and weakly with their race (Kaiser & Pratt-Hyatt, 2009, Experiment 2).

important than other identities, thus lowering participants' perceptions of his racial identification.

Additionally, research on cross-group friendships provides evidence that Whites react differently to strongly and weakly identified minorities. In one experiment, Whites were more willing to hire Black Americans with White friendship networks and less willing to hire those with Black networks compared to when no information about the individual's friendship network was available (Johnson, Kaiser, Rasheed, McElveen, & Cook, 2012). Importantly, the effects of friendship diversity on hiring decisions were mediated by perceptions of how racially identified that Black individual was with his group. Whites assumed that Black Americans were more identified with their racial group when they had primarily Black friends relative to when no information was known about their friends and that they were less racially identified when their friendship network was predominately White. And it was these inferences about identification that resulted in differential hiring rates.

Public and Private Expressions of Identification

More recently, some have argued that it is the public behavioral expression (rather than the private experience) of identity that drives much of majority group members' negative reactions to strongly identified members of devalued groups. In a set of experiments, White American participants learned about ethnic minority immigrants (Chinese immigrants to the United States) or White immigrants (Polish immigrants) who were strongly identified with their ethnic group but varied in the extent to which they expressed their identification publicly (Yogeeswaran, Dasgupta, Adelman, Eccleston, & Parker, 2011). Some participants learned that the immigrant target spoke his native language in public (in the public identity expression condition) and others learned that he spoke English in public and reserved his native language for use at home (in the private identity expression condition). When the target spoke his native language in public, participants were less likely explicitly to construe his ethnic group as American compared to when he spoke his native language only at home. Interestingly, at the implicit level, only Chinese immigrants were denied their rightful American identity when they spoke the native language in public rather than at home, suggesting that prejudice distribution effects may be most pronounced for non-White minorities. These effects have been replicated when implicit and explicit attitudes toward the target, rather than perceptions of Americanism, serve as the dependent measure (Yogeeswaran, Adelman, Parker, & Dasgupta, 2012).

Another set of experiments also points to the importance of public behavioral manifestations of identity in contributing to prejudice distribution effects. In one experiment (Van Laar, Bleeker, & Ellemers, 2012), White Dutch participants evaluated an ethnic minority job candidate who expressed either strong or weak private emotional ties to his ethnic group and who also declared that he behaved either in an assimilationist manner, like White Dutch citizens, or in an ethnic manner, consistent with his own culture, even when those behaviors were in opposition to typical Dutch behaviors. White participants were more threatened by the job candidate when he expressed either type of identification (affective ties or behavior typical of minorities) relative to when he expressed low levels of identification. However, participants extended negative evaluations only to the candidate who reported behaving like a typical ingroup member rather than a typical Dutch person, and not toward the individual who was only privately affectively tied to his group. Thus, White participants felt threatened by ethnic minorities who expressed their identities either publicly or privately but only behaviorally sanctioned those who publicly behaved in a manner consistent with their group.

When considered in conjunction with the Yogeeswaran studies, these data (Van Laar et al., 2012) suggest that it is behaviorally expressing one's identity in public that is most likely to set off prejudice distribution effects. Such minorities may be viewed as most likely to threaten the status of the majority group. Thus, majority group members are willing to accept minorities who identify privately with their group, so long as they conform publicly to the behavioral norms of majorities. This represents a nuanced type of cultural ideology— support for multiculturalism when it occurs exclusively in one's private sphere.

The data from Yogeeswaran et al. (2011, 2012) and Van Laar et al. (2012) seem, at first glance, to be inconsistent with the findings of Kaiser and Pratt-Hyatt (1999) and Dovidio et al. (2010), who report that simply identifying with a minority group is sufficient to set off prejudice distribution effects. However, both the former studies involved Whites' reactions to ethnic immigrant minorities, whereas the latter studies involved Whites' reactions to Black Americans. It is plausible that the stereotype of Black Americans differs on critical dimensions that cause participants to make the leap more quickly from identification to behavior with Black Americans relative to other minority groups. Because being Black is viewed as possessing a race as opposed to an ethnicity—and, indeed, a race with a longstanding history of political action in the United States—it is possible that the Black identity is seen automatically as public and political. These observations raise important questions about whether majority group members will react negatively to identity expression among all types of devalued groups, or whether identity expression means different things when expressed by different groups in various contexts.

PREJUDICE DISTRIBUTION IN INTERPERSONAL INTERACTIONS

Much of the existing research on the prejudice distribution perspective has examined the reactions of Whites to minority targets with whom they do not actually interact (e.g., minorities are presented on paper and video). If these are the only contexts where the prejudice distribution effect occurs, then it will be a narrow phenomenon that might dissipate in real life. Thus, as others have so thoroughly argued, it is important to test the generality of data from controlled laboratory settings in the messier, but more complex and rich, world of actual interactions (Hebl & Dovidio, 2005; Shelton & Richeson, 2006; Vorauer, 2006).

Intergroup interactions, however, are notoriously complicated with respect to predicting whether and in what manner majority group members will express discrimination. For example, when Whites harbor negative attitudes toward minorities, they sometimes employ self-regulatory efforts during intergroup interactions and express more favorable behavior than their private attitudes would suggest (Richeson & Shelton, 2003, 2007; Shelton, Richeson, Salvatore, & Trawalter, 2005; Vorauer & Turpie, 2004). Self-regulation of prejudice occurs in behaviors that are readily amenable to self-control, such as the explicit content of what one says (e.g., publicly expressing liking of a minority partner). It is more difficult, however, to regulate the expression of prejudice on other, more automatic behaviors, such as nonverbal behavior, and individuals who harbor such biases may continue to express them (Dovidio, Kawakami, & Gaertner, 2002).

These insights from research on the self-regulation of prejudice during interracial interactions may provide a stronger understanding of when majority group members will react negatively toward strongly identified minorities and when they will not. As strongly identified minorities are threatening to majorities (Kaiser & Pratt-Hyatt, 2009; Kaiser & Wilkins, 2010; Van Laar et al., 2012), majority group members may be especially concerned about expressing discrimination when interacting with minorities who appear (or are assumed) to be strongly identified with their group. When they are especially worried about expressing discrimination, they will regulate controllable aspects of their behavior, such as what they say during the conversation, and this self-regulation can result in an absence of negativity toward strongly identified minorities compared to weakly identified minorities (Shelton & Richeson, 2006). Their efforts to behave in an unbiased fashion may fail, however, despite their concern, when they are unaware of, or unable to gain control over, subtle aspects of their behavior that communicate their discomfort and bias (Dovidio et al., 2002). Thus majorities may struggle to control their behavior and will subsequently conduct themselves more negatively toward strongly identified members than weakly identified members of devalued groups.

A recent experiment provides evidence consistent with the notion that majority group members enact their self-regulatory goals and adjust their readily controllable behaviors during interactions with strongly identified minorities. In a field experiment (Barron, Hebl, & King, 2011), strongly and weakly identified racial minority (Black and Latino American) college students applied for jobs in retail stores at a mall. Identification was communicated with the applicants' hats, which contained logos expressing strong identification (e.g., "Black and Proud") or neutral content. Outgroup managers treated strongly and weakly identified minorities identically with respect to formal discrimination (e.g., interview offers, providing additional information about the position) and actually behaved *more positively* toward strongly identified minorities compared to weakly identified minorities on measures of interpersonal discrimination (e.g., positivity of the exchange as rated by observes in the store who witnessed the managers' verbal and nonverbal behavior). Barron and her colleagues reasoned that managers who interacted with strongly identified minorities were especially concerned to create an unbiased impression because they feared that strongly identified minorities would be litigious or confrontational with respect to negative employment treatment. Thus, the managers had strong reasons to exert control over their racial attitudes and behave especially positively toward strongly identified minorities. And it appears they did so successfully.

The research by Barron et al. (2011) provides an important insight into how the motivation to regulate prejudicial responses can moderate whether strongly identified minorities are especially likely to experience prejudice. By nature of its field study design, this experiment could not, however, offer opportunities to examine whether the store managers would have expressed bias toward strongly identified minorities on behaviors that are more difficult to control. Specifically, evaluations of their informal discriminatory behavior were based upon data provided by raters who were not blind to condition and who viewed the entire interaction, including the verbal nature of the exchange. Thus, the raters may have been most influenced by the managers' general positivity in the interaction (including their self-regulated positive verbal behavior with applicants), and it may have been these controllable aspects that contributed toward the managers' perceived positivity toward strongly identified minorities. On more subtle behaviors that are difficult to self-regulate, the managers may have behaved quite differently.

We recently tested these ideas in a laboratory interaction study in which unacquainted White and Black same-sex dyads engaged in a video-recorded interaction (Kaiser, Drury, Malahy, & King, 2011). In the weeks before the interaction, Black participants completed Luhtanen and Crocker's (1992) measure of the centrality of their racial group to their self-concept. During the interaction, participants had ten minutes to discuss their opinions about race relations (drawing upon methods used in Shelton, Richeson, Salvatore, & Trawalter, 2005). After the interaction, coders blind to hypotheses watched separate videotapes of each member of the dyad during the first few minutes of the interaction. One group of coders watched only nonverbal behaviors (the volume on the video was muted), while another group watched the video with audio accompaniment, evaluating the friendliness of each partner as expressed verbally and nonverbally. We reasoned that nonverbal behavior would be difficult to self-regulate, and that Whites' biases toward strongly identified Blacks would emerge on this type of behavior. However, consistent with Barron et al. (2011), we reasoned that Whites would not express bias through their verbal behavior, as this is easy to control when one is concerned not to show prejudice.

Figure 10.2 displays the results of hierarchical linear modeling analyses in which the relationship between the Black partner's level of racial identification and each partners' nonverbal behavior was examined (after accounting for reciprocity in both partners' behavior, as participants tend to mimic each other). As is evident in this figure, the more Blacks identified with their racial group, the more nonverbally unfriendly was the behavior of their White partners toward them. This finding is consistent with research showing that prejudice is particularly likely to be expressed in contexts where discriminatory behavior is difficult to control (Dovidio et al., 2002). Figure 10.2 also displays a striking paradox. Specifically, the more Blacks identified with their racial group, the *more* nonverbally friendly was their behavior toward their White interaction partner. This latter finding is consistent with research showing that devalued group members sometimes compensate for anticipated discrimination during the interaction by redoubling their effort and acting especially friendly to make the interactions progress more smoothly (Hebl & Dovidio, 2005; Miller & Kaiser, 2001; Miller & Myers, 1998; Shelton, Richeson, & Salvatore, 2005). These findings point to ironic processes in these interactions, as those Blacks trying the hardest and behaving the most positively toward their partners were precisely those who were treated the worst by Whites.

Consistent with Barron et al. (2011), this study found that Whites did not express bias toward strongly identified minorities on more easily controllable behaviors. That is, the coders detected nothing more prejudicial in the verbal content of what Whites said, irrespective of whether they were interacting with strongly or weakly identified Blacks. And strongly identified Blacks did not compensate verbally, suggesting that, irrespective of level of identity, they exerted effort to behave in a friendly manner on easily controllable behaviors. Together, these two separate investigations begin to identify the types of

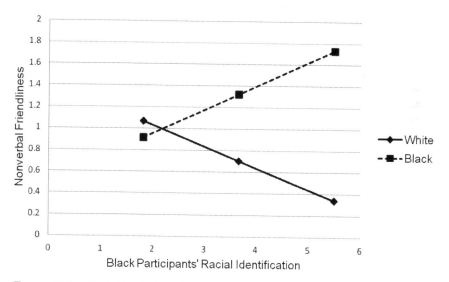

Figure 10.2   Blacks' level of racial identification predicts divergent nonverbal behavior among White and Black interaction partners (reprinted from Kaiser et al. [2011]).

behaviors on which strongly and weakly identified minorities will be more and less prone to experiencing discrimination.

Clearly, additional investigations on this topic will be needed to understand further the boundaries of the prejudice distribution effect in intergroup interactions. For example, studies could examine individual differences in majorities' motivation to control bias and examine whether this moderates majority group members' behaviors. Or majority members could undergo cognitive depletion prior to an interaction, and in this mentally exhausted context they may express bias toward strongly identified minorities on what would otherwise be easily controllable behaviors. Further, time series studies could be conducted that examine whether Whites are ultimately responsive to the positive nonverbal overtures of strongly identified Blacks. For example, if Blacks persist in their friendly nonverbal behavior, despite facing prejudice, they might ultimately bring their White partners on board in the interaction and engender positive reactions from them. Or, if Whites don't respond in turn to Blacks' positive overtures, Blacks may in turn reciprocate Whites' unfriendly behavior.

MODERATING FACTORS: DISARMING MECHANISMS

As research on the prejudice distribution perspective develops, it will be important for scholars to identify additional factors that exacerbate or mitigate prejudice against strongly identified minorities. As identifying with one's group is important for many members of devalued groups, strongly identified minorities likely utilize strategies to deflect prejudice without decreasing their identification with their group (see Miller & Kaiser, 2001). Further, to the extent that these strategies provide opportunities for remaining identified with one's group, members of devalued groups will be able to reap the psychological benefits offered by group identification (Branscombe et al., 1999; Leach et al., 2010).

One potentially important component of these prejudice-deflecting strategies may involve alleviating majority group members' fear of strongly identified minorities. Because minority group identification threatens majorities (Kaiser & Pratt-Hyatt, 2009; Van Laar et al., 2012), majorities may express less prejudice toward strongly identified minorities if their fears are mitigated. Livingston and Pearce (2009) discuss disarming mechanisms—"physical, psychological, or behavioral traits that attenuate perceptions of threat by the dominant group" (p. 1229)—as a strategy that Black men use to reduce Whites' fears of Black men. Steele and Aronson (1995, p. 803) discuss this type of disarming mechanism in their seminal paper on stereotype threat when describing how a Black American graduate student attempted to mitigate Whites' fearful reactions toward him by whistling Vivaldi when he walked in the streets. Although publicly expressing low levels of identification is itself a disarming mechanism, even minorities who are strongly identified can employ such mechanisms to head off prejudice. We suspect that there are numerous strategies used by strongly identified minorities to disarm the fears of majorities, and identifying these moderators of the prejudice distribution effect will be important. We discuss some of these below.

Status-Legitimizing Worldviews

Minorities' endorsement of status-legitimizing worldviews (SLWs) represents one type of disarming mechanism that causes Whites to react more positively toward identified minorities. SLWs are culturally shared beliefs that are created to explain and justify the unequal status hierarchy within a system (Crandall, 1994; Jost & Banaji, 1994; Major, Kaiser, O'Brien, & McCoy, 2007). Examples include the Belief in a Just World (Lerner, 1980), the Protestant Work Ethic (Katz & Hass, 1988), and the belief in individual mobility (Major, Gramzow, et al., 2002). By locating the causes of inequality within individual effort and deservingness, these worldviews function to legitimize status differences within a society. That is, these beliefs create the perception that, if a group has difficulty advancing, it must be because members of that group have not worked hard enough and are not as deserving of higher status.

Because majority group members are motivated to defend SLWs, a belief system that justifies their privileged position in the status hierarchy, they react particularly harshly toward individuals who question the accuracy of this worldview (Jost & Burgess, 2000; Kaiser, Dyrenforth, & Hagiwara, 2006). Thus, one reason why Whites react particularly negatively toward strongly identified minorities is because they assume that these individuals reject SLWs (Kaiser & Pratt-Hyatt, 2009). Indeed, when strongly identified minorities communicate that they endorse SLWs, they are viewed more positively compared to when they communicate that they reject SLWs or communicate nothing about them (Kaiser & Pratt-Hyatt, 2009). When majority group members encounter strongly identified minorities who endorse SLWs, they may redefine their understanding of minority identity to be something about those minorities' own culture and group rather than as a reactionary attitude against the majority's status position. This may in turn put majority group members at ease.

Counter-Stereotypic Traits

Another disarming mechanism minorities may employ is to present themselves counter-stereotypically—for example, by "whistling Vivaldi" (Steele & Aronson, 1995). Indeed, Van Laar et al. (2012) show that strongly identified minorities are well received when they behave counter-stereotypically (behave like the native-born Dutch). Similarly, minorities who assimilate by refraining from the use of their ethnic language in public are also engaging in a stereotype-disconfirming disarming mechanism that effectively mitigates majorities' biases (Yogeswaran et al., 2011). Similarly, a disarming mechanism might be in part responsible for why Blacks and Latinos who were strongly identified in the study by Barron et al. (2011) were so warmly received when they applied for jobs. In this study, these minority applicants all introduced themselves as

college students at a highly prestigious historically White university—
something that runs counter to negative stereotypes about ethnic minorities. In
short, strongly identified minorities who distance from negative stereotypes
about their group may be less threatening to Whites, and this may disarm the
biases that Whites would otherwise express toward these individuals.

Caveats

The disarming mechanisms described above focus on what targets of prejudice
can do to engender more positive treatment from majority groups. Although
disarming strategies like these are potentially beneficial to devalued group members, they can also carry psychological baggage, as they can involve behaving
discrepantly from one's own self-concept or beliefs (Festinger & Carlsmith,
1959). For example, minorities have good reason to reject status-legitimizing
beliefs, and some minorities embrace certain aspects of stereotypes as self-
relevant. Denying these aspects of one's authentic self in the service of improving
individual outcomes can be stressful (Shelton, Richeson, & Salvatore, 2005).
Further, disarming mechanisms require time and energy, both limited resources
that could go toward other pursuits. And employing disarming mechanisms
might engender frustration, as they require changing the self to deal with someone else's prejudice. Finally, disarming mechanisms may serve to legitimize
inequality, as they involve changing the self rather than mitigating the forces driving social inequality. Despite these costs, members of minority groups are sometimes motivated to reduce their personal exposure to prejudice, and these
disarming mechanisms can be important tools in dealing with prejudice (Miller
& Kaiser, 2001; Major, Quinton, McCoy, & Schmader, 2000).

Threat Reduction among Majorities

Clearly, it will also be critical to approach disarming the threat felt by majority
group members from the source of the problem—majority group members
themselves. Strategies that increase their comfort with strongly identified devalued group members should eliminate or reduce the prejudice distribution
effect. Self-affirmation, or reminding participants of the integrity and value of
their self-concept (Steele, 1988), is one process that may increase majority
group members' comfort, and those who are self-affirmed may be less threatened by and subsequently more accepting of strongly identified devalued
group members. Additionally, if majorities are able to attribute their fear of the
strongly identified to alternative causes, they may be more receptive toward
strongly identified individuals (Dutton & Aron, 1974). For example, if majority
group members interacting with strongly identified minorities are told that all
interactions in getting acquainted involve initial discomfort, they may be more
likely to attribute their fear to general aspects of having that interaction rather
than to the characteristics of their minority partner. Finally, if majorities are
taught that minority identification is not grounded in negative reactions toward

majorities, this too might reduce their prejudice toward devalued group members who identify with their group.

IMPLICATIONS FOR DIVERSITY

The first half of this chapter focused on the common assumption illustrated in Representative Wasserman-Schultz's quotation—that members of devalued groups understand discrimination because they consensually experience it. While no devalued individuals are fully immune from the experience of bias, the research described in this chapter highlights the potential error one would make in assuming that all members of a devalued group are equally exposed to, and subsequently equally in tune with, the pervasiveness of discrimination. In the second part of this chapter we explore how this erroneous assumption can lead to misjudging how members of these groups will react to injustice.

In arguing that judges from devalued groups typically act in ways that reduce inequality, Representative Wasserman-Schultz might have benefited from considering the current U.S. Supreme Court. Justice Clarence Thomas, an African American who is among the most conservative of the justices, has downplayed the role of racial animus as the cause of racial disparities and has frequently ruled against cases that would uphold civil rights for women and minorities. In contrast, Justice Sonia Sotomayor, a Latina and liberal member of the court, perceives discrimination as an ongoing problem and has ruled in ways that reduce injustice for disadvantaged groups. Although both of these justices would, according to Wasserman-Schultz, represent the interests of disadvantaged groups, their actual behavior is nothing alike when it comes to approaching injustice. As we explore in the remainder of this chapter, we believe that many people share the erroneous assumption that members of devalued groups consensually advance the interests of their own group. We further explore how this assumption, ironically, has the potential to undermine the success of diversity practices.

Specifically, we believe it is important to understand how the unequal distribution of prejudice can shape the way members of devalued groups behave in contexts where they have the opportunity to remedy or perpetuate injustice. If majority group members give weakly identified members of devalued groups more advantageous treatment than strongly identified group members, the weakly identified should advance in society to a greater degree than the strongly identified. For example, because Whites are disproportionately represented among the powerful ranks in organizations, they will often be in the position of deciding who should be hired, promoted, mentored, and otherwise geared for advancement within the organization. If weakly identified minorities are believed to possess beliefs that are advantageous to those in power (e.g., endorsing SLWs, assimilating with White norms), then they should be perceived as more palatable by management relative to strongly identified minorities. Because organizations are motivated to have at least some devalued group members succeed (Shin & Gulati, 2011), they may embrace the weakly identified and provide them with more opportunities to advance.

CLIMBING AND LIFTING OR CLIMBING AND KICKING?

What are the implications of selective advancement of the weakly identified for diversity? Most diversity efforts are grounded on trickle-down assumptions, contending that members of devalued groups who are first to advance in an organization will help to recruit, retain, promote, and contribute to policies that benefit their ingroup (see Carbado & Gulati, 2004, for a review). Carbado and Gulati (2004) refer to this pattern of assistance from more senior devalued group members as "climbing and lifting." However, if the early generation of successful devalued group members comes disproportionately from the ranks of the weakly identified, then this raises troubling implications for the success of diversity programs that rely on trickle-down effects. Specifically, when placed in an environment that threatens their group, weakly identified devalued group members are likely to pursue individualistic advancement strategies without helping their ingroup, whereas, in the same situation, highly identified devalued group members are more motivated to pursue actions that benefit the group (Ellemers, Spears, & Doosje, 2002). Indeed, when weakly identified group members learn that their group will have low status, they decrease their commitment to the group. In contrast, strongly identified group members maintain their commitment to the group in spite of its low status (Doosje, Spears, & Ellemers, 2002). Even more problematically, weakly identified devalued group members may "climb and kick" (Carbado & Gulati, 2004)—engage in preferential treatment of the outgroup over the ingroup—when they enter an environment in which their group's status is threatened, which contributes toward their group's disadvantaged position.

Although data indicative of climbing and kicking have appeared from time to time in the intergroup literature, this phenomenon has only recently begun to receive more thorough theoretical attention (see Jost, Banaji, & Nosek, 2004, for a review). As climbing and kicking runs counter to assumptions from prevailing models of intergroup relations which argue that individuals focus on maintaining positive identities and display ingroup favoritism in that pursuit (Tajfel & Turner, 1979; although see Marques, Yzerbyt, & Leyens, 1988), it is a prediction that has not always been at the forefront of research. The emerging system justification literature has tackled this issue and argues that, under some circumstances, climbing and kicking can be a response to one's disadvantaged status and that members of devalued groups can be co-opted into systems that oppress them, and in turn display more negative behavior toward their own ingroups compared to more powerful outgroups (for reviews, see Dasgutpa, 2004; Jost et al., 2004).

Several studies suggest that members of low-status groups do, under some circumstances, discriminate against their own group. In one study, White, Asian, and Latino participants were given the opportunity to select a timeslot for a future "getting to know you" interaction (Jost, Pelham, & Carvallo, 2002). Participants were told that another section of students had already signed up for times, so each timeslot had one name (a common Asian, White, or Latino name) listed as the potential partner for that time. Participants then rated each timeslot on a scale from 1 (most preferred) to 3 (least preferred). Asian and Latino participants showed preferences for times in which they would interact with a White partner over times in which they would interact with another member of their own group. Similarly, in another study, Black participants who expected to complete a task on which Whites stereotypically excel (i.e., a mathematically rigorous task) rated their potential task partner as more competent if he was White than if he was Black (Ashburn-Nardo & Johnson, 2008). Additionally, Blacks tip Black service providers less than White service providers, even when controlling for the quality of service (Ayres, Vars, & Zakariya, 2005; Lynn et al., 2008). These findings are not restricted to race but also extend to members of other low-status groups. For example, women have been observed to evaluate male leaders more favorably than female leaders in male-dominated contexts (Garcia-Retamero & López-Zafra, 2006).

Further evidence of climbing and kicking comes from organizational field studies. For example, women who succeed in disciplines in which their gender group is underrepresented show evidence of climbing and kicking. In one study, female full professors in the Netherlands (where women represent an extremely small fraction of full professors) reported that female PhD students were less committed to the field than male PhD students, while male professors did not show this bias—nor did male and female PhD students differ in their self-reports of commitment (Ellemers, van den Heuvel, de Gilder, Maass, & Bonvini, 2004). Similarly, women who reviewed NSF Economics Program grant applications (a field where women are underrepresented) rated proposals with female (but not male) principal investigators more negatively than men rated these proposals—even when controlling for proposal quality (Broder, 1993). And female subordinates in male-dominated fields feel this kick from their female bosses. For example, female law associates rate female law partners in their firms more negatively and as poorer role models when the firms have few women in the prestigious partner position (suggestive of a more stigmatizing context for women) compared to when the firms have a better gender balance of partners (Ely, 1994). Thus, across these studies, some women who thrive in male-dominated domains show climbing and kicking—as evidenced by their own behavior and the reports of ingroup members who work for them.

GROUP IDENTIFICATION MODERATES CLIMBING AND KICKING

We expect weakly identified women and minorities who advance in fields in which they are underrepresented will be likely to kick, whereas those who are strongly identified will lift. Indeed, research has begun to show that weakly identified women who have advanced in male-dominated fields may respond to discrimination they encounter in these fields by distancing themselves from other women and failing to support their advancement. In one study, women who held high-ranking nontraditional positions in companies throughout the Netherlands were surveyed about their gender and careers (Derks, Ellemers, van Laar, & de Groot, 2011a). Women who reported having weak gender identification when they began their careers and having experienced more discrimination during their professional lives were more likely to report that men were more committed to their careers than women. Strongly identified women who experienced discrimination did not show this effect, and nor did women at either level of identification when discrimination was not recalled to be pervasive.

An experiment that followed up on this survey finding provided stronger evidence that discrimination may contribute to kicking in weakly identified women (Derks, Ellemers, van Laar, & de Groot, 2011b). In this study, senior female police officers—women who had advanced in a field in which they are underrepresented—were primed with the presence or absence of gender discrimination by recounting either a time when they had experienced discrimination or a time when discrimination had not been a problem. When reminded of the presence of gender discrimination, the weakly gender identified police officers were more likely to deny the importance of discrimination against women, to describe themselves in masculine terms, and to distance themselves from other women. No differences between strongly and weakly identified women occurred when women were reminded of the absence of discrimination. In contrast, when reminded of the presence of gender discrimination, strongly gender identified police officers did not show these effects and were more likely to express support for collective action on behalf of women. Importantly, these results demonstrate that gender identification differentiates how women respond to bias within an organization and that weakly identified women are more likely to respond by distancing themselves from their group and their groups' interest, whereas strongly identified women are more likely to respond by advocating on behalf of the group.

To the extent that weakly identified devalued group members who are in threatening contexts deny the significance of discrimination and distance from their group, it is reasonable to anticipate that this behavior will produce climbing and kicking by giving preferential treatment to members of the high-status outgroup. We have recently begun examining directly whether advancement in a field in which low-status group members are underrepresented leads them to kick other members of their group. In one study (Spalding & Kaiser, 2012), female participants first completed a prescreening measure of gender identification (the centrality subscale of the Luhtanen and Crocker (1992) Collective Self-Esteem Scale) and then came into the lab to participate in a study about work groups and leadership. During the lab session, participants were told that they were completing the study along with two other participants, one male and one female, who were presented in computer profiles with photographs. After completing a management aptitude test, all actual participants were led to believe they scored higher than the other two participants and would subsequently be assigned to serve as the manager who would oversee the other two participants. In order to highlight that participants had advanced in a domain in which women were underrepresented, they signed a manager roster containing predominantly male names, which was intended to convey that men usually scored highest on the management aptitude test. Participants then selected clues to assist their male and female "subordinates" as they completed a test to serve as assistant manager, which required them to identify nonsensical phrases that rhyme with common phrases. The helpfulness of the clues given to the male versus the female subordinate served as the behavioral measure of kicking. Consistent with hypotheses, weakly gender identified participants were more likely than strongly identified participants to kick—i.e., give more helpful clues to the male subordinate than the female subordinate—than strongly gender identified participants, who were more likely to lift—i.e., give more helpful clues to the female subordinate.

In a second study, we examined whether advancing in a context in which they were underrepresented (i.e., an identity-threatening context) elicited the relationship between lifting and kicking. In this study, participants were assigned either to a condition that replicated the first study or to a condition in which they did not advance in the underrepresented domain but, rather, simply believed they were engaging with two other participants (one male and one female) on the same behavioral helping task. We found that the relationship between gender identification and kicking or lifting emerged only in the condition in which women advanced in a domain in which they were underrepresented. These data provide some initial clues that group identification may differentiate how members of low-status groups who advance in a field in which they are underrepresented treat members of the ingroup. Weakly identified members of low-status groups may kick when they advance in these fields, whereas strongly identified members may respond by lifting. Like the data from Derks et al. (2011b), these studies highlight how the presence of social identity-threatening environments is a necessary precursor to climbing and kicking.

POTENTIAL REASONS FOR CLIMBING AND KICKING

To date, sparse attention has been devoted to mechanisms that drive climbing and kicking, and outgroup favoritism more generally, and little is understood about why these processes occur. Climbing and kicking may be driven by both cognitive and motivational factors. Below we outline how both types of process may contribute to climbing and kicking.

COGNITIVE PROCESSES

Implicit Stereotype Endorsement

One possible reason for climbing and kicking is that weakly identified members of devalued groups harbor negative implicit stereotypes that majority group members are on average superior to fellow minorities in outgroup-dominated domains. Indeed, weakly identified Blacks are more likely to show implicit biases favoring Whites over Blacks relative to strongly identified Blacks (Ashburn-Nardo, Monteith, Arthur, & Bain, 2007). Likewise, women who are more weakly identified with their group on an implicit level are more likely implicitly to stereotype their group (Greenwald et al., 2002). As implicit stereotypes predict discriminatory behavior (Greenwald, Poehlman, Uhlmann, & Banaji, 2009), it may prove useful to examine further the role of such stereotypes in climbing and kicking (Dasgupta, 2004).

Overcorrecting for Ingroup Bias

Climbing and kicking could also occur through an overcorrection process (Wilson & Brekke, 1994) where, in an effort to avoid expressing ingroup favoritism, members of devalued groups readjust their attitudes toward the ingroup but anchor too far in the negative direction. This could also occur because of self-presentational concerns to avoid appearing prejudiced against majority group members—especially in front of them (Spears, Jetten, & Doosje, 2001)—or it could result because of internal personal standards to be fair (Plant & Devine, 1998).

MOTIVATIONAL PROCESSES

Conforming to Organizational Norms

Climbing and kicking might also represent conformity to the norms or perceived norms of the organization, even if those norms involve providing feedback that favors the outgroup over the ingroup (Branscombe & Ellemers, 1998). Social norms powerfully influence the expression of prejudice by members of both high-status (Crandall, Eshleman, & O'Brien, 2002; Sechrist & Stangor, 2001) and, more surprisingly, low-status groups (Shapiro & Neuberg, 2008). Indeed, when Black males perceive the expression of prejudice to be the norm for Whites, they publicly engage in racism against minorities by favoring a White job candidate over a Native American job candidate (Shapiro & Neuberg, 2008). Thus, if minorities perceive that the dominant organizational culture promotes discrimination against their own group, then they may, at least publicly, discriminate against their own group as well.

Expressing Loyalty to the Organization

Weakly identified devalued group members might harm their own group in part as a strategy for displaying loyalty toward their organization. By showing negativity toward the ingroup, devalued individuals communicate that they are team players who do not allow ingroup loyalty to interfere with organizational loyalty. Devalued group members might also think that being hard on the ingroup will lead their (often majority group) supervisors to like them more, and this could be personally advantageous.

Reifying Merit

Additionally, successful members of devalued groups, like most people, are motivated to maintain the belief that they advanced in society because of their own effort and abilities, and they derive esteem and pride from attributing their success to these internal factors (Weiner, 1985). This desire to have one's merit recognized may be particularly challenging for members of devalued groups as they carry the burden of others questioning their merit—for example, by believing that they unfairly benefited from affirmative action (Heilman & Alcott, 2001). This may cause them to act especially harshly toward their ingroup as a means of showing how they are particularly strong members of their group and that their group in general is not offered easy pathways to advancement. Doing this would also allow members of devalued groups to maintain their own unique status as individuals who have "made it" within the organization. Women and minorities who succeed in domains in which they are underrepresented may increase their achievement-related esteem by downgrading the achievements and abilities of other women and minorities in order to make their own success seem more exceptional (Eidelman & Biernat, 2007; Tesser, 1988).

Avoiding Stigmatization

Weakly identified women and minorities may climb and kick in order to avoid being "ghettoized" within the organization. They may fear that promoting and collaborating with other members of their ingroup may lead them to be seen both as more separate and on the fringe of the organization and more devalued in general. Indeed, the more a domain becomes occupied by members of devalued groups, such as women, the less status that domain garners (Reskin & Roos, 1990; Ridgeway, 2001). To the extent that members of devalued groups seek status within their field, they will be motivated to engage in actions that increase the perceived worthiness of their work.

Preparing Ingroup Members for Success

Climbing and kicking might also be driven by the belief that, in order to succeed in a threatening context, members of devalued groups must be exceptionally strong and capable of overcoming discrimination. Successful members of such groups might honestly believe that they are helping fellow ingroup members by behaving harshly toward them, as this treatment will help those who survive develop the ability to succeed despite obstacles and become thick-skinned as a result.

In sum, there are numerous potential reasons why climbing and kicking occurs. As research on this topic develops, it will be imperative to move beyond demonstrating the basic effect and to begin identifying reasons for why it occurs. By understanding the reasons underlying this type of treatment, we can begin to determine steps for mitigating climbing and kicking.

PREVENTING CLIMBING AND KICKING

Given that climbing and kicking can occur, it is important to understand how to prevent this type of behavior. This is particularly important in organizations, as they may be operating under the faulty assumption that simply having some key employees who belong to underrepresented groups will result directly in increased trickle-down diversity. If these individuals are strongly identified, then this assumption may be accurate. However, if those who advance come from the weakly identified ranks, then this assumption will need revision.

Preventing climbing and kicking will depend in large part upon why it occurs in the first place. Once these mechanisms are identified, efforts can be exerted to address factors that push weakly identified devalued group members in the direction of kicking. All of the motivational explanations offered for climbing and kicking above share a critical feature: The kicking behavior is assumed to stem from a reaction to contexts that devalue the social identities of low-status groups. To the extent that organizations make concerted efforts to create identity-safe spaces, then devalued group members who advance will be less worried about their status and value (Steele, 2010), and this should in turn promote less kicking among the weakly identified and less ingroup favoritism among the strongly identified.

For example, if climbing and kicking is caused by a need to reify one's merit, then organizations that explicitly correct faulty assumptions about affirmative action (e.g., that it involves hiring and promoting unqualified minorities; Heilman & Alcott, 2001) should be less likely to experience kicking compared to those that fail to correct these flawed understandings of affirmative action. That is, by removing the stigma that members of devalued groups are undeserving of high-status positions, those individuals will be able to enact decisions without fears that others question their qualifications and abilities.

Similarly, if climbing and kicking stems from devalued group members' desires to conform to organizational norms, then organizations that communicate openness to multiple perspectives should see reduced levels of kicking behavior. For example, if an organization offers a multicultural environment where group differences are valued and difference of perspective is viewed as a strength, then members of devalued groups will feel less pressured to comply with existing majority group members' norms and perspectives. In contrast, companies that present more colorblind environments, where the recognition of group-based categories is minimized, may send the message to devalued group members that their perspectives and life experiences are irrelevant to the organization's goals. Thus, devalued group members may feel that distancing from their identity is valued (or even rewarded). Under these circumstances, climbing and kicking is one way they express distance from their ingroup.

If climbing and kicking stems from more purely cognitive rather than motivational factors, then organizational diversity efforts aimed at reducing the influence of bias among majority group members might also be important educational tools for members of devalued groups. To the extent that individuals are aware of unconscious biases, for example, they can begin to exert control over these attitudes and subsequently reduce negativity toward members of their own group (Devine, 1989; Monteith, Ashburn-Nardo, Voils, & Czopp, 2002). Thus, even devalued group members might benefit from reminders about how implicit stereotypes leave people susceptible to expressing bias.

The recognition that climbing and kicking is triggered by the presence of a stigmatizing context is central to its prevention. It would be a mistake to attribute climbing and kicking to something dispositional among weakly identified members of low-status groups. For example, our own data (Spalding & Kaiser, 2012) show that weakly identified women do not always kick. They do so when their identity is devalued (the context sends clear signals that women do not belong) and not when identity-threatening signals are absent. Similarly, the research of Derks et al. (2011a, 2011b) demonstrates that weakly identified women showed indicators of climbing and kicking (e.g., rating men as more committed to their careers than women) only when discrimination was pervasive in their employment context, and not when discrimination was rare. This research is consistent with theoretical perspectives (Ellemers et al., 2002) contending that stigmatizing contexts are a key factor in determining when group identification will predict divergent responses among devalued group members. Thus, efforts to mitigate climbing and kicking will be most successful when they focus on removing stigma from the environment. Further, these efforts will facilitate the success of diversity programs that rely on the assumption that successful devalued group members have the interests of fellow group members at heart and exert effort to reduce discrimination.

CONCLUSIONS

As research on group identification develops, it will be important to incorporate further an interpersonal theoretical perspective that explicitly recognizes that strongly and weakly identified members of devalued groups experience different treatment from majority group members. Group identification is more than an internal psychological compass guiding one's construal of the social world; it is something to which others react, and such reactions shape the realities of members of devalued groups. Furthermore, these differential realities offer starting points for understanding how members of devalued groups treat one another. If the individual group members who rise up in underrepresented domains in which their group is devalued come disproportionately from the ranks of the weakly identified, this may ironically create greater obstacles for other members of devalued groups. For example, if assumptions like those made by Representative Wasserman-Schultz prevail within an organization, such organizations might prematurely believe that they are effectively improving diversity outcomes. However, given the variability in individuals' experiences with discrimination and their willingness to advocate on behalf of their group, it is important that organizations recognize that structural anti-discrimination measures are still needed, even when (and maybe especially when) devalued group members begin to break down historical barriers.

ACKNOWLEDGMENTS

Preparation of this chapter was supported by NSF BCS-0749159 and NSF BCS-1053732 grants to Cheryl Kaiser and an NSF Graduate Research Fellowship to Kerry Spalding. Address correspondence to Cheryl Kaiser, Psychology Department, University of Washington, Box 351525, Seattle, WA 98195-1525, ckaiser@uw.edu.

REFERENCES

Allport, G. (1954). *The nature of prejudice*. Cambridge, MA: Addison-Wesley.
Ashburn-Nardo, L., & Johnson, N. J. (2008). Implicit outgroup favoritism and intergroup judgment: The moderating role of stereotypic context. *Social Justice Research, 21,* 490–508.
Ashburn-Nardo, L., Monteith, M. J., Arthur, S. A., & Bain, A. (2007). Race and the psychological health of African Americans. *Group Processes & Intergroup Relations, 10,* 471–491.
Ayres, I., Vars, F. E., & Zakariya, N. (2005). To insure prejudice: Racial disparities in taxicab tipping. *Yale Law Journal, 114,* 1613–1674.
Barron, L. G., Hebl, M., & King, E. B. (2011). Effects of manifest ethnic identification on employment discrimination. *Cultural Diversity and Ethnic Minority Psychology, 17,* 23–30.
Branscombe, N. R., & Ellemers, N. (1998). Coping with group-based discrimination: Individualistic versus group-level strategies. In J. K. Swim and C. Stangor (Eds.), *Prejudice: The target's perspective* (pp. 243–266). San Diego, CA: Academic Press.
Branscombe, N. R., Schmitt, M. T., & Harvey, R. D. (1999). Perceiving pervasive discrimination among African Americans: Implications for group identification and well-being. *Journal of Personality and Social Psychology, 77,* 135–149.
Broder, I. E. (1993). Review of NSF economics proposals: Gender and institutional patterns. *American Economic Review, 83,* 964–970.
Carbado, D., & Gulati, M. (2004). Race to the top of the corporate ladder: What minorities do when they get there. *Washington & Lee Law Review, 61,* 1645–1693.
Crandall, C. S. (1994). Prejudice against fat people: Ideology and self-interest. *Journal of Personality and Social Psychology, 66,* 882–894.
Crandall, C. S., Eshleman, A., & O'Brien, L. (2002). Social norms and the expression and suppression of prejudice: The struggle for internalization. *Journal of Personality and Social Psychology, 82,* 359–378.
Dasgupta, N. (2004). Implicit ingroup favoritism, outgroup favoritism, and their behavioral manifestations. *Social Justice Research, 17,* 143–169.
Derks, B., Ellemers, N., van Laar, C., & de Groot, K. (2011a). Do sexist organizational cultures create the Queen Bee? *British Journal of Social Psychology, 50,* 519–535.

Derks, B., Ellemers, N., van Laar, C., & de Groot, K. (2011b). Gender bias primes elicit queen bee responses among senior police women. *Psychological Science, 22,* 1243–1249.

Devine, P. G. (1989). Stereotypes and prejudice: Their automatic and controlled components. *Journal of Personality and Social Psychology, 56,* 5–18.

Doosje, B., Spears, R., & Ellemers, N. (2002). Social identity as both cause and effect: The development of group identification in response to anticipated and actual changes in the intergroup status hierarchy. *British Journal of Social Psychology, 41,* 57–76.

Dovidio, J. F., Gaertner, S. L., Shnabel, N., Saguy, T., & Johnson, J. (2010). Recategorization and prosocial behavior. In S. Stürmer and M. Snyder (Eds.), *The psychology of prosocial behavior: Group processes, intergroup relations, and helping* (pp. 191–207). Malden, MA: Wiley-Blackwell.

Dovidio, J. F., Kawakami, K., & Gaertner, S. L. (2002). Implicit and explicit prejudice and interracial interaction. *Journal of Personality and Social Psychology, 82,* 62–68.

Dutton, D. G., & Aron, A. P. (1974). Some evidence for heightened sexual attraction under conditions of high anxiety. *Journal of Personality and Social Psychology, 30,* 510–517.

Eidelman, S., & Biernat, M. (2007). Getting more from success: Standard raising as esteem maintenance. *Journal of Personality and Social Psychology, 92,* 759–774.

Ellemers, N., Spears, R., & Doosje, B. (2002). Self and social identity. *Annual Review of Psychology, 53,* 161–186.

Ellemers, N., van den Heuvel, H., de Gilder, D., Maass, A., & Bonvini, A. (2004). The underrepresentation of women in science: Differential commitment or the queen bee syndrome? *British Journal of Social Psychology, 43,* 315–338.

Ely, R. J. (1994). The effects of organizational demographics and social identity on relationships among professional women. *Administrative Science Quarterly, 39,* 203–238.

Festinger, L., & Carlsmith, J. M. (1959). Cognitive consequences of forced compliance. *Journal of Abnormal and Social Psychology, 58,* 203–210.

Garcia-Retamero, R., & López-Zafra, E. (2006). Prejudice against women in male-congenial environments: Perceptions of gender role congruity in leadership. *Sex Roles, 55,* 51–61.

Greenwald, A. G., Banaji, M. R., Rudman, L. A., Farnham, S. D., Nosek, B. A., & Mellott, D. S. (2002). A unified theory of implicit attitudes, stereotypes, self-esteem, and self-concept. *Psychological Review, 109,* 3–25.

Greenwald, A. G., Poehlman, T., Uhlmann, E., & Banaji, M. R. (2009). Understanding and using the Implicit Association Test, III: Meta-analysis of predictive validity. *Journal of Personality and Social Psychology, 97,* 17–41.

Hebl, M. R., & Dovidio, J. F. (2005). Promoting the "social" in the examination of social stigmas. *Personality and Social Psychology Review, 9,* 156–182.

Heilman, M. E., & Alcott, V. (2001). What I think you think of me: Women's reactions to being viewed as beneficiaries of preferential selection. *Journal of Applied Psychology, 86,* 574–582.

Higgins, E. T., King, G. A., & Mavin, G. H. (1982). Individual construct accessibility and subjective impressions and recall. *Journal of Personality and Social Psychology, 43,* 35–47.

Jetten, J., Branscombe, N. R., Schmitt, M. T., & Spears, R. (2001). Rebels with a cause: Group identification as a response to perceived discrimination from the mainstream. *Personality and Social Psychology Bulletin, 27,* 1204–1213.

Johnson, J. D., Kaiser, C. R., Rasheed, H., McElveen, T., & Cook, C. (2011). A bridge over troubled corporate waters: How "Whitened" social networks enhance Black job applicants' hiring outcomes. Manuscript in preparation for submission.

Jost, J. T., & Banaji, M. R. (1994). The role of stereotyping in system-justification and the production of false consciousness. *British Journal of Social Psychology, 33*, 1–27.

Jost, J. T., Banaji, M. R., & Nosek, B. A. (2004). A decade of system justification theory: Accumulated evidence of conscious and unconscious bolstering of the status quo. *Political Psychology, 25*, 881–920.

Jost, J. T., & Burgess, D. (2000). Attitudinal ambivalence and the conflict between group and system justification motives in low status groups. *Personality and Social Psychology Bulletin, 26*, 293–305.

Jost, J. T., Pelham, B. W., & Carvallo, M. R. (2002). Non-conscious forms of system justification: Implicit and behavioral preferences for higher status groups. *Journal of Experimental Social Psychology, 38*, 586–602.

Kaiser, C. R., Drury, B. J., Malahy, L. W., & King, K. M. (2011). Nonverbal asymmetry in interracial interactions: Strongly identified Blacks display friendliness, but Whites respond negatively. *Social Psychological and Personality Science, 2*, 554–559.

Kaiser, C. R., Dyrenforth, P. S., & Hagiwara, N. (2006). Why are attributions to discrimination interpersonally costly? A test of system- and group-justifying motivations. *Personality and Social Psychology Bulletin, 32*, 1423–1536.

Kaiser, C. R., & Pratt-Hyatt, J. S. (2009). Distributing prejudice unequally: Do Whites direct their prejudice toward strongly identified minorities? *Journal of Personality and Social Psychology, 96*, 432–445.

Kaiser, C. R., & Wilkins, C. L. (2010). Group identification and prejudice: Theoretical and empirical advances and implications. *Journal of Social Issues, 66*, 461–476.

Katz, I., & Hass, R. G. (1988). Racial ambivalence and American value conflict: Correlational and priming studies of dual cognitive structures. *Journal of Personality and Social Psychology, 55*, 893–905.

Klandermans, B. (2002). How group identification helps to overcome the dilemma of collective action. *American Behavioral Scientist, 45*, 887–900.

Leach, C. W., Mosquera, P. M. R., Vliek, M. L. W., & Hirt, E. (2010). Group devaluation and group identification. *Journal of Social Issues, 66*, 535–552.

Lerner, M. J. (1980). *The belief in a just world: A fundamental delusion.* New York: Plenum Press.

Livingston, R. W., & Pearce, N. A. (2009). The teddy-bear effect. *Psychological Science, 20*, 1229–1236.

Luhtanen, R., & Crocker, J. (1992). A collective self-esteem scale: Self-evaluation of one's social identity. *Personality and Social Psychology Bulletin, 18*, 302–318.

Lynn, M., Sturman, M., Ganley, C., Adams, E., Douglas, M., & McNeil, J. (2008). Consumer racial discrimination in tipping: A replication and extension. *Journal of Applied Social Psychology, 38*, 1045–1060.

Major, B., Gramzow, R. H., McCoy, S. K., Levin, S., Schmader, T., & Sidanius, J. (2002). Perceiving personal discrimination: The role of group status and legitimizing ideology. *Journal of Personality and Social Psychology, 82*, 269–282.

Major, B., Kaiser, C. R., O'Brien, L. T., & McCoy, S. K. (2007). Perceived discrimination as worldview threat or worldview confirmation: Implications for self-esteem. *Journal of Personality and Social Psychology, 92*, 1068–1086.

Major, B., Quinton, W. J., & McCoy, S. K. (2002). Antecedents and consequences of attributions to discrimination: Theoretical and empirical advances. In

L. Berkowitz (Ed.), *Advances in experimental social psychology* (Vol. 34, pp. 251–330). San Diego, CA: Academic Press.

Major, B., Quinton, W. J., McCoy, S. K., & Schmader, T. (2000). Reducing prejudice: The target's perspective. In S. Oskamp (Ed.), *Reducing prejudice and discrimination* (pp. 211–237). Mahwah, NJ: Lawrence Erlbaum Associates.

Major, B., Quinton, W. J., & Schmader, T. (2003). Attributions to discrimination and self-esteem: Impact of group identification and situational ambiguity. *Journal of Experimental Social Psychology, 39,* 220–231.

Marques, J. M., Yzerbyt, V. Y., & Leyens, J.-P. (1988). The "black sheep" effect: Extremity of judgments towards in-group members as a function of group identification. *European Journal of Social Psychology, 18,* 1–16.

McCoy, S. K., & Major, B. (2003). Group identification moderates emotional responses to perceived prejudice. *Personality and Social Psychology Bulletin, 29,* 1005–1017.

Miller, C. T., & Kaiser, C. R. (2001). A theoretical perspective on coping with stigma. *Journal of Social Issues, 57,* 73–92.

Miller, C. T., & Myers, A. M. (1998). Compensating for prejudice: How heavyweight people (and others) control outcomes despite prejudice. In J. K. Swim & C. Stangor (Eds.), *Prejudice: The target's perspective* (pp. 191–218). San Diego, CA: Academic Press.

Monteith, M. J., Ashburn-Nardo, L., Voils, C. I., & Czopp, A. M. (2002). Putting the brakes on prejudice: On the development and operation of cues for control. *Journal of Personality and Social Psychology, 83,* 1029–1050.

Operario, D., & Fiske, S. T. (2001). Ethnic identity moderates perceptions of prejudice: Judgments of personal versus group discrimination and subtle versus blatant bias. *Personality and Social Psychology Bulletin, 27,* 550–561.

Plant, E., & Devine, P. G. (1998). Internal and external motivation to respond without prejudice. *Journal of Personality and Social Psychology, 75,* 811–832.

Quinn, D. M., & Chaudoir, S. R. (2009). Living with a concealable stigmatized identity: The impact of anticipated stigma, centrality, salience, and cultural stigma on psychological distress and health. *Journal of Personality and Social Psychology, 97,* 634–651.

Reskin, B. F., & Roos, P. A. (1990). *Job queues, gender queues: Explaining women's inroads into male occupations.* Philadelphia: Temple University Press.

Richeson, J. A., & Shelton, J. N. (2003). When prejudice does not pay: Effects of interracial contact on executive function. *Psychological Science, 14,* 287–290.

Richeson, J. A., & Shelton, J. N. (2007). Negotiating interracial interactions. *Current Directions in Psychological Science, 16,* 316–320.

Ridgeway, C. L. (2001). Gender, status, and leadership. *Journal of Social Issues, 57,* 637–655.

Schmitt, M. T., & Branscombe, N. R. (2002). The meaning and consequences of perceived discrimination in disadvantaged and privileged social groups. *British Review of Social Psychology, 12,* 167–199.

Sechrist, G. B., & Stangor, C. (2001). Perceived consensus influences intergroup behavior and stereotype accessibility. *Journal of Personality and Social Psychology, 80,* 645–654.

Sellers, R. M., & Shelton, J. N. (2003). The role of racial identity in perceived racial discrimination. *Journal of Personality and Social Psychology, 84,* 1079–1092.

Shapiro, J. R., & Neuberg, S. L. (2008). When do the stigmatized stigmatize? The ironic effects of being accountable to (perceived) majority group prejudice-expression norms. *Journal of Personality and Social Psychology, 95,* 877–898.

Shelton, J., & Richeson, J. A. (2006). Interracial interactions: A relational approach. In L. Berkowitz (Ed.), *Advances in experimental social psychology* (Vol. 38, pp. 121–181). San Diego, CA: Academic Press.

Shelton, J. N., Richeson, J. A., & Salvatore, J. (2005). Expecting to be the target of prejudice: Implications for interethnic interactions. *Personality and Social Psychology Bulletin, 31*, 1189–1202.

Shelton, J. N., Richeson, J. A., Salvatore, J., & Trawalter, S. (2005). Ironic effects of racial bias during interracial interactions. *Psychological Science, 16*, 397–402.

Shelton, J. N., & Sellers, R. M. (2000). Situational stability and variability in African American racial identity. *Journal of Black Psychology, 26*, 27–50.

Shin, P. S., & Gulati, M. (2011). Showcasing diversity. *North Carolina Law Review, 89*, 1017–1053.

Spalding, K. E., & Kaiser, C. R. (2012). *Climbing and lifting or climbing and kicking: Group identification moderates treatment of ingroup subordinates.* Manuscript in preparation for submission.

Spears, R., Jetten, J., & Doosje, B. (2001). The (il)legitimacy of ingroup bias: From social reality to social resistance. In J. T. Jost & B. Major (Eds.), *The psychology of legitimacy: Emerging perspectives on ideology, justice, and intergroup relations* (pp. 332–362). New York: Cambridge University Press.

Steele, C. M. (1988). The psychology of self-affirmation: Sustaining the integrity of the self. In L. Berkowitz (Ed.), *Advances in experimental social psychology* (Vol. 21, pp. 261–302). San Diego, CA: Academic Press.

Steele, C. (2010). *Whistling Vivaldi: And other clues to how stereotypes affect us.* New York: W. W. Norton.

Steele, C. M., & Aronson, J. (1995). Stereotype threat and the intellectual test performance of African Americans. *Journal of Personality and Social Psychology, 69*, 797–811.

Tajfel, H., & Turner, J. C. (1979). An integrative theory of intergroup conflict. In W. G. Austin & S. Worchel (Eds.), *The social psychology of intergroup relations*. Monterey, CA: Brooks/Cole.

Tesser, A. (1988). Toward a self-evaluative maintenance model of behavior. In L. Berkowitz (Ed.), *Advances in experimental social psychology* (Vol. 21, pp. 181–227). San Diego, CA: Academic Press).

Turner, J. C., Hogg, M. A., Oakes, P. J., Reicher, S. D., & Wetherell, M. S. (1987). Rediscovering the social group: A self-categorization theory. *American Journal of Sociology, 94*, 1514–1516.

Van Laar, C., Bleeker, D., & Ellemers, N. (2012). *Ingroup and outgroup support for upward mobility: Divergent responses to ingroup identification in low status groups.* Manuscript submitted for publication.

Van Zomeren, M., Postmes, T., & Spears, R. (2008). Toward an integrative social identity model of collective action: A quantitative research synthesis of three sociopsychological perspectives. *Psychological Bulletin, 134*, 504–535.

Vorauer, J. D. (2006). An information search model of evaluative concerns in intergroup interaction. *Psychological Review, 113*, 862–886.

Vorauer, J. D., & Turpie, C. A. (2004). Disruptive effects of vigilance on dominant group members' treatment of outgroup members: Choking versus shining under pressure. *Journal of Personality and Social Psychology, 87*, 384–399.

Weiner, B. (1985). An attributional theory of achievement motivation and emotion. *Psychological Review, 92*, 548–573.

Wilson, T. D., & Brekke, N. (1994). Mental contamination and mental correction: Unwanted influences on judgments and evaluations. *Psychological Bulletin, 116,* 117–142.

Yogeeswaran, K., Adelman, L., Parker, M., & Dasgupta, N. (2012). *In the eyes of the beholder: White Americans' national identification predicts differential reactions to ethnic identity expressions.* Manuscript submitted for publication.

Yogeeswaran, K., Dasgupta, N., Adelman, L., Eccleston, A., & Parker, M. T. (2011). To be or not to be (ethnic): Public vs. private expressions of ethnic identification differentially impact national inclusion of White and non-White groups. *Journal of Experimental Social Psychology, 47,* 908–914.

11

Oh the Places We Should Go!
Stereotyping and Prejudice in (Real) Mixed Interactions

EDEN KING

George Mason University

MIKKI HEBL

Rice University

As we have moved increasingly into the laboratory and away from the study of behavior, I believe we have been eroding the public's perception of the relevance of our findings to their daily activities. One of the best aspects of field research into naturally occurring behavior is that such relevance is manifest.

(Cialdini, 2009, p. 6)

In his recent "break up" with academic social psychology, Robert Cialdini cited its focus on laboratory over field research as a primary reason for his retirement. Despite recognition of the power of the situation and the value of triangulation of methods, a persistent favoring of tightly controlled laboratory studies conducted on college students over field studies conducted on general adult samples is evident in the premier social journals (see Henry, 2008; Norenzayan & Heine, 2005). One area in which this trend is problematic is research on stereotyping and prejudice, wherein scholars generally try to understand and improve interactions that happen in the real world by studying individuals in the lab (Hebl & Dovidio, 2005). Indeed, policy-makers and human resource personnel question whether the large body of experimental research findings on discrimination has any real-world implications (see Landy, 2008). The disconnect between the inherently social implications of this research and the methods we generally use might be reconciled through high-quality field research.

In this chapter, we will point out the potential value of field research for understanding stereotyping and prejudice, particularly as it fuels new questions and directions. In so doing, we note the folly of relying solely on laboratory research for understanding complex social interactions, given the lack of alignment between stated attitudes and behavior (see Crandall & Eshleman, 2003). We begin by briefly discussing a range of experimental approaches to understanding stereotyping and prejudice and then describe the frameworks and findings that have been applied to understanding these interactions in field research. We will also articulate new ideas that have been and can be drawn from field research on stereotyping and prejudice.

STEREOTYPING AND PREJUDICE IN EXPERIMENTAL RESEARCH

In their very first research methods classes, undergraduate psychology majors learn about the tradeoffs between experimental and correlational research and memorize the "correlation does not imply causation" mantra (see Black, 1955). Deeper appreciation for the implications of strategic methodological choices may not emerge until much later; indeed, some might argue that social psychology journal editors have not yet developed a full appreciation for a range of methodological choices. A content analysis of social psychological publications on prejudice showed that all but about 10% of articles in the *Journal of Personality and Social Psychology*, the *Journal of Experimental Social Psychology*, and *Personality and Social Psychology Bulletin* relied on student samples (Henry, 2008). Here, we describe the unique insights regarding stereotyping and prejudice that can be garnered through research using methodologies that vary with regard to experimental control and ecological validity (see Figure 11.1). We use our own research on weight-based stereotyping and prejudice to illustrate these tradeoffs and ultimately to advocate for more efforts to expand research that maximizes both experimental control and ecological validity (Quadrant IV); we believe that our best single studies are those that can be classified as experimental field research and that our most compelling papers involve a triangulation of methodological approaches.

Scholars of stereotyping and prejudice, many of whom are social psychologists, rely heavily on experimental research in laboratory settings with undergraduate participants.[1] As exemplified by the description of Hebl and Turchin's (2005) study on weight-based biases, studies of prejudice and stereotyping

---

1 We begin with the classic experimentalist perspective (Quadrant II), ignoring Quadrant I, as it implies low-quality research of which we hoped we would not find examples.

Methodological Choices

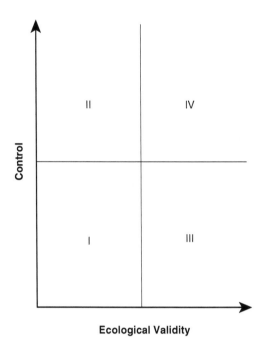

Figure 11.1   Methodological choices ranging in control and ecological validity.

often involve exposing undergraduate students to written stimuli ("paper people"):

> [Participants] were handed a writing utensil and an experimental booklet containing the instructions, the photograph stimuli, and the response sheet. The instructions indicated that participants would be viewing and giving their impressions of individuals provided on the response sheet. They then viewed 12 stimulus targets [which depicted previously tested thin, medium, and heavy women] presented in random order and rated them on the seven dimensions.
> (Hebl & Turchin, 2005)

The field has advanced substantially as a result of such studies, as they allow direct attribution of outcomes to social identity characteristics and other carefully manipulated factors. Take, for example, the majority of research on the phenomenon of stereotype threat. We have amassed a large body of data to demonstrate that (1) people behave and perform differently when in conditions under which stereotypes are relevant, (2) there are specific explanations for (mediators of) its effects, and (3) there are situational and individual factors that determine whether the effect emerges (see Schmader, Johns, & Forbes, 2008).

Nevertheless, the generalizabilty of these findings often comes into question in critical real-world settings such as cognitive ability testing in the employment setting (Sackett, Hardison, & Cullen, 2004; see also Stricker & Ward, 2004).

More recently, this type of scholarship has begun to address the neurological bases of prejudice and the experience of discrimination (see Amodio, 2009). For example, research in social neuroscience has revealed that the amygdala is activated under conditions of intergroup evaluations (Amodio, Harmon-Jones, & Devine, 2003). As another example, Derks, Inzlicht, and Kang (2008) explored the neurological sequelae of stereotype threat-inducing stimuli compared to neutral stimuli. This important area of research will tell us a great deal about the neurological correlates of stereotyping and potentially point to avenues through which attitude change can occur. Unfortunately, however, it tells us little about how people will behave outside of the scanning machine when they actually interact with targets of prejudice. In fact, one of our favorite quotes that illustrates this problem nicely is by Gilbert and Hixon (1991, p. 516), who state: "If we really want to know how persons think about persons, we may have to introduce our participants to some."

HIGH CONTROL, MODERATE ECOLOGICAL VALIDITY

Participants learned they would be assigned to the role of trainer or trainee and that they would engage in a computer-mediated training interaction with a partner who was in a different state (in reality both participants were in the same lab space). Thus, trainers and trainees never actually saw one another... Each trainer was presented with a digital photograph ostensibly depicting the trainee. The photographs were created using a Size 8 model (average weight for her height) seated on a couch... In one photograph, each confederate model posed as her natural size. In the second photograph, each confederate model posed wearing a professionally constructed obesity prosthesis underneath her clothing, generating a Size 22 figure.

(Shapiro, King, & Quiñones, 2007)

It is important to note that the categories implied in Figure 11.1 are not dichotomous and, instead, that both control and ecological validity might be better classified on a spectrum. In an effort to improve the generalizability of their findings, many experimentalists go to great lengths to create situations in the laboratory that might be more ecologically valid. In the study quoted above, participants engaged in genuine interactions that occurred virtually to allow for experimental manipulation of body size (Shapiro et al., 2007). Other researchers explore such interactions by assessing reactions to highly trained confederates or other actual participants who vary with regard to devalued social identity characteristics (e.g., gender, race). From these studies, we learn about intergroup interactions in whatever specific situation is created in the lab. Indeed, by showing that test performance was worse for participants who interacted with someone from a different ethnic group than for those who interacted with someone from their own ethnic group, Richeson and Trawalter (2005) highlighted the cognitive and emotional experiences associated with intergroup interactions. However, there are boundary conditions about the generalizability of even these kinds of rich findings; participants are typically students who are strangers but share a college affiliation in the context of a psychology lab. This raises questions about what happens when interaction partners know each other, when they share no relevant identity, or when they interact in natural settings.

LOW CONTROL, HIGH ECOLOGICAL VALIDITY

Approximately six weeks prior to attending their leadership development program, [CEOs, vice-presidents, and other organizational leaders] were asked to complete electronic survey measures on their performance ... personality ..., health-related behaviors, and demographics ... [Performance] assessment[s] were also sent to (and completed by) the direct reports, peers, and bosses that participants chose to serve as raters of their performance in this program. In addition ... participants were required to take part in a physical exam conducted by medical and certified fitness professionals ... regarding participants' physical activity, height, and weight.

(King, Rogelberg, et al., 2011)

Valuable real-world evidence of discrimination can be derived from field research that is typically situated in economics, sociology, and organizational psychology (Quadrant III). Such research typically relies on large-scale surveys or census information to make conclusions about discrepancies in jobs, salaries, and positions as a function of social-identity categories after controlling for potential confounds statistically. For example, after controlling for education, experience, occupation, and industry, sociologists conclude that women earn 91 cents for every dollar earned by men (Blau & Kahn, 2007). Some studies are even able to control for the potentially confounding effects of performance or productivity: Black men earn significantly less than White men even after controlling for human capital differences (Fugazza, 2003) and performance (Coleman, 2003; Kahn & Sherer, 1988). In our study quoted above, we were able to test for differences in performance evaluations of top executives as a function of their waist size and BMI after controlling for potential differences in personality and physical activity. These field studies provide compelling evidence that women, mothers, Black men, and obese people are discriminated against in the real world, but they cannot completely rule out alternative explanations that would be controlled methodologically in a laboratory study.

Field studies can also be useful in assessing genuine relationships as they develop over time. In explorations of same- and mixed-race college roommates over the course of a semester, Nicole Shelton and her colleagues have shown that ethnic minorities who have more negative racial attitudes also have fewer positive interactions with White roommates (Shelton & Richeson, 2006), that expectations of prejudice can lead to more negative interethnic interactions (Shelton, Richeson, & Salvatore, 2005), that mixed-race friendships decline over time when partners perceive low commonality (West, Pearson, Dovidio, Shelton, & Trail, 2009), that a roommate's anxiety about mixed-race interactions is a strong predictor of the other roommate's anxiety (West, Shelton, & Trail, 2009), and that efforts to build intimacy account for decreases in positive emotions among mixed-race roommates (West et al., 2009). These studies serve as examples of what can be learned about stereotyping and prejudice from high-quality field studies.

MODERATE/HIGH CONTROL, HIGH ECOLOGICAL VALIDITY

Ten female confederates (all Caucasian, 19-28 years of age) played the role of customers. In order to participate as customer confederates, the women had to be average-weight for their height, have somewhat round faces, and look natural in a size 22 professionally constructed prosthesis . . . The customer confederate turned on the tape recorder in her purse and then entered the assigned store. Once the customer passed the threshold of the store, the observer began timing the service lag time (time between the customer confederate entrance and a salesperson's offer of help) with the stopwatch function of her wristwatch . . . Once the customer confederate made contact with a salesperson, the confederate explained that she was looking to buy a gift for her sister who "was celebrating her 20th birthday and liked traditional and feminine things." Customer-observer pairs . . . [completed] questionnaires separately.

(King, Shapiro, Hebl, Singletary, & Turner, 2006)

We contend that experimental field studies can maximize both control and ecological validity (Quadrant IV). In the research described above, we were able to assess actual, behavioral responses to a target depending on their stigmatized status in customer service interactions (King et al., 2006). In a similar study on job applicants (Hebl, Foster, Mannix, & Dovidio, 2002), we were able to overcome potential experimenter biases by ensuring that confederates were blind to their condition; they wore hats that identified them as either gay or presumably heterosexual (i.e., "Gay and Proud" or "Texan and Proud").

These experimental field studies have strengths that are similar to the "audit studies" conducted by sociologists. In one such study, Bertrand and Mullainathan (2003) sent identical resumés labeled as from varying races and genders (i.e., Black: Lakisha, Jamal; White: Emily, Greg) in response to actual job postings. They found a 50% callback discrepancy between White and Black applicants across multiple cities and a wide range of jobs. This finding may be more compelling than that described in one of our own lab experiments using evaluations of fictitious resumés by undergraduate participants (King, Mendoza, Madera, Hebl, & Knight, 2006). In a similar audit study, Correll, Benard, and Paik (2007) considered the influence of gender and parental status on job callbacks. Whereas there was no difference in the callbacks received by men who were fathers and those who had no children, women who were described as childless received more than twice as many callbacks than did those who were mothers.

Experimental field research can help to address questions about how people behave in the real world without losing the power of attributing causal connections. Importantly, experimental field research may yield strikingly different conclusions than similar research conducted through other approaches. A classic example of this phenomenon in the intergroup literature was conducted by LaPiere (1934). In this study, the authors contrasted the behavior of hotel and restaurant staff when directly visited by ethnic minorities with the written responses to letters asking whether ethnic minorities would be allowed to stay at their establishment. The results showed that actual behaviors were starkly different than those that were described in written letters. More recent research reveals that participants show a similar disconnect in indicating that they clearly would not discriminate against applicants who disclose that they have survived childhood cancer but that their behavior indicates they do discriminate (Martinez, White, Mover, & Hebl, 2011). One further example is a series of masterfully constructed laboratory experiments that examined Whites' evaluations of Black and Hispanic individuals who were either strongly or weakly identified with their ethnic group (Kaiser & Pratt-Hyatt, 2009). The results suggested that experimental manipulations of the strength of fictitious targets' identification led to more negative evaluations by White participants. This can be contrasted with our own findings in a comparable experimental field study (Barron, Hebl, & King, 2011). When job applicants wore hats that indicated a strong ethnic identification (i.e., "Black and Proud" or "Black Student Association"), they were actually treated more positively by White managers than those in a control condition (i.e., a blank hat). We interpreted the stark difference in our findings to reflect, at least in part, the fact that ethnic identification might have a different meaning in a real-world, face-to-face job application context than in a laboratory setting. Consequently, we propose that such findings illustrate the need for research on stereotyping and prejudice outside of the laboratory. In the next section, we discuss specific contexts that we think should be explored in future research.

SO WHERE SHOULD WE GO? STEREOTYPING AND PREJUDICE IN THE FIELD

The two in-groups themselves set the stage for the friction phase of intergroup relations. During the last days of Stage 1, both the Rattlers and Eagles became insistent in their desire to challenge the other group of boys to play competitive games, especially baseball. The design of the experiment required a clear-cut stabilization of a definite structure within each group. While the staff ascertained this, the Rattlers and Eagles became impatient in their desire to engage in competitive games. When the staff members informed each group that there was another group in the camp area, the challenge was unanimous and enthusiastic... When the Rattlers heard the other group playing on "their" ball field, they made remarks expressing the feeling that they considered others playing there as intrusion. Even without coming into physical contact

with "those boys at the other end of the camp," the Rattlers had built up a
highly competitive mood in relation to them.
(Sherif, Harvey, White, Hood, & Sherif, 1954/1961)

In their inspirational field research quoted above, Sherif and his colleagues
(1954/1961) demonstrated that powerful negative outgroup attitudes and behaviors can emerge between two groups of young White boys at a summer camp.
This illustrates one of the most compelling aspects of social psychology: that it is
relevant for understanding interpersonal dynamics in any context in which individuals interact. Examining a full range of contexts is particularly crucial for the
area of stereotyping and prejudice, since these negative interpersonal dynamics
can be extremely destructive in any one of these settings. Social psychologists are
keenly aware of the power of the situation and thus should explore a range of
situations in which meaningful social interactions take place, including public
spaces, doctors' offices, jury rooms, retail settings, schools, and workplaces.

Public Spaces

Imagine all the places you go on any given day. You might walk through the
park before you hop on the bus to get to a museum. In each of these public
locations, you likely engage in verbal or nonverbal communication with the people you encounter. Our biases may be reflected by how far away we stand from
another person in line at the supermarket checkout or with much more overt
behaviors. These are everyday interactions in which we may let down our guard
and let our subtle preferences emerge (see Feagin, 1991).

Limited experimental field research has begun to explore stereotyping and
prejudice in such interactions. For example, in one study, confederates in either
pro-gay or neutral T-shirts asked people on the sidewalk for change for a park-
ing meter (Hendren & Blank, 2009). Confirming research on heterosexist attitudes, people were less likely to help the confederate when they wore a pro-gay
shirt than when they wore a neutral shirt.

Somewhat more common is experimental field research on strategies for
reducing prejudice in these public settings. As an example, a longitudinal
experimental field study showed that listening to a radio show featuring messages attempting to reduce prejudice, violence, and trauma (rather than a radio
show about health) both changed people's perceptions of what constituted such
behaviors and brought those behaviors more in line with the show's reflected
social norms (Paluck, 2009). In one of our own studies (Zitek & Hebl, 2007),
experimenters and confederates engaged in a scripted interaction to determine
whether people in public settings could be influenced to respond to a series of
questions in less prejudiced ways. When confederates clearly show egalitarian
preferences, participants display less prejudice. Because survey research shows
the negative consequences of everyday discrimination (e.g., Swim, Hyers,
Cohen, & Ferguson, 2001), research on prejudice in public spaces is critical.

Doctors' Offices

Persistent disparities in health and health outcomes between White and non-White people necessitate attention to biases in the health-care system. Indeed, critical interactions between physicians and patients can be affected by prejudice and stereotyping. Green and his colleagues (2007) found that internal medicine and emergency medicine residents with higher pro-White implicit biases were more likely to give an effective medication to White patients than to Black patients when they displayed symptoms of a heart attack. In another study focusing on the target's perspective of such interactions, Black patients rated interactions with physicians more negatively when those physicians were high rather than low in aversive racism (Penner et al., 2009). Physician biases have also been shown—in manipulated surveys of physicians themselves and in evaluative surveys by patients following their interactions with doctors—to impact their responses to (and treatment of) patients on the basis of their weight (e.g., Hebl & Xu, 2001; Hebl, Xu, & Mason, 2003).

Physician biases can have devastating effects on patients and their health, and research utilizing an experimental field approach may be helpful in teasing apart idiosyncratic differences in these interactions. For example, researchers might utilize "standardized patients" who act much like "secret shoppers" or confederates, following a standardized script in real interactions with physicians. In addition, such research might be useful in designing and testing the relative effectiveness of psychoeducational interventions.

Jury Rooms

In much the same way as disparities exist in health, ethnic minorities are hugely overrepresented in the U.S. penal system. As an example, according to the 2009 Uniform Crime Reports—a nationwide summary of data on crimes reported to law enforcement—28% of arrests were of African-American people, who comprise only 12.8% of the national population. Starker contrasts can be seen in data that show that African Americans comprise 40% of sentenced inmates (Bureau of Justice Statistics, 2011). Scholars have found strong evidence that stereotyping contributes to this discrepancy.

In a recent meta-analysis of research on mock juries' decision-making, Mitchell and his/her colleagues (Mitchell, Haw, Pfeifer, & Meissner, 2005) found that White defendants fare better than Black defendants. This corresponds to statistics from the Department of Justice that (arguably) show that Black defendants tend to receive harsher penalties than do White defendants (Bureau of Justice Statistics, 2011). Sam Sommers and his colleagues have studied the behavior of jury members and determined that, for example, mock juries comprised of diverse members were more likely to discuss the facts of the case, and were more lenient toward Black defendants, than all-White juries (Sommers, 2006) and that White mock jurors are more likely to demonstrate racial prejudice when race is not salient in the case (Sommers & Ellsworth,

2001). These and other findings confirm that stereotyping and prejudice likely play a role in real juries' deliberations and conclusions. Pairing such experiments with analyses of archival data on actual juries' decisions leads to strong arguments about the impact of racial stereotyping on ethnic disparities in the legal system.

To explore these disparities further, we would go beyond jury rooms into judicial chambers. This is a particularly touchy subject, given that the livelihood of judges relies on their pledge to be impartial arbiters of justice. Moreover, to admit that these impartial arbiters of justice may be vulnerable to the effects of stereotypes and prejudice is to admit that there may be flaws in the justice system as a whole. Some scholars of law and society and law and psychology have attempted to peek into judicial chambers by using the judges themselves as participants in experimental studies (see Rachlinski, Johnson, Wistrich, & Guthrie, 2008). More commonly, however, biases have been inferred only by the distribution of outcomes to defendants (e.g., Robbennolt, 2002). Here, too, pairing outcome data with the findings from experiments using actual judges as participants provides particularly strong evidence for the effect of bias on judicial decisions. Race, gender, and other biases continue to manifest in the judicial system, making this a critical area for our research (see Wrightsman, 1999, 2006).

Retail Settings

From a practical perspective, sales organizations should strive to make all customer service interactions as positive as possible in the interest of maximizing their sales receipts. Nevertheless, experimental field research has shown that even these kinds of interactions are plagued with the insidious effects of prejudice and stereotypes. Indeed, our cursory review of the literature suggests that experimental field research may be the most plentiful in the context of sales settings; thus, these studies can serve as prototypes for studies in other situations.

For example, when Black and White confederates in a "fair housing audit" requested information about housing, Black home-seekers were told that one-third fewer units were available than were White home-seekers (Yinger, 1986). As another example, an audit study at car dealerships showed race and gender discrepancies in the experiences of customers: White males were quoted lower starting prices than were Black or female shoppers (Ayres & Siegelman, 1995). In another traditional sales setting, female shopper-confederates encountered worse treatment in the form of decreased eye contact, rudeness, and hostility when they wore an obesity prosthesis (King et al., 2006).

In addition to demonstrating the incidence of discrimination, these studies provide evidence regarding the factors that underlie such experiences. In Ayres and Siegelman's (1995) work, there was some indication that car salespeople's quotes were based on their stereotypes about what White and Black people are able to pay. In our study on obesity bias (King et al., 2006), we found that discrimination was reduced when the confederate-shoppers claimed to be actively attempting to improve their appearance (e.g., by dieting and exercising). This demonstrates that beliefs regarding complacency likely underlie the stigma of obesity. Studying stereotyping and prejudice in sales settings has contributed and will continue to contribute to a broader understanding of intergroup relations.

Primary Schools

Studies of children in school contexts have clarified that prejudice emerges long before study participants are college sophomores, that the effects of stereotyping in school settings can impact a lifetime of achievement, and, more hopefully, that interventions can be effectively implemented to support diverse students. Foundational experimental field research in educational psychology explored the aftershocks of desegregation. Rosenfield, Sheehan, Marcus, and Stephan (1981) found that the proportion of ethnic minority students in a classroom was related to intergroup friendship formation, particularly when the White and minority students had similar achievement levels. Field research has also shown that the cognitive processes related to categorization develop across childhood in such a way that means the automatization of prejudice emerges in adolescence (Degner & Wentura, 2010).

If people learn about and perpetuate prejudice in school settings, schools may be an ideal place in which to target prejudice reduction efforts. Indeed, Aboud and Fenwick (2002) found that school programs designed directly to address race and prejudice can improve racial attitudes when supportive peer relationships are constructed. The argument that real change in intergroup attitudes and behavior begins with our children is compelling and hopeful.

Workplace Contexts

Work is a defining aspect of social life, as it gives rise to both status and identity. It is wholly appropriate, then, that scholars of stereotyping and prejudice should focus on the workplace as a context wherein discrimination emerges and perpetuates inequities. It is through research on the workplace that we have learned about contemporary manifestations of discrimination as incivility (Cortina, 2008), about the pernicious effects of demographic underrepresentation (Kanter, 1977; King, Hebl, George, & Matusik, 2010), and about real-world strategies for reducing inequities (such as diversity training and mentoring programs; Kalev, Dobbin, & Kelly, 2006).

Moreover, of critical importance is that research conducted in non-work settings does not always generalize to work situations. As mentioned previously, our own research on manifest ethnic identification conducted in job application contexts (Barron et al., 2011) contradicts similar research done in the lab (Kaiser & Pratt-Hyatt, 2009). But it is not just a "lab" versus "field" study distinction. In another study, we contrasted the experiences that women encountered when they wore a pregnancy prosthesis and applied for jobs to those in which they wore a pregnancy prosthesis and asked for help in a customer service setting (Hebl, King, Glick, Kazama, & Singletary, 2007). Our findings show starkly different experiences depending on context: Whereas pregnant shoppers experienced overly positive interactions (such as people saying, "Sweetie, let me help you with that!"), pregnant job applicants encountered hostility (people making incredulous comments such as "*She* is looking for a *job*?"). We interpreted these findings to suggest that hostile and benevolent sexism manifest in interpersonal punishments and rewards (respectively) to maintain traditional feminine gender roles.

To develop a comprehensive picture regarding actual experiences of stereotyping and prejudice, it is critical that we consider the emergence of these phenomena across situations and contexts. Exploring discrimination in coffee shops and cubicles will help us understand what actually happens in the real world and will give us clues about how to respond to this dynamic, yet persistent, challenge.

FUTURE DIRECTIONS

We fully acknowledge the value of other types of research and do not suggest the end of paper-and-pencil, laboratory, and other traditional methods . . . The increased reliance on interactive paradigms [however] will enable researchers to learn different sorts of information, to ask different types of questions, and to observe different sets of dependent measures (e.g., verbal vs. nonverbal, self-reports vs. actual behavior).

(Hebl & Dovidio, 2005)

Clearly, all methodologies have some value. The use of traditional methodologies has yielded volumes of insights about stereotypes and prejudice. But researchers may be limited in the questions they ask and the answers they find by restricting themselves to the use of only convenient and readily available laboratory settings, methods, and research participants. We propose, in this review, that there are so many more places researchers could go and that future research on stereotypes and prejudice should push beyond past settings of inquiry.

There are some critical avenues for future research, and one of the most important areas is that of identifying prejudice and discrimination remediation strategies. For instance, most Fortune 500 companies and major employers within the United States use diversity training programs, and many are mandatory, but the changes that they produce are often subtle to nonexistent (Kalev, Dobbin, & Kelly, 2006; Rudolph, 2010). The time is ripe for accumulating an empirical body of research on successful diversity training and other remediation strategies that individuals and organizations might adopt. Research is needed that goes beyond assessing simple attitude change in the lab to identifying critical content of such training, looking both at how actual person-to-person interactions are affected and at how factors such as organizational climate and manager buy-in might further influence the success of such training. As Rudolph (2010) notes, such research might further provide a guide for developing diversity and anti-bullying training in educational systems (e.g., Aronson & Patnoe, 1997). Kalev et al.'s (2006) survey data from 708 organizations further indicates that establishing social responsibility or designating an executive or task force for diversity may be particularly successful. Others have identified that the role of allies may be particularly effective (e.g., Zitek & Hebl, 2007). However, the empirical data on diversity training and other remediation strategies are simply lacking.

WHEREVER WE GO, THERE ARE *SOMETIMES* TRADEOFFS

In this chapter, we have made a case for the importance of considering external/ecological validity and not necessarily at the expense of internal validity. However, we are not suggesting that everyone should hang up their proverbial lab coats and leave their laboratories. If the zeitgest of conducting research were to collect data in real-world settings, we would likely be inspired to write another chapter about the utmost importance of internal validity and how we can easily gain it from laboratory settings.

In promoting researchers to go beyond their laboratory walls, then, we caution readers that experimental field research also can be limited. For instance, some of the experimental studies conducted in the field do not apply blind or even double-blind methodology (e.g., King et al., 2006), thereby introducing the increased possibility of experimenter bias. However, there are ways that researchers can deal with some of these limitations (see King et al., 2006; Quillian, 2006). In addition, experimental studies conducted in the field may capture participants who do not actually know one another, which may be a limitation in that people act differently when they do not know one another's history (see Landy, 2008). Furthermore, going beyond the safe laboratory can be tricky, requiring research assistance and introducing logistical challenges, and the lack of control can produce anxiety.

As with the college samples that are typically used in tightly controlled laboratory settings, there are limitations in the results we would obtain if we relied solely on data collection in the places we would like researchers to go. For instance, we know that participants exhibit very different behaviors in public than they do in private. Jury rooms have higher levels of anxiety and stakes than do laboratories. And workplace settings evoke very different behaviors from participants than do less professional and more personal settings. In addition, the people we might study in these places would not necessarily reflect the general population as a whole. Participants in doctors' offices may be older, sicker, and a more vulnerable clientele than college students (or people in general). Retail settings may include samples of participants who are wealthy, have time on their hands, or are more reckless with money. There are obviously great age restrictions where participants in primary schools are concerned. However, the limitations of any one sample could be nicely eliminated by collecting data across paradigms, settings, and differing ecological conditions.

Thus, we encourage researchers to continue using internally valid methodologies but, in addition, to consider balancing, blending, and introducing such methodologies with ones that are *also*, *sometimes*, and *more* externally valid. In this way, we do not have to compromise either the power of our theories or our ability to examine boundary conditions, identify underlying mechanisms, and test competing theories in ways that we know really work outside the laboratory.

CONCLUSION

Ultimately, we believe that what is critical is to capture the interaction from multiple perspectives and multiple approaches. We encourage researchers to use triangulation (Leslie, King, Bradley, & Hebl, 2008) and study the same phenomena from multiple perspectives, paradigms, and settings (see also Hebl & Dovidio, 2005). In so doing, we may very well uncover new and generalizable insights that hold both within and beyond the Ivory Tower.

REFERENCES

Aboud, F. E., & Fenwick, V. (2002). Exploring and evaluating school-based interventions to reduce prejudice. *Journal of Social Issues, 55*, 767–785. doi: 10.1111/0022-4537.00146

Amodio, D. M. (2009). Intergroup anxiety effects on the control of racial stereotypes: A psychoneuroendocrine analysis. *Journal of Experimental Social Psychology, 45*, 60–67. doi: 10.1080/10463280801927937

Amodio, D. M., Harmon-Jones, E., & Devine, P. G. (2003). Individual differences in the activation and control of affective race bias as assessed by startle eyeblink response and self-report. *Journal of Personality and Social Psychology, 84*, 738–753. doi: 10.1037/0022-3514.84.4.738

Aronson, E., & Patnoe, S. (1997). *The jigsaw classroom: Building cooperation in the classroom* (2nd ed.). New York: Addison Wesley Longman.

Ayres, I., & Siegelman, P. (1995). Race and gender discrimination in bargaining for a new car. *American Economic Review, 85*, 304–321.

Barron, L. G., Hebl, M., & King, E. B. (2011). Effects of manifest ethnic identification on employment discrimination. *Cultural Diversity and Ethnic Minority Psychology, 17*, 23–30. doi: 10.1037/a0021439

Bertrand, M., & Mullainathan, S. (2003). Are Emily and Greg more employable than Lakisha and Jamal? A field experiment on labor market discrimination. *American Economic Review, 94*, 991–1013.

Black, V. (1955). Laboratory versus field research in psychology and the social sciences. *British Journal for the Philosophy of Science, 5*, 319–330.

Blau, F. D., & Kahn, L. M. (2007). The gender pay gap: Have women gone as far as they can? *Academy of Management Perspectives, 21*, 7–23.

Bureau of Justice Statistics (2011). Prisoners in 2011. Retrieved from http://bjs.ojp. usdoj.gov/index.cfm?ty=pbdetail&iid=4559

Cialdini, R. B. (2009). We have to break up. *Perspectives on Psychological Science, 4*, 5–6.

Coleman, M. G. (2003). Job skill and Black male wage discrimination. *Social Science Quarterly, 84*, 892–906.

Correll, S. J., Benard, S., & Paik, I. (2007). Getting a job: Is there a motherhood penalty? *American Journal of Sociology, 112*, 1297–1338.

Cortina, L. M. (2008). Unseen injustice: Incivility as modern discrimination in organizations. *Academy of Management Review, 33*, 55–75.

Crandall, C. S., & Eshleman, A. (2003). A justification-suppression model of the expression and experience of prejudice. *Psychological Bulletin, 129*, 414–446.

Degner, J., & Wentura, D. (2010). Automatic prejudice in childhood and early adolescence. *Journal of Personality and Social Psychology, 98*, 356–374. doi: 10.1037/a0017993

Derks, B., Inzlicht, M., & Kang, S. (2008). The neuroscience of stigma and stereotype threat. *Group Processes & Intergroup Relations, 11*, 163–181. doi: 10.1177/1368430207088036

Feagin, J. R. (1991). The continuing significance of race: Antiblack discrimination in public places. *American Sociological Review, 56*, 101–116.

Fugazza, M. (2003). Racial discrimination: Theories, facts and policy. *International Labour Review, 142*, 507–541.

Gilbert, D. T., & Hixon, J. G. (1991). The trouble of thinking: Activation and application of stereotypic beliefs. *Journal of Personality and Social Psychology, 60*, 509–517. doi: 10.1037/0022-3514.60.4.509

Green, A. R., Carney, D. R., Pallin, D. J., Ngo, L. H., Raymond, K. L., Iezzoni, L. I., & Banaji, M. R. (2007). Implicit bias among physicians and its prediction of decisions for Black and White patients. *Journal of General Internal Medicine, 22*, 1231–1238.

Hebl, M. R., & Dovidio, J. F. (2005). Placing the "social" back in the examination of social stigma. *Personality and Social Psychology Review, 9*, 156–182.

Hebl, M. R., Foster, J. B., Mannix, L. M., & Dovidio, J. F. (2002). Formal and interpersonal discrimination: A field study of bias toward homosexual applicants. *Personality and Social Psychology Bulletin, 28*, 815-825.

Hebl, M. R., King, E. B., Glick, P., Kazama, S., & Singletary, S. (2007). Hostile and benevolent reactions toward pregnant women: Complementary interpersonal punishments and rewards that maintain traditional roles. *Journal of Applied Psychology, 92*, 1499–1511.

Hebl, M., & Turchin, J. (2005). The stigma of obesity: What about men? *Basic and Applied Social Psychology, 27*, 267–275.

Hebl, M., & Xu, J. (2001). Weighing the care: Physicians' reactions to the size of a patient. *International Journal of Obesity, 25*, 1246–1252.

Hebl, M., Xu, J., & Mason, M. (2003). Weighing the care: Patients' perceptions of physician care as a function of gender and weight. *International Journal of Obesity, 28*, 269–275.

Hendren, A., & Blank, H. (2009). Prejudiced behavior toward lesbians and gay men. *Social Psychology, 40*, 234–238. doi: 10.1027/1864-9335.40.4.234

Henry, P. J. (2008). College sophomores in the laboratory redux: Influences of a narrow data base on social psychology's view of the nature of prejudice. *Psychological Inquiry, 19*, 49–71.

Kahn, L. M., & Sherer, P. D. (1988). Racial differences in professional basketball players' compensation. *Journal of Labor Economics, 6*, 40–61.

Kaiser, C. R. & Pratt-Hyatt, J. S. (2009). Distributing prejudice unequally: Do Whites direct their prejudice toward strongly identified minorities? *Journal of Personality and Social Psychology, 96*, 432–445.

Kalev, A., Dobbin, F., & Kelly, E. (2006). Best practices or best guesses? Assessing the efficacy of corporate affirmative action and diversity policies. *American Sociological Review, 71*, 589–617.

Kanter, R. M. (1977). *Men and women of the corporation.* New York: Basic Books.

King, E. B., Hebl, M. R., George, J. M., & Matusik, S. F. (2010). Understanding tokenism: Negative consequences of perceived gender discrimination in male-dominated organizations. *Journal of Management, 36*, 537–554.

King, E. B., Mendoza, S., Madera, J., Hebl, M. R., & Knight, J. L. (2006). What's in a name? A multi-ethnic investigation of access discrimination. *Journal of Applied Social Psychology, 36*, 1145–1159.

King, E. B., Rogelberg, S., Hebl, M. R., Braddy, P., Shanock, L., Doerer, S., & Larsen, S. (2011). *When top dogs are fat cats: Do increased waistlines influence performance ratings?* Unpublished manuscript.

King, E., Shapiro, J. L., Hebl, M., Singletary, S., & Turner, S. (2006). The stigma of obesity in customer service: A mechanism for remediation and bottom-line consequences of interpersonal discrimination. *Journal of Applied Psychology, 91*, 579–593.

Landy. F. J. (2008). Stereotypes, bias, and personnel decisions: Strange and stranger. *Industrial and Organizational Psychology, 1*, 379–392.

LaPiere, R. T. (1934). Attitudes versus action. *Social Forces, 13*, 230–237.

Leslie, L. M., King, E. B., Bradley, J. C., & Hebl, M. R. (2008). Triangulating across multiple methods: All signs point to persistent stereotyping in organizations. *Industrial and Organizational Psychology, 1*, 399–404.

Martinez, L. R., White, C. D., Mover, K. A., & Hebl, M. R. (2011). *Fit for work? The hiring experiences of cancer survivors.* Unpublished manuscript, Rice University.

Mitchell, T. L., Haw, R. M., Pfeifer, J. E., & Meissner, C. A. (2005). Racial bias in mock juror decision-making: A meta-analytic review of defendant treatment. *Law and Human Behavior, 29*, 621–637. doi: 10.1007/s10979-005-8122-9

Norenzayan, A., & Heine, S. J. (2005). Psychological universals: What are they and how can we know? *Psychological Bulletin, 131*, 763–784. doi: 10.1037/0033-2909.131.5.763

Paluck, E. L. (2009). Reducing intergroup prejudice and conflict using the media: A field experiment in Rwanda. *Journal of Personality and Social Psychology, 96*, 574–587. doi: 10.1037/a0011989

Penner, L. A., Dovidio, J. F., Edmondson, D., Dailey, R. K., Markova, T., Albrecht, T. L., & Gaertner, S. L. (2009). The experience of discrimination and Black–White health disparities in medical care. *Journal of Black Psychology, 35*, 180–203.

Quillian, L. (2006). New approaches to understanding racial prejudice and discrimination. *Annual Review of Sociology, 32*, 299–328. doi: 10.1177/019027250807100103

Rachlinski, J. J., Johnson, S. L., Wistrich, A. J., & Guthrie, C. (2008). Does unconscious racial bias affect trial judges? *Notre Dame Law Review, 84*, 1195–1246.

Richeson, J. A., & Trawalter, S. (2005). Why do interracial interactions impair executive function? A resource depletion account. *Journal of Personality and Social Psychology, 88*, 934–947.

Robbennolt, J. K. (2002). Punitive damage decision making: The decisions of citizens and trial court judges. *Law and Human Behavior, 26*, 315–341.

Rosenfield, D., Sheehan, D. S., Marcus, M. M., & Stephan, W. G. (1981). Classroom structure and prejudice in desegregated schools. *Journal of Educational Psychology, 73*, 17–26. doi: 10.1037/0022-0663.73.1.17

Rudolph, D. (2010, April). Does diversity training work? Retrieved October 24, 2011, from http://news.change.org/stories/does-diversity-training-work

Sackett, P. R., Hardison, C. M., & Cullen, M. J. (2004). On interpreting stereotype threat as accounting for African American–White differences on cognitive tests. *American Psychologist, 59*, 7–13.

Schmader, T., Johns, M., & Forbes, C. (2008). An integrated process model of stereotype threat effects on performance. *Psychological Review, 115*, 336–356.

Shapiro, J. R., King, E. B., & Quiñones, M. A. (2007). Expectations of obese trainees: How stigmatized trainee characteristics influence training effectiveness. *Journal of Applied Psychology, 92*, 239–249.

Shelton, J. N., & Richeson, J. A. (2006). Ethnic minorities' racial attitudes and contact experiences with White people. *Cultural Diversity and Ethnic Minority Psychology, 12*, 149–164.

Shelton, J. N., Richeson, J. A., & Salvatore, J. (2005). Expecting to be the target of prejudice: Implications for interethnic interactions. *Personality and Social Psychology Bulletin, 31*, 1189–1201.

Sherif, M., Harvey, O. J., White, B. J., Hood, W. R., & Sherif, C. W. (1954/1961). Intergroup conflict and cooperation: The Robbers Cave experiment. Retrieved from http://psychclassics.yorku.ca/Sherif/

Sommers, S. R. (2006). On racial diversity and group decision making: Identifying multiple effects of racial composition on jury deliberations. *Journal of Personality and Social Psychology, 90*, 597–612.

Sommers, S. R., & Ellsworth, P. C. (2001). White juror bias: An investigation of prejudice against Black defendants in the American courtroom. *Psychology, Public Policy, and the Law, 7*, 201–229.

Stricker, L. J., & Ward, W. C. (2004). Stereotype threat, inquiring about test takers' ethnicity and gender, and standardized test performance. *Journal of Applied Social Psychology, 34*, 665–693.

Swim, J. K., Hyers, L. L., Cohen, L. L., & Ferguson, M. J. (2001). Everyday sexism: Evidence for its incidence, nature, and psychological impact from three daily diaries. *Journal of Social Issues, 57*, 31–53.

West, T. V., Pearson, A. R., Dovidio, J. F., Shelton, J. N., & Trail, T. E. (2009). Superordinate identity and intergroup roommate friendship development. *Journal of Experimental Social Psychology, 45*, 1266–1272.

West, T. V., Shelton, J. N., & Trail, T. E. (2009). Relational anxiety and interracial interactions. *Psychological Science, 20*, 289–292.

Wrightsman, L. S. (2006). *The psychology of the Supreme Court*. New York: Oxford University Press.

Wrightsman, L. S. (1999). *Judicial decision making: Is psychology relevant?* New York: Plenum Press.

Yinger, J. (1986). Measuring racial discrimination with fair housing audits: Caught in the act. *American Economic Review, 76*, 881–893.

Zitek, E. M., & Hebl, M. R. (2007). The role of social norm clarity in the influenced expression of prejudice over time. *Journal of Experimental Social Psychology, 43*, 867–876.

Index

Taylor & Francis

eBooks

FOR LIBRARIES

ORDER YOUR FREE 30 DAY INSTITUTIONAL TRIAL TODAY!

Over 23,000 eBook titles in the Humanities, Social Sciences, STM and Law from some of the world's leading imprints.

Choose from a range of subject packages or create your own!

Benefits for **you**

▶ Free MARC records
▶ COUNTER-compliant usage statistics
▶ Flexible purchase and pricing options

Benefits for your **user**

▶ Off-site, anytime access via Athens or referring URL
▶ Print or copy pages or chapters
▶ Full content search
▶ Bookmark, highlight and annotate text
▶ Access to thousands of pages of quality research at the click of a button

For more information, pricing enquiries or to order a free trial, contact your local online sales team.

UK and Rest of World: **online.sales@tandf.co.uk**

US, Canada and Latin America: **e-reference@taylorandfrancis.com**

www.ebooksubscriptions.com

ALPSP Award for BEST eBOOK PUBLISHER 2009 Finalist sponsored by

Taylor & Francis **eBooks**
Taylor & Francis Group

A flexible and dynamic resource for teaching, learning and research.

62587263R00170

Made in the USA
Middletown, DE
24 January 2018